CIVIL RIGHTS CROSSROADS

CIVIL RIGHTS
CROSSROADS

Nation, Community, and the
Black Freedom Struggle

Steven F. Lawson

THE UNIVERSITY PRESS OF KENTUCKY

Publication of this volume was made possible in part
by a grant from the National Endowment for the Humanities.

Editorial and Sales Offices: The University Press of Kentucky
663 South Limestone Street, Lexington, Kentucky 40508-4008

07 06 05 04 03   5 4 3 2 1

Library of Congress Cataloging-in-Publication Data

Lawson, Steven F., 1945–
    Civil rights crossroads : nation, community, and the Black
freedom struggle / Steven F. Lawson.
        p.   cm.
Includes bibliographical references and index.
    ISBN 0-8131-2287-2 (alk. paper)
    1. African Americans—Civil rights—History—20th century.
2. Civil rights movements—United States—History—20th century.
3. African Americans—Suffrage—History—20th century. 4. United
States—Race relations. I. Title
    E185.615.L375   2003
    323.1196'073—dc22   2003014585

This book is printed on acid-free recycled paper meeting
the requirements of the American National Standard
for Permanence in Paper for Printed Library Materials.

∞ ✿

Manufactured in the United States of America.

Member of the Association of
American University Presses

In appreciation of inspiring teachers

Menke Katz

Milton Belasco

Joseph A. Borome

William E. Leuchtenburg

Henry Hampton

CONTENTS

PREFACE

This collection spans twenty-five years of my writing about civil rights and African American politics. When I began writing I did not have a strategic plan for the direction of my scholarship. My first book, *Black Ballots: Voting Rights in the South 1944–1969*, established me as a scholar of black suffrage and particularly the role the federal government played in expanding the franchise. In a second book, *In Pursuit of Power: Southern Blacks and Electoral Politics 1965–1982*, I continued to chronicle the federal government and its implementation of voting rights programs. Nevertheless, these books did not focus on Washington alone, and a close look at them demonstrates the interconnection of national and local arenas in the formulation of civil rights strategies, tactics, and policies. A third book, *Running for Freedom: Civil Rights and Black Politics in America Since 1941*, was designed to highlight this federal and community interaction. A fourth book, *Debating the Civil Rights Movement*, provided an argument for the importance of the national government in explaining the origins and outcome of the civil rights movement, while at the same time recognizing its dependence on grassroots black activism.[1]

The essays in this volume reflect the trajectory of these books but also remain independent of them. In doing so, they mirror my conception of civil rights history as a freedom struggle operating on two parallel tracks that crisscross at crucial junctures. I have divided these essays according to various themes and not the chronological order in which they appeared. Beginning with "Studying the Civil Rights Movement," I review the historiography of the movement and outline the argument that forms the basis of *Debating the Civil Rights Movement*. Following this, a series of chapters focus on Lyndon Johnson and the ways in which a powerful president responded to and shaped the outcome of civil rights battles. Far from depicting an omnipotent chief executive who could manipulate and co-opt a social movement, they show the inability of a president as shrewd as Johnson to manage totally, however much he may have desired, the course of black militancy.

The chapters in the section "Civil Rights and Black Politics" caution scholars not to stop exploring the civil rights movement in 1965, as is now the custom. Although the civil rights coalition fractured and a number of important groups disbanded, movement advocates continued to organize politically and legally at the local and national levels. In the wake of the 1965 Voting Rights Act, African American electoral politics, which has produced over nine thousand elected officials throughout the nation, should be examined as an extension of the civil rights movement. It provides a critical way to analyze how many of the objectives were fulfilled. It also allows scholars to recognize how movement lawyers and lobbyists together with civil rights bureaucrats in Washington battled to keep affirmative action and the extension of black political power alive during an era of post–civil rights, conservative, presidential administrations.

The section, "From the Bottom Up," does more than provide a series of community studies. These chapters on Florida reflect the influence of those scholars who challenged the nation-centered model of civil rights history. As early as 1982, I published an article on Tampa, Florida, that traced the civil rights movement in the Cigar City and uncovered the local people who placed their own agenda for change above any national one. Even so, I found direct connections between community organizations and groups such as the National Association for the Advancement of Colored People (NAACP). The chapter on Groveland, Florida, shows that even the smallest communities were not isolated from the nation at large. The post–World War II wave of violence against blacks in Groveland and across the South garnered national and international attention that affected the United States' Cold War propaganda battles. The Cold War's Red-baiting tactics became intertwined with racial assertiveness in the South, and the chapter on the Florida Legislative Investigation Committee illustrates how the Sunshine State persecuted dissenters long after McCarthyism had been proclaimed dead.

I wrote exclusively about Florida largely because I lived and taught there for twenty years and had the opportunity to study its history closely. I learned that whatever reputation Florida had as a progressive southern state standing apart from the rest of the region was greatly exaggerated.

Florida and cities like Tampa were not exceptions within Dixie; rather, their history reveals the variety of ways white southerners sought to maintain their supremacy and civil rights activists maneuvered to overturn it. The Florida story shows how white moderates attempted to contain violence against blacks in order to control the shape and pace of racial equality. It further highlights how once the federal government began to exhibit less tolerance toward extralegal terror in the South, the use of state law and legal agencies, such as legislative investigation committees, became the chief weapons to retard challenges from African Americans. Echoes of Florida's history during the 1950s and 1960s reverberated throughout Alabama, Georgia, North Carolina, and Louisiana.

The final section, "New Paths of Exploration," attempts to broaden the discussion of race and civil rights. By looking at the payola scandal and rock 'n' roll music in the 1950s, one sees that the civil rights movement had a decided impact on political culture in places other than courts, legislative chambers, and street protests. Once the civil rights movement began to reap headlines during the mid-1950s, concerns about possible shifts in racial power manifested themselves in seemingly non-racial issues of politics and economics, such as in efforts to root out unsavory practices—payola—among radio and television disk jockeys. Indeed, the resurgence of black protest in the 1950s added fuel for congressional lawmakers who had seized on issues of conspiracies in American life to further their political objectives. The payola investigation, with a white segregationist congressman from Arkansas at its helm, constituted a form of racial McCarthyism and fit into a culture of investigation not only in Washington but also in the South where committees such as the Florida Legislative Investigation Committee operated. Instead of considering the civil rights movement as a separate historical unit, it is time to examine how it influenced and reflected the larger political and social contexts within which it functioned.

The essay on women, civil rights, and black liberation testifies to the explosion of literature in the past decade that identifies extraordinary women such as Fannie Lou Hamer, Ella Baker, Ruby Doris Smith Robinson, Jo Ann Gibson Robinson, and many others who quietly and at times not-so-quietly sustained the civil rights struggle in local communities throughout the South. Women activists are frequently underrepresented in popular treatments of the civil rights movement, overshadowed by powerful, charismatic men such as Martin Luther King, Jr., and Malcolm X. Nevertheless, without women's organizing skills and their presence at the center of social and cultural institutions in black communities, the civil rights struggle as a mass movement would have quickly fizzled.

All of these essays have been published before; the first appeared in 1976 and the last in 2002. Most of them remain the same as they were first published and reflect the current state of scholarship at the time. However, I have updated two of them: "Freedom Then, Freedom Now" and "The Unmaking of the Second Reconstruction." In the former, I have written a postscript that includes a discussion of some of the vast civil rights literature that has appeared since 1991. The second revised chapter brings the story of affirmative action, voting rights, and busing up to 2002. This sketch reveals that although the Second Reconstruction remains alive, it is far from well. Yet compared to events after the Civil War and the First Reconstruction, its longevity has been no small accomplishment. This volume also contains a select bibliography that emphasizes works published since 1990.

I wish to acknowledge and thank the editors and publishers of these essays for allowing them to be reprinted in this volume. To the collaborators on two of the articles, Mark Gelfand on one and David Colburn and Darryl Paulson on the other, I offer my sincere appreciation for this and many other contributions to my career. Among the friends and colleagues whose names do not appear next to mine on the title pages of these articles but without whose sage advice, inspiration, and friendship they would be less meaningful, I would like to salute Tony Badger, Ralph Carlson, Clay Carson, William Chafe, John D'Emilio, John Dittmer, Robert Divine, John Hope Franklin, David Garrow, Ray Gavins, Charles Hamilton, Darlene Clark Hine, David Levering Lewis, William Link, August Meier, Charles Payne, Louis Perez, Peyton McCrary, Paul L. Murphy, Robert "Doc" Saunders, Patricia Sullivan, Susan Thorne, Brian Ward, Deborah Gray White, and Howard Zinn. Singling out people is always a risky proposition, and I apologize to those I may have omitted and who helped me along the way. So let me say that none of these articles could have been written without the contributions of many great scholars of the civil rights movement who stimulated me to think more critically and creatively about my work. In preparing this collection for press, I owe a great debt of gratitude to Danielle McGuire, my research assistant at Rutgers, who will be a shining star in the next generation of civil rights historians. Steve Wrinn has been a guardian angel on this and previous publications and the main reason for the University of Kentucky Press' interest in this project. He is a model editor and publisher, filled with vision and encouragement.

The names of the people to whom this book is dedicated influenced me because they were great teachers at various stages in my life from elementary school through graduate work and beyond. Menke Katz, at Workmen's Circle School #10, taught me what a "mensch" was supposed to be; Milton Belasco, at William Howard Taft High School, turned history into more than a litany of names, dates, and places; Joseph Borome, at the City College of New York, taught me the importance of African Americans in history and the necessity of employing wit in teaching; William Leuchtenburg, at Columbia University, showed me what a consummate scholar and teacher does; and Henry Hampton, who produced "Eyes on the Prize," was a brilliant, sensitive, and gentle man who ensured that the history of the civil rights movement would reach the largest possible audience through his magnificent documentary films.

Most important of all, I thank Nancy Hewitt. Colleague, collaborator, critic, spouse, and dear friend, she has made my work and my life richer, more complicated, and ultimately more fulfilling. More than anything, she is with me for the long run.

PART ONE

STUDYING THE CIVIL RIGHTS MOVEMENT

FREEDOM THEN, FREEDOM NOW

The Historiography of the Civil Rights Movement

While the United States tilted in the direction of political conservatism during the past decade, the history of the civil rights movement
gained in popular appeal. Martin Luther King's birthday became a
national holiday. Hollywood fictionalized the events surrounding the
Mississippi Freedom Summer, drawing millions of customers to the
box office. The multipart documentary series, *Eyes on the Prize, I
and II*, portrayed this history much more accurately and won numerous awards and wide acclaim.[1] Much of this interest can be attributed to the regular cycles of nostalgia that prompt Americans to
recall the historical era of their youth. In this instance, memories
dredged up turbulent and unsettling times, yet they also harked back
to inspirational movements when ordinary people exhibited extraordinary courage. Images of civil rights heroes and heroines making
great sacrifices to transform their country and their lives contrasted
sharply with the prevailing Reagan-era mentality that glorified the
attainment of personal wealth and ignored community health. Returning to civil rights yesteryears made many Americans feel better
about themselves and what they might accomplish once again in
the future.

This recent popular curiosity about the subject follows on a
longer professional concern with charting the course of the civil rights
struggle. Scholars who began writing about the movement in the
late 1960s and 1970s focused on leaders and events of national significance. They conceived of the civil rights struggle as primarily a
political movement that secured legislative and judicial triumphs.
The techniques of social history, which were beginning to recon-

struct the fields of women's, labor, and African American history by illuminating the everyday lives of ordinary people, at first left the study of civil rights virtually untouched. Civil rights historians were not oblivious to these new approaches, but the most accessible evidence generally steered them in traditional directions. The documentary sources on which historians customarily drew, located in the archives of presidential administrations and leading civil rights organizations, revealed a political story that highlighted events in Washington, D.C.[2] Even the oral histories contained in these depositories, which could have remedied the political and institutional bias in written sources by uncovering the activities of common people at the community level, concentrated instead on civil rights leaders who gained some measure of national prominence.[3]

A second generation of scholars, writing in the late 1970s and 1980s, sought to reshape civil rights historiography. They questioned whether the civil rights movement could be properly understood as a coalition of national organizations pressuring Washington to correct racial injustices. They suggested that the focal point for investigation should shift to local communities and grassroots organizations. King and the other well-known players would not disappear from view, but they would take a back seat to women and men who initiated protests in small towns and cities across the South and who acted according to their own needs rather than those of central organizations headquartered in New York, Washington, or Atlanta. Given this reconfiguration of the struggle, the concept of a civil rights movement itself came under scrutiny. Once scholars moved beyond the notion of a protest "orchestrated by national leaders in order to achieve national civil rights legislation" and focused increased attention on grassroots efforts, Clayborne Carson argued, "black freedom struggle" more fully captured the object of study. More than a matter of semantics, this alternative expression signified that protest activities were not narrowly aimed at obtaining legal victories from the federal government but sprang out of waves of liberationist struggle in black communities. Nothing less was at stake in these battles, Carson asserted, than "to create new social identities for participants and for all Afro-Americans."[4]

In recent years, many researchers have begun pursuing a more interactive model, recognizing the need to connect the local with the national, the social with the political. They are attempting as well to expand these analyses by examining both external influences on the national political struggle, including nongovernmental institutions such as the media and liberal philanthropic foundations, and the internal dynamics of local movements, including relations between the sexes and the races. In addition, scholars are beginning to reexamine the ideological roots of the freedom struggle, exploring the legal, theological, and political legacies left by leaders and organizations of the 1930s and 1940s. Only by emphasizing the element of struggle—between national institutions and local activists, moderates and radicals, whites and blacks, women and men, predecessors and contemporaries—can we fashion more complete syntheses of the civil rights movement.[5]

5

The reworkings of civil rights historiography up to the mid-1980s are well illustrated in the eighteen-volume series edited by David J. Garrow. *Martin Luther King, Jr. and the Civil Rights Movement*[6] contains a gold mine of both classic and not-so-familiar works on the black freedom struggle. The works range over four decades from the 1950s to the 1980s, with most originating in the last twenty years. Included are published articles, many from journals little used by historians; unpublished doctoral dissertations

---

Martin Luther King and the Civil Rights Movement, David J. Garrow, ed. (Brooklyn, N.Y.: Carlson Publishing, 1989) 18 vols.

Vols. 1–3   *Martin Luther King, Jr: Civil Rights Leader, Theologian, Orator*

Vols. 4–6   *We Shall Overcome: The Civil Rights Movement in the United States in the 1950s and 1960s.*

Vol. 7.   *The Walking City: The Montgomery Bus Boycott, 1955-1956.*

Vol. 8.   *Birmingham, Alabama, 1956–1963: The Black Struggle for Civil Rights.*

Vol. 9.   *Atlanta, Georgia, 1960–1961: Sit-Ins and Student Activism.*

Vol. 10.   *St. Augustine, Florida. 1963–1964: Mass Protest and Racial Violence.*

Vol. 11.   *Chicago 1966: Open Housing Marches, Summit Negotiations, and Operation Breadbasket.*

Vol. 12.   *At the River I Stand: Memphis, the 1968 Strike, and Martin Luther King.*

Vol. 13.   *The Highlander Folk School: A History of Its Major Programs, 1932–1961.*

Vol. 14.   *Conscience of a Troubled South: The Southern Conference Educational Fund, 1946–1966.*

Vol. 15.   *Direct Action and Desegregation, 1960–1962: Toward a Theory of the Rationalization of Protest.*

Vol. 16.   *The Sit-In Movement of 1960.*

Vol. 17.   *The Student Nonviolent Coordinating Committee: The Growth of Radicalism in a Civil Rights Organization.*

Vol. 18.   *The Social Vision of Martin Luther King, Jr.*

and master's theses; undergraduate honors essays; and a state investigative agency report. An eclectic series, its contents are spread over the disciplines of history, sociology, political science, journalism, religion, and law. Those familiar with Garrow's own comprehensive trilogy on King will not be surprised by the author's efforts to identify and make readily available many scarcely known but informative sources; indeed, it feels as though the reader is taking a peek into the personal files Garrow used to compile his various works on King.

The collection consists of four volumes on King, three on various aspects of the civil rights movement, six on local communities, two on the sit-ins, two on predominantly white groups that actively supported civil rights, and one on the Student Nonviolent Coordinating Committee (SNCC). Three of the King volumes and the three concerning the movement as a whole mostly reproduce previously published essays in facsimile form. The contents of the remaining volumes have been reset for publication in this series. Eleven of the total consist of collections of sundry items, whereas seven are monographs. Each volume (or set of companion volumes) contains its own index, a very handy guide for a reference work so large.

The material gathered here illuminates the main historiographical themes. Many of the selections, especially the theses and dissertations, furnish observations based on oral histories with local blacks whose contributions have previously received little documentation. As might be expected in a project of this type, some of the essays are redundant, some outdated, and some deservedly overlooked. Fortunately, these are held to a minimum. Garrow briefly introduces each of the volumes and places them in context. Three of the works, those on Montgomery, Birmingham, and St. Augustine, provide insightful introductions by J. Mills Thornton, William D. Barnard, and David R. Colburn, respectively. The dissertations contain updated prefaces by their authors. Of this category, the most deserving of publication by virtue of their style and freshness of interpretation are by Joan Turner Beifuss (the 1968 Memphis sanitation strike), Irwin Klibaner (Southern Conference Education Fund), Emily Stoper (SNCC), and Ira G. Zepp, Jr. (King's philosophical roots).[7] Experts in the field may offer substitutions and additions, but overall, the series editor has made justifiable selections that should stimulate further research and writing.[8] For this, scholars and libraries will be appreciative.

Yet the reader must be wary of the ways that this collection, built as it is on past scholarship, reinforces rather than challenges mainstream themes. Those engaged in key debates for the 1990s, which entail questions of chronology, ideology, community dynamics, gender relations, and leadership, will find sporadic rather than thematic help here.[9] The theological roots of King's philosophy, for instance, are explored in depth, but the ideological roots of black liberation are barely noted. Beifuss's study of the Memphis sanitation strike in 1968 and the volume on the open housing demonstrations in Chicago during 1966 suggest the intertwining of economic and political agendas in the civil rights struggle, but few of the other works collected here explore this theme. Students of women's role in the movement or of labor and communist legacies from the 1930s and 1940s will not find many previously hidden gems here. Still, a close reading of these volumes offers more than a trip down memory lane for scholars in the field. By detailing the roads already taken, they can illuminate possible paths toward a new framework for civil rights historiography.

Even Garrow's continued fascination with King, reflected in the title as well as the contents of his collection, inspires some new approaches to the man and the movement. At a time when the nation has apotheosized the Reverend King alongside other revered heroes honored with national holidays, scholars have sought to measure the man and not the icon.[10] The King who emerges from public celebrations is a perennial dreamer, frozen in time at his most famous address during the 1963 March on Washington. Most Americans choose to celebrate and remember King's call for nonviolent, interracial cooperation in the face of festering racial injustices. What has been lost in this popular adulation is the recognition that the most prominent civil rights leader did not remain static in his thinking. Scholars have shown how, late in his career, King himself recognized that "the dream I had in Washington back in 1963 has too often turned into a nightmare," leading to his advocacy of a fundamental restructuring of American society.[11]

Contributors to these volumes who note the ways in which the persistence of American racism, materialism, and militarism transformed King's vision generally adopt the notion of "two Kings"—the reformer and the revolutionary—to capture the clergyman's shifts in emphases and outlook between the mid-1950s and the late 1960s.[12] Many of the authors included here, however, are more interested in tracing the roots of King's ideology than the trajectory of his politics. Standard accounts of King's intellectual roots have long followed the minister's own discussion of his development in *Stride toward Freedom*, which charted the influence of Henry David Thoreau, Georg Friedrich Hegel, Karl Marx, Walter Rauschenbusch, Reinhold Niebuhr, Mohandas Gandhi, and Edgar Brightman. What this chain of philosophical development omitted was the foundation of King's thinking: the biblical Jesus and the black church. King did not often write

7

about such matters because he aimed his publications mainly at white audiences. But scholars are now highlighting the primary impact of African American religious experiences on King.[13]

8

The Garrow collection adds to this approach by offering a number of detailed treatises on King's religious roots. Examples of this revisionism began to appear in the mid-1970s. Paul R. Garber analyzed King primarily as a "Black preacher who saw the modern Black freedom movement as a continuation of an ancient freedom movement in which, according to Exodus, God spoke through Moses, saying, 'Let my people go.'"[14] Whatever else he became, the Reverend King was foremost a Southern Baptist preacher. College and graduate school exposed him to formal intellectual traditions, but he made sense of them as they related to his upbringing in the home of Baptist ministers and his church-centered community. "The concept of a personal God of infinite love and undiluted power 'who works through history for the salvation of His children,'" Lewis V. Baldwin asserted, "has always been central to the theology of the black Church."[15] During times of crisis and moments of doubt, King derived strength from his Christian faith and not from school-bred systematic philosophy. Although Gandhi shaped King's approach to nonviolence, the spirit behind it came from Jesus's Sermon on the Mount. As James H. Cone explained, "black people followed King, because he embodied in word and deed the faith of the black church which has always claimed that oppression and the Gospel of Jesus do not go together."[16]

Digging out the roots of King's thinking does not create an either/or proposition that lines up a predominantly Western intellectual tradition against an African American religious heritage. The Hegelian King might have concluded that it is more likely a both/and situation. As August Meier wrote some twenty-five years ago, King was a master synthesizer who could interpret the African American struggle for freedom in language that struck responsive chords among blacks and whites.[17] More recently, scholars have discovered that King liberally borrowed ideas for his sermons and writings from both black and white Protestant ministers, often without attribution, and that his published books were produced with the helping hand of ghostwriters. These findings do not diminish his contribution to the movement, but they do suggest that future researchers will have to look even more carefully to follow the myriad influences on King.[18]

This reappraisal of King's ideological heritage, emphasizing his merger of seemingly disparate legacies, suggests that we might usefully reconsider the concept of "two Kings" that has been employed to explain shifts in his political vision. Even in the late 1960s, King abandoned neither his commitment to nonviolence and integration nor his core religious ideas and humanistic values. The great strength of King was his ability to adapt old ideals to changing situations. As demonstrated by Beifuss in her study of the Memphis sanitation strike, King's doubts about capitalism did not so much alter as deepen in response to urban revolts that highlighted the persistence of poverty.

As early as his seminary days at Crozer, King "thought the capitalistic system was predicated on exploitation and prejudice, poverty, and that we wouldn't solve these problems until we got a new social order."[19] In his first speech to a mass meeting during the Montgomery bus boycott, King signaled the profound changes that would have to sweep through American society. "We the disinherited of this land, we who have been oppressed so long, are tired of going through the long night of captivity," he thundered, "and now we are reaching out for the daybreak of freedom and justice and equality."[20]

The recognition that King embodied both moderate and militant political possibilities suggests a further recasting of civil rights historiography that has emphasized "two movements."[21] Here the Freedom Summer of 1964 and the passage of the Voting Rights Act in 1965 have served as the crucial markers. When neither interracial grassroots activism nor federal legislation ushered in the "beloved community" of black and white together, SNCC militants replaced the slogan of the Southern Christian Leadership Conference (SCLC), "freedom now," with "black power." At the same time, rebellions erupted in northern ghettos and for several years became an annual summer event. The failure of nonviolent protest to achieve results among economically depressed blacks in Chicago in 1966, the escalation of the Vietnam War, the assault of the FBI against black militants at home, and the concurrent retreat of the federal government in fighting the War on Poverty split civil rights forces and gave national prominence to the freedom struggle as defined in terms of black consciousness and autonomy.[22]

Yet here, as with King, the notion of a bifurcated identity may distort as much as it illuminates. Among those labeled moderate for their pursuit of legal and constitutional efforts in the late 1960s were women and men whose very lives were threatened for advocating the same goals in earlier decades. In the South, moreover, "black power" continued to mean electoral power for many rural blacks long after it took on other connotations in northern cities. And, though eschewing Marxism on both philosophical and religious grounds, many activist black preachers followed King in his move toward a version of democratic socialism rooted in Christianity. Their views presaged the liberationist theology of insurgent Latin American clergy; they spoke out forcefully against the Vietnam War as an immoral and colonialist adventure.[23] By 1968, "moderate" civil rights leaders were preparing a new march on Washington—this time on the side of poor people—that promised to increase the scale of civil disobedience and disruption. In addition, if moderates were willing at times to adopt militant methods and goals, it would become apparent by the 1980s that many former SNCC militants—including John Lewis, Julian Bond, and Marion Barry—were willing to step back from the threatening definitions of "black power" and embrace electoral solutions to second-class citizenship.

Once we shift the focus to shared rather than divisive elements in the struggle, two points of convergence are particularly visible. The first is the international concerns of all segments of the movement. Members of SNCC and later the Black Panthers self-consciously embraced a Third World perspective, demonstrated in their attire, hairstyles, names, and music as well as their political agenda. Leaders in the National Association for the Advancement of Colored People (NAACP), SCLC, and other civil rights organizations also attended to issues in Africa, Latin America, and Asia; nor was this only a response to their more militant counterparts. King's critique of the Vietnam War and neocolonialism after 1965 was foreshadowed by a sermon he delivered in the second year of the Montgomery boycott. He predicted "the birth of a new age" for people of color throughout the world who had "lived for years and centuries under the yoke of foreign power."[24]

This connection between racial injustice around the globe and in the United States was paralleled by a second shared concern of black activists: the link between discrimination and poverty. The economic issues that gained prominence in King's efforts after 1965 were long a part of the civil rights agenda. The backbone of the Montgomery boycott, the domestics and seamstresses who daily rode the buses to work, viewed economic woes and political disfranchisement as deeply intertwined. And the woman whose act of defiance initiated the boycott, Rosa Parks, traced her organizational roots not only to the NAACP but also to the Highlander Folk School, where radical labor activists had been training community organizers since the depression decade.[25] The man who bailed her out of jail following her arrest, E.D. Nixon, was not only a member of the NAACP but also of the Brotherhood of Sleeping Car Porters.

Scholars of African American history have begun to scrutinize more closely the ways in which the shared economic and political concerns evident in earlier decades, particularly as embodied in the radical wing of the labor movement and Communist party alliances with local black activists, provided ideological inspiration and even personnel to the postwar movement. These issues are largely missing from the Garrow Series but have been explored in recent works by Robin D.G. Kelley, Robert Korstad and Nelson Lichtenstein, and Karen Sacks.[26] As Kelley pointed out, when SNCC workers ventured into Lowndes County, Alabama, in 1965 to register voters, they revived, albeit unknowingly, a militant tradition established by Communist organizers thirty years earlier.

The Garrow Series takes 1954–1955 as the starting point of the struggle, as do most previous scholarship and such powerful visual records as *Eyes on the Prize*. Though made for good reason—the Supreme Court's landmark *Brown vs. Board of Education* ruling of 1954 and the Montgomery bus boycott of 1955—the decision to locate the beginning of the civil rights struggle in the midst of the McCarthy era may have led scholars to echo the silences imposed by anticommunist crusaders. Given the danger for activists of this era in owning up to previous affiliations with leftist movements, closer investigation of the backgrounds of grass-roots activists will be needed before evidence of links between post-*Brown* civil rights struggles and earlier radical campaigns emerges. Garrow's inclusion of Irwin Klibaner's dissertation on the Southern Education Conference Fund (SCEF) is especially welcome because it underscores the radical roots of the civil rights movement and the difficulties in sustaining support against anticommunist attacks orchestrated by state and federal authorities.

By aiming their sights at the grassroots level, where detailed examination of the culture of black communities is possible, scholars can address not only the legacy of black radicalism but also the larger and equally critical issue of whether the freedom movement of the 1950s and 1960s continued a previous protest tradition or started a new one. In one sense, the steady efforts of the NAACP since its founding in 1909 provide ample evidence of an unbroken line of challenges to racial discrimination in the twentieth century.[27] But the distinguishing feature of the freedom struggle emerging in the 1950s was the use of "direct action" techniques in villages, towns, and cities throughout the South. New organizations or rejuvenated chapters of old ones guided these assaults on the racial status quo in their local areas, apparently signaling a distinct break with the past.[28]

The argument for discontinuity was most forcefully presented by August Meier and Elliot Rudwick in a wide-ranging essay first published in 1976. They concluded that, despite a long and varied tradition of protest throughout African American history, "the use of [nonviolent] direct-action tactics has been episodic and characterized by sharp discontinuities."[29]

Each generation of black dissenters, they claimed, acted in response to current situations without drawing on history for guidance. Indeed, protesters usually initiated their struggles unaware they were repeating tactics that had been used before.[30]

The case for continuity, however, has received substantial support in recent years, building particularly on William H. Chafe's path-breaking study of Greensboro. Taking a life-cycle approach to local history, Chafe traces several generations of protest in the North Carolina city and finds important linkages from one era to another. An NAACP youth group established in the 1940s furnished participants for the sit-ins of the 1960s. Youngsters educated in black public schools during the 1950s joined the ranks of demonstrators in the 1960s. Two of the original four sit-in protesters attended the church of a clergyman who used his ministry to keep the message of freedom alive throughout the 1950s.

Chafe's approach must be applied to many other locations before we can gauge the various ways that protest movements emerged from the rich cultural heritage of black communities.[31] Garrow's collection offers studies on Montgomery, Birmingham, Atlanta, St. Augustine, Chicago, and Memphis, in each of which the traces of earlier crusades can be detected, often as faint but significant imprints on later struggles. These studies spotlight the importance of indigenous freedom struggles as well as of individuals whose courage was fired by their earlier participation in radical organizations and grassroots agitation. Among the civic and religious leaders who propelled the movement day by day, year in and year out, were many whose earliest efforts were linked to racially progressive organizations prior to the *Brown* decision. In Montgomery, this included not only Rosa Parks and E.D. Nixon but also the Reverend Vernon Johns. Even though he was replaced in the Dexter Avenue Baptist Church pulpit by King before the boycott erupted, he had worked vigorously against racial injustice throughout his four-year pastorate.[32]

Much the same situation existed elsewhere. In Atlanta in 1960, Lonnie King (no relation to Martin) and Julian Bond, students at Morehouse College, cleverly orchestrated sit-in demonstrations that led to the well-publicized arrest of Dr. King and created a political crisis for candidates during the presidential election campaign. Birmingham produced the fearless Fred Shuttlesworth, whose Alabama Christian Movement for Human Rights encountered bombs, bullets, and bricks years before the massive street demonstrations of 1963 led by the SCLC.

The local case histories included here reinforce the claims of sociologists Doug McAdam and Aldon D. Morris that black communities that mobilized their internal resources and marshaled them toward liberationist ends in the late 1950s and early 1960s were not reacting to discrimination either randomly or haphazardly. Rather, they were responding through established organizations and developing lines of communication. Underscoring the importance of black churches, colleges, and civic groups in fostering and maintaining a protest network, Morris concluded that the "sit-ins became a tactical innovation within the movement because they fit into the framework of the existing internal organization."[33] His conclusion is echoed in a recent essay by sociologist Lewis M. Killian demonstrating the ways in which seemingly spontaneous civil rights protests occurred within the context of preexisting organizations.[34]

Two other monographs in the Garrow Series—Klibaner's on SCEF and Aimee Isgrig Horton's on the Highlander Folk School—also focus on the pre-*Brown* roots of the freedom struggle. Employing an institutional rather than a community-based approach, they too demonstrate that the new groups and tactics, which seemed to appear spontaneously, actually emerged out of established organizations. At the same time, older groups and organizations were revitalized and transformed by newer ones as both joined in pursuit of common objectives. Before *Brown* and Montgomery, a tiny band of southern white racial progressives was committed to remaking their region along egalitarian racial and economic lines. Small in number, they were plentiful enough to form SCEF (and its predecessor, the Southern Conference for Human Welfare) and the Highlander Folk School. Their neighbors scorned them, and the authorities Red-baited them with charges of subversion. Despite their travail, liberal white southerners managed to provide valuable support for the movement through fund-raising, education, and organizing.[35]

By focusing on racially progressive whites, these studies highlight the diverse attitudes held by the South's dominant race. The bedsheeted bigotry of the Ku Klux Klan and the tie-and-jacket prejudice of the White Citizens' Councils have been ably described.[36] Yet many white communities were not monolithic. In a perceptive analysis of Montgomery, J. Mills Thornton argued that one cannot chart the ebb and flow of black protest without understanding the racial dynamics of the white community.[37] Whites usually lined up behind the banner of racial solidarity, but they also quarreled among themselves about how to respond to political challenges. Fearing that racial violence would interfere with their plans for urban economic redevelopment, the moderate white civic, business, and political leaders preferred to keep the peace through the give and take of biracial negotiation, for which they came under attack from obstructionist hard-liners.

Community histories are especially valuable in uncovering the coalitions and conflicts within and between black and white communities. The communities spotlighted in the Garrow collection display the same matrix of historical roots and contemporary organizations, civic and religious leadership and mass followings, political demands and economic goals. Together, they reveal many unheralded individuals who supplied indispensable leadership in initiating, directing, and keeping alive local protest activities through the network of black church, civic, and business organizations. Their lives demonstrate that blacks were not simply victims of separate and unequal policies; rather, they retained a measure of social, economic, and political autonomy that under the proper conditions could fuel demands for equality and power.[38]

Nevertheless, blacks' autonomy of action along with the breadth of their political and social agenda ensured that conflict as well as community would emerge within the black freedom movement. Conflicts occurred on several levels. Local blacks hoped to gain national attention by calling in recognized leaders such as King, but disagreements developed between community activists and outside leaders over when and at what cost a settlement should be reached. In campaigns such as those in Birmingham, the SCLC sought mainly to convince national lawmakers to enact legislation eradicating de jure racial discrimination and characteristically left the scene upon accomplishing this mission. Black locals benefited from the legislation thus secured, but they were deprived of vital support for sustaining their own organizations.[39]

Whatever tensions may have existed, local blacks clearly ignited struggles to which King reacted. In St. Augustine, Dr. Robert Hayling, a dentist and a leader of the local NAACP, mobilized protests against segregation and courageously fought the Klan for a year before calling King for assistance in 1964. When King turned northward to Chicago in 1966, he stepped onto fertile territory already plowed by Al Raby and the Coordinating Council of Community Organizations. In Memphis in 1968, black sanitation workers in alliance with civil rights veterans such as James Lawson precipitated the struggle that brought King to that city to fight his final battle.

Crisis-induced unity did not remove underlying differences over strategy and tactics among black civil rights activists that stemmed from generational, ideological, and economic cleavages. Predictably, they resurfaced after victory was achieved. These splits were not always destructive, however. Jack L. Walker, investigating the Atlanta sit-ins of 1960, concluded that the division of labor between black student activists and more cautious adult negotiators brought about a peaceful and substantial resolution to the conflict.[40]

As community studies reveal the masses of individuals at the heart of the movement, the efforts of women have been recovered alongside those of men. In general, racial solidarity seems to have muted sexual conflict within the freedom struggle. And, where gender differences did emerge, they might have provided some of the same advantages as did the differences between young militants and older moderates outlined by Walker. Yet any definitive analysis of gender relations in the movement awaits basic research on female participants, leaders, and followers.

Reading through the diverse works in the Garrow Series, one finds the names of numerous women who made important contributions to the movement. Jo Ann Robinson, Ella Baker, Diane Nash, Fannie Lou Hamer, Septima Clark, and Rosa Parks are some of the more prominent figures whose efforts are recorded here. Nevertheless, we need systematic studies of how ordinary women, in their roles as mothers, wives, workers, churchgoers, and professionals affected the nature of the movement.[41] Indeed, there are important connections to be made between the black church as the institutional bedrock of civil rights protest and the significant place of women inside it.

When *Eyes on the Prize* broadcast an episode on the Montgomery bus boycott, film footage revealed the extensive presence of women at mass meetings and on the streets walking to work. However, the narration, as in most scholarly studies, failed to analyze the sexual politics of racial struggle. A doctoral dissertation by Steven M. Millner in 1981 suggests that the heavy involvement of women stemmed, in part, from the fact that black females outnumbered black males in Montgomery's population and rode the bus much more frequently than did men. Moreover, the rude behavior black women suffered from white male drivers was doubly insulting by virtue of their sex and race. Rosa Parks's arrest galvanized the black community, in part, because she had a reputation as both an activist and a "lady." Yet, on occasion, Montgomery's female activists chose "unladylike" behavior to exhibit their passion for equality. When black male leaders were arrested for violating an anti-boycott law, for instance, a group of older women came to the courthouse, "wearing men's hats and dresses rolled up," and warned a gun-toting policeman who tried to disperse them: "[We] don't care what you got. If you hit one of us, you'll not leave here alive." It will take further research to uncover the multiplicity of roles women played in Montgomery alone.[42]

The most notable controversy concerning women in the larger free-dom struggle focuses on SNCC. Sara Evans has argued that many of the white women who worked with SNCC in the Deep South later became in-strumental in developing the women's liberation movement. She attrib-uted the awakening of their feminist consciousness to a variety of factors: the egalitarian ethos of SNCC, the inspiration of black women in local com-munities who provided the movement with strong female role models, and the revolt against male chauvinist attitudes that relegated women to con-ventional female tasks. Only the third argument has produced disagree-ment. Mary King, a SNCC staffer who along with Casey Hayden drew up a feminist manifesto in 1965 critical of sexism within the organization, has recently claimed that Evans misinterpreted the meaning of this protest. King insists that she and Hayden were not complaining about their role as women in SNCC but were questioning whether the civil rights movement could tolerate "differing political and social concerns, as various groups and, in our case, women defined them."[43] Reconciling King's contempora-neous and retrospective statements remains problematic, but scholars are beginning to measure the impact of SNCC on the lives of black and white women in order to determine just how much conflict grew out of gender as distinct from race differences.[44]

One fruitful approach to the controversy over women's treatment within SNCC may be to focus on the way in which women helped forge the unique character of the organization and then worked to sustain their place within it. Ella Baker is widely acclaimed for her critical role in bridging genera-tional divides and in shaping the structure and style of SNCC. Still, no full biography of Baker exists. Such a work might usefully draw on Karen Sacks's study of union organizing among both black and white hospital workers at Duke Medical Center. Sacks argued that, in large part, it was women's and men's different definitions of leadership that led to their particular roles in community struggles. Women in the Duke struggle focused on creating and sustaining support networks; men on drafting statements, controlling the highest organizational offices, and serving as public spokesmen. Be-cause men's definition more closely fit that of the media, they were per-ceived by outsiders as the preeminent leaders of the movement.[45]

The emphasis in SNCC on establishing and sustaining community net-works and encouraging grassroots leadership supplied a ready arena in which women could flourish. And it is not surprising that Baker should have served as the midwife at the moment of SNCC's birth. Other women also felt at home with SNCC's style of activism and organization. But ten-sions could be expected to surface nonetheless because, even with all the important positions held by women, men most often spoke to the public and controlled the majority of formal leadership positions. Moreover, the turn toward "black power" after 1965 enhanced the status of masculine forms of militancy as it muted feminine elements of organizing within SNCC, particularly as black power moved north.

Clearly, most women thrived in SNCC, as did many men, during those years when a female style of activism and leadership prevailed. Indeed, it was perhaps the combination of a feminine model of organizing—at which men like Bob Moses excelled—with a masculine model of leadership—which women like Fannie Lou Hamer learned to use—that lent SNCC its uniqueness and force. SNCC was, after all, the civil rights group with the shortest life span but the greatest transformative power.

From its beginnings in 1960, the group recognized the truth of Baker's advice to fight for "more than a hamburger" and attacked the very structure of racial subordination. SNCC fieldworkers encountered brutal forms of white repression in remote sections of the Deep South. They experienced firsthand the abject poverty that kept rural blacks in virtual bondage. The iconoclastic group considered the NAACP too stodgy, criticized the SCLC's charismatic leadership style, and snickered at Dr. King as "de lawd."[46] SNCC also clashed with sympathetic northern white liberals and national government officials who tried to compromise their political objectives. Starting out idealistically committed to nonviolence and an interracial beloved community, by the late 1960s SNCC's battle-toughened troops endorsed retaliatory self-defense, black nationalism, and the overthrow of capitalism. The group's rising identification with Third World anticolonial struggles made it an early, outspoken critic of the Vietnam War.

Like King, SNCC has attracted many thoughtful chroniclers. Howard Zinn, Clayborne Carson, James Forman, Cleveland Sellers, and Mary King have written noteworthy accounts charting SNCC's trajectory from reform to revolution over the course of the 1960s.[47] To this list, the Garrow Series adds political scientist Emily Stoper. Her work helps explain why SNCC's strength also made the group vulnerable to collapse during the late 1960s. She categorizes SNCC as a "redemptive organization," whose members exhibited a "moral ethos" of righteous anger forged from mutually shared experiences of struggle and persecution. Having undergone ordeals by fire in harsh southern battlefields, SNCC staffers regarded each other as a "band of brothers [and sisters], a circle of trust." Wary of outsiders and alienated from the mainstream, SNCC members were not equipped to deal with the bottom line of American politics—compromise. Moreover, the tightly knit organization could not withstand an influx of newcomers, however well-meaning. Thus the appearance of large numbers of white volunteers as participants in the Mississippi Freedom Summer campaign of 1964, though invited by SNCC, "brought to the surface a great deal of the pathology of black-white relations."[48] While Stoper charts the organizational strains within SNCC, many of the group's troubles must also be attributed to the federal government, first for its hesitancy in providing adequate protection and then for waging a repressive counterintelligence program against militant blacks.

Stoper's work, based largely on interviews with SNCC adherents, offers valuable hints for further research. In focusing on the political culture of SNCC and that of the larger society, she suggests we look more carefully at the way values, symbols, and language shaped the freedom struggle. In many instances, civil rights activists succeeded in conveying images of struggle reflecting the democratic and egalitarian ideals that Americans celebrate, at least in theory. This was certainly true with SNCC's early history. Yet the group's communitarian ethic ultimately conflicted with the competitive, individualistic values of those who controlled political discourse, including government officials and representatives of the media.[49] Furthermore, in examining how organizations such as SNCC operated within the broader, predominantly white society, one must not fail to evaluate how civil rights groups conformed to and transformed southern black conceptions of freedom. Local black southerners were instrumental in shaping SNCC's definition of liberation and black power, but they did not necessarily interpret these terms in the same ways.[50]

Redirection of scholarly studies to the local level, which Garrow and others have called for, should not obscure the need to move from the particular to the general, from case study to synthesis. Clayborne Carson characterized the movement "as a series of concentric circles, with liberal supporters on the outside and full time activists at the center."[51] This assessment appropriately emphasizes grassroots efforts, yet it is crucial to acknowledge that the federal government could both strengthen and limit possibilities for change. Indeed, it ultimately required the power of Washington to break the segregationist stranglehold on first-class citizenship in towns across the country. Moreover, although the aims of national and local groups sometimes differed, in many instances they coincided. Often, local groups called for outside assistance at the same time national organizations sought test cases or local showplaces. Rather than concentric circles, the image of overlapping spheres sharing a common segment might more accurately reflect the shape of the struggle. The shared zone of cooperation expanded or contracted according to pressures from below and political considerations from above.[52]

Differences of interpretation are as evident among civil rights scholars as they were among civil rights activists. In part, this explains why interest in civil rights history shows little sign of abating. Scholarly texts are still rolling off the presses along with autobiographical accounts of individual activists to expand our view of the movement against racism.[53] If the studies of the next thirty years are as rich as those of the previous three decades, as sampled in the Garrow collection, we all have something to look forward to. Among forthcoming works are the volumes from the Martin Luther King Papers Project and studies on women, the international dimensions of the freedom struggle, and its pre-1954 antecedents found in the labor movement and in black nationalist and racially progressive interracial groups. In addition, more in-depth explorations of the movement in Mississippi and other southern states will soon appear.[54] These promise to add a critical edge and greater complexity to the portraits of protest presented here.

FREEDOM DOWN TO NOW

In the ten years since publication of this article, books on the civil rights movement have continued rolling off the presses. These works have maintained the high quality of research and writing that characterized the first several decades of scholarship on the movement. They have explored many of the themes sketched out in the original essay. Several informed readers of community struggles, some of which made great headlines and others that did not. Others addressed civil rights struggles in the context of national and even international politics, and a few sought to connect the two. As might be expected, books on Martin Luther King, Jr., continue to flourish, but a large number of autobiographies and biographies have examined a broader range of characters, black and white, women and men, who shaped the movement independently of Dr. King. Furthermore, scholars have pushed out in new directions and studied topics that had been virtually ignored or underdeveloped in the first forty years of writing. In the process, they have continued to expand the chronology of civil rights and black emancipation. My purpose here is to outline a few of the most significant works, those that speak most closely to issues raised in my original essay and some of those that chart new opportunities for research.

Two of the books that I mentioned as forthcoming in 1991, John

Dittmer's *Local People* and Charles Payne's *I've Got the Light of Freedom*, have both achieved the high standards of community studies first set by William H. Chafe, Robert J. Norrell, and David R. Colburn. Dittmer and Payne deal with Mississippi, the former with the entire state, the latter with the Delta. The Magnolia State offered a laboratory for experimentation with social movements, and these two exceptional books deepen our understanding of the hardships freedom fighters faced as well as the extraordinary resources that black Mississippians marshaled to overthrow white supremacy.

Though focusing on "local people," Dittmer provides a great deal of evidence of how important the federal government and national civil rights groups were in opening some doors to racial equality while closing others. Dittmer also continues the trend of pushing the chronology of the civil rights movement back into the World War II era, when veterans such as Medgar Evers returned home from the military to challenge Theodore Bilbo's racist politics. From the outset of this period, local blacks sought assistance from the federal government, in this case Congress, which held hearings to bar Bilbo from taking his seat. In the end, divine intervention and not the national government settled the matter, as Bilbo died of cancer. However, it ultimately took more federal effort and human perseverance than divine retribution to end racial apartheid in the Magnolia State.[55]

Payne spends much less time on national politics than does Dittmer. As an historical sociologist, Payne is interested in constructing a model of social movements. Fortunately for historians, he has eschewed the jargon that often accompanies social science research and has presented a rich and readable analysis of how local people in the Delta developed their own goals, networks, and leadership styles to challenge their oppressors. Characteristic of the best civil rights studies, African Americans occupy these pages not as victims and objects of white supremacy but as agents and subjects of their own destinies. What Payne calls the "organizing tradition" buttresses his portrayal of how the movement in Mississippi helped shatter the walls of racial inequality and disfranchisement. Furthermore, Payne argues the merits of the slow, painstaking organizing tactics practiced by SNCC over the hit-and-run, publicity-oriented mobilizing style undertaken by King and the SCLC.

In a provocative bibliographic essay at the end of the book, Payne offers a trenchant critique of historians and journalists who have utilized what he calls a "normative" approach to the movement. According to Payne, these authors privilege integration over nationalism, Martin Luther King over Malcolm X, and a national over a local focus. Payne is certainly correct in calling upon scholars to pay greater attention in their narratives to indigenous black activism; however, rather than seeking this adjustment for the sake of balance, Payne would discard one norm he opposes with another that he favors. Merely substituting a "local determinism" for a "top-down determinism" will not furnish the complicated and multi-dimensional understanding of the civil rights movement that is still needed.[56]

21

Indeed, several scholars have blazed new trails that take us beyond both the local and national into the international context of the movement. Among this group, Mary Dudziak, Thomas Borstelmann, Michael Krenn, Penny Von Eschen, and Brenda Gayle Plummer have led the way in demonstrating the connections between the black freedom struggle and American foreign policy. They have shown that African Americans were knowledgeable and concerned about anti-colonial developments in Africa and raised their voices in protest against European imperialism on the continent. Moreover, as Dudziak and Borstelmann in particular have contended, the need for the United States to acquire allies among recently liberated, non-white nations in its Cold War propaganda battles with the Soviet Union prompted presidents from Harry Truman to Lyndon Johnson to take forceful measures for racial equality that deprived the Soviets of rhetorical ammunition against this country. Nevertheless, because of Cold War priorities, chief executives were sometimes just as anxious to stifle civil rights dissent, as John Kennedy unsuccessfully attempted with the freedom rides, than to press ahead for rapid change. Although scholars have helped broaden our perception of the civil rights movement and its place in the world arena, for the most part they have yet to connect the shaping of foreign policy with the actions of blacks on the local level. The role of the NAACP usually garners attention, but foreign policy–related concerns of groups such as the SCLC and more importantly SNCC, CORE, and their grassroots constituents have hardly been explored.[57]

In presenting the Cold War as providing ideological opportunities for African Americans to exploit, these authors have departed from those who emphasize the restrictions on social reform that the Cold War imposed at home. Patricia Sullivan's *Days of Hope: Race and Democracy in the New Deal Era South*, argues that the spread of anti-communism dealt a debilitating blow to the incipient, interracial, liberal-labor alliance of the Popular Front Era that was in the process of transforming the South politically and economically during the 1930s and 1940s. Sullivan contends that the Progressive campaign for president of Henry Wallace in 1948 marked the turning point for the possibility of racial democracy in the region. Wallace's defeat and the Red-baiting that accompanied it shattered the Popular Front coalition that had been gaining ground in challenging segregation, disfranchisement, and economic inequality. Like Robert Korstad and Nelson Lichtenstein, Sullivan suggests that this defeat dealt a crushing blow to the civil rights movement by removing organized labor as a force for reshaping the South's system of economic exploitation. In his case study of organized labor and race relations in Memphis, Michael Honey generally supports this view.[58] Yet even without the Cold War there remains a good deal of doubt that white southern workers in the late 1940s would have discarded their racial antipathies to align themselves with the black freedom struggle.[59]

This "lost opportunity" thesis needs to be tested more extensively by studying local communities and the agendas of national politicians and civil rights organizations. Peter Lau, in a recent doctoral dissertation on the black freedom struggle in South Carolina during the first half of the twentieth century, concludes that the Cold War did not force black South Carolinians to pursue political and legal goals at the expense of economic aspirations. Indeed, one was always embedded in the other: blacks did not seek the right to vote merely to exercise a legal right; rather, they considered it as a chief means of securing tangible economic results. Unlike historians such as Alan Brinkley who view World War II as a watershed in the shift away from class-based liberalism to identity politics, Lau perceives this as a false dichotomy.[60] Timothy Thurber in his study of Hubert Humphrey and civil rights agrees with Lau. He demonstrates that throughout his career, the Minnesota defender of civil rights insisted that the struggle against racial inequality was inextricably linked to the struggle against economic inequality.[61]

Despite differing interpretations, the authors just noted all reinforce what has become the consensus view that the civil rights movement did not suddenly spring up in 1954 or 1955. The most common points of origin are located in the 1930s or 1940s. However, some historians have pushed back the chronology even further. Adam Fairclough, both in his study of Louisiana and his survey of the black freedom struggle, locates the beginning of the civil rights movement in the 1890s with Ida B. Wells's militant campaign against lynching followed a decade later by the founding of the NAACP. Kevern Verney digs even deeper to discover the movement's origins. He begins his text on black civil rights in America with the introduction of slavery in the seventeenth century, but like Fairclough he focuses more on the turn-of-the-twentieth century.[62] In contrast, Glenn Eskew views the early stirrings of the civil rights movement in Birmingham, Alabama immediately following World War II and finds that the movement led by the Reverend Fred Shuttlesworth ten years later "marked a clear departure from traditional black protest" in the city.[63] Eskew's study raises a cautionary flag for those seeking to extend the traditional civil rights chronology too far back. First, campaigns for civil rights, even in the same locale, did not always proceed without interruption and often moved in fits and starts. Second, a useful distinction should be made between the black freedom struggle and the civil rights movement. The civil rights movement if it has any contextual meaning must be seen as a distinct and coherent part of the longer freedom struggle. It roughly coincides with the acceleration and upward climb of organized local and national black protests for equal treatment and first-class citizenship. There were obviously civil rights components to the black freedom struggle in earlier times—during Reconstruction and with the founding of the NAACP. Nevertheless, the modern phase of the movement, which absorbed so much attention during the 1950s and 1960s and achieved much of the protest agenda, needs to be identified for the characteristics that made it distinct from earlier efforts without forgetting the links that connected them.

Civil rights historians have long called for treatments of individuals who though less known than established leaders shouldered much of the burden of the civil rights movement. Three biographies of Bayard Rustin, who played a key, behind-the-scenes role as one of the shrewdest tacticians in the movement, have appeared. Ella Baker, whose vision of community organizing and participatory democracy guided SNCC, has attracted two biographers. Bob Moses, who put into operation Baker's principles in Mississippi and SNCC's Ruby Doris Smith, the first female chair of the organization, have each found a biographer. Fred Shuttlesworth, who courageously guided the Birmingham movement a decade before Dr. King launched demonstrations in the city, and Harry T. Moore, the NAACP's chief representative in Florida in the 1940s who may have been the first martyr in the postwar civil rights movement, have gained the attention they deserve. Complementing these books, a growing number of memoirs of black and white activists have offered a personal glimpse of the difficulties encountered in fighting for equality and the strength of character it took to overcome them.[64]

Two biographies of African Americans stand out for their significance in broadening our understanding of personal challenges the movement presented to civil rights activists. Tim Tyson's biography of Robert F. Williams, the North Carolina advocate of armed self defense in the late 1950s who fled into exile in Cuba and China during the 1960s, demonstrates what has rarely been acknowledged before: the link between civil rights and black power. Tyson convincingly shows how Williams not only grew out of the

23

soil of the black freedom struggle emerging throughout the South during and after World War II, but also that Williams's brand of radical politics originated from the same roots as that of the civil rights movement. In doing so, he helps narrow the gap that many scholars have commonly perceived as existing between the civil rights and black power movements. This book also punctures easy generalizations about the place of nonviolence as a weapon in the freedom struggle. In fact, Tyson creatively shows that self-defense, as advocated by Williams, had a longstanding tradition in southern, rural black communities. It would take the genius of Dr. King and others to fashion a movement that elevated nonviolence over retaliation.[65]

Furthermore, Tyson explores the role of gender in Williams's militant approach. He points out the importance for men who sought to defend their families and neighbors with weapons if necessary as a critical means of asserting their manhood. In a white supremacist culture that had systematically attempted to castrate black males physically and symbolically, armed retaliation replaced an identity of submissiveness with one of masculine power.

Black women faced a similar dilemma. Perceived as possessing a more heightened sexuality than white women, they became targets of white male sexual aggression. White on black rape was rarely punished, for black women were considered the legitimate recipients of white male lust. In her intimate biography of Fannie Lou Hamer, Chana Kai Lee uncovers the personal hardships of one of the movement's greatest indigenous leaders. For Hamer the personal meshed with the political from the stories she was told about her grandmother's rape by a white man, from her own forced sterilization when she went to have a stomach cyst removed, and her beating by white policemen in the Winona, Mississippi jail, which left her feeling violated. More than any other biography to date, Lee's demonstrates the terrible cost for women who challenged and ultimately transformed southern racial and psycho-sexual norms, while at the same time trying to fulfill expectations of them as wives and mothers. Lee reminds us that people like Hamer endured intense disappointment and pain "for freedom's sake."[66]

In addition to these and other black contributors to the movement, historians have also written about white sympathizers and opponents. These include Jon Daniels and Viola Liuzzo, two whites who gave their lives for the cause. Segregationist governors such as George Wallace and Orval Faubus have received probing treatments that place their racist appeal within the wider political context of the conservative South and nation. In an attempt to complicate the responses of white southerners to the struggle, Charles Marsh and Diane McWhorter have presented tough-minded but sensitive accounts of their fathers' responses to the battle for desegregation. In a recent article, Charles Eagles has called upon scholars to study the variety of responses, positive and negative, white southerners exhibited during the movement, and it appears that through biography and autobiographies the effort is well under way.[67]

White and black women have continued to reap a great deal of attention in the civil rights literature of the past decade. A fuller account of the outpouring of works on this subject appears in the final essay of this collection, "Women, Civil Rights, and Black Liberation." Here it is necessary to mention that the new works explore the variety of women's leadership roles, confirming that women tended to thrive at the local level and that the movement arose on the foundation of women's social networks already established in their communities. Though sexual chauvinism among men certainly existed, what is more remarkable given the dominant culture is the degree of cooperation and role sharing among men and women, especially in more progressive organizations such as SNCC. Yet it is important to note that even more male-centered groups such as the NAACP and SCLC contained strong women in leadership positions, such as Ruby Hurley and Constance Baker Motley in the former and Dorothy Cotton and Septima Clark in the latter. Moreover, the widely reported conflicts between black and white women activists, especially in Mississippi in 1964, appear more the result of racial concerns over autonomy and safety than gendered considerations of appropriate roles.[68]

With respect to gender, more needs to be done about uncovering attitudes about masculinity and femininity as well as sexuality within the movement. Tyson has opened the way in his study of Robert Williams, and scholars should continue to look at the way tactics and ideologies reflected and challenged traditional conceptions of gendered behavior. Notwithstanding the connections between civil rights and black power that Tyson underscores, researchers should also investigate the impact that the heightened masculinity of the latter had on women's participation in the liberation struggle.[69] In addition, historians have begun to look at same-sex sexuality as it affected perceptions of and relations within the movement. John Howard has paved the way with his analysis of Mississippi, and Stacy Braukman has introduced the connections between attacks on civil rights and homosexuality in Florida. Biographers of Bayard Rustin and Allard Lowenstein, too, have raised the issue of homosexuality as they examine relations between the personal and political for their subjects.[70]

A good deal of work still needs to be done in examining the interaction between the civil rights movement and mass culture. The movement gained considerable momentum and reached its peak during an era of expanded material consumption and a marketing strategy designed to attract the purchasing power of the burgeoning baby-boom generation. Brian Ward has written a pioneering study that carefully charts the push for integration and nationalism respectively in the production and consumption of popular music styles from rhythm and blues, rock 'n' roll, soul, rap and hip-hop. In *Just My Soul Responding*, Ward offers a penetrating analysis of the connection between internal black cultural forms and the external political contexts in which they were shaped.[71] As such, it paves the way for further investigation of the interrelationship between the black freedom struggle and popular culture as represented in black comedy, radio broadcasting, theatre, dance, and art.[72]

Another fruitful area of research that has captured increased attention is religion. Most of the early studies of the religious foundations of the civil rights movement centered around the Reverend King's liberationist Christian theology. Recent studies have expanded to include white clergy and their congregations. The importance of this subject can be paraphrased in Dr. King's reflection that the most segregated hour in America was 11:00 on Sunday mornings when Americans attended church. The centrality of religion in the South and the prominence of Judaeo-Christian values in American life beg the question of how predominantly white churches accommodated segregation and what some of them finally did to move toward racial brotherhood and sisterhood. Studies of the past decade have branched out to include how various religious denominations and clergy related to the civil rights movement. James Findlay Jr. has chronicled the National Council of Churches as a powerful lobbying organization for civil rights as well as its efforts in sustaining organizing in the Mississippi Delta. Findlay's book also offers a useful example of combining the national with the local that still eludes most work on the movement. We know much more today than in 1990 about the experiences of southern white Presbyterians, Methodists, Episcopalians, and Jews during the civil rights era.[73]

Despite the emphasis on localism in the movement, historians have continued to write about the national government and civil rights. In the past several years books have appeared about the presidencies of Harry Truman, Richard Nixon, and Ronald Reagan, specifically related to their civil rights policies. They suffer from the limitation of previous studies by focusing almost exclusively on the White House as the central agency for orchestrating the movement or, in the cases of Nixon and Reagan, nearly liquidating it.[74] There is every reason to study the implementation of the landmark civil rights laws, executive orders, and judicial decisions that accompanied the black freedom struggle; however, historians have to take into account not just high administration officials and bureaucrats in Washington who initiated and carried out these policies, but also the residents of local communities who were affected by them. In this vein, J. Morgan Kousser has written a painstaking study of how black litigants in local communities battled attempts to limit the application of the 1965 Voting Rights Act. James Patterson has performed a similar feat in reexamining the implementation of *Brown v. Board of Education*.[75]

"Freedom Then—Freedom Now" originally was inspired by the publication of David Garrow's multi-volume anthology of Martin Luther King, Jr., and the civil rights movement. It is appropriate to conclude this update with a discussion of the King literature. Although scholars of the past decade have heeded the call to abandon the King-centered approach to civil rights history, the fascination with King persists. Charles Eagles has criticized movement scholars for failing to detach themselves sufficiently from their subject. For example, in the year 2000, he argued that "[for] all the attention to Martin Luther King Jr., scholars have been rather cautious in their treatment of the Nobel Laureate."[76] However, much evidence challenges this assertion. Eagles was referring to the putative downplaying of charges against King of plagiarism and womanizing. A look at the literature of the 1990s, as Eagles acknowledges, finds a thematic issue of the *Journal of American History* devoted to King's plagiarism as well as two important books that discuss in detail King's "borrowing" in preparing his sermons. A new book by Michael Eric Dyson does not spare King from an examination of his plagiarism and adultery.[77] Thus, recent historians have not avoided these sensitive subjects, though it remains unclear what light they shed on the internal development of the civil rights movement.

Rather the problem for current and future historians is not to lose sight of King's critical role in the movement and still demonstrate that he was part of a larger and longer black freedom struggle. In whittling King down to size, historians run the risk of being unable to explain to a new generation of students, born some two decades after King's death, what he meant to most ordinary people inspired by the movement. In his second volume on America during the King years, Taylor Branch manages to write more about the times than the life of the civil rights leader. Indeed, King virtually disappears from this account for long stretches of time.[78] Branch reinforces the view that there would have been a civil rights movement without Martin Luther King, which is undoubtedly true. However, scholars should not lose sight of the reality that King's presence had an enormous impact on how the movement progressed and was received. Fortunately, Peter J. Ling's one-volume biography of King strikes a reasonable balance between the minister and the movement. He views the dynamic interaction between the two and concludes that King was a more innovative leader for the movement after 1965 than before. Acknowledging his strength as a mobilizer rather than an organizer, Ling justly argues that whereas King's successes should be shared with countless others in the movement, so should responsibility for his failures be equally distributed.[79]

Studying King's life continues to be relevant for understanding the power of the civil rights movement. As Dyson has affirmed, by looking closely at King one witnesses the transformative effect the movement had on its participants. Issues of moral lapses pale beside the strength of character people like King exhibited in the face of constant danger. They showed uncommon courage in their willingness to embrace revolutionary solutions that would threaten their relationship with former allies and powerful government officials who could cause them a great deal of harm.

Looking back over the past forty years of civil rights scholarship there is little question that authors have sympathized with the goal of overthrowing white supremacy. Yet even with this egalitarian consensus historians have had healthy disagreements over the focus, scope, and conceptualization of the movement.[80] New subjects for exploration have been included—gender and class come easily to mind—a variety of individuals and organizations have gained attention, and the chronology of struggle has broadened considerably. If historians continue to build upon and challenge the work of the past, the future of civil rights studies will continue to thrive.

PART TWO

LYNDON B. JOHNSON AND THE BLACK FREEDOM STRUGGLE

EXPLORING JOHNSON'S CIVIL RIGHTS POLICY

Lyndon Johnson spent the final months of his life filled with memories of the civil rights struggle that had greatly influenced his political career. In December 1972, at a symposium held at the Johnson Library, the former president heard an array of notable civil rights leaders commemorate his achievements in promoting racial justice. Several weeks later, during his last televised interview, Johnson spoke about civil rights. With the sound of explosions in Southeast Asia fading and in the relaxed one-to-one format in which he clearly excelled, the retired chief executive passionately recalled for Walter Cronkite the way it was in demolishing Jim Crow. These farewell appearances, unlike so many other presentations during his presidential years, did not generate charges of a credibility gap. Indeed, Johnson's remarkable performance in the area of civil rights commanded overwhelming praise during his lifetime and the accolades have continued seven years after his death. The Texas politician who so zealously courted consensus would be pleased with the widespread acclaim for his civil rights record.

Most commentators have agreed that the passage of three pieces of civil rights legislation in 1964, 1965, and 1968 provided ample testimony of the president's political skills and humanitarian instincts. Even those who found Johnson offensive personally or philosophically have commended his actions in behalf of black Americans. The list of admirers contains the names of members of both races and representatives of both ends of the American political spectrum. Bayard Rustin, a leading theorist in the civil rights movement, remembers "that the Johnson Administration . . . had done more . . . than any other group, any other administration. . . . I think Johnson was the best we've ever had."[1] Doris Kearns, whose psychoportrait of Johnson does not flatter the man, best states the white liberal point of view: "His position on racial issues was more advanced than that of any other American President: had he done nothing else in his entire life, his contributions to civil rights would have earned him a lasting place in the annals of history."[2] From the conservative side, which has preferred to move cautiously in expanding federal jurisdiction over race relations, George F. Will approvingly calls Johnson "the man who was more right than anyone since Lincoln on the permanent American problem, race."[3] Seconding these judgments of Johnson on the left, Bruce Miroff, a radical critic of Kennedy-Johnson liberalism, concludes that "no other administration accomplished so much in the way of civil rights legislation; no other President undertook such a rhetorical commitment to the black cause."[4]

This historical consensus, however, has not guaranteed unanimity. Detractors of Johnson's civil rights efforts generally have attacked from the left. Some dissenters have attributed the failure to eradicate racial inequality to the liberal capitalist system and its most successful practitioner of reform. Ronald Radosh discerns an "Administration plan for keeping the Negro movement tied to the corporate system" and deplores "politicians of the Democratic Party [who] have co-opted the Negroes and used sentiment and the vote to reinforce the predominance of the Washington consensus."[5] Others have condemned President Johnson for not pursuing stronger measures than he did within the prevailing politico-economic system. According to this view, Johnson could have wielded presidential authority to protect civil rights workers in the South, to realign the Democratic party in Dixie, and to enforce more vigorously the powerful civil rights legislation he had helped place on the books. "To overcome the tendency of states' rights to hurt the cause of civil rights for black people," James C. Harvey contends, "strong presidential leadership was needed. It never was forthcoming."[6] These critics ascribe Johnson's weakness to a traditional conception of the limits of national power in a federal system, a failure to develop and support effective enforcement machinery within the executive bureaucracy, a cautious response to the political backlash of disgruntled white voters, and a preoccupation with the Vietnam War. For these reasons, John Herbers, a perceptive journalist for the *New York Times*, charges that once civil rights laws were enacted "it was the Johnson Administration that instituted, in 1965, a gradualism of its own and passed along the whole process to its successor."[7]

Most appraisals of the Johnson presidency and civil rights have been written without benefit of research at the Lyndon B. Johnson Library. Contemporary accounts relied extensively on data gleaned from the public record and from personal interviews with individuals who played leading roles in shaping administration policy. The civil rights revolution of the 1960s attracted intensive and high-caliber media coverage; reports sketched the broad outlines of Johnsonian strategy and its execution. The first-rate quality of investigative journalism provided inside accounts of public policy making that in the past were seldom available until historians invaded dusty archives years after the events. In scooping stories from historians, journalists fortunately dug up raw materials that might never have found their way into manuscript collections. Considering Johnson's fondness for conducting business over the telephone, the enterprising reporter who pieced together unrecorded conversations based on interviews with a network of informants blazed an important historical trail. Information leaked by unnamed sources must be evaluated carefully, but scholars looking for valuable leads ignore such evidence only at their peril.

Today researchers do not have to rely exclusively on the columns appearing in newspapers and journals. In addition to periodical literature, the Government Printing Office has cranked out reams of paper documenting activities within each branch of government. Efforts to extend to blacks constitutional guarantees of equality required extraordinary exertions from presidents, members of Congress and judges. Civil rights advocates demanded from Washington an exercise of national power that would assist African Americans in reversing centuries of discrimination. Thus, writing a history of the racial struggle during the Johnson years demands a substantial expenditure of energy just to collect and read through accessible published works. The president's public papers, transcripts of congressional proceedings, agency reports, particularly the volumes put out by the United States Commission on Civil Rights, and the opinions of the Supreme Court abundantly mark the course for historians to follow. The problem for current researchers stems from abundance rather than shortage.

Those interested in probing beyond the massive public record will also encounter a huge collection of documents deposited at the Johnson Library. Open since 1973, the library has swiftly processed manuscripts related to civil rights. The rapid availability of these papers attests to Johnson's deep personal faith in the cause of civil rights and, perhaps, to his confidence that the documentary evidence would demonstrate that no other chief executive had exceeded him in furthering racial equality. Over the past seven years, researchers have not rushed to dispute the glittering evaluation offered by Clarence Mitchell, an NAACP official whose oral memoir is stored at the library. Johnson "made a greater contribution to giving a dignified and hopeful status to Negroes in the United States than any President including Lincoln, Roosevelt, and Kennedy," Mitchell rhapsodized.[8]

34

The general agreement on Johnson's sponsorship of the civil rights cause has not closed off considerable opportunities for original research. The holdings of the Johnson Library have lured an increasing number of investigators in recent years; however, only a few monographs on race relations have appeared in print. Historians seem reluctant to enter a field which has received so much prior attention from journalists, participant-observers, and analysts in such sister disciplines as sociology and political science. Nevertheless, many aspects of Johnsonian policy toward African Americans await careful study based on a fresh reading of the large quantity of archival sources. The task involves an exploration of the fields of education, employment, housing, voting, military service, criminal justice, and public accommodations. While examining the political arena in Washington, investigators must also keep track of forces at the grassroots level—demonstrations, riots, backlash—beyond the direct control of the federal government. Writers who manage to thread together the diverse strands of the civil rights mosaic will weave a rich design surpassing previous compositions.

An accurate assessment of President Johnson's role in civil rights must take into account the distance traveled by the Texan since the beginning of his political career. Johnson developed gradually into a forceful advocate of racial emancipation. He was not a Negrophobe, but until 1957 he faithfully followed the southern congressional coalition in opposition to civil rights legislation. In 1957 and 1960, however, he used his position as Senate majority leader to maneuver passage of the first civil rights bills enacted since Reconstruction. At the time, commentators speculated that Johnson had changed his mind, hoping to enlarge his appeal nationally and to increase his availability as a Democratic presidential candidate.[9]

On the basis of a review of Johnson's congressional papers dealing with civil rights, historians have deemphasized personal ambition and have stressed that Johnson showed a capacity for growth as he represented broader constituencies than those in the Lone Star State. Monroe Billington has authored the most complimentary appraisal of Johnson's early years as a director of the National Youth Administration and a congressman from the tenth district in Texas. Although Johnson "did not support civil rights legislation in the 1930's and 1940's," Billington concludes, "there is no reason to believe that he did not sincerely desire to help blacks. The practical situation tempered his private attitudes."[10] This account does not focus on the period when Johnson served as majority leader and his public stand shifted. Examining his performance during that era, Steven Lawson and Mark Gelfand contend that Johnson desired to preserve peace between the warring factions of the Democratic Party. He attempted to accomplish this aim by molding a civil rights bill acceptable to northern moderates and southern conservatives.[11] In contrast, Joe B. Frantz pays less attention to the political considerations influencing Johnson's decisions. Drawing upon interviews from the Johnson Library Oral History Project, Frantz argues that Johnson advanced "in a remarkably straight line, a generally progressive line, with now and then an aberration that might be inexcusable but no more damnable than the aberrations that most of the remainder of us sometimes perpetrate."[12] The availability of Johnson's congressional papers on civil rights should encourage a continuation of the inquiry into how he balanced regional loyalties and national aspirations to move beyond the parochialism of his southern colleagues.

The support Johnson gave to civil rights legislation paralleled his climb up the political ladder. Having shed some of the stigma that frustrated the presidential ambitions of other Dixie politicians, this grandson of a Confederate soldier teamed with John F. Kennedy, a senator from Yankee New England, to capture the White House in 1960. As vice-president, Johnson continued to mature as a proponent of equal rights, but this process has received scant attention. His thousand days in the number two spot were not happy times, because, as T. Harry Williams points out, "Johnson, who knew about power and had exulted in its use, now had none and could only watch others use it, most of them younger men, the courtiers of Camelot who ignored or patronized him and out of his hearing called him Uncle Cornpone."[13] Nevertheless, life in the Kennedy administration offered him new opportunities to expand his understanding of the moral dimensions of the quickening black struggle.

During those years, Johnson headed the President's Committee on Equal Employment Opportunity (PCEEO). Charged with this responsibility, he worked closely with Plans for Progress, a project designed by the administration to persuade government contractors to correct racially biased employment practices. Journalist Leonard Baker and historian Carl Brauer have commented upon the vice-president's role in civil rights. Both acknowledge the limited effectiveness of the job programs which depended upon voluntarism and conciliation. Whereas Baker observed Johnson assuming a more activist position on civil rights by the middle of 1963, Brauer did not hear the vice-president raise his voice within Kennedy councils in defense of strong legislative measures. He pictures Johnson as a cautious advisor urging the president to avoid the prospects of a disastrous fight over the civil rights bill introduced in June.[14]

An extraordinary document contained in the prepresidential files of the Johnson Library reveals LBJ's reservations about Kennedy's civil rights strategy. On June 3, 1963, the vice-president and Theodore Sorenson, a top White House aide, held a lengthy telephone conversation which Johnson recorded on a dictaphone machine. The tape and transcript of the talk offer fascinating insights into Johnson's views of racial politics. Almost uninterrupted for over thirty minutes, Johnson criticized the Kennedy people for failing to do their legislative homework in paving the way for legislation. "I think it can be more constructive," he lectured, "and I think it can be better . . . I don't know who drafted it; I've never seen it. Hell, if the Vice President doesn't know what's in it how do you expect the others to know what's in it? I got it from the *New York Times*." According to the former majority leader, the question centered on timing. A poorly planned congressional fight would sacrifice the rest of the New Frontier measures. If Kennedy sent up his civil rights proposals immediately, Johnson warned, "Howard Smith is going to be in the lead in one place and Dick Russell in the other place, and they're going to sit quietly in these appropriation committees and they're going to cut his outfit off and put it in their pocket and never mention civil rights. So I'd move my children on through the line and get them down in the storm cellar and get it locked and key, and I'd make my attack. I'd tell the Negroes what I'm doing."[15]

Johnson's approach to racial problems was clearly evolving. This native son of Dixie believed that white southerners could be persuaded to listen to reason, and he recommended that President Kennedy travel to a southern city, look its residents "in the eye," and articulate "the moral issue and the Christian issue." At the same time, the vice-president maintained the blacks felt uncertain that the federal government stood behind their struggle. Thus, Johnson urged a strong presidential expression on the morality of racial equality to show blacks that "we're on their side . . . and . . . until they receive that assurance, unless it's stated dramatically and convincingly, they're not going to pay much attention to executive orders and legislative recommendations."[16] Eight days after the Johnson-Sorenson discussion, President Kennedy delivered his most fervent civil rights address on national televison; however, it is unknown whether this message reflected Johnson's advice.

Vice-President Johnson's thinking on this subject needs further study. The Johnson Library's prepresidential files contain records of the PCEEO and the files of George Reedy and Hobart Taylor, Johnson's closest advisers on racial matters at the time. A review of these papers will help illuminate the vice-president's performance in carrying out his major civil rights assignments, his role in fashioning administration responses to racial confrontations, and his outlook toward the escalating pace of those conflicts. Given the former majority leader's successes in shepherding two civil rights acts through Congress and his ongoing contacts on Capitol Hill, investigators should look for clues to explain why Kennedy refrained from utilizing him to push strong legislative measures before a wave of terrorism rolled through the South in the summer of 1963.[17]

Several months after a long, hot season of demonstrations culminating in a mammoth march on Washington, D.C., tragedy presented Lyndon Johnson with the opportunity and power to prove how deep his concern for racial equality had grown. The murder of President Kennedy gave Johnson a chance to fulfill what he had come to recognize as his "moral obligation to every person of every skin color" and also to help his native South cast aside the oppressive race issue.[18] The extension of freedom to blacks carried the potential of liberating white southerners from a caste system which economically and socially impoverished both races in the region. Tom Wicker, a native-born North Carolinian and an astute columnist for the *New York Times*, observes that Johnson *"as a Southerner* . . . was better placed than any man to recognize that full national unity and sweeping national progress . . . was not possible until the South had somehow been brought back into the Union."[19] Building on this journalistic analysis, Professor T. Harry Williams remarks, "It has been insufficiently appreciated that Johnson believed the elimination of segregation would lift an onus from his section, would enable southern whites to stand as equals with that majority that had looked down on them for their racial practices."[20]

Over the next five years, President Johnson signed into law three civil rights measures aimed at crushing the barriers of racial separation in public accommodations, education, and housing; extending equal employment opportunities; and expanding the right to vote. Their passage tested the President's ability to construct a consensus around controversial proposals and to patch up the coalition when it showed signs of cracking. President by virtue of assassination, Johnson had much to prove. Doris Kearns recalls his saying, "I knew that if I didn't get out in front on this issue, [the liberals] would get me. . . . I had to produce a civil rights bill that was even stronger than the one they'd have gotten if Kennedy had lived. Without this, I'd be dead before I could even begin."[21] At the outset, the martyrdom of John Kennedy and vivid memories of southern blacks suffering "Bull"

Connor's racist brutality in Birmingham created the right political atmosphere for Johnson to work his miracles in Congress. However, the chief executive had to exercise his formidable skills in a hostile climate once the feeling of national bereavement wore off and liberals attacked the administration's escalation of the war in Vietnam. Thus, passage of a series of monumental civil rights bills occurred under varying circumstances within a short span of years.

When Johnson took office on November 22, 1963, his predecessor's civil rights bill lay stalled in the Rules Committee of the House of Representatives. The Kennedy administration had conducted intensive negotiations with members of Congress in order to write legislation with sufficient clout and favorable chances for enactment. Such a proposal had emerged from the House Judiciary Committee, which was dominated by civil rights proponents. Committed to its passage as a memorial to the slain Kennedy, on November 27 President Johnson delivered a stirring civil-rights-as-redemption message to a grieving Congress. However, neither the preliminary work done in the preceding months nor the sorrow gripping the nation ensured swift approval of the administration-backed Judiciary Committee bill. Before Johnson signed the measure into law on July 2, 1964, civil rights advocates had painstakingly broken fifty-seven days of filibustering in the Senate. At the same time, they had kept momentum for the bill rolling over the presidential primary bandwagon of George Wallace, the Alabama governor whose bigoted appeals found increasing acceptance in the North.

The Johnson administration finally overcame traditional congressional roadblocks and an incipient white backlash, but its achievement has attracted little interest from scholars. A few brief accounts of the parliamentary maneuvering leading to passage of the act have appeared, but they are limited in scope. The most detailed treatment to date, Daniel Berman's *A Bill Becomes a Law*, follows the legislative routes taken by the Civil Rights Act of 1960 and, to a lesser extent, the 1964 statute. The author describes proceedings on Capitol Hill, largely ignoring events outside the halls of Congress.[22] For some specialists of the Kennedy years, neglecting the Johnson White House has not constituted much of a loss. They have implied that Johnson's presence as chief executive made little difference in obtaining the ultimate victory. "What might have happened had Kennedy not been assassinated is of course impossible to establish," Carl Brauer asserts, "but many of those closest to the legislative process later reflected that essentially the same goal would have been reached."[23]

Johnson has minimized his own efforts in battling for the bill. Writing in *The Vantage Point*, he remembers, "I deliberately tried to tone down my personal involvement in the daily struggle so that my colleagues on the Hill could take tactical responsibility and credit."[24] This strategy has partially obscured the diligence with which the president commanded the congressional offensive. Whether courting the indispensable Everett Dirksen, the Senate Republican leader, or making public speeches, Johnson never ceased guiding the long legislative fight. One of the most crucial reasons for success was Johnson's refusal, uncharacteristic of his style as a legislator, to accept compromise. Indeed, he insisted that Congress postpone other business until it had favorably disposed of the omnibus civil rights bill. Patience paid off as liberal senators outlasted their loquacious southern adversaries and Dirksen lined up his followers behind the measure.[25]

The Johnson Library offers documentation of some of the activities initiated by the executive branch to clear passage of the bill. Administrative histories furnish a good place to start. Compiled by departmental officials in the waning months of the Johnson term, these accounts consist of a narrative appended with selected material from bureau files. Although these annals exude self-congratulation, they shift attention away from the pervasive White House and refocus it on the routine work of the federal bureaucracy. These chronicles trace internal policy deliberations which preceded a final recommendation conveyed to the president by the top agency chief.

According to the *Administrative History* of the Justice Department, major policy decisions concerning the bill had been made during the Kennedy regime. After November 1963, the Justice Department concentrated on "Congressional liaison and preparation of materials in support of the Administration bill."[26] Civil Rights Division lawyers helped lawmakers to understand and defend critical provisions of the proposal, while the White House rounded up support in its behalf. Lee White, who advised both Kennedy and Johnson on racial affairs, reported that there "have been countless meetings, discussions, phone calls to Congressional leaders, minority group representatives, and Administration personnel." Some of those conversations involved attempts to obtain enough votes to impose cloture in the Senate. To win over Carl Hayden of Arizona, "who [would] carry several other votes with him—such as the two Nevada Senators," the administration promised to negotiate a favorable solution to a controversial water project in Hayden's home state, "contingent upon the promise of a cloture vote by Hayden on civil rights."[27] One oral history interview indicates that Johnson also exerted pressure on his reform allies. Hubert Humphrey recalled that the president prodded him to show that liberal "bomb throwers" could depart from their customary speech making long enough to produce tangible results.[28]

Passage of the 1964 act came at a crucial juncture in the administration's involvement with the civil rights movement. Preparing to campaign for the presidency, Johnson did not want chaotic scenes of black agitation to frighten white voters into the camp of Barry Goldwater, the conservative Republican candidate who had voted against the civil rights bill. After the ceremony signing the measure into law, the president spoke privately with a group of civil rights leaders and admonished "that there be an understanding of the fact that the rights Negroes possessed could now be secured by law, making demonstrations unnecessary and possibly even self-defeating."[29] Agreeing with the chief executive, each of his listeners except representatives from the Congress of Racial Equality (CORE) and the Student Nonviolent Coordinating Committee (SNCC), the most militant of the groups, urged blacks to suspend large-scale protests until after the November election. Although sporadic violence flared both in the South and the North, Johnson easily won the contest. However, brutal assaults on civil rights workers spending a summer in Mississippi and riots by blacks in urban ghettos of the North flashed ominous warnings that racial strife would bring new problems for the administration.[30]

Elected president in his own right, Johnson preferred to postpone further legislative action on civil rights, but the resumption of mass protests in Selma, Alabama, in 1965 forced him to change his mind. The struggle for passage of the 1965 Voting Rights Act has received the fullest treatment of any aspect of Johnson's civil rights policies. Using documents in the Johnson Library, David Garrow's *Protest at Selma* and Steven Lawson's *Black Ballots* conclude that before Martin Luther King launched his demonstrations in Alabama, Johnson had authorized the Justice Department to sketch possible legislation removing obstacles that impeded black voter registration in the South. Lawyers at the Justice Department were roughing out their drafts when state troopers viciously assaulted a parade of protesters attempting to walk from Selma to Montgomery on Sunday, March 7, 1965. Both authors conclude the bloody attack ensured that the eventual bill "would be enacted into law, and with only minimal delay and no weakening amendments."[31]

In a most interesting departure for others to follow, Garrow compares the unusually prompt passage of the Voting Rights Act with the prolonged deliberations that had preceded approval of the civil rights law a year earlier. He suggests that Congress reacted with greater speed to the Selma demonstrators than those in Birmingham because the former remained nonviolent and stuck to a single issue. This analysis emphasizes the impact of media coverage in shaping congressional responses to racial confrontations. Consideration should also be given to Johnson's augmented influence with the eighty-ninth Congress, which seated far more liberal members than those who had watched events unfold in Birmingham. Furthermore, a bill devoted to voting rights, long considered the foundation of representative government, had political advantages over a measure addressing the more controversial issues of education and employment. A comparison of mail received by the White House during the course of debates on the two civil rights bills might reveal the differences in public perception of the need for each piece of legislation. Nevertheless, in both instances, the violence inflicted upon peaceful civil rights activists in due course swung sentiment behind reform measures.

In contrast, the moral indignation that fostered enactment of these two powerful measures had subsided by the time a third proposal became law in 1968. The final legislative component in Johnson's civil rights trilogy, it combatted racial discrimination in housing and jury selection and punished those who interfered with civil rights workers encouraging the exercise of constitutionally guaranteed rights. Reflecting changing times, the act also included penalties for individuals who traveled across state lines to foment or participate in a riot. The consensus that sustained earlier legislative victories had fractured under the stress of the Vietnam War and ghetto riots, thus making passage of this omnibus bill a significant feat. A full investigation of the attempts to secure this controversial proposal from 1966 through 1968 can offer insight into Johnson's endurance in extending first-class citizenship to blacks, and it may also provide a glimpse of the president's attitudes toward the altered contours of the civil rights movement.

Unlike the situation in 1964 and 1965, no single crisis with the drama of Birmingham or Selma mobilized the administration into action. However, a series of well-publicized slayings of civil rights workers in the South and the subsequent acquittal of the accused murders did prompt the Justice Department to search for ways of strengthening impartial jury selection. After Alabama prosecutors failed to obtain a conviction in the murder case of Viola Liuzzo, a pilgrim to Selma, Joseph Califano, who coordinated the president's domestic legislative programs, reported to his boss on October 25, 1965, that there was "an increasing likelihood . . . that we will have for consideration in the civil rights area next year proposals on jury selection systems."[32] Before the end of the year, Attorney General Nicholas Katzenbach had added to the legislative list items for expanding "federal jurisdiction to investigate civil rights crimes and enhance personal security."[33] By the time President Johnson delivered his civil rights message to Congress on April 28, 1966, the administration had broadened its proposal to include provisions banning racial discrimination in housing, the most controversial features of the omnibus measure.

The protracted, uphill struggle to obtain passage of the bill has received the least detailed treatment of any of Johnson's civil rights laws.[34] Perhaps the shift in emphasis after 1965 from integration toward the development of a separate black consciousness has lessened interest in studying the persistence of traditional civil rights goals in the late 1960s. Nevertheless, James C. Harvey has outlined the basic chronology of events leading to enactment of the 1968 statute. Written before the Johnson Library officially opened its doors, the description in *Black Civil Rights during the Johnson Administration* relies on data from newspapers, periodicals, and government documents. Since then, the library's civil rights papers have become available; they await inspection by scholars attempting to explain how the measure passed with powerful odds against it. In doing so, researchers will evaluate Harvey's conclusion that while "the president did utilize a number of levers at his disposal, . . . [in] the case of the Civil Rights Act of 1968 . . . Clarence Mitchell [the NAACP's Washington lobbyist] deserves more credit for its passage than Johnson himself."[35]

A large collection of archival sources covers the 1968 Civil Rights Act, permitting an inquiry from several directions. The Justice Department, the White House staff, officials of civil rights groups, congressional leaders, and the president assumed key roles in the battle. The Justice Department's *Administrative History* describes the successive stages in drafting the measure to satisfy civil rights organizations and to meet objections raised by Senator Dirksen, without whose support once again, Attorney General Ramsey Clark reported, "we are pessimistic about being able to vote cloture."[36]

During congressional deliberations on the bill in 1966, the House of Representatives added an antiriot amendment, thereby weakening the measure. Although the president opposed it, he still had to answer the clamor for tough action in the wake of summer uprisings in northern ghettos. His concern was reflected in late November and December as an intergovernmental task force on civil rights met to map out plans for the coming legislative session. Summoned by Joseph Califano, this group of representatives from the White House staff and the Department of Justice advised the president that a civil rights bill "would probably not pass unless an 'anti-riot' proposal is included." In plotting strategy, the task-force members recommended that "it might be better to include an acceptably narrow 'anti-riot' provision in the proposal—over which we would have a degree of control—than to have a broader 'anti-riot' provision added by Congress."[37]

The housing sections posed another serious problem for the administration. The White House came under intense pressure to adopt even stronger civil rights provisions than it had originally introduced. The most forceful suggestions emerged from the White House Conference on Civil Rights held in early June 1966. The vast records of the conference, including working papers, transcripts of proceedings, and reports, reveal that recommendations adopted by the panelists exceeded in scope those authorized by the task force and accepted by the president.[38] At the same time, the real estate industry organized a potent lobby against the housing measures, and its efforts seemed to strike a responsive chord in public opinion. Some White House aides bluntly warned that the "housing proposal will be impossible to enact," but the president stood by his original proposal. He emphatically insisted that support must be built "for all of the package and not just for parts of it."[39]

Johnson maintained this stance for two years, and in March 1968, he watched his supporters choke off a filibuster after three unsuccessful cloture attempts. The bill was about to clear its final congressional hurdle in the House when large-scale rioting broke out following the assassination of Martin Luther King. The impact upon Congress of King's death and the disorders that it unleashed remains undetermined, but the judgment of Barefoot Sanders, the President's legislative liaison, is instructive. The murder of King did not have much effect, Sanders recall, "because the yeas and nays cancelled each other out."[40] Much of the sympathy for the bill prompted by the slaying gave way to anger as members of Congress on their way to the Capitol inhaled smoke from burning buildings torched by mobs rampaging through Washington, D.C. When the civil rights leader died in Memphis, the House was considering what route to take on the administration bill already approved by the Senate. The lower chamber could endorse the measure or call for a conference committee which would delay final acceptance and probably result in dilution of the bill. The lawmakers chose the first alternative. Apparently, the administration broke the legislative stalemate by holding in line the votes secured before the tragic killings and the subsequent turbulence.

The most important issues arising from a study of the Civil Rights Act of 1968 concern Lyndon Johnson's responses to the changing configuration of the racial struggle. As the civil rights coalition diminished in size and white reactionary forces grew, Johnson refused to order a major retreat on the legislative front. However, in honoring his moral commitment to extend first-class citizenship, the president had to take into account the political considerations upsetting his legislative consensus. Critics have accused him of backing away from his firm support of civil rights after northern white voters exhibited their hostility not only to riots but to black militancy in general. James Harvey speculates that Johnson did not push the civil rights bill in 1966 because "he was thinking about the growing white backlash."[41] However, such a conclusion, besides requiring verification, ignores the possibility that black agitation may have stiffened Johnson's resolve to persist in prying loose the civil rights bill from Congress.

The effects of rising black aggressiveness on White House policy offer exciting avenues for research. As SNCC and CORE abandoned white liberals and blacks in the ghettos spontaneously released their rage against symbols of white authority, the Johnson administration rushed to reinforce advocates of peaceful change. The prospects of racial violence in the cities, beginning with the summer of 1964, prompted Johnson advisers to find ways, as Eric Goldman notes, "to help the established Negro leaders, who may well be losing control of the civil rights movement, to reestablish control and keep the movement going in its legitimate direction."[42] To accomplish this aim demanded sensitivity and finesse. Harry McPherson, who succeeded Lee White as Johnson's principal counselor on race, recalls the problem facing his boss: "Johnson . . . understood that while he needed [Whitney] Young and [Roy] Wilkins and [A. Philip] Randolph and [Bayard] Rustin, that his embrace of them would endanger them after a short time with the Negro community. And yet he needed them and did use them in urgent situations."[43] An exchange of memoranda in September 1966 between McPherson and Attorney General Katzenbach delineates this thorny dilemma. The White House aide pointed out that "our lines of communication to the movement run generally . . . to the older Negro establishment. We have very few contacts with younger Negro leaders. We *must* develop these contacts." Katzenbach responded on a note of pessimism, contending that the "younger leaders who now exist are precisely whose who . . . have consistently chosen an 'outside course': that is, Stokely Carmichael." Nevertheless, he did recommend that the NAACP, the Urban League, and the Southern Christian Leadership Conference (SCLC) consider "establishing a militant but peaceful organization of young people who could successfully compete with SNCC."[44] Nothing specific came of the idea, but the administration's attempts to develop alternatives to black violence and to bolster the position of conventional civil rights leaders merit a full investigation.

The annual outbreak of summer riots made matters worse for the White House. In contrast to the brutality suffered by peaceful protesters, the violence perpetrated by black mobs preaching physical retaliation hurt the administration politically. Recognizing that"every night of rioting costs us the support of thousands," one Johnson lieutenant suggested that the chief executive "appeal to the good sense and conscience of the country both white and Negro. Denounce violence, but recognize frustration. Be firm in the insistence on obedience to law"[45] Plagued by urban upheavals that increased in intensity each year during his second term, Johnson adopted a moderate course of action. Aimed at extending victories won by his loyal civil rights allies, the President's program also acknowledged the fears for personal safety voiced by Americans, white and black. McPherson echoes the difficulty liberals experienced in striking a delicately balanced response: "'By God, there's law and order here. You can't get away with this,' followed by 'Of course we understand why you rioted. We know you could hardly do anything else.'"[46] How to respond to social and economic maladies infecting the ghettos without "rewarding the rioters" continuously perplexed the president and his advisers.[47]

Disorders in Watts, Newark, and Detroit raise a number of questions. Did the White House learn from the initial explosions any lessons that it applied to later problems? Did partisan political considerations, such as the presence of a Democratic or Republican governor, affect Johnson's handling of particular riots? A comparison of the strife in Newark with that in Detroit offers a good case study of this point. In pacifying insurrections in the North, did the administration follow the same principles as it did in answering requests by civil rights workers in the South for federal protection from white racists? Besieged by demands to repair the breakdown of law and order that hampered the civil rights movement in Dixie, the Justice Department customarily refrained from intervening, contending that the federal system delegated law enforcement duties to local officials.[48]

In the past, presidents had established commissions to study volatile civil rights problems and to recommend solutions. Following this tradition, Johnson created a group of inquiry headed by Otto Kerner to examine the urban disorders. However, when the panel suggested strong measures and condemned white racism, the White House ignored its proposals. Why did Johnson choose to scuttle the Kerner Commission's report? By doing so, he left the impression that he viewed it "as an attack on [his] administration calling for too much Federal spending while the Vietnam war is going on."[49]

The Vietnam War earned some dividends for civil rights advocates while it also unsettled their ranks and drained funds and attention from their struggle. The need to build and maintain a consensus in support of escalation in Southeast Asia may have influenced Johnson's support of additional civil rights measures after 1965. Although SNCC and CORE attacked the administration's Vietnam policy from the start, the NAACP, the Urban League, and the SCLC attempted to divorce foreign and domestic affairs. Whitney Young of the Urban League derided white liberals who ignored the president's "impressive record of accomplishing what they have been fighting for for years and work themselves into a lather over Vietnam." NAACP Executive Secretary Roy Wilkins spent "a considerable amount of his time . . . keeping the 'peace in Viet Nam movement' from becoming too big a factor in the civil rights movement."[50] In defending the war, the majority of black leaders sought to maintain Johnson's backing for their unfinished programs in housing, employment, and education. Vietnam and the riots isolated the president from black radicals, but drew him closer to such moderates as Wilkins and Young.

It remains for historians to estimate the impact of the Vietnam War on civil rights. The heavy combat load shouldered by blacks overseas gave civil rights leaders ammunition to use in fighting their battles on the home front. "For the first time," a black adviser to the president declared, "the U.S. has fielded a truly democratic team in Vietnam," a situation that provided the premise for arguments for extending racial equality.[51] The threat posed to this ideological weapon by antiwar groups urging withdrawal from Vietnam may help explain the vehemence with which black leaders loyal to the President attacked the dissenters. In selling the war to their constituents, Negro leaders cemented presidential support for their goals, but they paid a high price for their endorsement. Not only did the conflict splinter the civil rights forces, but the war also crowded vital domestic programs off the list of top priorities. By 1968, according to Ramsey Clark, Johnson had shifted "his concerns and time . . . so far toward Vietnam that his involvement [in civil rights] was very, very limited."[52]

One of the casualties lost in the war was the president's association with Martin Luther King. In winning some of his greatest victories from 1963 through 1965, King had come to depend on the power of the federal government. Although viewed as a militant, he was considered a responsible leader who usually listened to White House reason. King enjoyed administration cooperation as long as he kept private his reservations about the war. The breach that developed between Johnson and King after 1967 closed off to each side options for pursuing racial advancement.[53]

Public opposition to the Vietnam War soured King's relationship with Johnson. Soon after passage of the Voting Rights Act in August 1965, administration advisers began expressing concern over King's "trying to get into the Vietnam act."[54] Over the next two years, presidential aides tried to compute the most "difficult part of the equation: . . . what Martin Luther King will do next."[55] During that time, King's name continued to appear on White House invitation lists, and he or one of his assistants attended high-level strategy sessions on civil rights. However, by April 1967 King had openly denounced Johnson's policy of escalation, and the White House and its black allies sought to discredit "the crown prince of the Vietniks."[56] Shortly before King's assassination, some of the president's people responded to King's plans for a poor people's march on Washington by angrily lumping together the winner of the Nobel Peace Prize with such purveyors of violence as Stokely Carmichael and Rap Brown.[57] An inquiry into the administration's response to the subsequent march may pinpoint some of the consequences resulting from the deterioration of the alliance between the chief executive and the black leader.

Johnson's disenchantment with segments of the civil rights movement can also be discerned by examining the events surrounding the White House Conference in 1966. A speech delivered by the president to the graduating class of Howard University on June 4, 1965 triggered plans for a conference to address the unfinished business remaining on the nation's civil rights agenda. Beginning a new phase in pursuit of racial emancipation, the address emphasized affirmative action to remove the remnants of past discrimination. The president declared, "We seek not just freedom but opportunity—not just legal equality but human equity—not just equality as a right and a theory, but equality as a fact and a result."[58] In preparing to deliver these remarks, Johnson explained to his principal speechwriter: "It was like you couldn't pick up the blanket off a Negro at one corner, you had to pick it all up."[59]

However, the bright expectations aroused by the president's stirring message soon dissolved into acrimony. Disputes erupted over whether to schedule workshops at the projected conference on the controversial Moynihan report, a treatise widely misinterpreted as attributing the plight of African Americans to a degenerate family lifestyle. Although the conference planners finally scratched the topic from the scheduled discussions, other sources of discord persisted. The conference took place amidst undercurrents of tension between the administration and civil rights militants over Vietnam and black power. Over two thousand delegates attending the meeting ratified far-reaching proposals for massive governmental and private action, but in contrast to the year before, the president now showed little enthusiasm for jumping into "the next and most profound stage of the battle for civil rights."[60]

The standard account of the White House conference appeared a year after the event in Lee Rainwater and William L. Yancey's *The Moynihan Report and the Politics of Controversy*. The authors criticize Johnson for intentionally orchestrating the conference to persuade black Americans "that he was now in charge of the civil rights movement."[61] A valuable book based on conversations with key public officials and civil rights leaders, it can nevertheless be updated. Fresh answers are needed to explain why Johnson called the conference and what degree of control the White House exerted over the proceedings. Some have charged that Johnson intended the affair to drive a wedge in the civil right movement, allowing him to lessen pressures "to produce such a major program at the time he was escalating the war in Vietnam and couldn't do both." Harry McPherson, who helped organize the gathering and wrote his own version of it, dismisses this charge. He insists that until the middle of 1967, the president thought he could wage wars simultaneously at home and abroad.[62] Still unaccounted for are Johnson's reasons for shelving the suggestions offered by the conferees.[63]

In siding with the moderates over the militants, Johnson tried to guide the course of the civil rights struggle. Sharing the sentiments of Rainwater and Yancey, Bruce Miroff suggests that the president sought to manipulate the sometimes unruly forces for racial advancement into acceptable avenues of progress. "Threatened by the independence, dynamism, and unpredictability of black political activity," Miroff asserts, "the White House attempted to find means of directing this activity into safer and more controlled channels."[64] Civil rights proponents believed that American government was crisis oriented, that it responded most rapidly to direct confrontation. Following outbursts of militancy, officials in Washington sought to accomplish reform in piecemeal fashion, only to have a new crisis precipitate calls for more immediate and sweeping action. Critics on the left, like Miroff, aimed their attacks more at the pluralist system than at the particular chief executive who presided over it. Condemning liberals for striving to reduce conflicts through rational negotiations between competing interest groups, they preferred instead a decision-making process which encouraged a heightening of tensions through mass political demonstrations.[65]

Although seeking to keep turbulent civil rights pressures from shattering its fragile reform consensus, the Johnson administration seriously doubted that it could harness black activism. According to Nicholas Katzenbach, the president was "the country's leader toward civil rights, but this is something different from being a civil rights leader." The attorney general warned that "one of the principal difficulties of established Negro leadership has been and will continue to be taking positions that are at the same time responsible and practical—and clearly independent of the Administration."[66] Nevertheless, the White House intended to exert a calming influence on civil rights protesters. Before a discussion with Martin Luther King in 1964, Lee White suggested that "some thought should be given to providing . . . constructive channels to energies for the summer," and he endorsed the holding of religious rallies, voter registration drives, and community job programs.[67]

The desire of presidents to ameliorate disruptive social conflicts is not surprising; more importantly, historians should analyze what policy choices are selected from the available options. Two separate questions must be raised: How skillfully and imaginatively did Johnson and his staff operate within the existing framework of political institutions? How effectively did the solutions devised by liberal reformers promote genuine equality of opportunity? These queries furnish different yardsticks for measuring the overall performance of the Johnson administration in responding to black unrest.

Those judging the ability of Johnson to obtain remedies for curing racial ills must also consider how well he administered the prescribed treatments. An evaluation from this perspective turns the spotlight away from the White House and toward the departments in the executive branch. Gary Orfield has correctly pointed out that enactment of a law "means very little until the resources of the executive bureaucracies are committed to its implementation."[68] Thus, studies of the way federal agencies enforced congressional legislation are essential for reaching conclusions about the progress of civil rights during the Johnson years.

A full-scale analysis of these efforts can be undertaken with only partial assistance from the Johnson Library. Enforcement responsibilities centered primarily in the Justice Department; the Department of Health, Education and Welfare; the Department of Housing and Urban Affairs; and the Equal Employment Opportunity Commission. Their records are destined for deposit in the National Archives. Without looking through these office files, it is impossible to document substantially how agencies promulgated their guidelines and carried out their rules and regulations. Nevertheless, the Johnson Library affords the researcher opportunities to gather additional data from administrative histories, the White House central files, and transcribed interviews with department chiefs.[69]

Investigations of federal enforcement efforts provide an added dimension to the examination of the Johnson administration's responses to convulsions within the civil rights movement. Implementation activities took place mainly during a period when black radicals directed their anger against white liberals, and the mood of whites across the nation swung from sympathy for civil rights activists to hostility against black militants. In this highly charged political atmosphere, Johnson had to calculate the risks not only to his legislative program but also to his enforcement plans.

Johnson has been sharply criticized for not paying closer attention to the vital details of bureaucratic operations. Allan Wolk contends that the president "used his legislative skills to get Congress to act, but then assumed somewhat of a laissez faire attitude in which he allowed enforcement to proceed without his help or hindrance."[70] James Harvey also chides the chief executive: "Without his pressure and support the bureaucracy was often unable or unwilling to cope with counter-pressures of strategically placed southern Congressmen and the recalcitrance of their white constituents in opposition to implementation of civil rights laws."[71] Gary Orfield agrees that federal agencies performed cautiously, but he argues that moderation was occasionally necessary to ensure lasting changes within a federal system which put a premium on cooperation between Washington and local governments.[72]

Some commentators have implied that the president deliberately thwarted strong enforcement endeavors. They bemoan a decision by Johnson in late 1965 assigning overall supervision of civil rights activities to the Justice Department. In doing so, the chief executive reversed a short-lived experiment designating Vice-President Humphrey as civil rights coordinator for the White House. Critics maintain that enforcement was handicapped by this transfer of duties away from Humphrey, known as an innovator in civil rights, to Attorney General Katzenbach, who was inclined to pursue a methodical, legalistic approach.[73] The reorganization decision came at a time when Johnson and the civil rights movement had reached a crossroads; thus, researchers might consider whether it was a signpost indicating new departures in administration policy.

Two excellent monographs have already discussed the swirling currents of change affecting the performance of the bureaucracy. Orfield's penetrating study of Title VI of the 1964 Civil Rights analyzes executive operations within a dynamic political context. The author demonstrates that to a large extent enforcement efforts depended on congressional approval. Agency officials either had "to come to terms with its existing constituency or to try to create a new constituency able to generate broadly based support in Congress."[74] After 1965, legislators were horrified by the ghetto riots sweeping the nation, and they took out their wrath by pinching needed funds from federal programs. James Button's *Black Violence* suggests that admin-

istration responses to black revolts varied according to the level and intensity of the disturbances, the attitude of public officials toward the groups
participating in the disorders, the availability of government money to satisfy the protestors' demands, the clarity of the demonstrators' goals, and
the concomitant deployment of nonviolent forms of dissent. Using these
criteria, Button discerns a generally sympathetic reaction from Washington to urban unrest from 1963 to 1965 in contrast to a position of retrenchment in 1967 and 1968. These findings, along with those of David Garrow's
on Selma, indicate that the effects of violence on administration policy
shifted with the political moods of Congress and the nation.[75]

51

Explorations of the Johnson years naturally focus on Washington as
the seat of governmental power. However, scholars have studied official
business transacted in the nation's capital without examining political life
in the city itself. The District of Columbia offers a microcosmic view of
Lyndon Johnson's pursuit of racial equality. Deprived of home rule, the
district, when Johnson took office, was governed by three commissioners
appointed by the president. However, Congress made crucial decisions affecting the city, including those involving finances. The House and the Senate each had a committee which closely monitored Washington affairs. The
House Committee on the District of Columbia provided the chief stum-
bling block for home-rule advocates. Traditionally chaired by white Southerners, the House panel had resisted attempts over the years to extend
self-government to a city whose black residents comprised a majority of
the population.

Under these circumstances, Washington resembled a southern city
depriving blacks of an effective voice in government. After 1965 Washington Negroes listened carefully to exhortations on black power by Stokely
Carmichael, a graduate of the district's Howard University, and they increasingly sought to apply his lessons to their city. Although the absence of
self-government also handicapped whites living in Washington, the home-
rule issue revolved around race. The white chairman of the Board of Commissioners, an advocate of autonomy, declared that the "real reason for
opposition to home rule is the fear that Washington might be run by its
Negro citizens."[76] One northern member of Congress considered home rule
as "a sort of 'civil rights' issue" and recommended that it "might do a little
coat-tail riding in a successful civil rights fight in the House."[77]

As president, Johnson sponsored self-government measures in Congress, culminating in an intense legislative battle that narrowly failed in
1966. After the House declined to modify its own version of a bill to con-

form with one passed in the Senate, the chief executive took other steps toward home rule. In 1967, he won congressional approval for a reorganization plan dissolving the three-member governing board and replacing it with an appointed mayor and city council. Adoption of this halfway measure did not reflect a desire on Johnson's part to stop short of pursing the goal of "full elective local government"; rather, the president insisted, "successful operation of the new government will strengthen our case before the Congress."[78]

Despite obvious implications for civil rights, historians have neglected the home-rule fight. One of the rare acknowledgments of its importance, Robert Sherrill's *The Accidental President*, portrays Johnson unfavorably. Sherrill argues that the president felt scant enthusiasm for home rule and gave little help to extend it to "the only major city in America where black power could become an immediate fact."[79]

A plentiful supply of documents exists in the Johnson Library for investigators wanting to test the validity of Sherrill's harsh judgment. Details of administration strategy in managing the issue can be located in the files of several White House aides, most notably in those of Charles Horsky, who advised the president on District of Columbia matters through most of the home-rule campaign. Additional information can be found in the White House Central Files as well as in the oral histories of Charles Diggs, a black member of the House district committee; Barefoot Sanders, the legislative liaison; and Joseph Rauh, a civil rights lawyer active in the Democratic Party organization in the nation's capital. A perusal of these materials will add to an overall estimation of Johnson's role in advancing equal rights for African Americans. Attention should be devoted to the impact of the black power persuasion on presidential thinking concerning home rule. Furthermore, scholars examining the riot in Washington following Martin Luther King's assassination and the subsequent assembly of poor people can determine how, after five years of siege, the administration regarded continuing racial unrest and civil rights protests.

The Johnson years were a watershed in the struggle for racial equality in the United States. More than any president before him, Lyndon Johnson helped blacks discard the legal barriers blocking the attainment of first-class citizenship. Most of the uncompleted civil rights items on the legislative agenda he had inherited upon taking office in 1963 were enacted by the time he retired to his Texas ranch in 1969. The kind of president capable of ordering the public execution of Jim Crow, Johnson was not Eric Goldman's "wrong man from the wrong place at the wrong time under the wrong circumstances."[80] Combining moral fervor and a finely honed sense of political timing, Johnson translated the ideals of civil rights protesters into practical statutory language.

53

However, as the goals of the racial struggle leaped beyond integration and strict equality under law, the president displayed the limitations of modern liberal reformers. By philosophy and style, he was suited for achieving legislative breakthroughs within the traditional boundaries of the constitutional system. But, when administration achievements boosted black expectations of immediate economic and political power, the conventional remedies of color-blind treatment decreed by law were inadequate. The Civil Rights Act of 1964 opened up public accommodations to black patrons, but it did not enable them to acquire the funds to afford admission. The 1965 Voting Rights Act removed discriminatory suffrage requirements in the South, but it stopped short of eliminating methods of diluting the franchise, and it did not supply the resources for mobilizing the potency of black ballots. The Civil Rights Act of 1968 outlawed racial bias in the sale of houses and the rental of apartments, but it did not address the problem of furnishing adequate incomes so that blacks could escape the slums. In this second Reconstruction as in the first, the unconquered frontier bordering full emancipation was economic.

The Johnson administration's approach to solving racial problems by a redistribution of economic and political power should be examined. In his Howard University address, the president passionately asserted the need to transcend ordinary solutions. He pointed the way toward affirmative action to compensate for past abuses, and investigators should search for documentary clues to measure how much success his regime had in reversing the effects of previous discrimination in education, politics, and employment. How did the chief executive view busing? What did he do to foster realignment of the Democratic Party in fulfillment of its 1964 convention pledge to encourage increased representation by minorities?[81] How did the administration view quotas for hiring? These questions and others must be asked to determine how far Johnson was willing to move in challenging the vestiges of racial inequality.

By literal standards, Lyndon Johnson was the foremost practitioner of civil rights ever to occupy the White House. His greatest successes, T. Harry Williams notes, emerged from "measured manipulated change within the system and a consensus built on compromise."[82] However, in staking out a middle ground of reform between white conservatives and black militants, he had trouble holding the center together. The challenge for future historians of the Johnson administration is to improve upon these extemporaneous comments of Harry McPherson:

> Johnson and I and Bill Moyers and many of us around the White House were Southern liberals. We believe in integration, we believe in reason, we believe that things are going to be fine if men of good will get together and if we put down the racists. We thought that if we could be a sort of super YMCA saying "You can go to school with us, we'll educate you, train you, will get better housing" and all that sort of stuff. But we haven't really fixed it at the base which is money, security, families holding together, some power that is given to them by money.[83]

In utilizing the archives of the Johnson Library to reach an assessment of civil rights during the Johnson years, researchers should heed several warnings. Researching a history of the Johnson administration uncovers the thinking of the White House staff and agency officials more than it does the president's. The files contain volumes of evidence testifying to the opinions of presidential advisers who counseled their boss or wrote letters for his signature, but they usually lack statements penned in the chief executive's hand. The Johnson system of answering staff memoranda by checking off "yes," "no," or some other possible listing at the bottom of the page precluded an extensive written dialogue. Although one might safely assume that a presidentially scrawled check mark constituted Johnson's point of view on a particular issue, historians must allow the chief executive's actions to speak louder than his written words.

Aggravating the problem of deciphering Johnson's personal beliefs is the president's predilection for conducting important business over the telephone. Fortunately, Johnson's assistants maintained a detailed log of incoming and outgoing calls, including those at the Texas White House, and these records are deposited at the Johnson Library. In most instances, however, the subject of the conversation is not listed, though sometimes an aide jotted down on a sheet a brief description of the discussion. This practice occurred more frequently with respect to personal meetings involving the president. Notations outlining these sessions come closest to documenting the president's private thoughts. Although most conversations were unrecorded, the Diary Backup Files nevertheless help identify the individuals who advised the chief executive on routine matters and in time of racial crisis. (It was later revealed that Johnson taped his calls.)[84]

Oral histories may also fill in some of the gaps in the written materials. More than forty transcribed interviews in the Johnson Library touch upon the subject of civil rights. The respondents include government officials and private citizens, and supporters and opponents of civil rights measures. However, these interviews suffer from some shortcomings. They vary in quality depending on the pertinence of the questions raised and on the candor and memory of the interviewees. Furthermore, the library needs to supplement its collection by arranging to add oral memoirs of a number of individuals presently absent from the project.[85]

Presidential libraries have inherent drawbacks. Like its counterparts, the Johnson Library presents a view of the past from the top, obviously reflecting in its records the presidential vantage point of social change. This tendency stems from the organization of manuscript collections around specific administrations, an arrangement that may misdirect the civil rights researcher by suggesting presidential omnipotence in shaping race relations. In choosing to focus on the Johnson administration, one orients a study toward Washington and away from the grassroots level from which the civil rights struggle derived most of its creative energies. In countering the presidential bias, investigators must carefully examine the interplay of forces, governmental and private, national and local.

To date, the initial judgment that Lyndon Johnson played a striking role in promoting racial equality remains intact. The 1972 symposium that unveiled the civil rights papers brought to the speaker's rostrum Julian Bond, a former SNCC member, a caustic critic of Johnson's Vietnam policy, and one of the few blacks elected to the Georgia legislature before the Voting Rights Act of 1965. Addressing an audience gathered at the Johnson Library, the young lawmaker remarked about the library's namesake that "when the forces demanded and the mood permitted, for once an activist, human-hearted man had his hands on the levers of power and a vision beyond the next election. He was there when we and the Nation needed him, and oh my God, do I wish he was there now."[86] After inspecting the library's holdings it may be asked, are these words any less timely three [seven] presidential regimes later?[87]

THE IMPROBABLE
EMANCIPATOR

Lyndon Johnson was, as T. Harry Williams observed a few months after the former president's death, a "tormented man from [a] tormented region who had such large visions of what his country might become." Born and raised in the South, Johnson had only gradually come to recognize the hardships blacks endured under the racial caste system in Dixie. But as he became aware of their plight, and as he acquired power and spoke to a constituency beyond his region, the Texan dedicated himself to realizing the American dream for African Americans. That commitment, however, had to be fulfilled in the context of Johnson's penchant for what Professor Williams has called, "measured, manipulated change within the system and a consensus built on compromise."[1] In the process, Johnson shaped some of twentieth-century liberalism's greatest triumphs but also some of its bitterest disappointments.

Both Lyndon Johnson's contemporaries and those historians who have dared to venture into the very recent past have praised his civil rights legislative achievements as outstanding. In less than six years he guided to passage three measures that destroyed public segregation in the South, made good the promise of the Fifteenth Amendment, and attacked the nation's discriminatory residential patterns. Clarence Mitchell, who, as the legislative representative of the National Association for the Advancement of Colored People (NAACP), closely observed Johnson's performance in Washington, concluded, "[Lyndon Johnson] made a greater contribution to giving a dignified and hopeful status to Negroes in the United States than any other President, including Lincoln, Roosevelt and Kennedy."[2] This judgment has been seconded by Carl Degler, who wrote of Johnson that as "President his record on Negro rights surpassed that of any

President since Lincoln; his public avowal of Negro equality more than matched that of John F. Kennedy."[3]

Yet, despite the widespread plaudits Johnson has received for his efforts to rectify the nation's racial wrongs, some critics have questioned his prescriptions for change. Generally, these commentators do not doubt Johnson's sincerity, but they find the New Frontier's and Great Society's liberal remedies inadequate cures for the ills that have plagued blacks for generations. They believe that in dealing with southern white obstructionists Washington policymakers have unduly stressed conciliation and negotiation and held a traditional conception of the federal system when nothing less than compulsion, massive intervention, and a restructuring of the political order was needed. Furthermore, these dissenters maintain that much of the radical protest against the system which surfaced in the late 1960s reflected disillusionment with the reformist approach. As political scientist Charles V. Hamilton has contended, "Notwithstanding the eloquent argument of liberals—white and black—that American politics required compromise, it is also the case that there are limits beyond which a theoretical political democracy cannot go and expect unswerving loyalty from those who perceive themselves to be the perpetual victims of the democratic process."[4]

Johnson's strong advocacy of civil rights while in the White House is all the more striking when compared to his early record in Congress. As a member of the House, he had opposed proposals to abolish the poll tax, create a fair employment practices commission, and make lynching a federal crime. When Johnson assumed his Senate seat in 1949, he quickly lined up with his southern colleagues against the Truman administration's civil rights program, which he attacked as "sadistic" and "designed more to humiliate the South than to help the black man."[5] During his tenure on Capital Hill, however, Johnson never played the role of Negrophobe, a practice popular with the other politicians from his region. Rather, for the Texan, progress in race relations would come slowly, and Negroes would have to be patient before they secured their constitutional rights. Explaining his philosophy to one of his black constituents after the delivery of his maiden speech to the Senate—a defense of the filibuster—Johnson wrote, "Personally it is my hope to see the day when the atmosphere throughout the South and the nation is such that the laws the Negro wants are laws for the good of the entire populace, not for individual and distinct segments.[6]

Over the next several years, the pressure increased for action on civil rights. In 1954, the Supreme Court's *Brown v. Board of Education* ruling struck down desegregation in the public schools, and a year later blacks in the Deep South, most notably in Montgomery, Alabama, rallied to confront Jim Crow. Furthermore, northern Negroes began to exert a potent political force for equal rights. In the decade since the outbreak of World War II, the black population in the North had nearly doubled, swelled by the heavy exodus of southern blacks searching for jobs and first-class citizenship. Northern Negroes were able to use their ballots as a balance of power in close congressional elections, and they might swing their states with large numbers of electoral votes into the winning presidential column. Thus, as southern Negroes petitioned the federal government to combat racial discrimination, their enfranchised northern brethren influenced both political parties to listen carefully to this request.[7]

When the Eisenhower Republicans introduced a comprehensive civil rights bill in 1957, Johnson was majority leader of the Senate. In this position he tried to bridge the gulf between regional and national politics as he worked to maintain harmony among the Democrats and to steer his party on a middle course. "The American people," Johnson had remarked in 1953, "will never long tolerate a political party dominated exclusively—nor one that appears to be dominated—by any special groups—be it labor, capital, farm, North, South, East, or West."[8] The senator feared that the administration's civil rights plan, especially Title III, which was designed to help implement the Brown decision, would disrupt the Democratic Party. Johnson tried to shape a bill with which the warring factions of his party could live. By trimming the proposal down to a mild right-to-vote bill, he hoped to assist the southern Democrats in forestalling the omnibus Eisenhower measure from becoming law. In addition, the majority leader, as his press secretary George Reedy noted, would partially satisfy the need of his northern colleagues to "take some of the edge off the Negro groups— who are the only ones with a direct interest."[9]

Johnson's strategy worked. The final piece of legislation that emerged under his skillful maneuvering was a suffrage law. He led the forces to remove the controversial Title III, which he claimed would result in "new and drastic procedures to cover a wide variety of vaguely defined so-called civil rights."[10] On the other hand, the senator perhaps was willing to endorse a suffrage measure, because he believed that the Fifteenth Amendment specifically shielded voting rights from racial discrimination, and he thought that disfranchisement made a mockery of the constitutional principle of representative government. Moreover, Johnson reasoned that southern blacks, by casting their ballots effectively, could gain first-class citizenship for themselves without the need for further federal action. Yet even in this instance Johnson would only vote for a franchise plan that had "proper safeguards." Consequently, he forged a coalition behind an amendment granting a jury trial to those accused of criminal contempt in defiance of the civil rights law. Most of the reformers argued that this provision would seriously weaken the bill, since southern juries seldom convicted whites of violating blacks' civil rights. In the end Johnson had his way, and he led sixty senators including three from the South in passing the first civil rights measure since Reconstruction.

In 1960, when civil rights again received congressional attention, Johnson operated in the center once more. Of the many proposals under scrutiny, the Republican administration and Democratic leaders chose to concentrate on the franchise. The approved bill authorized the appointment by the federal courts of referees to enroll qualified blacks who were disfranchised by hostile local officials. Most suffragists found the referee procedure less satisfactory than the alternative of presidentially selected registrars, recommended by the Civil Rights Commission. Although the bill that Johnson shepherded into law disappointed most of the liberals, it did keep the Democratic Party united for the approaching presidential contest.[11] The Texas senator had traveled a great distance since 1949. No longer a strictly regional spokesman, Johnson had voted for two civil rights statutes and gained for himself the Democratic nomination for vice president.

Lyndon Johnson had come to speak for equality because he thought it would liberate Negroes and his native South. As he climbed higher up the political ladder and addressed a wider audience he became aware of the severe handicap that racism inflicted upon African Americans. By the time he ran for vice president, he had already promised a group of liberals that he intended to meet his "moral obligation to every person of every skin color."[12] Johnson also believed that if the southern racial caste system were dismantled the alienation of the region from the rest of the country would come to an end. In discarding the race issue, Dixie leaders might realistically tackle the economic and social problems of the South unencumbered by the shibboleths of white supremacy. Otherwise, a "further embittered South, defiant and implacable," Tom Wicker, the *New York Times* columnist, perceptively noted, "would be a dead weight on the Democratic party, on the nation."[13] In 1960, Johnson thought the healing process of bringing the South back into the Union would be aided by the creation of a community reconciliation service. This agency would bring to the troubled South the same types of soothing persuasion the majority leader had utilized so well in Washington.

In his thousand days of service as second in command of the nation, Johnson rounded out his education on race relations. The vice president supervised the Committee on Equal Employment Opportunity, which handled more cases in its first year than its forerunners had examined in six years, and he privately counselled President Kennedy to issue a sweeping fair housing order. To some liberal critics, however, Johnson's performance was too timid. They faulted the committee for seeking compliance through conciliation rather than compulsion, and they were dismayed that Johnson, as president of the Senate, refused to render a parliamentary ruling that would have aided cloture reform. Nevertheless, in the months before November 1963, the vice president had strongly committed himself in favor of the most far-reaching civil rights bill to be considered seriously by Congress since Reconstruction. One hundred years after the Emancipation Proclamation went into effect, this grandson of a Confederate soldier remarked, "The Negro today asks justice. We do not answer him . . . when we reply . . . by asking 'Patience.'"[14]

After John Kennedy's death, Lyndon Johnson made civil rights his top legislative priority. In 1964 he signed the omnibus civil rights law containing most of the measures he had fought against as a congressman and incorporating one feature he had cherished—the organization of the Community Relations Service. Holding the nation's top office just as the civil rights revolution was reaching its peak, Johnson translated into statutory language ideas that had been discussed in Washington for decades.

Nowhere, perhaps, was the Negro's advance greater than in the area of voting rights. Indeed, the registration figures bespeak a revolution in Negro suffrage. When Johnson entered the White House in 1963, approximately one-quarter of adult blacks were on the voter rolls in the South; by the time he left office, the proportion was approaching two-thirds. In some counties in Mississippi, Alabama, and Louisiana where no blacks had cast a ballot since the turn of the century, thousands of Negroes were participating in the electoral process by 1969, and some were even winning office.[15] Before his death, Johnson would see two southern blacks, one of them from Texas, take seats in the House of Representatives, and in the fall of 1973, ten years after Johnson picked up the civil rights banner left by John Kennedy, a Negro was elected mayor of Margaret Mitchell's Atlanta.

The franchise issue, however, also illustrated the limitations of what President Johnson could or would do on the Negro's behalf. As a politician, Johnson possessed deep faith in the redemptive powers of the ballot box and believed that once blacks had unfettered access to the voting booth their integration into American society—his Great Society—would be facilitated.[16] But also as a politician, Johnson realized that such changes in the United States did not come swiftly or easily: the public had to be prepared to accept them, the Congress had to be convinced of their necessity and the legislature's institutional barriers to reform had to be surmounted, and vital resources such as presidential prestige had to be rationed so as to be available for another day and another battle. So long as black southerners confined their efforts to prodding the national government to safeguard the constitutionally shielded franchise they found their champion in the White House, but when they demanded a share in running Democratic Party affairs or when they requested federal protection for their registration workers, the president did not always respond quickly or adequately. His two outlooks—the politician as reformer and the politician as realist—came into conflict within Johnson in 1964 and 1965 as he faced the issue of black political power.

The challenge of the Mississippi Freedom Democratic Party (MFDP) to the regular party organization in the Magnolia State pointedly raised this dilemma. Together with Alabama, Mississippi had long been the citadel of white supremacy; the disfranchisement of blacks was nearly complete and the Democratic Party was lily white. The Council of Federated Organizations (COFO), a civil rights conglomerate, had begun registration drives in the early 1960s to get Negroes on the voter lists and into the party structure that governed the state. Counselled by Joseph Rauh, the attorney of the United Automobile Workers and former chairman of Americans for Democratic Action, the Freedom Democrats tried to participate in the precinct, county, and state conventions of the regular Mississippi Democratic Party. Encountering nothing but rebuffs and hostility from the officially recognized state organization, the MFDP decided to force a confrontation. Following the prescribed rules of the Democratic National Committee, the insurgents elected forty-four delegates and twenty-two alternates to attend the national convention in Atlantic City. Unlike the lily-white faction that refused to commit itself to whomever the national convocation nominated, the interracial reformers went to the seaside resort pledged to the re-election of Lyndon Johnson and the creation of his Great Society.[17] The Freedom Democrats believed that they had a legal right to representation, because they belonged to the only freely chosen party in Mississippi, and their delegates would take the loyalty oath.[18]

Before the trip to New Jersey, the Mississippi suffragists had asked the president for help. During the registration campaign, their staff had been intimidated by local law enforcement officers and vigilantes. The actions ranged from arrests on minor charges to beatings and the murder of three COFO workers. Because they believed that their constitutional rights were being trampled upon, these suffragists clamored for protection from Washington. The COFO received support for its contention from some noted constitutional lawyers who argued that under Title 10, Sections 332 and 333, of the United States Criminal Code, the president could send the armed forces. But the militants did not insist on an invasion of federal soldiers. Historian Howard Zinn, an adviser to the Student Non-Violent Coordinating Committee (SNCC), one of the most militant groups in the COFO, was among those who argued that the president had the authority to dispatch "marshals in civilian dress . . . [to] prevent the more flagrant constitutional abuses . . . with more effectiveness and less irritation than the presence of uniformed federal forces or even nationalized units of the local National Guard."[19]

The administration was aware of the volatile situation in Mississippi but continued to reject the suffragists' pleas for assistance. In early June 1964, Attorney General Robert Kennedy, without making any recommendation, reported to the president that Mississippi "law enforcement officials are widely believed to be linked to extremist anti-Negro activity or at the very least to tolerate it."[20] Parents of a group of students working on the summer project asked for federal protection "before a tragic incident takes place." On June 17, however, four days prior to the killing of three suffrage campaigners, Lee White, Johnson's White House specialist on civil rights, remarked that it was "incredible that those people who are voluntarily sticking their head into the lion's mouth would ask for somebody to come down and shoot the lion," and suggested that the chief executive reject such requests for intervention.[21]

The president's legal counsellors argued that the federal system prevented action in the manner urged by COFO. "When a civil rights worker engaged in voter registration asks the Justice Department for federal protection," Assistant Attorney General Burke Marshall later explained, "he is told that there is no national police, that federal marshals are only process servers working for the federal courts, that the protection of citizens is a matter for local police."[22] Privately, however, Deputy Attorney General Nicholas Katzenbach espoused a slightly different theory. On July 1, he confided to the president that he could find "no specific legal objection to sending federal civilian personnel to guard against possible violations of federal law." Nor did he think that Johnson was prevented from deploying the militia if there was a complete breakdown of law and order. But for practical reasons Katzenbach did not recommend such federal intervention. He maintained that the Justice Department did not have enough personnel to do the job, but most important, the deputy attorney general contended, a massive national intrusion would result in the displacement of local policemen who were "most crucial . . . in maintaining law and order in a community gripped by racial crisis."[23]

Although the suffragists were disappointed by the response of the Johnson administration to their demands for protection, they still expected the national Democrats to approve the MFDP challenge. When the battle-fatigued MFDP delegates arrived in Atlantic City at the end of August, they reinforced their legal arguments for representation with strong moral appeals. Should the convention not admit the MFDP contingent, John Lewis, chairman of the SNCC, wrote Johnson, "the Democratic Party and the Federal Government can never become the instruments of justice for all citizens that they claimed to be."[24] Mrs. Fannie Lou Hamer, a delegate from Sunflower County, Senator James Eastland's home district, tearfully related to the Credentials Committee how state troopers had viciously beaten her up when she attempted to help other blacks register. How, asked the MFDP, could the president and the political party that had promoted the landmark Civil Rights Act of 1964 now turn around and give legitimacy to the very leaders and institutions in Mississippi that denied hundreds of thousands of blacks the exercise of their most fundamental right as Americans?[25]

In the highly charged atmosphere of the summer of 1964, this type of question stirred sympathetic responses from a significant number of northern delegates. Never before had a Democratic Convention replaced an all-white delegation with an integrated one, and many of the men and women gathered at the New Jersey resort seemed disposed to set a precedent. But the final answer to the MFDP's challenge could only come from the person directing the convention's proceedings: Lyndon Johnson. The chief executive knew that a political party did not always respond to the wishes of its presidential leader, as his mentor Franklin Roosevelt had discovered in 1938. Most of the time it functioned as a loose amalgam of fifty distinct organizations often going their separate ways. Quadrennially the party gathered to reaffirm its common identity and rally around its presidential nominee. When a popular incumbent like Johnson was in charge, the faithful were inclined to listen. Theodore White, a chronicler of presidential elections, reported about the Atlantic City affair, "There was no moment when the Convention machinery of Johnson . . . might not have imposed a solution."[26] Had Johnson backed the insurgents, the assembled Democrats probably would have assented.

For the president it was an agonizing, yet preordained, decision. Although sensitive to the principles on which the Freedom Democrats grounded their case and aware that support for the challengers would enhance his reputation among northern liberals, Johnson also believed that to back the MFDP would seriously endanger the national consensus he was trying to build. The Goldwater candidacy guaranteed that the liberal Democrats would stick with their president. The South, on the other hand, was very insecure, and the chief executive had no desire to assist the GOP by throwing the region's white politicians out of the Democratic Party.[27]

Characteristically, Johnson sought to avoid the appearance of victory or defeat for either side in the dispute. For a time he dallied with the idea of having a few members of the regular delegation come down with a "virus" so that their places could be taken by MFDP people.[28] Perhaps this scheme was too contrived, because the president ultimately adopted the more customary tactic of a compromise. The MFDP was offered two at-large seats, while those from the lily-white group would have to pledge their loyalty to the national ticket before receiving official recognition. In addition, the Credentials Committee suggested that guidelines be established to prevent future discriminatory practices in party operations.[29]

Johnson assigned Hubert Humphrey, whose civil rights record was impeccable, the task of convincing the MFDP to accept the bargain. The Minnesota senator's staff reportedly informed Humphrey's old friend and ADA colleague, Joe Rauh, that unless an agreement was reached Humphrey would lose his chance to be Johnson's running mate. Charles Diggs, a black congressman from Detroit and a member of the Credentials Committee who had originally backed the MFDP, later explained why he and other black leaders went along with the compromise: "There is no question in my mind that the package . . . helped the President in his desire to nominate Humphrey. . . . Had a divisive floor fight developed the President would have been forced to select as his Number Two man a person less identified with the liberal wing of the party."[30]

The MFDP, however, was not satisfied by Johnson's attempt at conciliation. The challengers rejected what they derisively labeled the "back of the bus proposal."[31] Johnson's preference for consensus politics held little attraction for the young civil rights workers whose heads had been bloodied in their frustrated efforts to shake up southern politics. "We must stop playing the game," declared the MFDP, "of accepting token recognition for real change and of allowing the opposition to choose a few 'leaders' to represent the people at large." After all, the challengers maintained: "That is the way things have been done in Mississippi for a long time."[32] The insurgents were not irreconcilables, however. They were prepared to go along with the plan suggested by Oregon Congresswoman Edith Green to count the "loyal" Democrats of both delegations.[33] Since many more MFDP members than regular Democrats would swear their allegiance, the blacks would have won the power and recognition for which they had risked their lives.

But if Johnson was not ready to encourage this upheaval in southern political arrangements, he was setting the stage for change. Although the president's plan did not halt the walkout of most of the Mississippi delegation, it averted a widespread Dixie defection at the convention. Johnson may have diminished his moral credibility in his managing of the MFDP challenge, but the compromise strengthened his long-range legislative plans. Wise to the ways of Congress, LBJ realized that the cooperation of powerful southern committee chairmen was indispensable for the passage of his expensive and far-reaching socio-economic reform program. To this end, Johnson's forging of the Atlantic City bargain soothed the Dixie solons and added to his political capital in Congress.[34] And in November, despite the loss of five Deep South states, including Mississippi, he carried a majority of the old Confederacy. This smashing electoral victory afforded him increased leverage in pursuit of his Great Society.

New federal action was necessary to give Negroes a place in the Great Society, and both Johnson and black leaders agreed that extension of the franchise was a top priority. The MFDP and integrated groups in other states, the president thought, would never be able to dislodge the lily-white factions peacefully unless they could fortify their moral fervor with votes at the ballot box. Johnson believed, furthermore, that such electoral strength would add to the Negro's self-esteem, since the changes that followed from enfranchisement would be "a consequence of the black man's own legitimate power as an American citizen [and] not a gift from the white man."[35] The president's reformist and realist instincts were acting in tandem, but there was still the delicate question of timing to be settled.

In the euphoria immediately following his 1964 landslide re-election triumph, Johnson cranked the engine of the federal government to begin producing new voting rights legislation, but his aides were soon counselling a slowdown. Lee White advised Johnson not to embark on any innovative civil rights ventures in 1965; the nation, White explained, had to have a period of rest so it could absorb the changes wrought by the 1964 act.[36] Similar advice came from the Justice Department. The 1964 measure had bestowed great responsibilities upon the agency, and the recently appointed attorney general, Nicholas Katzenbach, wanted to get the department's new machinery running smoothly before taking on another task. Moreover, the department's Civil Rights Division hoped that some of the voting suits it was litigating in the courts would demolish the methods of southern resistance without more legislation.[37] If additional authority was required, the department's preference was not for another suffrage statute but a constitutional amendment prescribing a universal franchise.[38] The amendment route would take a minimum of two years, but it would probably moderate southern opposition in Congress and head off a filibuster that might threaten the rest of Johnson's ambitious Great Society programs.

As the president pondered his course, events in Selma, Alabama, suddenly and dramatically altered the environment of his decisionmaking. In early January 1965, Martin Luther King, just back from Oslo where he had received the Nobel Peace Prize, had launched a series of demonstrations in this capital of the Black Belt to protest the biased practices that kept 98 percent of the community's adult Negroes from the polls. Along with the local SNCC workers, King led hundreds of blacks in daily marches to the Dallas County Courthouse to get their names on the voter lists. The Board of Registrars was open two days a month and during its office hours processed only a small fraction of the black applications. Compounding the tensions created by the board's dilatory behavior were the provocative actions of Sheriff Jim Clark and his armed deputies. By the beginning of February, the sheriff had arrested over two thousand protesters, including the Nobel laureate.[39]

King's incarceration focused national attention on the denial of black voting rights. In the early 1960s, the sit-ins, freedom rides, and the Birmingham demonstrations had concentrated popular outrage on the indignities blacks were forced to suffer when they attempted to utilize public accommodations. Similarly, the riot at the University of Mississippi in 1962 had given impetus to the drive to end segregation in the schools. The 1964 Civil Rights Act struck hard at Jim Crowism in public places and schools, but significantly the one section of the bill that was substantially watered down dealt with the franchise. This alteration had occurred without much notice, but King, with the unwitting cooperation of Sheriff Clark, George Wallace, and the Alabama Ku Klux Klan, rectified this oversight in the winter and spring of 1965 as the plight of Selma's voteless blacks shared the news spotlight with the administration's escalation of the war in Southeast Asia.

Johnson and the Justice Department lawyers had begun 1965 by preparing mild legislation on voting rights; by mid-February they were working feverishly to come up with stronger measures.[40] Republican congressmen on both sides of Capitol Hill were demanding prompt action, and Minority Leader Everett Dirksen, appalled by the viciousness of the Alabama police, told Attorney General Katzenbach that he was ready for a "revolutionary" bill.[41] Adding to the pressure for new legislation, Dr. King posted bail and flew to Washington for a meeting with the president. On February 9, he urged upon Johnson a voting rights proposal that would establish automatic machinery to eliminate the arbitrary power of the local officials, prohibit literacy tests, and provide for enforcement by federal registrars.[42] A few days later, representatives of the NAACP informed the president that the planned constitutional amendment "would not be a satisfactory approach."[43] In this climate, the administration started searching for statutory language that would satisfy Congress and the civil rights groups, end the machination of southern officials, and survive the scrutiny of the courts.

Before the administration could get its legislation finished, the confrontation in Selma exploded, and Johnson had to deal with another crisis. Soon after being released from jail, King had announced plans for a "Freedom March" from Selma to Montgomery; almost immediately Governor Wallace banned all demonstrations on state highways. On Sunday, March 7, a showdown took place. With FBI agents and Justice Department observers scribbling notes on the sidelines, 525 orderly marchers were savagely attacked by state troopers and Sheriff Clark's deputies as they crossed the Edmund Pettus Bridge just outside Selma. Pictures of men on horseback beating women and children were splashed over the next morning's front pages, leading to nationwide demands for the dispatch of federal soldiers to safeguard black rights in Alabama. Hospitalized with a skull fracture, SNCC's John Lewis complained, "I don't see how President Johnson can send troops to Viet Nam . . . and can't send troops into Selma, Alabama."[44] More violence appeared to be in the offing when King, who had been in Atlanta on "Bloody Sunday," announced his intention of leading a second march in two days.

The president's response was swift—and characteristic. He sent Leroy Collins, director of the Community Relations Service, to Selma to avert a clash between King and the Alabama authorities. Working against a short deadline, Collins, with the assistance of John Doar, the Justice Department's mediator par excellence, fashioned an agreement that allowed King and his followers to cross the Pettus bridge and then stop and pray in front of a heavily armed line of state troopers before turning back.[45] Neither the marchers nor the state police were happy with their assigned roles, but the scenario was played out peacefully. That evening, however, an enlistee in the freedom struggle, the Rev. James Reeb, a white minister from Boston, was fatally beaten by racist assailants on a Selma street.

The question of federal police action in Selma revived the controversy between Johnson and the suffragists which had begun the previous summer in Mississippi. Once again the president and his advisers opposed such intervention. Katzenbach worried about the precedent that would be set, doubted that a federal presence would actually promote calm or be effective, and feared that once troops or marshals were involved it would be extremely difficult to get them out. Johnson shared these concerns and had some political ones as well. Intervention by Washington, he believed, would make a martyr of Wallace, resurrect bitterness between the North and the South, and destroy the chances of passing voting rights legislation.[46]

The president apparently reconciled whatever contradictions he may have discerned between the politics and the morality of his decision. He never deviated from his ultimate goal of extending the ballot to the mass of southern blacks, but he was anxious to achieve his objective without stirring up the wrath of the opposition. Unlike the suffrage crusaders filled with burning rage against their racist oppressors, LBJ did not view southern white leaders as evil men whose sin must be painfully exorcised with righteous indignation. Instead, he preferred to reason, negotiate, and cajole—the famous "Johnson treatment." The Texan presented his ideas for racial change in a highly charged atmosphere where southerners wielded great power in Congress and elected officials in Dixie whipped up popular resistance. Thus, he sought to expand first-class citizenship for southern blacks and, at the same time, convince the white South to make the required adjustments peacefully and permanently. It was a task for a modern day Samson and a Solomon, and no political leader could have the strength or wisdom to satisfy both sides completely.

The chief executive, however, showed that he would use the armed forces as a last resort. When King won a federal court order allowing him to proceed with his march, Johnson met with Governor Wallace at the White House and bluntly informed him that the federal government would protect the marchers if Alabama did not. On March 18, Wallace telegraphed the president that he did not have the available resources to ensure the marchers' safety, hence Johnson federalized the Alabama National Guard to patrol the fifty-mile route from Selma to Montgomery.[47] However, even the presence of troops did not prevent three nightriders from shooting and killing a white volunteer from Detroit, Viola Liuzzo.

Amidst the Alabama turbulence, Johnson personally presented his voting rights program to the Congress. On March 15, adopting the battle cry of the freedom struggle, he told the legislators and a nationwide prime time television audience, "It is not just Negroes, but really it is all of us, who must overcome the crippling legacy of bigotry and injustice. And we *shall* overcome."[48] Generally accepted as Johnson's finest hour, the president's performance touched even his harshest critics. "Your address," wrote John Lewis, a battle-scarred veteran of Selma, was "historic, eloquent, and more than inspiring."[49]

The administration's bill was just as impressive; the Justice Department lawyers had done their job well. The measure replaced the cumbersome court procedures outlined in the 1957 and 1960 Civil Rights Acts with an automatic formula to wipe out discrimination. In states and counties where a literacy test was utilized and less than 50 percent of the population had gone to the polls in November 1964, the bill would suspend educational requirements for voting. Furthermore, it authorized the attorney general to assign federal examiners to register qualified voters in the designated areas. After some minor changes, the bill would be back on the president's desk for his signature by early August.[50]

The passage of the Voting Rights Act of 1965 demonstrated how reformist Johnson could be when his ethical and political senses coincided. The tremendous rise in black voting after 1965 was impressive, and its impact was felt throughout the South—Sheriff Jim Clark would be among the first to feel its strength at the polls. The days of wanton violence against southern blacks appeared to be coming to an end, and black neighborhoods were receiving a more equitable share of community services. The year 1968 would even see the seating of thirty-six black delegates as part of the reform Mississippi delegation at the Democratic Convention.[51]

Yet having employed much of the authority of his office to help clear away the *legal* barriers to the exercise of the ballot by blacks, the president's political instincts and his perception of the nature of the federal system kept him from utilizing the act's full potential as a catalyst for change in southern politics. Federal examiners were sent only to fifty-eight out of one hundred eighty-five counties where less than a majority of the adult blacks were signed up to vote in 1965. Without a federal presence, many blacks reared in an environment of repression and brutality experienced extreme difficulty in remembering that politics was no longer for whites only. Nor did Johnson employ the full facilities of the federal government to bring blacks to the polls. As the civil rights organizations pointed out, he might have authorized various federal agencies such as the Department of Health, Education, and Welfare, the Department of Labor, and the Department of Agriculture to sponsor nonpartisan programs in citizenship training.[52] The administration decided against a postcard campaign directed toward black neighborhoods that would inform residents when registration offices were open.[53] Furthermore, the president did not encourage reorganization of his party in the South so that blacks could gain an equitable share of the leadership posts, and as the presidential term drew to a close in 1969 they remained virtually excluded from high Democratic councils in Dixie.[54]

If, on balance, the president had significantly transformed the political world he had inherited from his predecessors and in which he had once thrived, Johnson was also a victim of his very successes. Under the Great Society, southern blacks enrolled to vote in record numbers. But with each new gain, Negro aspirations soared higher than the Johnson administration could fulfill them. The passage in 1968, for example, of a statute empowering the Justice Department to protect civil rights organizers was no longer relevant to many of the former COFO workers because they had already repudiated liberal reform ideology in favor of the exclusionary doctrines of black nationalism and black power. Furthermore, the president's escalation of the conflict in Vietnam diverted vital energies away from pursuing justice at home. As the bomb blasts reverberated ever more loudly from Southeast Asia, influential activists like Martin Luther King joined the chorus of voices protesting Johnson's war policies. Whereas the chief executive never accepted the arguments of the antiwar critics, like the militants he realized that the job of extending full freedom remained unfinished. In December 1972, shortly before his death, he confessed to a National Archives sponsored symposium on civil rights, "The progress has been much too small; we haven't done nearly enough. I'm ashamed of myself that I had six years and couldn't do more than I did."[55] Lyndon Johnson had broken the lock on the ballot box, but he did not open the door widely enough to complete emancipation.

MIXING MODERATION
WITH MILITANCY

When Lyndon Johnson left the White House in 1969, America stood divided over his handling of affairs related to war and peace. Disturbed by the deteriorating quality of life in their cities and confounded by the intractability of combat in the swamps and jungles of Vietnam, they doubted the credibility of the president and the Great Society he had pledged to create. By the mid-1970s both the war against poverty and against the Vietnamese had ended, neither successfully, and the underlying problems of racism and foreign interventionism persisted. Over the two-and-one-half decades after Johnson stepped down from office, the racial policies of his successors ranged from "benign neglect" to outright hostility. Whatever his shortcomings, and they were many, LBJ was the last president to offer committed leadership that challenged racial injustice. The inferno of ghetto uprisings that ignited Miami and Los Angeles during the 1980s and early 1990s dramatically refocused national attention on the unfinished legacy bequeathed by the Johnson administration. Although Johnson's failures remain evident from the vantage point of today's hindsight, it is easier to see them as the result of a flawed vision of black emancipation rather than of a deliberate disengagement from civil rights concerns.

President Johnson exhibited leadership for social change that suited his background and ideology. A consummate legislator, he placed great faith in the passage of laws to obliterate racial discrimination. Having climbed his way up the electoral ladder from congressman to president, it is hardly surprising that LBJ conceived of reform in such a traditional manner. He summed up his fundamental political philosophy to the Mississippi civil rights leader Charles Evers: "If you want to change the system, get in it and make what you want to make out of it."[1] If legislation held the key to unlocking the door to racial justice, then success depended upon cultivating basic skills in lobbying and building alliance. To the pragmatic Johnson, the bottom line consisted of counting votes, for as he informed Clarence Mitchell, the chief representative on Capitol Hill of the National Association for the Advancement of Colored People (NAACP): "Clarence, you can get anything that you have the votes to get. How many votes have you got?"[2] Johnson drew energy from the lawmaking process and never seemed to tire from participating in it. His presidential assistant Joseph Califano recalled him poring over projections of congressional roll calls after a hectic day and "devour[ing] these tally sheets like a baseball fanatic reviewing the box scores of his home team."[3]

Artful in the give-and-take of legislative horse trading, Johnson sought out black leaders who knew how to strike a bargain. His political upbringing had taught him to recruit allies who represented identifiable constituencies and could deliver votes. According to Joseph Rauh, the liberal lawyer who lined up with the president on civil rights but broke with him over the Vietnam War, "Johnson always had this idea, . . . if you deal with the right person and get him, then the issue will go away."[4] On racial matters this meant consulting the Big Six civil rights officials, A. Philip Randolph, the revered labor and protest leader, and the heads of the National Urban League, NAACP, Congress of Racial Equality (CORE), Southern Christian Leadership Conference (SCLC), and Student Nonviolent Coordinating Committee (SNCC).[5] Just as the president invited spokespersons of important interest groups to the White House to plot legislative strategy, so too did he consult the heads of national civil rights groups. "It was like bringing George Meany and Walter Reuther and four labor leaders in to talk for labor," presidential counselor Harry McPherson explained. "You had the six in to talk for the Negroes."[6]

Johnson felt comfortable negotiating with black leaders who often willingly joined him in playing by the rules of the legislative game. If the president believed that by summoning these designated representatives to the Oval Office he heard the opinions of African Americans who counted politically, the chief executive was carrying on the practice of his predecessors who listened to delegates from virtually the same groups. Johnson was astute enough to realize that he could not stage-manage the rapidly unfolding civil rights drama, however; he discerned that civil rights leaders would have to retain their independence or their credibility would be challenged by more militant blacks. Realizing that the black leaders with whom he conferred could be dismissed as "Johnson people" and thereby lose some of their effectiveness, the president encouraged those leaders he trusted to keep up the pressure on him. He reportedly told Roy Wilkins, the executive secretary of the NAACP, "You can hit me a little bit. You can take a pot shot at me. I can understand that."[7] For the crafty Johnson, bargaining was a two-way street: Civil rights leaders would make demands on him, and he would "use them when he wanted support to push for something or 'raise a little hell.'"[8] Naturally there were limits to Johnson's tolerance of criticism, and his patience with individuals lasted as long as they shared his fundamental values and faith in working through the political system.

From the outset of his administration, the president welcomed civil rights leaders into the White House. Within two weeks after the Kennedy assassination, Johnson huddled with the NAACP's Wilkins, Whitney Young of the Urban League, Martin Luther King, Jr., of SCLC, James Farmer of CORE, and A. Philip Randolph. (There is no record of a SNCC representative meeting with Johnson during this same period.) The new chief executive was familiar to most of these leaders, having dealt with them as a senator and then as vice-president, when he directed Kennedy's program to promote equal employment opportunity. The Texan quieted any lingering doubts that African Americans had reason to worry about a southerner in the White House. Farmer remembered the president encouraging him "that whenever we had a problem in this movement or wanted to talk to him, call; the call would get through to him. . . . And it did."[9]

The NAACP's Roy Wilkins occupied the position of Johnson's number-one civil rights confidant.[10] McPherson recalled that the "president really loved Roy Wilkins," and apparently the feeling was mutual. After a particularly memorable address by Johnson in March 1965, the NAACP chief declared: "I had waited all my life to hear a President of the United States talk that way. And at that moment, I confess, I loved LBJ."[11]

Wilkins personified the kind of leader whom Johnson trusted. Like LBJ, he advocated legislative lobbying, litigation, and lining up new voters as the preferred means to achieve racial equality. Wilkins approached politics with the pragmatic toughness that Johnson appreciated. A moderate in a movement that was growing more militant throughout the 1960s, Wilkins steadfastly backed up the president in defending his domestic and foreign policy programs from attack by black dissidents. Presidential counselor George Reedy, who had been with Johnson since his Senate years, advised his boss early on to consider Wilkins as "*the* Negro leader." Reedy summed up the White House consensus in praising Wilkins for his "judgment and sense of fair play."[12]

Next to Wilkins, Johnson developed the closest ties with Whitney Young. As chair of President Kennedy's Committee on Equal Employment Opportunity, Vice-President Johnson had touched base regularly with the director of the Urban League, an organization devoted to opening up the job market to African Americans. Young, like Wilkins, regarded LBJ as a far more capable leader on civil rights than Kennedy, whom he believed was slow to exhibit the necessary "political conviction [and] guts" in confronting racial inequality.[13] The chief executive thought so highly of the Urban League official that he tried to persuade him to accept a position in his administration, an offer Young declined.[14]

Refusing a governmental appointment, Young successfully resisted the president's legendary arm-twisting by convincing Johnson that he could be of greater assistance to him from the outside. Young argued persuasively that he could better fulfill their common objectives if he remained in his "present spot, that it was a unique position and one from which I could exercise a maximum influence and control."[15] Moderate, responsible, and levelheaded, the Urban League director expressed "his total support" for LBJ and vowed to "do anything . . . to help him."[16] He meant it. When black and white liberals began abandoning the president over the Vietnam War, Young stuck by him. On a tour of Vietnam sponsored by the Urban League in mid-1966, Young took the opportunity to trumpet the administration's civil rights achievements during a period when most of the news that black GI's received from home stressed heightened racial tensions.[17]

A. Philip Randolph rounded out the triumvirate of black leaders among the Big Six whom the president most admired. The founder of the Brotherhood of Sleeping Car Porters, Randolph had merged his role as a labor leader with that of an independent champion of civil rights. A socialist and one-time radical, by 1963 the seventy-four-year-old Randolph had become the elder statesman of the movement. His "natural eloquence," advocacy of an interracial labor-liberal coalition, and sponsoring of the 1963 March on Washington gave him standing among all segments of the freedom movement. The White House respected him as a sensible and reliable leader and turned to him when it wanted to keep quarreling civil rights factions in check.[18] Having observed the national political scene since the Great Depression and organized protests against discrimination that grabbed the attention of several presidents, Randolph considered LBJ the most supportive. "President Roosevelt didn't have the contact with the Negro leaders that President Johnson has had," he recounted from firsthand experience and added: "President Truman was a man committed to civil rights, but he was not as accessible as President Johnson."[19] Together with Wilkins and Young, Randolph backed the president on such thorny issues as Vietnam, and in 1964 Johnson awarded him the Presidential Medal of Freedom.

One consequence for black leaders such as Wilkins, Young, and Randolph who identified so closely with Johnson was that the relationship narrowed the limits within which they might disagree with the White House. Those individuals who strayed too far from the acceptable boundaries risked falling out of presidential favor. The case of James Farmer is both instructive and somewhat puzzling.

The head of CORE, the interracial group that had pioneered nonviolent direct-action techniques in the postwar black freedom struggle, Farmer started out on excellent terms with Johnson. A native of Marshall, Texas, the hometown of the president's wife, he contrasted LBJ's cordiality to him with Kennedy's aloofness; in discussions with Johnson shortly after he became president, Farmer found him open, enthusiastic, and responsive. For the next year, Farmer received the flattering "Johnson treatment"—his phone calls got through and his "written communications reached him without languishing on the desks of aides."[20] Unlike Wilkins and Young, however, Farmer led a group that relied principally on confrontational demonstrations. This approach had brought CORE into conflict with the Kennedy administration over the Freedom Rides in 1961, and it eventually proved troublesome for the Johnson regime as well. With comprehensive civil rights legislation meandering its way through Congress in late 1963 and 1964, the administration emphatically wanted CORE to refrain from "staging street demonstrations which might get people's backs up." The White House wanted Farmer's organization to function instead like traditional interest groups, lobbying for legislation and trying "to coordinate its activities through the White House."[21]

Though CORE gladly joined the successful coalition behind passage of the Civil Rights Act, by late summer 1964, Farmer's congenial relationship with the president had begun to suffer. The precise reason is difficult to ascertain. Farmer attributed the rift to his unwillingness to agree to a call initiated by Wilkins in June for a civil rights moratorium on mass demonstrations until after the November presidential election. Wilkins, reflecting Johnson's thinking, feared that further agitation would fuel a white backlash and benefit the Republican nominee, Barry Goldwater, a foe of the 1964 Civil Rights Law. Farmer believed that the president was "furious" with his dissenting position and retaliated by reducing his access to the White House. "The president's political career had led him to equate disagreement with disloyalty," Farmer complained.[22]

Farmer's assessment may be correct, but it needs some qualification. Though the number of the CORE leader's recorded contacts with the president decreased after June 1964, it did not fall off significantly.[23] Of course the quality rather than the quantity of these interactions may have declined, as Farmer asserted, yet documentary evidence in the Johnson Library suggests that the situation was more complicated. Farmer refused to toe the administration's line on the moratorium, but he continued to cooperate with the White House to defuse potentially troubling confrontations. On July 30, a day after Farmer joined civil rights leaders in discussing Wilkins's suggestion for a halt to demonstrations, presidential assistant Lee White spoke with the CORE director about "how frustrating it is that those who apparently want to defeat Senator Goldwater take action that can only result in aiding him." Farmer reportedly agreed and "expressed the view that it was mighty tough to combat, but he would do his best"[24] Apparently, the CORE chief kept his word. In early August White inquired about whether the group would picket the president on his trip to Syracuse, New York, in protest of the failure of the federal government to solve the murders of three civil fights workers in Mississippi, two of whom were CORE staff members. Farmer replied that the local chapter would not embarrass Johnson and instead would quietly turn over a petition to the president's staff.[25] In late October, several weeks before the election, Farmer again assisted the administration. White House aides heard a rumor that four hundred CORE members from New York City were traveling to Maryland to participate in a protest that might cause a serious disturbance. On October 22 White informed the president that "our relations with Farmer are good enough to ask him for his cooperation in seeing to it that this not be done at this time." Several days later, Farmer assured White that "the top leadership of CORE squelched the plan."[26]

The moratorium controversy by itself did not produce an irreparable breach between Johnson and Farmer, but it accentuated the widening gap between them. Given CORE's increasing militancy, Johnson never felt comfortable with Farmer again, who, in contrast to Wilkins, Young, and Randolph, did not show the kind of loyalty the president demanded. The CORE leader had been helpful, but LBJ probably did not consider him totally reliable. Farmer subsequently campaigned with the other civil rights leaders for the president's suffrage legislation in 1965 and was invited to the signing ceremony in August. Yet Johnson, who could be as petty as he was generous, tried to snub Farmer by refusing to give him one of the souvenir pens.[27]

Farmer did not fall from presidential grace by himself; the Reverend Martin Luther King, Jr., experienced an even more volatile relationship with the president. From the beginning King and Johnson never felt entirely at ease with each other, nor did they develop the personal rapport

LBJ shared with Wilkins and Young. Part of the difficulty stemmed from a clash of two dominant personalities. King's close assistant, Andrew Young, believed that the chief executive and the minister had trouble communicating because the president liked to do all the talking. "Of course Dr. King was a talker himself," Young recounted, so they had trouble establishing "a give and take kind of relationship."[28]

Yet the uneasiness between King and Johnson involved more than conflicting personalities; they differed fundamentally in their attitudes toward social reform. Johnson favored measured change produced through lawsuits and legislation. King found these methods useful, but he chose to wage his struggle through mass demonstrations and civil disobedience, tactics designed to spotlight white racism, make liberal officials in Washington uncomfortable, and force them to heed black demands. Johnson's desire to undertake reform while preserving social order collided with King's readiness for disruption through provocative nonviolent protests.[29]

Nevertheless, these tensions did not keep Johnson and King from cooperating on common objectives. They needed each other. The civil rights activist required the power of the federal government to shatter entrenched white opposition to equality, and the president used King's demonstrations to rally support for his legislative plans. In 1964 the Atlanta minister, unlike Farmer, did not attack Wilkins's suggestion for a moratorium during the presidential campaign, and he supported the Johnson-orchestrated compromise at the Democratic nominating convention that left civil rights forces from Mississippi angry with the administration.[30] The 1965 protests in Selma, Alabama, climaxed friendly relations between the two as King took a respite from conducting voting-rights demonstrations to confer twice with the president and otherwise kept in touch by telephone.[31] Johnson's performance in securing passage of the Voting Rights Act deeply pleased King, and one of his associates told presidential assistant Richard Goodwin that the minister "now felt the Negro cause was actually going to succeed."[32]

During this period conflicts arose, but generally they were settled easily. Louis Martin recalled that there were "protocol" problems in scheduling appointments with the president because King wanted to see him alone, without Wilkins and Young, whom he believed took advantage of his international prestige.[33] After King won the Nobel Peace prize in 1964, the president had to decide whether to attend a November banquet in his honor; LBJ chose against it because, as Attorney General Nicholas Katzenbach pointed out, King and Wilkins were "locked in a power struggle" and Johnson's attendance would "elevate King over" his close NAACP friend.[34] Instead the president met alone with the Nobel laureate the following month.

By mid-1965 the scheduling problems Martin referred to had been resolved. Lee White reported to Johnson with some satisfaction that King had learned not to announce unilaterally "that he is coming to meet the President," behavior that in the past had disturbed the publicity-conscious and secrecy-minded White House.[35]

The uneasy alliance fractured as Dr. King increasingly shifted his attention from traditional civil rights matters and voiced opposition to the president's escalation of the war in Vietnam and the consequent weakening of his domestic Great Society programs. In August 1965 he urged President Johnson to halt the bombing of North Vietnam and negotiate with the Viet Cong. He also began to focus on the economic misery in northern urban ghettos inflamed by rioting, a concern that led him to link American militarism abroad with materialism and racism at home. Privately Johnson cautioned the minister, but according to King he "never asked me not to speak out on Vietnam."[36] Over the next year King continued to criticize the president's Southeast Asian policy, but he refrained from becoming an active leader in the antiwar movement until 1967; by then the two leaders had ceased meeting with each other. They had not spoken face-to-face for about a year, and Andrew Young remembered that the last time they talked over the phone had been around Thanksgiving 1966 when King called LBJ to denounce the war. Actually the initiative for curtailing the relationship came from King, not Johnson; the disgruntled civil rights leader declined several invitations to come to the White House.[37]

Although the president appeared willing to keep open the lines of communication, he grew increasingly furious with King. Throughout the 1960s the FBI had been investigating King's possible connections with Communists, and the bureau's director, J. Edgar Hoover, eagerly furnished the president with reports reinforcing his belief that "King might be subject to communist manipulation."[38] In April 1967, after King delivered a blistering attack against the United States as "the greatest purveyor of violence in the world today," the administration became hysterical: John P. Roche, the Brandeis University professor and White House intellectual-in-residence, privately informed Johnson that King "has thrown in with the commies" and characterized him as "inordinately ambitious and quite stupid."[39] Yet Johnson was less concerned about King's alleged role as a subversive or a sexual pervert (Hoover's eavesdroppers had picked up "evidence" of King's extramarital affairs) than about traditional political considerations. The president fretted, Joseph Califano has explained, that the minister's impassioned antiwar broadsides "would provoke a conservative backlash, not just against King but against the Great Society."[40]

To reduce the negative fallout from King's assaults, LBJ looked to the black leaders he trusted. The White House delighted in the efforts Wilkins and Whitney Young made, albeit unsuccessfully, to convince King to put aside the antiwar issue for the greater good of the civil rights movement. The president dispatched Young to South Vietnam as part of a team of observers to monitor national elections, and his glowing reports served to counter King's criticism and to drive a wedge between the minister and the other moderate civil rights leaders.[41]

Relations deteriorated sharply over the Vietnam War, and King's growing radicalism on domestic issues added to the cleavage. As David Garrow and Adam Fairclough have shown, after the ghetto uprisings in 1965 the civil rights leader increasingly moved to the Left in analyzing the connection between capitalism and racism. A putative democratic socialist, Dr. King condemned the Johnson administration for retreating on the battlefields of the war on poverty and urged the chief executive to establish a massive jobs program providing employment for everyone, black and white, who needed it. On this issue, unlike Vietnam, the White House could not argue that King had no business meddling. LBJ's response was not to take any new departures but to try to line up King behind the administration's programs, believing "that King should work harder to get Congress to pass his legislation already on Capitol Hill."[42] In this instance as in others, the president preferred to deal with King on the terrain he knew best—the legislative arena. Growing more radical and disillusioned with the political mainstream, however, the Atlanta minister found little common ground to occupy with his former presidential ally.

Moving in the opposite trajectory from King and Farmer, Bayard Rustin saw his welcome improve at the White House. A former Communist and a pacifist who had served a prison term for failing to comply with the draft during World War II, Rustin helped pioneer CORE-initiated freedom bus rides in 1947. During the 1950s he acted as an adviser to King and helped him organize the SCLC. His radical background alone would have made him suspect to the federal government, but his homosexuality compounded the distrust. Nevertheless, by 1963 Rustin had become a close associate of A. Philip Randolph, some of whose esteem rubbed off on him. He ran a labor institute bearing Randolph's name, and Rustin served as a useful liaison between King, with whom he maintained good relations, and the administration. Over Johnson's five-year tenure, Rustin received an increasingly more favorable reception from White House officials as he shared their positions on important matters concerning civil rights strategies and especially the Vietnam War. Although he faulted the administration for limiting spending on its poverty program, the value of Rustin's political stock with the president generally rose as King's dropped.[43]

Least acceptable of the Big Six were the leaders of SNCC, who reflected precisely the kind of style that differed most from Johnson's. Showing an antielitist bent, they expected leadership to emerge from local communities and decisions to grow out of group-centered deliberations. Given SNCC's orientation, neither John Lewis, its chairman, nor James Forman, its executive secretary, could have developed the same relationship with Johnson as did Wilkins, Young, or even King.

More than any other organization in the early 1960s, SNCC mobilized young people to challenge racial discrimination in innovative and exciting ways. Its militancy was well know, but as long as the group adhered to a nonviolent, interracial vision of achieving equality the Johnson administration tolerated its iconoclasm. The president, however, remained skeptical of SNCC's moralistic and generally uncompromising posture, which did not conform to his brand of pragmatic politics. The 1964 bargain related to the seating of Mississippi Freedom Democratic Party (MFDP) delegates, which had been hammered out in the time-honored manner of national conventions, satisfied Johnson's election agenda but left SNCC convinced of the duplicity of white liberals and the federal government.[44]

The shaky peaceful coexistence broke down by mid-1966. SNCC took an early lead in denouncing United States involvement in Vietnam, questioning whether young men should cooperate with the draft. Encouraging civil rights work as an alternative to military service, in January 1966 the organization berated the United States for murdering the Vietnamese people by "pursuing an aggressive policy in violation of international law."[45] Privately, Vice-President Hubert Humphrey spoke for the administration in condemning SNCC's statements as "the most outrageous attacks on the President." He also echoed the dismay expressed by Wilkins and Young, Johnson's staunchest defenders, that the White House treated SNCC "with a sort of benevolent equality on a par with the NAACP and Urban League."[46] The tenuous link between SNCC and the administration finally severed in May when the group withdrew from the planned White House Conference on Civil Rights, indicating that it considered white liberals as no better than southern white racists.[47]

SNCC's position of noncooperation reflected significant internal changes within the organization. Stokely Carmichael replaced John Lewis, and his election signaled the transformation of SNCC from an interracial group supporting the tactic of nonviolence into one dedicated to black nationalism and retaliatory self-defense. Lewis, an admirer of Dr. King, had cooperated in planning the White House Conference scheduled for June; and though Johnson administrations officials viewed him as a radical, he was the type of "restrained" leader they could deal with. Under Lewis, McPherson remarked, "SNCC was still an organization that you could invite to the White House without getting a hand grenade thrown through the window before they came."[48] In contrast, Carmichael led SNCC along an all-black course and delivered incendiary speeches with menacing antiwhite overtones. He also offended the White House in a personal way: SNCC prepared to lead antiwar demonstrations in Washington on August 6, which coincided with the wedding of the president's daughter Luci. Johnson's civil rights allies rushed to denounce SNCC's plan as "in poor taste" and "politically untenable." In turn, SNCC dismissed their complaint and called them "messengers . . . for the Boss Man."[49] Subsequently, in a September 1966 recommendation concerning a meeting between civil rights leaders and the president, McPherson advised: "There is no longer any need to have SNCC . . . represented."[50]

Over the next few years, the administration entered into an adversarial relationship with SNCC. As the group shifted its sights from the rural South to the urban battlefields of the North, Carmichael and his successor, Hubert "Rap" Brown, became targets of government surveillance, especially through the FBI's provocative counterintelligence program (COINTELPRO).[51] Carmichael's black-power rhetoric appeared to federal officials to fuel violent uprisings in black ghettos, and his unauthorized travels to Cuba, North Vietnam, and China in 1967 aroused their anticommunist suspicions.[52]

Johnson and his White House advisers strongly encouraged the Justice Department to prosecute Carmichael for inciting riots. The usually sensible McPherson did not much care whether the SNCC leader constituted a "clear and present danger" or that his inflammatory statements might have been protected under the First Amendment; civil liberties aside, he wanted Carmichael behind bars "because he was helping to destroy the consensus on which progress depended."[53] As violence rocked black ghettos in summer 1967, concern with agitators such as Carmichael surfaced within Johnson's cabinet. Secretary of State Dean Rusk asked, "Don't we have any remedy for these people?" and Secretary of Health, Education and Welfare John Gardner queried, " Surely there must be a limit to what a man can say?"[54]

Despite these views, which Johnson shared, the federal government did not indict Carmichael; the president reluctantly accepted the counterarguments presented by Attorney General Ramsey Clark. A fellow Texan whose father had sat on the United States Supreme Court, Clark resisted the intense political pressure to make an example of Carmichael and display the administration's toughness in fighting crime. After a thorough investigation of Carmichael's statements, Clark concluded that the government lacked the necessary evidence, to "support the prosecution under an interpretation of the law that was constitutionally valid." Nor could the Justice Department dig up any other statute that might produce a conviction of Carmichael based on his trips to Communist countries that were off limits to American citizens.[55] Johnson abided by the attorney general's decision despite the conservative political attacks it generated. Nevertheless, privately he took a dim view of Clark's constitutional caution; the president confided to Califano that if he "had ever known that [Clark] didn't measure up to his daddy, I'd never have made him Attorney General."[56]

Even if Carmichael had been less outspoken in his criticism of administration policies, the White House would have clashed with SNCC over its efforts to develop grassroots leadership that challenged the political establishment. The controversy over the Child Development Group of Mississippi (CDGM) provides a case in point. An outgrowth of the movement to organize disfranchised and impoverished blacks in the Delta State, the CDGM became a Head Start program funded through Johnson's War on Poverty agency, the Office of Economic Opportunity (OEO). Veterans of SNCC and the MFDP saw in the preschool education project a means of building upon the political organizing drives that years of voter registration had begun. They hoped to expand the notion of political participation to include control over decisions affecting the daily lives of poor people customarily neglected by the electoral system. Following intensive recruitment, by the end of summer 1965 CDGM operated over eighty centers serving six thousand children in forty towns throughout the state.[57]

Recognized for its innovative approaches to education, the CDGM nonetheless ran afoul of powerful Mississippi politicos. United States senator John Stennis, the chair of the Appropriations Committee and a Johnson supporter on Vietnam, frowned upon the close involvement in the Head Start program of civil rights activists, particularly those militants associated with SNCC. He prevailed upon Sargent Shriver, the OEO director, to launch an investigation into charges that CDGM had managed its projects in a fiscally irresponsible manner and had failed to include a sufficient number of whites in its ranks. In effect, Stennis claimed that CDGM was masquerading as a black nationalist front. White House staff member McPherson became convinced that CDGM consisted of "dedicated and sensible people" who clearly performed good deeds, but he was concerned about the unfavorable political repercussions that would occur if the administration did not assuage Stennis.[58]

As it had done at the 1964 Democratic National Convention with respect to seating the MFDP, the administration fashioned a compromise that preserved the CDGM but in weakened form. After first cutting off its funds for violating OEO management procedures, in late 1966 Shriver relented and agreed to funnel poverty money to a reformed CDGM, which would share supervision over Head Start programs with a rival group of moderate whites and blacks.[59] Rather than endanger the rest of the War on Poverty from budget slashing by Stennis's Appropriations Committee, the White House chose to reach an accommodation that safeguarded measured economic and political change in Mississippi. While keeping the radically inclined CDGM alive, the administration endorsed a more conventional brand of interracial leadership, one more in tune with its version of political pragmatism.

This entire episode has received too little notice from historians. By examining the administration's handling of the problem, scholars can open up new vistas on approaches the federal government used to influence the shape of the black freedom struggle in the South. Decisions reached in Washington had a profound effect upon which groups of blacks and whites would obtain vital resources, thereby influencing the course of racial advancement. The resolution of the CDGM conflict suggests that the issue involved not only considerations of race but also of class, a pattern that John Dittmer has sketched concerning the MFDP convention settlement.[60]

The CDGM resolution illustrates the Johnson administration's inclination to handle civil rights issues through regular political channels and according to traditional methods of negotiation. In contrast to seemingly unpredictable protest leaders who spelled trouble for the president, Johnson leaned more frequently on black elected officials. Shortly after the crushing defeat of Goldwater in 1964, Hobart Taylor, Jr., a black presidential adviser, pointed out a theme that would become constant during LBJ's term: the need to increase the number of minority elected officials. Taylor wanted Johnson to deemphasize his reliance on established civil rights leaders who, he asserted, were "no substitute in the long run for the development of effective political leadership in the traditional sense."[61] LBJ declined to abandon his loyal civil rights allies, but at the same time his advisers sought to achieve closer contact with elected black officials at the local level. Following passage of the 1965 Voting Rights Act the number of black officials began to swell both in the South and the North. Johnson confidant and deputy director of the Democratic National Committee, Louis Martin, urged the chief executive to "find ways and means to tie these newly elected legislators and other Negro officeholders to the President and the national party."[62]

It did not take any arm-twisting to convince Johnson to cultivate these officials. He appeared at gatherings arranged by Martin and Clifford Alexander, swapping stories with members of the audience as one elected politician to another. McPherson remembered that the president never had a better time than at these receptions; they spilled over into the White House Rose Garden and were like "a love feast every time."[63] The chief executive felt a special bond with these officials because they too had campaigned for office and exercised the skills it took to win. Moreover, they met Johnson's definition of responsibility. "Here were people," Alexander explained, "elected by other people who had to go back . . . [and] would be held accountable in a few years."[64]

We know about Johnson's feeling for black political officials in general, but the record reveals much less about his relations with specific elected leaders. In fact, much more evidence exists about the administration's interaction with national civil rights leaders than with black politicians. Part of the discrepancy stems from the circumstances: Relatively few black elected officials were serving in Washington.[65] Furthermore, it was not until late in his term that African Americans began winning important posts at the local level, most notably Carl Stokes as mayor of Cleveland, Ohio, and Richard Hatcher as mayor of Gary, Indiana. The administration took special delight in the victory of Stokes, whom one Johnson aide described as "a great guy and an extremely valuable political property [who] represents the kind of 'black power' we need in the Democratic party."[66] Those observers interested in studying the complex relationship between the White House and the most influential black elected leader during this period, Adam Clayton Powell, should consult Charles V. Hamilton's judicious biography on the controversial Harlem congressman.[67] From examining this and other such relationships one can evaluate how the administration and African American elected officials each balanced their civil rights concerns with other political interests.

One elected official who after 1966 gained increased notice from the White House was Barbara Jordan. The president took a keen interest in the Texas state senator from Houston, who later became a U.S. congresswoman, and "was peacock proud" of this "role model he often claimed to have discovered." The archives, however, do not yield much data on Jordan that illuminate her budding leadership role; it would be helpful to investigate and identify the political qualities that brought Jordan to her fellow Texan's attention.[68]

Little information exists on the administration's dealings with female civil rights leaders. Except for Dorothy Height, the head of the National Council of Negro Women, an organization founded by Mary McLeod Bethune, a close associate of Franklin and Eleanor Roosevelt, the representatives of national civil rights organizations consulted by the White House were men. This situation clearly reflected the president's conception of the civil rights struggle as a form of interest-group politics. For him, social change came from the top down, with the president expected to provide the necessary political and moral leadership; thus conceived, the chief executive's contact with black women would be limited. Women played crucial roles within the freedom movement, but they tended to exert their greatest influence at the grassroots level and in a manner that often did not garner extensive publicity or media attention.[69]

Despite an affinity with black male leaders who acted moderately and responsibly, White House officials realistically understood that they could not call the shots and control a dynamic, independent African American freedom movement. As Bruce Miroff, a scholarly critic of the president's style of leadership acknowledged, the Johnson administration did not engage in a "conspiracy to manipulate black activists" but at most "attempted to keep on top of [constantly] changing issues."[70] This was especially true starting in summer 1964 when violent racial uprisings swept through black ghettos of the urban North. Although the administration tried to defuse potential trouble spots before they exploded and to keep the lines of communication open, presidential advisers admitted that "a lot of this is essentially uncontrollable. It will happen no matter what the federal government does.[71]

The president derived scant assistance from his chosen black leaders, who themselves had no effective control over these racial outbursts. As the black liberation struggle rejected integration and nonviolence, leaders such as Wilkins, Young, Farmer, and King became less relevant as peacekeepers. A resident of Detroit, whose streets erupted in violent fury in summer 1967, exhorted African Americans to cease being "house niggers and slaves like Whitney Young and Roy Wilkins—and to stand up and fight like Stokely Carmichael and [heavyweight boxing champ] Cassius Clay [Muhammed Ali]."[72] Recognizing this leadership vacuum, presidential aides sought to figure out how to recruit young leaders whose voices meant something to the new rebels; they failed ultimately to discover an acceptable alternative to Carmichael. Indeed the quest was impossible, and McPherson finally had to admit that the administration could not anoint any leader who would be respected by disillusioned blacks. Anyone whom the White House touched was "poison" to them, he asserted, because the "hand of the Man's authority on their shoulder was damning . . . to the real militants."[73]

The administration held few options. During the years of urban insurrections from 1964 to 1968, federal officials struggled to decipher the meaning of the turmoil in communities about which they knew almost nothing. The rage manifested in ghetto revolts came predominantly from a younger and poorer element whose experiences remained foreign both to white liberals and their older, middle-class black allies. Desiring to expand its network of informed black sources, the administration nevertheless wanted nothing to do with Carmichael or other black nationalists; White House officials refused even to consider black power advocates as legitimate leaders. Although Rap Brown and Carmichael "are trying to stir rebellion," McPherson advised the president, "they have few troops to call their own; they represent bitterness not people."[74] Along with Louis Martin, he believed that black power advocates were "not interested in dialogue," and even those who were not terrorists "seemed to be visionaries who have no real appreciation of the realities of American life save for the suffering that Negroes experience."[75]

Johnson's assistants did not think the president could talk with militants spouting black power slogans, and they hatched a plan to find out for themselves what was happening in the nation's racial battlefields. McPherson confessed that it was a "desultory way" of gathering information; however, neither the president nor his civil rights loyalists "had maintained a political apparatus in each city, through which intelligence flowed continuously to" the White House.[76] Without publicity, in 1967 presidential assistants fanned out through inner-city streets in Baltimore, Chicago, Cleveland, Detroit, Los Angeles, New York City, Oakland, Philadelphia, and other cities, spending several days in each location talking to people who reflected all shades of opinion. Much of what they heard inspired pessimism. After touring Chicago, Sherwin J. Markman reported that it "was almost like visiting a foreign country—and the ghetto Negro tends to look on us and our government as foreign."[77] Accompanied by Clifford Alexander and Louis Martin, McPherson visited Brooklyn's Bedford-Stuyvesant section and discovered just how out of touch the established leadership was; listening to an angry woman whip up an enthusiastic crowd in defense of retaliatory violence, McPherson remarked, "I would bet she knows her neighborhood better than any organization politician in it."[78]

Nevertheless, the president's emissaries detected some hope. Despite encountering palpable hostility, they found the president still popular among ghetto residents, at least among those people who believed in taking constructive measures to relieve bleak conditions. Men such as the Reverend Louis Sullivan of Philadelphia, who ran a successful job-training program out of his church, furnished the kind of leadership that appealed to the White House; he was "the essence of the best of the new Negro middle-class . . . [who] are responsible, articulate, and deeply involved in the problems of their race," according to Markman. Moreover, Sullivan and others like him had particular appeal for the president because he "is solely concerned with civil rights and does not become involved in Vietnam debates."[79] Johnson's observers were heartened that if the administration cooperated with leaders such as Sullivan and stayed the course in waging the War on Poverty (as well as that in Vietnam), then progress would continue to be made.[80]

What did these impromptu forays accomplish? Probably not very much besides proving what the administration already knew—that its leadership ties to the ghetto were thin. The visit to Detroit in May 1967 did not turn up a clue that a disastrous riot would break out only two months later, nor did the travelers to Oakland in March mention the Black Panther party, a gun-toting cadre of youths whose efforts to combat excessive force by the police resulted in several deadly encounters with law officers.[81] Yet some good came out of these eyewitness accounts. Alexander thought that the president used them in support of legislation to improve living conditions in the ghetto. Johnson insisted that although measures to exterminate disease-carrying rodents or to subsidize apartment rents would not immediately forestall violence, they would show his determination to forge ahead for the long haul. "If men of good will keep their eyes on the main thing," McPherson explained the president's thinking, "we would pass the laws that would speed the process."[82] Ultimately, however, the Great Society never lived up to its promises, and more effective programs would have done a great deal toward reducing the administration's credibility gap among disgruntled African Americans.

Better communication still might have narrowed some of the divide between the federal government and militant blacks, but the administration proved incapable of closing the split that had grown into a huge gulf. Political considerations played a large part as the White House tempered its concern for the plight of blacks with the calculation that it would alienate disaffected white voters who were showing signs of defecting from the Democratic party. Yet the rift was fundamentally irreconcilable. The president and the new black activists inhabiting the ghetto spoke a different language, one distinct from that which Johnson customarily heard from Wilkins and Young. The chief executive could enter into a dialogue with middle-class black leaders whose notion of civility and decorum conformed to his own, yet he had no way of speaking to young, impoverished African Americans who rejected his standards of behavior and rhetoric. Johnson could not possibly communicate with angry black rebels, as Farmer persuasively noted, "who would tell it like it is and call him an MF [motherfucker]."[83] As Sherwin Markman pointed out after visiting Chicago: "There is even a language of the ghetto. . . . As one man put it to me, 'Why should we have to speak the white man's language?'"[84] When Johnson heard these unfamiliar and dissonant voices, Clifford Alexander declared, it did not "hit his ear too well."[85]

The Johnson who might encourage criticism from Wilkins and Young could not abide it from outsiders who did not share his values and faith in the system. Though he once remarked to Richard Goodwin that he did not "expect gratitude" from African Americans, the president's bruised feelings belied these words. Those aides and civil rights allies who knew him best agreed that Johnson took the ghetto rebellions as a personal insult. According to Young, "he seemed to feel . . . what man has done more and why doesn't everybody know this and why aren't they appreciative?"[86] Needing to explain why ungrateful blacks tarnished his Great Society, the president believed despite considerable evidence to the contrary that the riots were instigated by an unspecified conspiracy. "Even though some of you will not agree with me," he lectured the cabinet in summer 1967, "I have a very deep feeling that there is more to that than we see at the moment."[87] Without conjuring up the possibility of sinister outside forces lurking behind the riots, how else could Johnson explain to himself why blacks did not give him sufficient thanks?

The work of the Kerner Commission illustrates the limits of Johnson's understanding. In the wake of a round of destructive riots in summer 1967, the president created the National Advisory Commission on Civil Disorders to study conditions in the ghetto that bred despair and violence. Headed by Democratic governor Otto Kerner of Illinois, the bipartisan membership included two African Americans, Roy Wilkins and Republic senator Edward Brooke of Massachusetts. The appointment of Wilkins and Brooke to the panel of eleven reflected Johnson's continued faith in moderate black leaders, a faith not shared by ghetto dwellers. A distressed McPherson reported to his boss after a visit to Harlem that residents there considered the two appointees as "'office' leaders—they have no following on the streets; they neither understand nor are understood by people on the streets."[88]

Given the moderate composition of the body, the president received a jolt when the commission issued its report the following March. Attributing the blame for the riots to white racism, the group recommended a massive federal spending program to deal with the manifold problems. As he had responded to the outbreak of the riots, Johnson bristled at what he perceived to be the commission's failure to recognize his many accomplishments in fighting racial discrimination. Feeling personally aggrieved, he confided to Califano that the report was "destroying his interest in things like this."[89] Neither his reliable friend Wilkins nor his devoted assistant McPherson could convince the hurt chief executive that the commission's handiwork showed him no disrespect, and the stubborn Johnson basically ignored the panel's findings.[90]

89

Events occurring shortly after the release of the Kerner Commission's report further tested the administration's relations with black leaders. The assassination of Dr. King on April 4, 1968, unleashed a spontaneous wave of rioting throughout the country, including within the nation's capital. Califano and McPherson persuaded the president to convene a White House meeting the next day with African American and congressional leaders. Johnson, who had not seen the slain minister for two years and whose estrangement from him was virtually complete, decided to set aside his personal pique and use King's death to help heal the nation's racial wounds. He turned "instinctively" to those leaders who, unlike Dr. King, had stuck with him throughout the years. Led by Wilkins and Young, the list included Bayard Rustin, Dorothy Height, Clarence Mitchell, Leon Sullivan, and two city officials who exhibited the political leadership he admired, Walter Washington, appointed by Johnson as mayor of the District of Columbia, and Mayor Richard Hatcher of Gary, Indiana. Walter Fauntroy represented the SCLC, and King's grieving father regretfully declined an invitation to attend but wanted the president to know that "his prayers are with [him]."[91]

The White House also invited Floyd McKissick, the director of CORE. Following Farmer's departure as head of the group in March 1966, McKissick had guided the organization on a black power and antiwar path. For nearly two years the administration had excluded him from the White House but in this instance relented, perhaps because it wanted to include one representative from a group at the forefront of the new black activism yet whose ties went back to the old civil rights coalition. And McKissick, for all his expressed militancy, was no Stokely Carmichael or Rap Brown. Whatever the intention, McKissick never made it to the meeting. When he arrived at the White House gate with two assistants who had not received invitations, the guard cleared McKissick but not his companions. The CORE director refused to participate without the unauthorized pair, and Johnson aides, hearing about the brouhaha during the meeting, apparently decided that to allow all three in would disrupt the affair.[92]

Had McKissick attended, the president quite likely would not have satisfied him. Johnson greeted his guests by asking their support "as responsible Negro leaders." After listening to them reaffirm their commitment to nonviolence and urging "concrete and meaningful action to counter dialogue in the streets," the chief executive reminded them of all that he had achieved. Still upset with the Kerner Commission, he reiterated his long list of accomplishments in reversing racial discrimination. He realized that more remained to be completed, and he pledged to pursue what he did best—to obtain legislation for fair housing and to press Congress to appropriate additional funds to wipe out poverty. His most telling remarks came at the end of the forty-seven-minute session because they indicated that he expected the moderate black leaders he had relied upon to share the responsibility for his failures as well as successes. "I have taken every opportunity to get through to the young people. How well I have gotten through remains to be seen," LBJ declared and than pointedly asked those leaders assembled: "But also—how well have you gotten through?"[93]

"Not very well," was the answer shouted back from the riot-torn streets of the cities. Following King's assassination, a week of violence plagued more than one hundred communities, leaving forty-six people dead, over three thousand injured, and twenty-seven thousand incarcerated and costing in excess of $45 million in property damages; it required twenty-one thousand federal troops and thirty-four thousand National Guardsmen to restore peace.[94] The violence did not cause Johnson to retreat, however. Facing the white backlash whipping through Congress, he managed to secure additional civil rights and housing legislation already in the congressional hopper. Even with Johnson's political world collapsing around him under the weight of Vietnam and urban rebellions, he continued to pull the legislative strings that he had mastered during his thirty-odd years in Washington.[95]

Holding the line also meant that Johnson did not intend to entertain new legislative initiatives while under siege, especially those proposals from black activists outside his recognized leadership circle. The Poor People's Campaign, originated by Dr. King, underscored this point. Mobilized as a nonviolent, interracial army of several thousand poor people to descend upon Washington, D.C., and to expose the inadequacy of the nation's skirmish against poverty, the protest began on May 12, a little over a month after King's death. The SCLC chief had not drawn up a long list of specific demands; instead he wanted poor people to gain pride from forming their own collective movement that would publicize their plight and prod the nation to action. King's successor, the Reverend Ralph D. Abernathy, implemented the hazy plan whose centerpiece became the construction of "Resurrection City," where the poor from diverse racial and ethnic backgrounds "would live together in peace and mutual respect."[96]

The Johnson administration greeted the campaign with patient apprehension. Coming so soon after the April riots, the president thought the demonstration would prove both dangerous and futile. Yet the chief executive ordered his cabinet secretaries to prepare a review of their programs and when visited by delegations of the poor they should "listen very closely and sympathetically to their appeals."[97] The Justice Department carefully monitored the activities of the protesters, and Attorney General Clark together with other administration officials attempted to cooperate with Abernathy, whom they considered a moderate leader within the context of this potentially disruptive confrontation. Fearing that the campaign was attracting hard-to-control militants who "would be pleased to see this 'peaceful' approach fail," Clark sought to find "a constructive purpose . . . to make it work so that the country sees that nonviolence can achieve something."[98]

The administration generally achieved its goal of maintaining peace. Widespread bloodshed was avoided, Washington escaped massive dislocations, and the president did not go down in history as another Herbert Hoover who brutally ejected depression-era Bonus Marchers from the nation's capital.[99] The administration made some minor "changes and improvements" in federal programs to give Abernathy "something to report back to his people."[100] In effect, the White House waited the protesters out. Besieged by conflicts in internal leadership, drenched by rain, and mired in mud, Resurrection City mocked Abernathy's plan for creating a model city of racial brotherhood. Federal officials allowed the demonstrators to convene a "Solidarity Rally" on June 19, but by then the impoverished, makeshift community was about to collapse. A few days later, D.C. police arrested the small remaining band of diehard protesters, including Abernathy, which did spark a brief outbreak of violence in Washington's black neighborhoods.[101]

Although Johnson exhibited considerable forbearance, he could not bring himself to show forgiveness. He refused to agree to several advisers' requests that he meet personally with Abernathy; as he had with King, the president felt his successor failed to display the proper gratitude. Speaking to a gathering of fifty thousand people on Solidarity Day, Abernathy criticized the administration's record over the past five years as a series of "broken promises," thereby guaranteeing that Johnson would shun him.[102] The president abhorred the protest but tolerated it. Ramsey Clark's comments serve as a useful touchstone:

> Resurrection City appalled Johnson. He loves Washington. It represents everything good that he believes in . . . physical beauty, grace in government, heroic monuments, human dignity. To see these pitiful poor people with . . . their ugliness and misery sprawled on the monument grounds—really hurt him—deeply hurt him. I think he was quite courageous in controlling himself and in letting us proceed as we did.[103]

To the end Johnson remained faithful to his vision of civil rights leadership. A moderate in militant times, he tried to keep the political center from crumbling. Amid a turbulent racial revolution, he steadfastly attempted to direct social change along conventional lines, and the black leaders most closely associated with him did little to shift him off course. No more than he did they control the new outrage and militancy that fueled the ghetto upheavals and the movement toward black nationalism. The issue of racial justice grew more complicated. No longer a southern problem with middle-class blacks at the forefront, as the battleground shifted northward it became marked by class and generational conflicts. The president and his black advisers did not speak or comprehend the language of the militants, either in a literal or a symbolic sense. To them, as with most other Americans, civil disorders meant wanton riots, not political rebellions, and black power signified "kill Whitey," not racial pride. Aware of the communication problem, the White House could still do little to improve the situation.

Johnson's definition of social reform compounded the problem. Tolerating mass demonstrations as a necessary evil, he believed that what really counted was the power of interest groups to apply concerted pressure on congressional lawmakers to swing votes in their favor. From this vantage point, the black revolt could be mediated in Washington by leaders who knew their way around the legislative chambers. Thus, the White House cut itself off from many grassroots activists directly responsible for providing direction and meaning to the black freedom struggle. Unlike most issues that appeared before Congress, the black revolt could not be handled simply through manipulation of the well-worn machinery of pluralistic politics.[104]

Johnson sided with moderate black leaders not only because they displayed their loyalty to him but also because of his historical experiences. Having cut his political teeth during the New Deal, he consumed certain lessons about the perils of waging reform. At the height of ghetto insurrections in 1967, when militants scorned traditional civil rights leaders, McPherson reminded the president of how the Left had hurled abuse at Franklin Roosevelt. "To the Communists," he noted, "Roosevelt was a fascist, because he wanted to preserve a voluntary life in America."[105] Picking up on this theme, United Nations Ambassador Arthur Goldberg, a former secretary of labor and U.S. Supreme Court justice, warned the chief executive against dismissing the NAACP as "outdated." After all, the rising strength of organized labor in the 1930s reminded him that the "radical leadership of that movement has largely vanished with time, or become part of the social mainstream."[106]

Looking back over Johnson's career, one is struck by his remarkable growth on civil rights issues. The transformative power of the black freedom struggle converted him from a routine defender of African Americans into the most vigorous advocate of racial equality ever to occupy the Oval Office. This progression, however laudatory, did not prepare him for the bitterness and anger that accompanied the black revolution in its later stages. An intensely prideful man who felt no better than when he was fully in control of events, Johnson did not fathom that black leaders could have their own separate agendas; nor was it their style to pay him gratitude for actions they thought he should have been carrying out in the first place. Like most white leaders of his period and region, the Texan retained, as James Farmer commented, "an element of paternalism" in dealing with a generation of blacks who prized their autonomy and self-direction.[107]

Even had Johnson's personality and ideology not been an obstacle, the president faced formidable practical constraints in collaborating with black leaders. Independent of Johnson, the freedom struggle generated a white political backlash that turned increasingly hostile to the goals of black advancement. Legislative wizard that he was, the president still could not magically make disappear the mounting congressional opposition to extension of the Great Society. From the perspective of the 1990s it hardly seems possible that even by embracing leaders more militant than Wilkins and Young could Johnson have deflected the onrushing force of conservatism, which would propel Republicans into the White House for twenty of twenty-four years following Johnson's retirement from office.

President Johnson left an ambiguous legacy of racial reform. He aroused great passions in Americans who hailed him as a second great emancipator or derided him as "Lynchum B. Johnson."[108] That he was neither goes without saying. Indeed he was a committed centrist, a liberal reformer by the standards of his era, who responded to a mighty social revolution sometimes too cautiously and defensively but with much more compassion and enterprise than any president before and after him. The animosity he elicited should be tempered by a recognition of his great worth. Roger Wilkins, Roy's nephew and director of the Justice Department's Community Relations Service, poignantly expressed the ambivalence toward Johnson of many African Americans who saw their racial consciousness raised during the 1960s. Wilkins had grown more radical than his uncle and felt sorely disappointed that the moderate president had failed to come sufficiently to terms with the anger manifested in black militancy. When he stepped down in 1969 and thought about Johnson, the younger Wilkins had "hated him." Yet decades later he admitted that "if you ask most knowledgeable blacks who was the best President for blacks, most of them will answer Lyndon Johnson." And after years of painful soul-searching, he candidly acknowledged, "That is my answer."[109] This bittersweet feeling captures both the agony and the triumph accompanying President Johnson's troubled leadership.

PART THREE

CIVIL RIGHTS AND
BLACK POLITICS

FROM BOYCOTTS
TO BALLOTS

In 1946 southern black soldiers returned from having fought in World War II, only to encounter white racism at home. A Georgia veteran expressed the sentiments of black GIs throughout the region, many of whom marched to county courthouses demanding their right to vote. "Peace is not the absence of war," he declared, "but the presence of justice which may be obtained, first, by your becoming a citizen and registered voter." The following decade, as the pace of the civil rights movement was quickening, some twenty-five thousand people rallied at the Lincoln Memorial in Washington, D.C., to celebrate a "Prayer Pilgrimage for Freedom." On 17 May 1957 the Reverend Martin Luther King, Jr., who had recently led a pathbreaking bus boycott in Montgomery, Alabama, emphasized suffrage as the key weapon for black liberation. "Give us the ballot," King predicted, and African Americans would use it to secure their basic rights, ensure justice, and guarantee responsible government. Over a quarter of a century later, more than ten times the number of people who heard King in 1957 assembled in the same location to honor his memory and listen to one of his disciples update his message. On 27 August 1983 with the ballot long won, the Reverend Jesse L. Jackson proclaimed: "We can have change through elections and not bloody revolution. Our day has come. From slaveship to championship . . . [f]rom the outhouse to the courthouse to the White House, we will march on."[1]

These expressions of the black veteran, minister, and presidential candidate represented separate but interconnected dimensions of black politics. Each sought to combine traditions of protest with the use of the franchise to achieve racial equality. For African Americans the ultimate aim of politics, either protest or electoral, has been liberation. Seeking emancipation from the bondage of white supremacy, disfranchised southern blacks challenged the political system for admission, even as they hoped to transform it by their participation. Toward this end marches, rallies, and demonstrations became political instruments to obtain a share of power to shape public policy, just as casting a ballot was aimed at making the political process more responsive to their demands.

Scholars of the civil rights struggle have furnished a full but as yet incomplete picture of the political aspects of the black freedom movement. For over twenty years political scientists, sociologists, historians, and journalists have filled library shelves with volumes investigating the origins of the movement, the individuals who led it, the groups that mobilized it, the tactics they employed, and the legislation and litigation they pursued. In general, the literature in the field can be divided according to the scholarly discipline of the researchers. Sociologists have concentrated on analyzing the civil rights phenomenon, including its political ramifications, within the framework of the formation and development of other social protest movements. Political scientists, who have written most extensively about black politics, have tended to focus on minority electoral behavior and the responses of the executive, legislative, and judicial branches to civil rights pressures. For their part, historians have written biographies of major leaders, the organizations they guided, and the issues they pursued, and most recently they have begun to examine case studies of the movement as it originated and matured in various communities throughout the South.[2] Drawing upon many of these works, this chapter offers a historical perspective on the development of black electoral politics and its relationship to civil rights protest.

During the post–World War II period, black southerners have moved through four stages of political development: reenfranchisement, mobilization, competition, and legitimacy. Judged by voter registration, participation at the polls, campaigning, and officeholding, the overall gains have been impressive. Yet one must remember that these advances have occurred unevenly and at different rates. In some areas blacks already have passed through all four phases of this political cycle, whereas in others they have barely moved beyond reacquiring the suffrage. In most places, southern black political development has fallen somewhere along the spectrum short of full legitimacy.[3] The civil rights movement has never taken root in many locations and has been abandoned prematurely in others; but where it has operated, blacks generally have gained increased influence to affect or power to mold decisions vital to their lives.

However, with the legal barriers to political participation mainly overcome, many African Americans still have found their economic hardships resistant to cure through the ballot box. Though political empowerment has meant a great deal to most southern blacks, it has been much less successful in lifting the burdens of class from their shoulders. Ironically, the political advances of the civil rights struggle, which have most benefited the burgeoning black middle class, have heightened differences between the most affluent and the more impoverished segments of the black community. This interplay of race and class concerns remains the most vexing issue for both practitioners and students of black politics.

Civil rights proponents have long believed that blacks could not be free without obtaining the right to vote. At the turn of the century. W.E.B. Du Bois set the standard for rejecting racial solutions that excluded the exercise of the franchise. Attacking Booker T. Washington for his strategy of postponing black participation at the ballot box, Du Bois insisted that the right to vote was intimately connected to first-class citizenship. Without it blacks would never command respect, protect themselves, and feel pride in their own race. To Du Bois, a scholar of the freedom struggle after the Civil War, Reconstruction provided vital evidence that black elected officials could transform the lives of their constituents. From this experience they derived the historical lesson, summarized by Eric Foner, that "it was in politics that blacks articulated a new vision of the American state, calling upon government, both national and local, to take upon itself new and unprecedented responsibilities for protecting the civil rights of individual citizens."[4]

The end of Reconstruction and the subsequent disfranchisement of blacks did not extinguish the yearning of African Americans to regain the right to vote and once again become active political agents. Beginning in 1910, the National Association for the Advancement of Colored People, with Du Bois among its leaders, launched a judicial attack on various techniques aimed at depriving southern blacks of their ballots. Following an early victory against the grandfather clause, the association waged a protracted campaign that eventually succeeded in overturning the white primary in 1944. By gaining a voice in the process of choosing candidates in the one-party Democratic South, blacks secured access to the only election that counted. Assessing the potential implications of this decision, a prominent black lawyer concluded that the "Supreme Court released and galvanized democratic forces which in turn gave the South the momentum it needed toward ultimate leadership in American liberalism."[5]

Unfortunately this triumph fell short of such optimistic expectations. Instead of the white primary, southern states employed a variety of surrogates—literacy tests, poll taxes, and the discriminatory administration of voter registration procedures—that kept the overwhelming majority of blacks from the ballot box. On both the national and local levels suffragists struggled to remove the remaining political obstacles. In 1957 and 1960 the NAACP, together with its liberal white allies, persuaded Congress to enact legislation challenging discriminatory registration practices. Meanwhile, black southerners themselves were organizing to recover the franchise. NAACP branches filed lawsuits and sponsored voter registration drives and voter education workshops. Independent civic leagues often joined in these enterprises, as did freedom-minded clergy who used their pulpits to preach the virtues of the ballot. When the Reverend Dr. King and his ministerial colleagues formed the Southern Christian Leadership Conference in 1957, they immediately launched a "Crusade for Citizenship" to sign up three million new voters in two years.[6]

The long history of the struggle to obtain the right to vote suggests the strength of the consensus of civil rights advocates that reenfranchisement constituted the decisive step toward political equality. Participation at the polls was expected to yield the kinds of basic benefits that groups exercising the franchise customarily enjoyed. Yet for black Americans much more was at stake. With their systematic exclusion from the electoral process, the simple acquisition of the vote constituted an essential element of liberation from enforced racial subordination. The political scientist Charles V. Hamilton, who studied the voting rights struggle both as a participant and scholar, found this passion for the ballot very understandable. "White America had spent so much effort denying the vote to blacks," he observed, "that there was good reason to believe that they must be protecting some tool of vast importance. Perhaps it was reasonable to put so much emphasis on the one fundamental process that clearly distinguished first-class from second-class citizens."[7]

In focusing on reenfranchisement, blacks sought to validate the principles of the American creed. To this extent, their aims were easily comprehensible to white Americans. By working for the suffrage, blacks committed themselves to the established rules of electoral politics, thereby seeking to make them work in their own behalf. Rather than attempting to overthrow the liberal ideology of republican self-government, black suffragists tried to gain admission to the democratic polity as an equal participant. As long as they moved in this direction, social change, by implication, would be seen as coming from the ballot box rather than from the barrel of a gun. In emphasizing the vote, therefore, blacks tacitly agreed to enter a political contract with the ruling order. Grievances could be settled slowly, peacefully, and with little disruption. Armed with the ballot, blacks would achieve respect and begin to compete for the fruits of the equal opportunity previously denied them.

Yet while sharing the values of liberal democracy, some black suffragists also held a more radical vision of political emancipation. The Student Nonviolent Coordinating Committee survived less than a decade, but it had a profound effect on shaping an alternative approach to black political empowerment. Founded in 1960, SNCC operated mainly in the rural, black-belt areas of the South, where racial oppression usually was most extreme and well entrenched. Living amid abject poverty and vigilante violence, SNCC fieldworkers came to see the ballot more as a means of transforming existing political institutions than as merely gaining access to them. They viewed the suffrage not as an end in itself but as an instrument for organizing local communities. Through voter registration efforts, SNCC members hoped to identify indigenous leaders who could then mobilize friends and neighbors to join in actively addressing the issues directly affecting them. Their vision of participatory democracy was premised on collective involvement in determining policies. In SNCC's scheme of community-oriented decision making, political governance signified more than the right of individuals to cast an unfettered vote; it meant the power of the group to define and execute its own agenda.[8]

Those touched by SNCC and recruited for grassroots leadership shared both traditional and radical notions of the suffrage. They combined a faith in the possibility of the ballot's potential to improve their individual lives with the hope that it would enable them to collaborate in overcoming their oppression. Bob Moses, SNCC's architect of voter registration in Mississippi during the early 1960s, built his community-organizing approach around the suffrage, because "every person, every black person, felt it was right." He believed strongly that civil rights organizers should take their cues from local people, who would then respond more favorably to their efforts. A seventy-year-old minister in Greenwood, Mississippi, experienced a personal transformation in reaching the decision to become a registered voter. "I am tired of being a second-class citizen," he told a SNCC fieldworker. "All of my life I have wanted to go [to register] and I ain't been able to. I am glad you are here. I am going to register to vote." Fannie Lou Hamer, who in 1962 had been evicted from her job on a plantation in Sunflower County, Mississippi, for attempting to register, ruminated on the relationship between racial esteem and the ballot. Before she obtained the franchise, she said, "some white folks . . . would drive past your house in a pickup truck with guns hanging up on the back and give you hate stares." But now this had changed because she and the majority of blacks in her community had become empowered to vote. In words that echoed Du Bois's views half a century earlier, she asserted: "These same [white] people now call me Mrs. Hamer, because they respect people who respect themselves."[9]

Voter registration campaigns connected electoral and protest politics. Though in the early days SNCC's members split over the relative merits of conducting direct-action demonstrations and canvassing for black suffrage enrollment, the distinction between the two rapidly faded. In many areas of the Deep South, registration drives themselves became a form of mass protest. In the rural black belt and in cities like Birmingham, Alabama, attempting to register voters led to violent white responses. Mass marches then ensued and produced confrontations and arrests that focused a national spotlight to their plight. In fact, voter registration drives brought civil rights activists into closer contact with individuals than was usually the case in protest demonstrations. Franchise workers went directly into people's homes, where they observed firsthand the daily problems of racism and poverty.[10] Thus, as a vehicle for rallying blacks to engage white racism directly and expose it to public scrutiny, voter registration drives took their place alongside sit-ins, freedom rides, and other forms of non-violent protest.

Electoral politics also reinforced a variety of protest tactics. The Montgomery bus boycott of 1955, for instance, was preceded by increased black voter registration and participation. Black ballots had begun to influence the outcome of some local contests and raise expectations about the improvements that voting would bring. When the pressure of the black vote failed to convince white officials to resolve the bus problem voluntarily, black political activists like E.D. Nixon and Jo Ann Robinson took the lead in organizing the boycott. Similarly, in 1957 in Tuskegee, Alabama, those most actively involved in voter registration activities launched a boycott to protest a racially motivated legislative gerrymander. Three years later, the sit-in movement began in Greensboro, North Carolina, a city that several years earlier had elected a black man to serve on the municipal council. The successful sit-ins, August Meier observed, "almost invariably occurred in places where Negroes formed a significant share of registered voters."[11] Electoral activities helped to heighten awareness among blacks that they could organize to challenge Jim Crow. Yet scholars have scarcely explored the connection between the two. For example, under what conditions did local blacks redirect their energies away from conventional political efforts at the polls to direct-action protests in the streets?

Combining protest and electoral activities, civil rights proponents thus waged more than a moral struggle; they conducted a political movement.

They did not limit their appeals to matters of conscience but depended on the political techniques at their disposal to force changes in the status quo. Persuasion without provocation was not enough, and conversion without power did not work. As Adam Fairclough has written about Dr. King, the civil rights leader "explicitly rejected the notion that blacks . . . could overcome their subjugation through ethical appeals and rational argument: they also needed an effective means of pressure."[12] As a political struggle, the civil rights movement, through protest, electoral activity, or a combination of the two, attempted to exert the necessary force to restructure power relationships between the races.

Inevitably, the reenfranchisement of black southerners gave impetus to the political mobilization of African Americans. The hundreds of voter registration drives throughout the South in the early 1960s, especially under the auspices of the Voter Education Project, succeeded in signing up some 688,000 black registrants. The proportion of eligible blacks registered jumped from approximately 29 percent in 1962 to 43 percent two years later.[13] Subsequently, the battle to register blacks in Selma, Alabama, in the face of severe repression by obstructionist white officials focused national attention on the distress of the disfranchised throughout Dixie and culminated in the passage of the Voting Rights Act of 1965. Having won this landmark piece of legislation through the persistent pressure of collective action, blacks could not take their hard-earned voting rights for granted. Rather, they had to continue mobilizing people to register and go to the polls in order to gain real power.

The Voting Rights Act suspended literacy tests in specified jurisdictions and provided the federal government with the option of dispatching examiners to register blacks in designated counties in seven southern states. This landmark law produced dramatic results. Within four years about three-fifths of the eligible black population managed to register. Nevertheless, Washington left the job of promoting voter registration to the civil rights organizations that had done so in the past, placing a heavy burden on grass-roots civil rights organizations.[14]

Although civil rights groups lacked adequate finances and personnel to complete the task, they had created the foundation for mobilizing the black electorate. For generations the South had buttressed its structural obstacles to voting with extralegal violence and intimidation, creating a well-founded fear among blacks concerning the costs of trying to become involved in politics. Civil rights associations provided a source of solidarity, a sense that individuals did not have to feel so alone and vulnerable in the face of danger; consequently, they helped to reduce the level of fear to manageable proportions. This, in turn, boosted black confidence in removing the political barriers that impeded racial advancement.[15]

The campaigns yielded impressive results. After 1965 the gap between white and black registration shrank. In 1966 the proportion of adult whites registered in the seven states originally covered by the Voting Rights Act exceeded that of blacks by a margin of nearly 30 percent; in 1982 the differential had closed to an average of about 9 percent. The estimated difference in turnout in presidential elections was even less. In 1968 black participation in the South lagged behind whites' by 10 percent, but in 1984 blacks trailed by only 5 percent.[16] Even more striking than the narrowing of this racial divide, blacks actually engaged in political activities at a much higher rate than would have been predicted from their socioeconomic profile. Because a larger portion of blacks than whites occupied the lower end of the income and educational scales, they lacked the resources usually associated with high levels of political involvement. Yet blacks showed a greater incidence of political participation compared with whites of similar socioeconomic status.[17]

This surprising finding can be attributed in large measure to the heightened black consciousness aroused by the civil rights movement. Collective action had demonstrated the power of oppressed groups to reshape their political world, and the racial pride that developed convinced blacks that politics concerned them as much as it did whites. In Mississippi, where the black registration figure jumped from 6 percent in 1964 to 60 percent in 1971, a black observer touring the Magnolia State remarked "That we are casting aside the feelings of inferiority and shame and realizing what a strong and beautiful people we are."[18] In conducting voter registration drives, erecting citizenship schools, holding mock elections, and directing protests, civil rights groups mobilized black southerners, many of them impoverished and poorly educated, to overcome these handicaps and band together for increased political action.

Along with the civil rights movement, the federal government also played a significant role in galvanizing group consciousness and black political mobilization. The power of Washington in economic and diplomatic affairs had expanded steadily during the New Deal and World War II; from 1944 on, the civil rights movement diverted some of that influence to the cause of racial equality. Reformers aimed to tip the balance of power in the federal system from the southern states to the national government. Because the states typically regulated the areas of education, public accommodations, law enforcement, and voter registration requirements, civil rights groups needed federal force to destroy racist practices in the South.

Demonstrations were designed to disturb the racial peace, create crises, and compel federal intervention on the side of civil rights protesters. Generally, this strategy worked. Presidents John F. Kennedy and Lyndon B. Johnson helped convince liberal foundations to sponsor and sustain the most important collaborative suffrage enterprise in the South, the Voter Education Project, which joined the NAACP, SNCC, SCLC, and Congress of Racial Equality.[19] Furthermore, the Justice Department filed suits against discriminatory registration practices, and in 1965 the passage of the Voting Rights Acts resulted in the enrollment of the majority of blacks.

The extension of federal responsibility that emerged out of the civil rights struggle carried over to the implementation of legislation as well. After the Supreme Court interpreted the Voting Rights Act as ranging beyond unfair voter registration procedures to the prohibition of discriminatory election procedures, the federal bureaucracy expanded its surveillance of the South and began investigating the biased use of at-large elections, multimember districts, reapportionment, and municipal annexations. Under the 1965 law, all changes in electoral rules had to be submitted to the Justice Department for approval. Despite the increasingly conservative outlook of successive presidential administrations in the 1970s and 1980s, voting rights enforcement became an institutionalized and regular feature of the political process. Scholars disagree about whether the Justice Department's civil rights overseers have monitored discriminatory electoral practices strongly enough, but there is little doubt that government officials scrutinized state action to a degree unthought of a generation earlier.[20]

Nevertheless, the civil rights movement caused a reallocation of power in the federal system without undermining it. In general, Washington acted cautiously, choosing to interfere in state affairs only as a last resort. The national government refused to intervene to shield civil rights activists from the racist intimidation and terror they experienced on a daily basis in well-known southern locales. Neither federal marshals nor troops stormed into the South until massive violence occurred and it was clear that local officials could not or would not maintain order. Even after passage of the Voting Rights Act, federal registrars went into only some threescore of the most recalcitrant counties, leaving most of Dixie untouched. Furthermore, the Justice Department allowed the overwhelming majority of southern electoral laws submitted for its prior clearance to stand. Whatever increased authority the national government possessed was administered in a spirit of cooperation with the states.[21]

This federal sensitivity to states' rights unintentionally spurred the growth of black consciousness, the driving force behind political mobilization. Ironically, by failing to heed the appeals of suffrage workers for increased federal protection in the South, a move that would have shifted law enforcement from local to national hands, Washington radicalized civil rights activists. Disappointment with white liberals prompted some of the most dedicated civil rights proponents to rethink their strategy and goals. Out of this reexamination, groups such as SNCC and CORE moved away from supporting integration with whites to building autonomous political bases within their own communities. This emphasis on black power, whatever negative, antiwhite connotations it carried, reflected the positive growth of heightened black solidarity. The black power impulse served to mobilize the newly enfranchised to become politically active and advance their collective racial interests.[22]

With federal law guaranteeing reenfranchisement and black racial consciousness becoming increasingly politicized, African Americans sought to compete for electoral power. In the past, the minority of southern blacks who had the freedom to vote, including those in scattered cities like Atlanta, Durham, and Tuskegee, used their ballots to support moderate white candidates against their race-baiting opponents.[23] Now as a result of the increased availability of the suffrage and the intense struggle needed to secure it, black southerners looked to members of their own race to represent their interests. This was especially true in areas with a large number of blacks among the eligible voters, where the chances of electing a black candidate were high. Just as acquisition of the ballot furnished a necessary step toward advancing first-class citizenship, so too did the election of blacks serve as a badge of equality. "A race of people excluded from public office," a black political leader in South Carolina asserted, "will always be second class."[24] The running of black candidates both reflected growing racial pride and presented a stimulus of further black political mobilization. The election of a black candidate to a post in a rural county in Mississippi, the winner declared, "will give the Negro race the feeling . . . like they can progress, and this in itself [will make] more people run for public office."[25]

The extension of the suffrage and the racial esteem that accompanied it broke the hold of whites over selecting black political leaders and setting their agendas. According to Louis Martin, a prominent black journalist and presidential adviser, the Voting Rights Act ushered in a new breed of minority politician who understood "that political power is generated in the black precincts and does not come from the hands of the great white father."[26] Many of the black contestants and elected officials had participated in some aspect of the civil rights struggle and viewed their role as an extension of the movement. In contrast to the white officials they challenged or replaced, they typically considered politics an arena for continuing the transformation of black communities that the civil rights movement had sparked. As Fannie Lou Hamer put it, she expected black officials to respond "to human needs" and "save [their] people."[27]

However, the transition from civil rights to electoral politics did not necessarily move this smoothly. Mass demonstrations depended on emotional appeals, tended to be episodic, and soon lapsed after resolution of the particular crisis. In contrast, the competition for public office, as a political scientist has observed "is more mundane and requires both longterm political skills and the ability to consistently draw the black electorate."[28] Candidates had to get elected by spending long hours campaigning door-to-door and shepherding large numbers of people to the polls. Once elected, they had to master the techniques of bargaining and compromise, often settling for solutions hammered more out of pragmatism than morality. Despite the humanistic concerns they often brought to their positions, black elected officials had to accommodate to the constraints imposed upon them by the political system they entered.[29]

Operating within these limitations, black public officials nonetheless achieved notable accomplishments. Their candidacies stimulated increased black political mobilization, and their elections have provided significant minority access to city halls and county courthouses, where most black officials hold power. They also succeeded in opening up jobs and allocating government contracts to their black constituents, improving the quality of municipal services, and reducing racist rhetoric and violence. Reaping tangible and symbolic gains, they helped tear down the psychological and physical walls that kept blacks in confinement. A retired worker in Tuskegee, Alabama, clearly recognized the difference they made: "Everything's better. In the old days, before black officials ran the county, most black people steered clear of white enclaves. They used to arrest you over there if you went through," but not anymore.[30]

Still, the attainments have fallen short of the needs. Perhaps the limitations of the ballot were clearer to black officeholders than to those who put them in office. As Richard Arrington, the black mayor of Birmingham, Alabama, remarked, "there are the expectations of the black community that expects you to do more than you can do." In most cities and counties of the South (and the rest of the country as well) black elected officials have been in the minority and thus could not deliver political rewards without the cooperation of white colleagues. Even in those rural, black-belt areas where blacks controlled a majority of government positions, the blacks lacked the economic resources to affect significantly the material conditions of the impoverished population. Even in more prosperous major cities presided over by black mayors, such as Atlanta, Birmingham, and New Orleans, economic power remained in white hands. "Blacks have the ballot box," an Atlanta newspaper editor admitted, "and whites have the money." Consequently, urban black politicians aligned with white businessmen to promote downtown redevelopment projects and gentrification of their cities, resulting in the displacement of poor residents from their neighborhoods, making it harder for them to find adequate housing and jobs.[31]

The failure to achieve further success stemmed in part from the inability of blacks to win a greater share of elected positions. The number of black elected officials in Dixie has skyrocketed since 1965, leaping from less than seventy-five in 1965 to 3,685 in 1987. Yet, of the more than eighty thousand elected officials in the former Confederate states, only 4.6 percent were black by the latter year, far less than the proportion of blacks in the population of the region. Moreover, in twenty-one of eighty counties where blacks constituted a majority of the population in the original seven states covered by the Voting Rights Act, no member of their race held elective office in 1980.[32]

Reenfranchised southern blacks failed to realize their electoral potential for a variety of reasons. In some places, they had not yet acquired the economic resources and political skills to mount effective campaigns. The civil rights movement, which had been so instrumental in mobilizing political participation, scarcely operated in many areas of the South and failed to stay long enough in others. Furthermore, blacks encountered resistance from whites who attempted to weaken the strength of their newly acquired ballots. The existence of such electoral procedures as at-large elections and multimember districts diluted minority voting power, making it more difficult for blacks to elect representatives of their own choosing.[33]

The numerical underrepresentation of black elected officials did not necessarily leave them without important political leverage. If they wished, blacks could use their votes to help elect white representatives and gain concessions from them. Indeed, increased black electoral participation served to make outspoken racist appeals in political contests a thing of the past and forced aspiring white candidates to campaign for black ballots.[34] However, black citizens wanted not only influence but power, a condition they associated with the election of African Americans to represent their communities.

This issue of fair representation brought to the surface tensions within the civil rights coalition over individual versus group-centered goals. "At a time of rising civil rights consciousness," the political scientist Abigail M. Thernstrom commented, "the question of proper representation for at least certain groups—those defined by race, ethnicity, and political marginality—was bound to arise."[35] The Voting Rights Act furnished the opportunity for blacks to cast their ballots, but it did not guarantee their election. Traditionally, liberals believed that the chief aims of the civil rights struggle were to eliminate discriminatory barriers to equality under the law and to utilize the Constitution as a color-blind instrument. Having achieved these goals with the legislative victories of the 1960s, many whites deserted the civil rights coalition in opposition to race-conscious entitlements that treated blacks not as individuals but as members of a historically exploited group. With respect to the franchise, critics of affirmative action policies worried that "categorizing individuals for political purposes along lines of race and sanctioning group membership as a qualification for office may inhibit political integration."[36] According to this view, as long as blacks were free to cast their votes and influence the outcome of elections, the constitutional guarantee of equal opportunity for all citizens was fulfilled.

In contrast, civil rights leaders redefined liberal norms. While eschewing advocacy of official quotas mandating proportional representation, they argued that in a society in whose institutions racism persisted, it was appropriate to fashion remedies that took race into account. It did not suffice to give blacks the right to vote and then tolerate supposedly neutral electoral rules that had the effect of diluting the impact of their ballots. Forged through collective action, the communitarian outlook of the freedom struggle shaped blacks' political aspirations. For most of American history elected positions had been reserved for whites by virtue of their race. After years of struggle and sacrifice, African Americans claimed legal and moral justifications for a larger share of the electoral representation than they possessed.

Blacks also waged this battle for representation within the structure of the Democratic Party. Though not entirely successful, they managed to pry open its doors to more extensive black participation. They accomplished this as a direct consequence of the civil rights movement in the South. In 1964, when the SNCC-inspired Mississippi Freedom Democratic Party contested for delegate seats at the Democratic national convention, it set in motion a process that transformed the party organization. The MFDP did not gain official recognition that year, but national party leaders promised to bar discrimination within their southern ranks and to ensure that blacks had ample opportunity to participate in the selection of Democratic functionaries in the future. In 1968 party leaders kept their word and awarded seats at the convention to a biracial delegation from Mississippi, as well as to those from several other southern states. Within the next four years, reform reached its peak as the party adopted affirmative action guidelines requiring "representation of minority groups on the national convention delegation in reasonable relationship to the group's presence in the population of the State."[37]

The effects were impressive. In four years the percentage of black convention delegates had more than doubled, to 14.6 percent. For the most part, the delegations at the 1972 convocation containing the highest ratio of blacks came from states designated by the Voting Rights Act. Mississippi led the way with 56 percent, and in each of the covered states the proportion of black representatives equaled or exceeded the percentage of blacks in the population. The Democratic party had been so much altered by the addition of blacks and other traditionally underrepresented groups, such as women and young people, that one older, white male delegate could barely recognize it. "I never thought I'd see the day," he exclaimed, "that middle-aged white males would be our biggest minority."[38] Though the figures for black delegate representation dropped at subsequent conventions, they continued to reflect the greatly increased presence of blacks in the Democratic party—and nowhere more than in the land of Dixie, the center of the civil rights movement.

As blacks gained increased representation in governmental and partisan institutions, minority participation in the political process acquired added legitimacy. Where African Americans won public office, including those instances where they captured a majority of the available positions, whites generally accepted the validity of their rule. This is not to suggest that whites completely abandoned their efforts to hamper or subvert blacks from exercising power, especially in those rural, black-belt counties of the South traditionally most hostile to racial equality.[39] But in most locales whites either resigned themselves to or actively cooperated with black governance. White businessmen found black officials supportive of their plans for economic modernization, and because of their overwhelming population advantage in most communities and in every state, whites learned that fears of living under black domination had been greatly exaggerated. For those whites who refused to concede the legitimacy of black political rights, the enforcement of the Voting Rights Act kept their resistance in check.

Yet white cooperation with black participation in the political process stemmed from more than self-interest or federal coercion. Segregationists had an increasingly difficult time defending disfranchisement in a political culture that considered the right to vote essential to republican government and that viewed restrictions founded on race as unacceptable. It was true that basic principles of the democratic ethos had not changed between the end of Reconstruction and the beginning of World War II, the period during which the South had encountered relatively little opposition from the national government in circumventing the guarantees of the Fifteenth Amendment. However, the subsequent wartime struggle against Nazi fascism and the ensuing Cold War campaigns to line up nonwhite nations behind America's anti-Soviet foreign policy helped undermine the racist premises upon which black disfranchisement had been sustained in the South. Furthermore, whereas other civil rights issues like school desegregation and fair employment generated serious disagreement, protection of the suffrage encountered fewer objections. Clearly, the struggle for enfranchisement produced legislative conflicts in Washington and fierce hostility in the South, but overall, Americans accepted the principle of majority rule and the sanctity of free elections. In sum, whites have largely recognized the legitimacy of black political representation, as Peter Eisinger noted, "by explaining it as a product of democratic processes" and the norms of fair play.[40]

At the same time, by adopting electoral competition as the chief means of pursuing racial advancement, African Americans have stamped their own legitimacy on the established political order. With ballots in hand, blacks resorted less often to the kinds of protest activities that were the only methods available for influencing policy when they were disfranchised. "Black political participation," one observer declared, "is to the civil rights movement what the protest movement was in the 1960s." In this vein, elected officials became "the principal agents of implementation" of the benefits blacks obtained through the political system. As a consequence, more disruptive forms of agitation seemed anachronistic. "There was no longer a need to march in the streets against the policies of big city mayors," Manning Marable concluded, "because blacks were now in virtually every municipal administration across the nation."[41]

The process of black political legitimization has further served to absorb into the electoral mainstream some of the most radical impulses of the civil rights era. The experience of the Mississippi Freedom Democratic Party provides a case in point. As the organizers of the MFDP conceived of this group, it represented economically dispossessed sharecroppers and domestic workers. Reflecting the philosophy of SNCC, they did not just desire delegate recognition from the national Democratic party; rather they sought also to transform political and economic relations in the Magnolia State. "We want to be on the ground level, where the decisions are made about us," Bob Moses asserted. "We don't want to [be] mobilized every four years to vote. We want to be in the actual running of things." Their chal-

III

lenge rejected in 1964, they did see blacks gain representation in the Democratic Party, albeit in altered form. In 1968 the biracial Loyalist delegation that gained the seats at the national convention consisted of fewer MFDP veterans than four years before. They had been replaced by more moderate blacks and whites. By the end of the 1970s, this Loyalist faction exchanged its national recognition for incorporation with the mostly white Democratic regulars, who controlled the party apparatus within Mississippi. Little remained of the original spirit or membership of the MFDP by the time of fusion. Although unity accorded blacks acceptance as political partners within the Democratic party, the progressive goals that the early civil rights militants had envisioned remained unfulfilled.[42]

As the influence of protesters gave way to the power of professional politicians, black elected officials increasingly entered coalitions with whites. At the local level, in those places where blacks constituted a majority of the electorate they needed fewer white votes to triumph. Nevertheless, throughout the South (as well as the North), blacks needed white allies to govern effectively. Where African Americans had numerical strength, they still lacked control of economic resources. Without the cooperation of white businessmen and financiers—and this was as true in rural Lowndes County, Alabama, as in metropolitan Atlanta, Georgia—black officials could not raise the funds to carry out their programs. Consequently, they had to devise policies to improve black living conditions without threatening white community elites. For example, in 1981 Birmingham mayor Richard Arrington explained: "What I had to decide as mayor was not whether I was going to pursue civil rights goals, but how to do it. If I alienated all the white leadership, I began to realize that it was going to be twice as hard to achieve the goals."[43]

Under such circumstances, whites often played a pivotal role in shaping black politics. As black candidates began competing with each other in areas containing black majorities, the minority white electorate helped determine the outcome. In Atlanta and New Orleans, for example, some victorious black officials have failed to win a majority of black votes but clinched their election by capturing the bulk of white ballots. These politicians faced the delicate task of representing black interests without offending the whites who had tipped the balance of electoral power in their favor. In many areas of the South, particularly in small towns and rural areas, blacks still assumed that whites only voted for blacks to manipulate and control them. In one such hamlet, a losing black candidate expressed his skepticism about his black opponent who received most of the white votes:

"Doc is not classified as black to me. You black when black folks elect you. White folks don't vote for black folks."[44]

At the state level, where blacks everywhere were in the minority, they necessarily had to forge coalitions with whites. In most instances this meant black support for white candidates; in the former Confederacy, only in Virginia has a black won statewide election to the top executive post of governor.[45] Blacks won a rising share of seats in state legislatures, but they remained outnumbered by white lawmakers and therefore had to form biracial alliances to obtain benefits for their constituents. As a rule, they have joined forces with moderate white "New South" politicians, who supported both desegregation and the expansion of industrial and commercial ventures. These policies favored middle-class whites and blacks, leaving the poor of both races behind. In general, the representatives of impoverished blacks and whites failed to construct biracial coalitions along common class lines. As in the past, very different perspectives on race continued to divide those most economically depressed. A recent study by a team of political scientists confirmed this point: "Nearly all . . . white subgroups opposed the positions on current racial issues that are preferred by majorities of southern blacks."[46]

Yet the widespread participation of black voters in the South also altered the racist outlook of the Democratic Party in the region. With the growth of the Republican Party within Dixie and its appeal among conservative white voters, Democratic politicos scrambled for black votes to compensate for white flight from their ranks. A senior Democratic officeholder in Mississippi remarked: "When the blacks stay with the Democrats, we can just about win, but when they leave, we can't."[47] In return for this support, white southern Democratic lawmakers increasingly took positions favorable to their black constituents. The shift in backing for civil rights legislation was especially striking. In 1975 and 1982 southern white Democratic congressmen lined up solidly behind renewal of the Voting Rights Act, reversing the situation of a decade earlier when the overwhelming majority had opposed the measure. In 1987 the defeat of Robert Bork for nomination to the Supreme Court hinged on the refusal of key southern Democratic senators to approve it. Blacks perceived Bork's judicial philosophy as endangering the civil rights advances they had so recently made. As Senator Richard C. Shelby of Alabama, who owed his election to the black electorate, declared: "In the South, we've made a lot of progress. We do not want to go back and revisit old issues."[48]

At the same time, white southern Democrats still tended to be more conservative on economic and class-related issues than their northern counterparts. The significance of the black electorate notwithstanding, whites composed from three-quarters to over four-fifths of the registered voters in the South. With the changing racial complexion of his party, a white Democratic official from South Carolina warned about the perils of ignoring this white majority. "Within a short time," he remarked in early 1988, "we would be a black party in the South, deserted by the whites, a band of hopeless people waiting for favors from Washington." To defeat Republicans, the Democrats had to hold onto the bulk of black votes while obtaining a substantial minority of white electors. Because whites held much more conservative opinions than did most blacks, Democratic politicians had to balance their positions somewhere between the liberal and conservative ends of the spectrum. As a result, successful southern white Democrats typically cast themselves as moderates.[49]

In the American political system, perhaps the ultimate sign of legitimacy comes in the presidential arena. In this respect, the campaigns of Jesse L. Jackson for the Democratic nomination in 1984 and 1988 indicated the arrival of blacks as active agents in national electoral politics. In the past, the black electorate had contributed winning margins to Democratic standard-bearers—most recently for Jimmy Carter in 1976. But never before had a black candidate mounted as strong a challenge for the top office in the land as did Jackson.[50] Building upon a solid foundation of black votes, especially in the South, Jackson attempted to fashion what all national politicians must ultimately create: a winning coalition. For him this meant an alliance with whites as well as with other exploited minorities. Though Jackson's campaigns emerged from the tradition of protest and reenfranchisement in the civil rights era South, they have become part of the respectable electoral mainstream. His platform included not only social and economic issues of special interest to blacks but also foreign and domestic policies that mattered to whites. Born out of the reawakened racial consciousness of the freedom movement, the Jackson candidacies tried to construct a "Rainbow Coalition" that united people of all races around common economic and political concerns. His two defeats notwithstanding, the Reverend Jackson helped confer on black political aspirations a renewed measure of legitimacy.[51]

Despite some splendid accomplishments, the acquisition and utilization of the ballot did not solve some fundamental problems. The ballot has proved a necessary but insufficient tool for achieving racial equality in theory as well as practice, and black political power is wider than it is deep. Entry into politics had limited effectiveness in relieving the economic distress that blacks endured disproportionately to their presence in the population. Whereas the poverty rate among black families declined over the decade of the 1970s (from 41 percent to 30 percent), the percentage of impoverished blacks was still more than four times that of whites (7 percent). Blacks experienced a higher incidence of unemployment than did whites, and the figures for young black male adults reached depression-era levels. In Lowndes County, Alabama, one of the first places in the rural South where blacks came to political power, their median family income rose slightly in comparison with that of white residents (from 33 percent to 41 percent); nevertheless, the median family income of blacks, $7,443, trailed far behind that of whites, $18,350. Accordingly, in 1985 the black sheriff of the county, John Hulett, summed up the obvious lesson: "Until people become economically strong, political power alone won't do. For most people, it's like it was sixteen years ago."[52]

The economic news was not all bad. Expanding opportunities resulting from desegregation and affirmative action programs swelled the size of the black middle class. From this group, with its access to economic resources and educational skills, new black political leaders emerged. Only recently risen from the lower rungs of the economic ladder, these middle-class black politicians tended to identify with the plight of those less fortunate. In addition, their newfound upward mobility was not entirely secure, and they remained more vulnerable than their white counterparts to downswings in the economy. For this reason and because they were products of the same emancipatory forces that shaped the racial consciousness of poor blacks, middle-class blacks continued to share with them mutual concerns associated with race.[53]

In the long run, this growing class stratification in black communities may erode racial solidarity, though to what extent remains unclear. During the civil rights era, southern blacks, no matter what their economic class, encountered a monolithic structure of racial segregation. Conflicts over tactics and strategy existed among various civil rights organizations, but they usually managed to subordinate their rivalries to the common fight against Jim Crow and disfranchisement. Having achieved many of their aims, blacks became freer to divide politically along conventional lines of class, section, generation, and gender. Even Jesse Jackson's presidential bid in 1984 failed to unite black elected officials. Those black politicians most closely tied to national Democratic Party affairs were more likely to support one of the established white candidates in the primaries than those who operated chiefly on the local political stage and supported Jackson, the acknowledged outsider.[54] The degree to which the political cleavage among blacks is occurring and the forces behind it offer rich possibilities for future research.[55]

This process of fragmentation was slowed down by the enduring significance of race in American politics. The United States has not yet become a color-blind society, and race looms large as a category for determining political choices. Public opinion surveys indicated that blacks and whites disagreed sharply over a broad range of policy issues, especially those that deal with federal efforts to reverse the economic and social effects of past racial discrimination and seem to give preferential treatment to blacks. "Even those blacks who have 'made it' economically," Thomas Cavanagh reported,"are more likely to support the views of poor blacks than those of well-to-do whites." Furthermore, racial polarization accompanied reenfranchisement. The emergence of southern blacks into the electorate initially sparked a political countermobilization of southern whites to sign up to vote.[56] While blacks flocked into the Democratic Party in the South, whites deserted to the Republican Party and joined newly transplanted northerners to turn it into a competitive force in the traditionally one-party region. In presidential elections, a majority of white southerners have not supported a Democratic presidential candidate since 1964, in contrast to the overwhelming mass of black voters. In addition, this sharp racial split at the polls also existed in local contests where black and white candidates directly competed against each other.[57]

In order to assess further both the strengths and the weaknesses of electoral politics as a vehicle for black advancement, historians should expand upon current themes as well as branch out into new fields of research. One fruitful line of investigation would continue the present trend of studying the evolution of black politics at the community level. The black-led freedom struggle originated and derived its power from people in small towns and cities throughout the South, and it is impossible to evaluate the political consequences upon them without looking closely at the places in which they lived. For the most part, scholars who have studied crisis spots in the South, such as Birmingham, Selma, and Albany, have only examined them during the few months they were in turmoil. Broader more systematic treatments of communities over a period of a generation or two would measure more fully the impact of civil rights politics. Such case studies will help us distinguish between short- and long-term changes as well as discern areas that have remained largely unaffected by the movement. By doing so, we can compare the levels of political development that have occurred in different places and determine the forces that have promoted or retarded racial advancement.

Toward this end, it is important to integrate local accounts with events in the national arena. The federal government greatly affected the movement of black politics through its various phases. Black activists helped shape the formation in Washington of public policies, which, in turn, had to be implemented at the local level. Yet it is not enough merely to place community and national issues side by side; one must seek to demonstrate the interaction between them. In this respect, Robert J. Norrell's study of Tuskegee provides a holistic model for researchers to follow.[58]

A virtually neglected aspect of black politics has been the role of women. Scholars should explore the contributions of women, especially blacks, in regaining the right to vote and in participating in the political mobilization that accompanied it. The careers of Jo Ann Robinson in Montgomery, Fannie Lou Hamer and Unita Blackwell in Mississippi, and Ella Baker with the NAACP, SCLC, and SNCC suggest the importance of women in assuming a multiplicity of tasks during the civil rights period.[59] In every community less well known but no less courageous women joined the struggle. It does appear that black women played a more prominent part in the reenfranchisement and mobilization phases of political development than they have in competing for elective positions. Although it appears that black females have participated politically at a higher rate than did black men, in 1987 they held only 649 offices in the South, which constituted 17.8 percent of the number occupied by blacks.[60] Thus, we need to explore the impact of women on shaping the civil rights movement as well as the freedom struggle's effects on their political lives.

In addition, there is a need for a comprehensive study that compares the women's and black suffrage movements. It might be asked what effect the acquisition of the ballot had on directing grievances of race and gender into socially and politically sanctioned channels. For instance, what happened to the diverse economic and social goals of black and women activists that ranged beyond the legal right to register and vote? Given the persistence of sexual discrimination in the seventy years following the adoption of the Nineteenth Amendment, how have African Americans, male and female, fared by comparison in the two decades since passage of the Voting Rights Act?[61]

In integrating community and national histories and looking more closely at women, scholars should also study the relationship between the political aims and economic results of the civil rights movement. The success of the black middle class has heralded the gains achieved by the breakdown of racial barriers to economic opportunity, but the persistence of substantial black poverty and unemployment has attested to the cleavage between electoral expectations and financial rewards. By committing themselves to the suffrage as a central tool for emancipation, blacks, implicitly if not explicitly, accepted the ground rules of the American political system. In doing so, black politicians have downplayed the more radical collective side of the reenfranchisement strategy as envisioned by SNCC. As a result, they have become part of the dominant political culture whose values have benefited the black middle class while leaving the economic fortunes of lower-class blacks largely unchanged.[62]

Notwithstanding the limitations of the suffrage as an instrument of liberation, the political emancipation of blacks made a critical difference, as a story recounted by Bob Moses poignantly shows. He told of a woman he remembered working with in Mississippi, Hazel Palmer, who had not been elected to any office or gained material success by objective standards. But that was beside the point. "It didn't matter that she did not make it in any other way that society thinks people make it," Moses insisted. "But she had won something in her spirit that no one could take away from her."[63] Combining protest with electoral politics, the civil rights movement succeeded in reawakening black consciousness and transforming individuals and their communities through collective action. Future generations of African Americans struggling to gain the undelivered promises of racial equality will build upon this precious legacy.

PRESERVING THE
SECOND RECONSTRUCTION

The passage of the Voting Rights Act of 1965 climaxed a long struggle to restore the ballot to southern blacks. For over a half century civil rights advocates had litigated, legislated, and demonstrated against barriers erected to evade the Fifteenth Amendment. Although the judiciary had overturned the grandfather clause and the white primary and Congress passed two pieces of legislation increasing the power of the federal government to challenge discriminatory suffrage practices, by 1965 less than 40 percent of the black adults in the South had been enrolled on the voter lists, and less than seventy-five elected officials in the region were non-white. Within ten years after the Voting Rights Act went into effect, approximately 60 percent of black southerners had qualified to vote and more than fifteen hundred blacks held public office. Not since the period after the Civil War had blacks participated so extensively in the political process.

In flocking to the polls, African Americans evoked contrasting images of the Reconstruction Era. The Voting Rights Act elicited in some white southerners painful memories. Supreme Court Justice Hugo Black of Alabama decried one section of the statute as a revival of "'the conquered province' concept . . . reminiscent of old Reconstruction days when soldiers controlled the South and when those States were compelled to make reports to military commanders of what they did."[1] Negroes held a more favorable impression of Reconstruction. "In ten years," Chuck Stone, a journalist and political commentator, predicted in 1968, "the black South is going to be the leading force among black people and, as was true during Black Reconstruction, spawn a race of brilliant and articulate black men whose capacity for innovative social legislation may well help to save America from the self destruction of its own white racism."[2]

The history of Reconstruction also held bitter lessons for blacks. White commitment to racial equality, never wide or deep, was short lived, and a caste system which kept southern blacks segregated socially, impoverished economically, and impotent politically was the era's ultimate legacy. If by the mid-1960s the shroud of oppression was beginning to lift, few blacks could forget the hopes raised and the hopes dashed a century earlier. On the eve of the harshly contested presidential election of 1968, A. Philip Randolph found the similarities to the earlier epoch disturbing. "In 1876," he commented, "the basic needs of all black people were sacrificed for the alleged corruption of the Reconstruction governments of the South. Today all black people are being blamed for the destructive rioting and the violent words of a few. Then as now it was charged that the black people were not ready for full equality."[3] Victims once before of a change in political climate, blacks were naturally fearful of the anger and devisiveness that characterized the American landscape in the late 1960s and early 1970s.

So far, the political gains of the Second Reconstruction have outlasted those of the first. Maintenance of the suffrage during the Second Reconstruction reflected the continuing consensus on enfranchisement. Unlike the era following the Civil War when extension of the vote to blacks was considered an extreme measure, the period since the end of the Second World War has witnessed an acceptance of the ballot as a moderate instrument for social change. When the tactics of the civil rights movement shifted from litigation to direct action confrontation, the ballot assumed conservative overtones. Registering to vote and going to the polls provided less of a threat to public peace and the established order than did massive street demonstrations and boycotts. Furthermore, compared to such goals as the desegregation of schools, public facilities and housing, and the removal of racial bias in employment, extending the franchise posed less direct challenges to prevailing social and economic patterns.[4]

Nor did southern whites feel nearly as threatened by a black electorate as they had during the First Reconstruction. In the modern civil rights era, black enfranchisement was not accompanied by any white disqualification as was the case during Radical Republican rule. Moreover, demographic changes reduced the potential for black control. The huge migration of blacks northward since World War I diminished the possibility that whites could be substantially outnumbered at the polls. In fact, while the gap between the percentage of registrants of each race has narrowed, the proportion of eligible whites placed on the voting rolls has increased since the mid-sixties. In the southern states blacks fell far short of constituting a majority of the electorate, and in many of the counties where blacks predominated in absolute numbers, they did not command a majority of the crucial voting-age population.[5] Thus, the continued participation and influence of southern whites in local, state, and national politics throughout the Second Reconstruction, despite their opposition to it, has conferred a legitimacy on civil rights measures that was lacking during the First Reconstruction. Federal military intervention to protect first class citizenship rights for blacks has been the exception rather than the rule.

Although both Reconstructions involved national management of racial policies in the South, the earlier version required a much sharper break with prevailing conceptions of the federal system. The national government proved unwilling to make a sustained constitutional departure from the past. The Civil War may have smashed the doctrines of states rights and nullification, but the Union victory only briefly altered the traditional roles state and national governments played in domestic affairs. Reconstruction did not create permanent machinery in Washington geared to supervise civil rights in the South. Furthermore, many of the innovative congressional measures that might have rearranged the balance of federal and state control of race relations were eviscerated by an unsympathetic judiciary. A century later the situation had changed dramatically to the benefit of black enfranchisement. The New Deal and World War II had thrust the federal government into assuming responsibilities previously handled by the states and created expectations among Americans that Washington could provide solutions for a variety of problems. At the same time, circumstances surrounding the Cold War abroad and realities of domestic politics nudged the federal government to the side of promoting racial equality.[6] Toward this end and under constant pressure from blacks, the judiciary reversed itself and furnished the necessary precedents for congressmen and presidents to enact and enforce civil rights legislation.

When the Voting Rights bill swept through the national legislative halls in 1965, it encountered less opposition from southern white politicos than any of the other four civil rights measures enacted from 1957 to 1968. With a flourish of historical symbolism, Lyndon Johnson held the bill-signing ceremony in the same Capitol Rotunda room where Abraham Lincoln put his name to a document granting freedom to Confederate-owned slaves. The tough measure Johnson approved on August 6 contained a formula to suspend literacy test requirements for voting, authorized the attorney general of the United States to appoint federal registrars and observers for designated jurisdictions, required the covered governmental units to submit all suffrage regulations passed after November 1, 1964, to the Department of Justice or the District Court for the District of Columbia for clearance, and maintained these extraordinary provisions in effect for at least five years. Accordingly, six southern states and parts of a seventh were slated for a degree of direct federal intervention in their electoral affairs unmatched since the 1870s.[7]

The consensus supporting passage of this strong remedy for disfranchisement remained intact as other issues growing out of the Vietnam War and urban riots cracked the civil rights coalition. The escalation of the conflict in Southeast Asia diverted funds and attention away from civil rights. Attorney General Ramsey Clark recalled that by 1968, the president's "concerns and time had shifted so far toward Vietnam that his involvement [in civil rights] was very, very limited."[8] Also, the war split the ranks of the civil rights movement. First SNCC and CORE, and then Martin Luther King's SCLC attacked the administration's Vietnam policy, leaving the NAACP and the Urban League lined up behind Johnson. *The New Pittsburgh Courier* voiced the disappointment of moderate blacks: "Our criticism of Dr. King is specifically because he has mixed the matter of civil rights with the complex and confusing issue of foreign policy. And in so doing, he has caused some damage to the former, where the issue is so clear against the fuzziness of the latter."[9]

The expansion of the war aggravated tensions already brewing within the civil rights movement. Since the 1964 Mississippi Freedom Summer and the subsequent failure to seat an insurgent, interracial delegation from Mississippi at the Democratic national convention, liberal whites had come under a barrage of criticism from militant blacks. The divisions within the movement over war and peace, violence and non-violence, integration and separatism were dramatized in the slogan of black power. Along with the eruption of riots in the urban ghettoes of the North, the controversy surrounding black power fostered the development of a white backlash. With the radicalization of elements of the civil rights alliance and the extension of racial issues such as equal housing to the North, the enthusiasm that had accompanied passage of the Voting Rights Act waned. By mid-1966 southern white lawmakers were riding the crest of the backlash to thwart enactment of a new civil rights package including a controversial fair housing proposal. Congressman Howard W. Smith of Virginia crowed: "I hope [this civil rights bill] is the straw that will break the camel's back and bring home to the people in states other than the South the serious infractions of constitutional principles contained in much of the Civil Rights legislation."[10]

It was too soon to write an epitaph for the civil rights struggle. Despite expectations to the contrary, an omnibus civil rights bill became law in 1968. The Johnson administration worked closely with the remnants of the civil rights coalition—the NAACP and the Urban League. The president's continued moral commitment was reinforced by practical considerations. Concerned about the growth of black militancy and the white backlash, the White House attempted to guide the civil rights forces in a moderate direction, thereby retaining the loyalty of the majority of blacks without further estranging whites. This strategy carried risks, because as one presidential aide remarked: "We've done a lot to try to bolster the . . . responsible Negro leadership, which then has the effect of making them seem like Uncle Toms, and the younger black element becomes alienated."[11]

The extension of the vote played a crucial part in White House efforts to steer the civil rights movement on a centrist course.[12] Speaking for the Johnson Administration, Attorney General Nicholas Katzenbach reminded civil rights activists after the passage of the Voting Rights Act that demonstrations in the streets were no longer "the only type of democratic expression possible for Negroes." He remarked that the time had arrived "when the civil rights movement can and should turn from protest to affirmation, from a force against discrimination to a major affirmative force in the life not only of the Negroes of the South but of all the South."[13] For the president, enfranchisement furthered the goal of racial harmony and greater legitimacy for the political system he so cherished. Echoing the words of his Civil War predecessor, Johnson praised the Voting Rights Act for making "it possible for this Government to endure, not half slave and half free, but united."[14] These comments also reflected the thinking of those blacks who viewed the interracial, liberal coalition working non-violently with the Johnson administration as the most appropriate method for achieving racial equality. Bayard Rustin, a chief spokesman for this strategy, observed approvingly: "What began as a protest movement is being challenged to translate itself into a political movement."[15]

This channelling of energies from civil rights protest into political organizing, which Rustin recommended, likewise had some appeal to critics of the Johnson administration. Martin Luther King, Jr., whose relations with the White House ranged from cool to frigid, did not believe "everything Negroes need will . . . like magic materialize from the use of the ballot. Yet as a lever of power," he insisted, "if it is given . . . attention and employed with the creativity we have proved through our protest activities we possess, it will help to achieve far-reaching changes during our lifetime."[16] Harsher adversaries than King of Johnson's Great Society reforms also saw great possibilities in the ballot. "The *act* of registering to vote," argued black power advocates Stokely Carmichael and Charles V. Hamilton, "marks the beginning of political modernization by broadening the base of participation," a prerequisite for the eradication of racism."[17] The definition of the black power slogan voiced by Carmichael and his comrades in the Student Non-Violent Coordinating Committee lacked precision, but it was initially understood to mean, as one black Mississippian asserted, that "black communities should have people running for public office so that they would control the communities."[18] Thus, although serious disagreements over tactics and goals split the civil rights movement after 1965, moderates and radicals alike viewed the ballot as one important weapon for black liberation.

The main task for the Johnson administration was to render the provisions of the Voting Rights Act into an operational program. The Justice Department, which drew the primary assignment under the statute, took as its goal the creation of a sizable black electorate capable of influencing the choice of southern officials who would thereby acquire a stake in perpetuating black enfranchisement. In pursuit of a new status quo, as political scientist Gary Orfield has pointed out, the federal bureaucracy needed "time to defy the normal political gravity of the American political system toward localism while Federal power is used to transform the local conditions."[19] Toward this end, the Justice Department sought to satisfy the expectations of civil rights groups without unduly alarming southern white political leaders.

The department delicately balanced its obligations to southern blacks with political and constitutional considerations.[20] Its Civil Rights Division (CRD), established in 1957, had attracted a talented staff of lawyers who spent much of the time before 1965 enforcing the voting rights laws already on the books. A top priority of Kennedy's civil rights program, suffrage litigation gave division attorneys expertise in combating disfranchisement. No one knew the terrain better than did John Doar, a field lawyer who became chief of the division in 1965. Through his exploits in the Deep South, Doar had won the confidence of civil rights activists. Tireless in his devotion to the cause of broadening the right to vote, he insisted on operating prudently. Two weeks after the Voting Rights Act went into effect, Assistant Attorney General Doar expressed the rationale for future enforcement of the law: ". . . our objective was to obtain full compliance with the '65 Act in all states . . . but to attempt to do this with a minimum amount of federal intrusion into the registration business of the states."[21] The new law had not altered the Justice Department's long-standing policy of holding to a minimum federal intervention in local affairs.[22] To be sure, the Justice Department did not intend to allow its belief in federal-state comity from interfering with a free black suffrage; however, its staff stressed "how important it is to convince our friends in these [covered] states that they should do the job themselves."[23] Thus, sensitive both to the aspirations of the suffragists and the legitimate concerns of state and local officials, agency staff attempted to administer the statute so "people would say that the Department of Justice . . . was fair . . . rational and objective."[24]

Moving cautiously, Attorney General Katzenbach and his successor, Ramsey Clark, used the discretionary power bestowed upon them by the 1965 act to designate selectively the counties to which federal examiners were dispatched. Over three and one-half years, the Justice Department singled out sixty-four counties of the 185 where less than 50 percent of eligible blacks were enrolled. Initially, the attorney general appointed examiners where there was "past evidence of discrimination," and subsequently he targeted counties were "obstacles of literacy, delay, and inadequate access" persisted despite departmental objections.[25] In no instance did the CRD conclude that examiners automatically were needed if a marked disproportion existed between the ratio of white and black registrants. The attorney general declined to send registrars to locales having "a substantial racial imbalance, where every other indication in the county is that the registrar is in full compliance with the Voting Rights Act and the imbalance is rapidly being eliminated."[26]

In negotiating with state officials to remedy abuses voluntarily and offering them a chance to avoid an influx of federal personnel, the Department of Justice utilized affirmative action principles. Overcoming the consequences of past discrimination did not stop with suspension of literacy tests, but it also required the adoption of procedures insuring "all persons eligible under the Act have an opportunity to become registered and to vote." Hence, the department informed southern registrars: "Compliance means not only that local officials may not practice distinctions based on race, but that they are under a duty to take affirmative steps to correct the effects of past discrimination."[27] Local enrollment boards were instructed to compensate disfranchised blacks by keeping their offices open for longer hours, on evenings and Saturdays, providing extra days of registration throughout the year, employing additional clerks to conduct registration in convenient places, and publicizing registration schedules. Failure to act accordingly resulted in the appointment of federal examiners.

The Justice Department adopted affirmative action techniques more as a standard by which to encourage and measure voluntary compliance than as a means of fostering maximum black registration and political participation. John Doar justified compelling local registrars to set up additional offices to enroll blacks who lived in outlying areas far from the county courthouse headquarters, but he insisted: "we are not in the mobile registrar business and we do not want to appear that we are."[28] The assistant attorney general contended that private civil rights organizations had to shoulder the burden of voter registration, otherwise, "when the Federal Government builds and takes over, when it leaves the whole thing caves in."[29] Doar's successor, Stephen Pollack, shared these attitudes and maintained that he "never considered we were given a responsibility by the law to work to promote pressures to go out and register," but rather "to make sure those who want to register can." Pollack adhered to his policy because "people with whom you deal must feel there is a certain neutrality."[30]

By the time Johnson stepped down from the Oval Office, his administration had made a notable but somewhat cautious advance in maximizing the potential for southern black suffrage. In 1964 less than one-third of voting-age blacks had registered in the seven states eventually covered under the Voting Rights Act; five years later nearly three out of five black adults had signed up. Furthermore, during this time, black elected officials in these states numbered over 265. While acknowledging this significant progress, civil rights advocates, including the most temperate, criticized the Johnson administration's performance. Suffragists faulted the Justice Department for not interpreting the affirmative action concept more aggressively. Roy Wilkins of the NAACP worried about the "danger of 'administrative repeal'" of the 1965 statute if it did not receive more vigorous enforcement, and along with Whitney Young of the Urban League complained: "there is no more money available in either organization for . . . [an] intensive voter and registration drive in the South."[31] Strapped for funds, civil rights workers looked to Washington for assistance in stimulating black applicants to enroll and came up empty handed. Having experienced this frustration, Vernon Jordan, director of the Voter Education Project sponsored by the Southern Regional Council, labeled the implementation of the Voting Rights Act "moderate" and "partial" and asked, "How much more might have been accomplished if the Act had been fully enforced?"[32] These friendly critics of the Johnson administration worried that the force of the suffrage statute would be deflected prematurely ushering in a repeat of post–Civil War history when "through a series of stratagems, fraud and violence, Negroes were effectively cut out of all the political life in the South."[33]

The Johnson administration could be held only partly responsible for the slowdown in black voter registration. The rate of enrollment had dropped after the most highly motivated blacks placed their names on the rolls in the first few months after the Voting Rights Act went into effect. Many of those who remained disfranchised suffered from the same socio-economic handicaps curtailing political participation by the poor and ill-educated throughout the nation. In addition, fear and intimidation continued to hamper prospective black registrants in the South. To break down the habit of non-voting, instilled through generations of white supremacy, required not only increased federal intervention, but also the resumption of local civil rights activities like those conducted in the early 1960s.[34] Yet, the concerted efforts necessary to remove the vestiges of racial deference never materialized in the wake of the disintegration of several of the most effective civil rights groups. SNCC and CORE, ruptured from within by ideological disputes, virtually abandoned the South, and the SCLC, unable to recover from the assassination of the charismatic Martin Luther King, barely survived. Thus, the demise of these private organizations heightened the dependence of civil rights advocates on the federal government for vigorous implementation of the Voting Rights Act.

The test of the durability of black enfranchisement and the Second Reconstruction came with the transfer of presidential regimes in 1969. In occupying the White House, Richard Nixon owed his nomination and election to elements hostile to a robust execution of civil rights laws. His southern strategy which undercut traditional Democratic electoral support in the South and reduced the third party appeal of George Wallace allied him with perennial foes of civil rights such as Senator Strom Thurmond. During the 1968 campaign the South Carolina Republican had exacted a pledge from Nixon to treat the South "like the rest of the Nation. If they are going to pass a Federal voting rights law to apply to the South," Thurmond coaxed, "let it apply to the rest of the Nation." After Harry Dent, Thurmond's legislative aide, joined the White House staff in 1969, he looked forward to throwing the voting rights "monkey . . . off the backs of the South."[35] Similarly, Democratic Senator Richard Russell of Georgia, noting "that there is now a different person in charge of the [voting rights program] in the new administration [was] hopeful that he will be somewhat more reasonable in his attitude toward our part of the country."[36]

Indeed, Nixon's Justice Department was prepared to be "more reasonable" than its predecessor. Concerning racial equality, neither Attorney General John Mitchell nor Jerris Leonard, assistant attorney general in charge of CRD, measured up favorably to their counterparts in the Johnson Administration. As Nixon's campaign manager, Mitchell had skillfully deployed the southern strategy, and one of his deputies, Kevin Phillips, subsequently promised southern Republicans that the administration would "change the approach" on the Voting Rights Act to please them.[37]

Nixon policymakers did not take long in making their intentions per-

127

fectly clear. Only six months in office, the administration had attempted to slow down the pace of school desegregation in Mississippi and weaken the potency of the Voting Rights Act which was up for renewal. The attorney general hoped to accomplish the latter by rewriting the prescription and reducing the dosage of the suffrage medicine. In mid-1969 Mitchell proposed to Congress recommendations for a *nationwide* ban on literacy tests until January 1, 1974, removal of restrictions on state residency requirements for presidential elections, and authority for the attorney general to send voting examiners and observers anywhere in the nation. In place of the vital triggering formula and pre-clearance sections of the 1965 statute, he proposed that the Justice Department depend upon litigation to challenge and put a freeze on the adoption of new suffrage restrictions. Mitchell argued "that voting rights is not a regional issue. It is a nationwide concern for every American which must be treated on a nationwide basis." Congressman William McCulloch, an Ohio Republican, replied for all suffragists that the provisions of the Mitchell bill "sweep broadly into those areas where the need is least and retreat from those areas where the need is greatest."[38]

Although the civil rights troops had few allies in the White House, they still possessed enough clout in Congress to defy the administration's wishes. Initially, the Justice Department's proposal squeaked to victory in the House, but the Senate passed a version extending the key sections of the Voting Rights Act for another five years. The lower chamber assented, and after a year long battle, a bipartisan coalition succeeded in retaining firm protection for southern black participation in the electoral process. On June 22, 1970, a month and one-half before the most effective provisions of the Voting Rights Act for all practical purposes would have expired, a reluctant Richard Nixon resuscitated them. The bill he signed into law was very different from what his administration had wanted, including a proviso enfranchising eighteen to twenty year olds, but he could boast that the final draft submitted for his signature no longer suffered from a regional stigma. The revised statute suspended literacy test requirements for voter registration throughout the country and contained a supplementary triggering mechanism which snared three counties in New York City and parts of Wyoming, California, and Arizona. Citing the progress made during the previous five years, the president justified an extension of the legislation as evidence "that the American system works." The figures showing an impressive rise in black voter registration, Nixon asserted, "stand as an answer to those who claim that there is no response except to the streets."[39]

President Nixon had followed a circuitous route in fulfilling his campaign pledge to "bring us together," but his final decision to okay the 1970 bill appealed to blacks without angering white southerners. *The New Pittsburgh Courier* congratulated the chief executive and exclaimed: "Nothing Mr. Nixon has done since his advent to the White House is as reassuring to black citizens. . . ."[40] Although Dixie legislators ultimately lost the fight to "get the South out from under this sectional application," they did appreciate the Nixon administration's efforts and the slight success in extending geographically the act's coverage. Moreover, with the base of the electorate broadened since 1965, some southern lawmakers had little incentive to block a renewal of the statute. For example, Senator Ernest Hollings of South Carolina remarked privately: "Don't ask me to go out and filibuster. I'm not going back to my state and explain a filibuster against black voters."[41] Thus, extension of the Voting Rights Act in 1970 indicated that defense of the suffrage had become part of the status quo, severely hampering those who sought to reverse this now entrenched policy.

Fresh from its rebuke over renewal of the Voting Rights Act in 1970, the Nixon Administration maneuvered to regain some of the ground it had lost. In early 1971 the Justice Department planned to promulgate guidelines for implementing section five, the preclearance provision which had virtually been neglected during the Johnson years. It was leaning toward drawing up a blueprint that shifted the burden of proof in the review of election laws from local jurisdictions to the federal government. This proposed realignment of responsibility came at a time when the covered areas were engaged in reapportionment, redistricting, and, in the case of Mississippi, reregistration, thereby placing black southerners at a disadvantage in retaining and possibly extending their political power.[42] The Supreme Court had liberally construed the language of section five to apply to a second generation of suffrage barriers—those designed with the purpose or having the effect of diluting the influence flowing from increased voter registration. In this category were such devices as gerrymandering, switching from single-member to multi-member and at large elections, and annexation of predominantly white territory adjacent to majority black areas or those locations likely to become so. In a pathbreaking ruling in 1969 Chief Justice Earl Warren declared that the Voting Rights Act "was aimed at the subtle as well as the obvious," and he interpreted the right to vote to mean "all action necessary to make a vote effective."[43] The high tribunal's expansive reading of section five opened the way for a shift in enforcement of the landmark statute. Hence, the act was conceived less as a means of handling registration problems and more as a tool for extending to blacks an opportunity to make their ballot count to the fullest extent. With the first phase of enfranchisement considered virtually finished, a cadre of career attorneys in the CRD had welcomed the judicial strengthening of section five so as to make it effective in blocking artful forms of discrimination; but top administration policymakers wished to rein in federal interference.[44]

The bipartisan coalition that had been so successful in 1970, once again mobilized its resources and forced the administration to retreat. Armed with favorable federal court rulings and threatening to hold congressional hearings, the suffragists persuaded the administration to write section five guidelines in a fashion they advocated. The voting rights consensus again remained in place. In contrast to such divisive racial conflicts as busing and preferential treatment in hiring, a sympathetic congressional aide observed, "everyone is for letting a guy have his full power to vote."[45]

Until Watergate forced the president's resignation, the Nixon Administration took its cue from the 1970–71 voting rights battles and breathed new life into section five. From 1965 through 1974, of 4,226 suffrage submissions, the attorney general interposed 166 objections, eighty-seven percent of which came after 1970. The CRD contained a dedicated and resourceful band of attorneys who had evolved as experts in the field and were able to recognize sophisticated practices designed to diminish the influence of the black electorate. Although the Nixon administration received few accolades from suffragists, its civil rights lawyers generally followed the administrative approach handed down by Johnson's attorneys. As William E. Leuchtenburg correctly notes, "much of the positive activity under the Nixon Administration came not because of the enterprise of Nixon and his immediate aides, but rather from momentum developed by the federal bureaucracy, a momentum which no president could easily halt."[46]

Some of the continuity stemmed from a holdover of CRD personnel, but much of it reflected a common attitude concerning the proper role of law enforcement within the federal system. Jerris Leonard, who was recruited from outside the Justice Department, declared that he could not "overlook an obvious enactment clearly unequivocally contrary to Federal law," but he candidly admitted to a Dixie congressman: "Since I have been in this Division . . . I have done my very best to lean over backwards to give the benefit of the doubt to southern communities with respect to those submissions pursuant to Section 5."[47] David Norman, who replaced Leonard as assistant attorney general in 1971 and who had served in the CRD since its creation in 1957, sounded very much like his Johnson administration predecessors upon testifying: "In my opinion, and as a matter of policy of this administration, it is far more advantageous to implement the law by voluntary agreements reached by the parties because once they make these agreements you have a much better chance locally of their being carried out." Norman insisted that the Nixon regime enforced the law "vigorously," but he also believed that the attorney general should neither appoint federal examiners on the basis of disproportionately low black enrollment nor dispense funds to encourage minorities to register.[48] These policies exasperated civil rights advocates just as they had during the Johnson years. John Lewis, a battle-scarred veteran of numerous civil rights confrontations and a director of the Voter Education Project, discerned the major difference to be one of style rather than of substance: "During the Johnson Administration, we did have some people we could talk with. During the Nixon-Ford years, we just haven't had anything. But for the most part, it's not a vast difference."[49]

From 1965 to 1975 the Justice Department under the direction of both Democratic and Republican chief executives stamped a cautious brand of affirmative action on black suffrage advancement. Although the Nixon administration attempted to institute procedures which would have retarded enfranchisement, basically it enforced the key provisions of the Voting Rights Act in much the same way as had the Johnson attorneys. Negotiation and voluntary compliance were favored because the Department of Justice, as a team of scholars has observed, "does not want to dramatically interfere in local policymaking processes and much prefers to work with local officials in the covered jurisdictions in a cooperative effort."[50] Such deference to the smooth functioning of the federal system encouraged conformity with the law. Southern white election officials grumbled about the special burdens section five placed upon them, but usually tendered the required submissions secure in the knowledge that Washington rejected only a small fraction of their offerings.

This process avoided much of the friction that existed between national and state governments during the years following the Civil War, but it necessitated ongoing vigilance on the part of the civil rights groups. Twice they succeeded in convincing congress and the president to renew the Voting Rights Act, and they exerted sufficient pressure to ensure that the Department of Justice did not stray far from its obligations under the statute. Civil rights litigants utilized the courts to identify subtle forms of racially biased voting practices, thereby enabling the CRD to attack most of the artful schemes invented to restrain the power of the black electorate. Local civil rights groups in the South also proved adept at monitoring and reporting to Washington changes in election requirements that might otherwise have gone undetected.[51]

To some extent, the vagaries of Republican enforcement of the Voting Rights Act can be traced to partisan considerations. The votes of newly enfranchised blacks figured little into the calculations of the GOP's southern strategists in the White House, for the bulk of blacks in the South cast their ballots for Democratic candidates. Nevertheless, the Nixon administration caved in easily on the issues of perpetuating and implementing the Voting Rights Act. Actually, congressional Republicans from the North never wrote off the black vote. They sided with northern Democrats to thwart Nixon from successfully practicing his southern strategy on the Voting Rights Act. After ten years, the statute had become a bipartisan fixture, in contrast to the identification of black suffrage with a single political party during the First Reconstruction.[52]

By 1975 a national consensus continued to sanction federal enforcement of black enfranchisement. President Gerald Ford, who on two occasions as Republican minority leader in the House, had unsuccessfully labored to weaken the act, signed into law a seven year extension of the landmark statute. More remarkably, counted in the overwhelming legislative triumph for the bill were the majority of southern white lawmakers. Their approval reflected the editorial comment of the Birmingham *News*: "Black votes . . . are . . . a significant factor—and a force which exerts pressure on elected officials regardless of race to represent blacks fairly."[53] Recent experience had shown white southerners that the federal government could extend black suffrage without disrupting their lives or forcing substantial federal intrusion into Dixie. They also had little reason to be dissatisfied with the growing number of blacks elected to office. Still very much in the minority, and holding office mainly in predominantly black areas, these public officials performed their duties without threatening white political or economic domination.[54]

For black southerners the payoffs from the ballot varied according to circumstances. Where they won the majority of elected offices and exercised power over governments with an adequate supply of economic resources, their chances of upgrading living conditions were greatest. Services such as garbage collection, street maintenance, sewage and sanitation, and police and fire protection have shown the most notable improvement. Too often blacks failed to capture control of positions in all but the poorest areas. In most places, obtaining the franchise has resulted only in marginal economic gains. In contrast, the political process has benefitted more from black ballots. Race baiting has virtually ceased, white candidates campaigned regularly for black votes, and the lines of communication between the races have opened. Overall, the main achievement cannot be quantified. Enfranchisement has made a striking contribution to black self-esteem. Lawrence Guyot, a black political organizer in Mississippi, accurately observed, "that the number of victories isn't as important as the fact that they symbolize a bit of black authority, a gradual return to respect for those accustomed to having their lives manipulated by white hands."[55]

The election of a larger number of southern blacks to public office possibly would have yielded increased dividends on the suffrage investment. Comprising approximately 20 percent of the voting age population of the seven covered southern states, blacks held only about 3 percent of the elected posts. The legislative and judicial victories in the 1960s and early 1970s did not eradicate all the barriers hampering the suffrage, and black registration and voter turnout lagged behind that of whites. Subtle forms of discrimination replaced blatantly biased practices and overt intimidation. In many areas of the South, the electoral process diluted the strength of black votes, and whites persisted in their discriminatory efforts. On the eve of a congressional decision concerning whether to extend the Voting Rights Act for a third time, in September 1981, the United State Commission on Civil Rights issued a report documenting "white resistance and hostility by some State and local officials to increased minority participation in virtually every aspect of the electoral process."[56] Furthermore, although the Second Reconstruction has legitimized the black franchise, like the first it has failed to solve the serious economic disabilities that reduce the liberating qualities of the franchise.

Furthermore, expansion of the suffrage helped defuse black militancy and channel protests into traditional political processes. Having fought hard and sacrificed much to obtain the right to vote, southern blacks did not regard it lightly as a weapon for liberation. In the late 1960s, a young voter registration worker with a "revolutionary perspective," insisted "that black people have to gain control of the existing structures where they can. Political activity is not a dead horse, and never will be in a place where we have so much potential as the South."[57] In utilizing electoral politics as a legitimate exercise toward obtaining freedom, southern blacks gradually moved away from reliance on the disruptive direct action techniques that were their only means for social change when they were excluded from the ballot. The shift away from civil rights confrontations to political participation had narrowed the choices considered suitable for racial advancement. Charles Evers of Mississippi, who successfully made the transition from civil rights agitator to politician, affirmed: "There's no cause to riot if you can vote. I don't care how much you riot, how much you pray—that white man fears only one thing: your power to replace one official with another by the ballot box."[58]

On balance, the Second Reconstruction has been displayed most vis-

133

ibly in black ballots. Southern black political power has not reached the level of strength achieved during Radical Republican rule, but it is based on a more solid foundation of acceptance. The principle of correcting the consequences of past discrimination has unleashed an enormous storm of controversy; however the type of affirmative action applied to black enfranchisement has generated much less bitter conflict. Nevertheless, this general agreement has been approaching its limits as the emphasis on enforcement of the Voting Rights Act shifted from the right to register to the opportunity to get elected. Serious questions remain as to how far Washington should or legally can go in restructuring the electoral process so that blacks may maximize their potential power in winning election to public office.[59] The lesson suggested by the First Reconstruction is that a premature withdrawal of federal supervision poses a serious danger to the achievement of racial equality. Neither the fears of white southerners nor the hopes of the suffragists have been realized. Vigilance thus remains necessary, and the political system still needs to be made more responsive to the aspirations of the recently enfranchised.

THE UNMAKING OF THE SECOND RECONSTRUCTION

In early 1960 four black college students in Greensboro, North Carolina, challenged Woolworth's to serve them equally alongside whites at its lunch counter. The demands for justice seemed relatively simple then. If treated without regard to color, blacks were expected to take advantage of the available opportunities to free themselves from the bondage that had lasted a century beyond the end of slavery. The matter proved to be more complex. Although blacks would obtain equality before the law, they discovered that the law did not automatically confer equality. The barriers of racism fell, but the remnants of Jim Crow in political, social, and economic institutions kept blacks from competing equally with whites for positions of power and prestige. In seeking remedies for this vexing problem, blacks called into question the meaning of traditional notions of equality and suggested answers that inflamed anew racial animosities in the country.

The movement galvanized by the lunch counter sit-ins was a special kind of revolution. Southern blacks, segregated by law and custom and subject to unequal treatment, merely sought to gain the rights and privileges exercised by other Americans. They aspired not to overturn the system—unless it was the one that maintained apartheid—but, rather, to enter it as fully as possible. Desiring integration into American life, they pressed the nation to live up to its own democratic ideals of equal opportunity and justice for all. A charter member of the Student Non-Violent Coordinating Committee (SNCC), the interracial organization created in 1960 following the sit-ins, summed up the attitude of activists at the time. "The ache of every man to touch his potential is the throb that beats out the truth of the American Declaration of Independence and the Constitution," Marion Barry declared. "We seek a community," the future mayor of

Washington, D.C., asserted, "in which man can realize the full meaning of self which demands open relationship with others."[1]

No one expressed a greater commitment to interracial fellowship than did Martin Luther King, Jr. Having risen to prominence as a leader of the Montgomery bus boycott in 1955, the Reverend King moved on to his native Atlanta to guide the Southern Christian Leadership Conference (SCLC), a group dedicated to "achieving full integration of the Negro in all aspects of American life." From a variety of Christian and secular sources, including Jesus and Karl Marx, Walter Rauschenbusch and Reinhold Niebuhr, Friedrich Hegel and Mahatma Gandhi, Frederick Douglass and A. Philip Randolph, Dr. King constructed a set of strategic aims from which he rarely wavered. At the center of his objectives was the establishment of "the 'beloved community' in America where brotherhood is a reality." In working toward this end, SCLC had as its "ultimate goal genuine intergroup and interpersonal *living—integration*."[2]

Martin Luther King's value to the civil rights movement came not so much as a philosopher but as a translator and communicator of ideas. He spoke to the intensely religious mass of southern blacks in language they could easily understand. His sermons took the message that blacks would find redemption for their suffering in the next world, the traditional preaching of black ministers, and transformed its meaning to the here and now. "One day the South will know that when these disinherited children of God sat down at lunch counters," he wrote, "they were in reality standing up for the best in the American dream and the most sacred values in our Judeo-Christian heritage."[3] At the same time, King's religious homilies contained soothing words for whites. Their emphasis on nonviolence, redemption, and reconciliation offered whites an opportunity to cleanse themselves of the sickness of racism and to live up to their democratic faith. This creed, which placed the main burden of suffering and loving one's enemies on blacks, posed little threat to white sensibilities. The historian August Meier attributed much of the influence of Dr. King to his "combination of militancy with conservatism and caution, of righteousness with respectability."[4]

In striving for inclusion into the mainstream of American life, blacks did not intend to relinquish their racial identity. W.E.B. Du Bois provided the classic analysis of the black yearning for assimilation and preservation. "One feels his twoness," Du Bois wrote in 1903,

an American, a Negro, two souls, two thoughts, two unreconciled strivings; two warring ideals in one dark body, whose dogged strength alone keeps it from being torn assunder. . . . The history of the American Negro is the history of this strife,—

this longing to attain self-conscious manhood, to merge his double self into a better and truer self. . . . He simply wishes to make it possible for a man to be both a Negro and American, without being cursed and spit upon by his fellows, without having the doors of Opportunity closed roughly in his face.[5]

The civil rights movement highlighted each element of this dualism. In directly confronting racist institutions, blacks not only demanded full equality as American citizens, but in the process they also heightened their sense of worth individually and collectively. Franklin McCain, one of the four students who originally sat in at the Greensboro Woolworth, remarked: "I probably felt better that day than I've felt in my life. I felt as though I had gained my manhood . . . and not only gained it, but . . . developed quite a lot of respect for it."[6]

The tactics employed by the protesters enhanced the feeling that they could determine their destiny. Customarily the objects of white-controlled decision-making processes, African Americans became active participants in shaping events that directly affected them. As lawyers and lobbyists working mainly through the National Association for the Advancement of Colored People (NAACP), they had already won some noteworthy judicial and legislative battles against discrimination in education, transportation, and the suffrage. By 1960, however, the South had manufactured ways to contain these victories, and the majority of blacks still endured segregation and disfranchisement. The adoption of nonviolent direct-action campaigns enabled southern blacks to regain the offensive. Such protest activities built grassroots support among blacks, thereby maximizing the human and financial resources available to keep the challenges going. In addition, on the local level they circumvented the existing channels of communication between white elites and traditional black leaders that had brought changes in race relations gradually, paternalistically, and within a segregated context. Demonstrations forced white officials to deal with black demands that they previously had not heard and would rather have avoided considering.[7]

Initially, the practitioners of nonviolent civil disobedience aimed their efforts at convincing white southerners to abandon their Jim Crow ways. Their optimism proved unfounded, and whites frequently reacted with more brutality than brotherhood. Anne Moody, a black student at Tougaloo College in Jackson, Mississippi, described the perils that awaited demonstrators attempting to integrate Woolworth's lunch counter there. "We kept our eyes straight forward and did not look at the crowd except for occasional glances to see what was going on," she recalled. "We bowed our heads, and all hell broke loose. A man rushed forward . . . and slapped my face. Then another man who worked in the store threw me against an adjoining counter. . . . The mob started smearing us with ketchup, mustard, sugar, pies, and everything on the counter. . . . About ninety policemen were standing outside the store: they had been watching the whole thing through the window, but had not come in to stop the mob or do anything." She came away with this painful lesson: "After the sit-in, all I could think of was how sick Mississippi whites were."[8]

In areas of the region where civil rights activists did not encounter such vicious displays of prejudice, they found more sophisticated means of preserving white hegemony. In contrast with Jackson, civic leaders in places like Greensboro succeeded in moving protests off the streets and resolving disputes around a negotiating table. "Somewhere a Southern community must find a way to deal with civilities as well as civil rights," the Greensboro *Daily News* editorialized. Toward this end white officials hoped to avoid the violence that had plagued other cities, maintain the progressive image of their town as they pursued an economic and cultural renaissance, and preserve control over the pace of racial change. Led by influential businessmen in cooperation with moderate black leaders, these local communities dismantled some of the machinery of segregation, but only as much as necessary to keep the peace and head off a new round of disruptive protests. Such was the case in Tampa, Florida, one of the first cities in the South to create a biracial committee to settle disputes amicably. Reflecting the attitude of civic leaders, its principal newspaper asked: "What new industry would decide to go into a city which seethes with murderous racial conflict?" Nevertheless, not until passage of the 1964 Civil Rights Act were black Tampans permitted equal access to most of the "Cigar City's" hotels, restaurants, bowling alleys, and hospitals.[9]

This "middle way" did more to ensure peace and harmony than to promote justice. In raising their voices for moderation, white elites intended to continue exercising responsibility for local governance and not allow decisions to be dictated by civil rights militants or their extremist opponents. Although these enlightened urban communities discarded some of their blatantly racist practices, progress came unevenly. Except for municipal facilities and large chain department stores, public accommodations remained segregated or off limits completely to black customers. Nowhere more than in education were the narrow bounds of voluntary cooperation exposed. Despite the historic *Brown* decision in 1954, most school districts in the South operated a dual system of education. States with progressive reputations, such as North Carolina, led the way in devising techniques that followed the letter of the law while violating its spirit. Attempting to present the illusion of desegregation, they adopted pupil placement regulations that permitted black students to apply for admission to previously white schools and allowed local school boards the option of turning them down for reasons other than race. In practice these so-called "freedom of choice" plans left the overwhelming majority of blacks to attend segregated schools as they had in the past.

Reliance on voluntary cooperation and goodwill had not brought blacks very far toward achieving their goals during the early sixties. If their situation had improved in a handful of progressive cities, it remained as bleak as ever in the rest of the South. Experience had proven that thoroughgoing social changes should not come without outside intervention. Since World War II the federal government had moved slowly and somewhat unsurely to the side of civil rights. Presidential orders by Harry Truman and Dwight Eisenhower had desegregated the armed forces and facilities on federal military installations in the South; Congress had enacted two civil rights laws dealing with disfranchisement; and the Supreme Court had toppled the doctrine of "separate but equal" in public education. However, by 1960 the national government had yet to use its powers forcefully enough to demolish racial discrimination in the South. Civil rights advocates, hoping to involve the federal government more fully in their cause, turned their attention increasingly to Washington.

The election of John F. Kennedy was auspicious. During his presidential campaign, Kennedy had staked out some advanced positions on civil rights. He threw his support behind the black protesters whose activities were shaking up the South. "It is in the American tradition to stand up for one's rights," he declared, "even if the new way is to sit down." Hurling criticism at Eisenhower for not providing moral leadership against racial bias, Kennedy remarked that "moral persuasion by the President can be more effective than force in ending discrimination against Negroes."[10] Not content to rely on rhetoric alone, he drew up a specific agenda to have ready if elected to the White House. It included the desegregation of federally-assisted housing "by the stroke of a presidential pen" and the drafting of legislative proposals to attack discrimination in education and the suffrage. Late in the campaign, the Democratic nominee dramatically portrayed his sympathy with the civil rights struggle. After Martin Luther King was arrested for a minor traffic offense following his participation in a demonstration in Atlanta, Kennedy telephoned the minister's wife to console her, and his aides helped secure her husband's release.[11] With this gesture Kennedy cemented the allegiance of the black electorate, which became a major factor in his slender margin of victory.

Once in office President Kennedy did not immediately translate his lofty campaign pledges into action. The chief executive backed away from incorporating into his legislative program the civil rights measures that had been drawn up at his initiative, and a bill to limit abuses in the administration of literacy tests for voting died on the congressional floor for lack of White House support. For nearly two years, the president failed to issue the promised executive degree against housing discrimination, prompting black skeptics to send him pens lest he had forgotten. Finally, in late November 1962, Kennedy issued an order, albeit a very limited one. Needless to say, his early record brought disappointment to black leaders who had been led to expect much more from the new president. Martin Luther King, previously the recipient of Kennedy's favor, nevertheless concluded that the White House "waged an essentially cautious and defensive struggle for civil rights."[12]

King's assessment hit the mark. Although Kennedy continued to express sympathy for the goals of the civil rights movement, he chose mainly to react to events rather than provide the kind of forceful executive leadership he had pledged. His priorities were elsewhere. He devoted much of his energy to matters of foreign policy, playing his role on the world stage with a daring he did not exhibit at home. In domestic affairs Kennedy felt hamstrung by the conservative coalition of southern Democrats and northern Republicans whose strategic grip on the legislative machinery had long frustrated reform. Furthermore, in waging the Cold War against the Soviet Union, Kennedy needed the support of these powerful lawmakers, and thus, he sought to avoid offending their racial sensibilities. When the administration did move in a liberal direction on the legislative front, it preferred to fight for expansion of existing social welfare measures—such as minimum wages and social security—that would benefit blacks economically without directly raising the controversial racial issue.

However much Kennedy would have liked to postpone dealing with troublesome civil rights problems, he could not set the timetable for action. The struggle for black equality had gained a momentum all its own. Although five major organizations—NAACP, the Urban League, SCLC, SNCC, and the Congress of Racial Equality (CORE)—directed legislative and legal strategies, the impetus behind the demonstrations came at the local level. The Greensboro sit-in had given birth to hundreds of others, and these indigenous movements had devised wade-ins, kneel-ins, drive-ins, and other imaginative techniques to confront segregation directly. Building on this ferment from below, the NAACP, CORE, SLC, and SNCC mobilized their forces to pressure the national government and to prick the consciences of whites throughout the nation to guarantee black emancipation.

The Kennedy Administration responded warily to the racial conflicts sparked by heightened black protests. Although believing in integration and worried that vicious displays of racism tarnished America's international image, the president nonetheless counselled moderation in handling civil rights disputes. Preferring reason to coercion and order to agitation, Kennedy hoped to persuade southern officials to act responsibly and to convince civil rights activists to refrain from participating in disruptive confrontations. "Tell them to call it off. Stop them," President Kennedy responded upon first hearing about a proposed interracial freedom bus ride through the South in 1961, and he remarked privately, " I don't think we would ever come to the point of sending troops."[13] The chief executive eventually did dispatch federal marshals to protect the freedom riders when they came under attack in Alabama, and in 1962 he mobilized the armed forces to quell an uprising at the University of Mississippi following the matriculation of its first black student, James Meredith. However, he did so only as a last resort. In such instances Kennedy hardly showed a greater willingness to throw the full weight of federal power behind the civil rights cause than had Eisenhower in Little Rock, and when he did react it was more to restore law and order than to recognize the justice of black demands.

As an alternative to disruptive civil disobedience campaigns, the Kennedy administration offered the conventional enterprise of voter registration drives where the laws protecting the right to vote were clearly on the activists' side. Guaranteed by the Fifteenth Amendment, the suffrage was considered the cornerstone of the nation's democratic foundation. Furthermore, the franchise would foster racial progress in the orderly fashion that Kennedy found acceptable. The ballot also had great appeal for black strategists who believed that it might provide the key to unlock the door to liberation. "Give us the ballot," Martin Luther King declared in 1957, "and we will no longer have to worry the Federal government about our basic rights."[14] In 1962, to promote enfranchisement, the Kennedy regime encouraged the formation of the Voter Education Project, thereby bringing together white liberal philanthropic foundations and civil rights organizations to conduct suffrage drives in the South. At the same time, the Justice Department stepped up litigation in the courts against discriminatory registration practices.

The voting rights campaigns met with neither much success nor tranquility. Less dramatic than direct action protests, door-to-door canvassing of prospective registrants nevertheless aroused the same kind of white hostility that accompanied sit-ins and freedom rides. A virtual reign of terror existed in much of the rural southern black belt, where whites firebombed civil rights headquarters, cracked the skulls of suffragists, and jailed them for minor infractions of the law. The prospects in the judiciary were only slightly better. Although the Kennedy Justice Department brought suits against biased electoral practices, unsympathetic federal judges in the South threw them out of court or delayed processing them as long as possible. The civil rights forces felt this hurt even more because President Kennedy had appointed several of the most obstructionist judges. Although the efforts of the executive branch did increase the number of black names on the registration lists, the majority of blacks were still unable to vote.

By 1963 civil rights leaders had concluded that federal intervention would come primarily in response to crises. "Civil rights workers knew that as long as there was no disorder," the historian Catherine Barnes has noted, "the administration would not move vigorously."[15] Consequently, in May 1963 Martin Luther King led demonstrations in Birmingham to provoke a confrontation that would increase the pressure for federal action. His strategy worked. "Bull" Connor's police force broke up nonviolent protest marches with excessive force, and the use of attack dogs, water hoses, clubs, and cattle prods created an ugly scene. Racial tensions reached a breaking point when the home of Martin Luther King's brother and the headquarters of SCLC became the targets of firebombers, and in retaliation rampaging mobs of blacks temporarily abandoned nonviolence and assaulted white people and property. In June the situation was much the same in Jackson, where NAACP Field Secretary Medgar Evers was ambushed and killed by a sniper, precipitating a near riot by black mourners. Attempts by the Kennedy administration to mediate these conflicts produced an uneasy peace but did not redress black grievances.

For two and one-half years, President Kennedy had tried to maintain a delicate balance between his personal commitment to the objectives of the civil rights movement and his political obligations to powerful southern leaders within his party. With racial turbulence rapidly rising, the president finally asked Congress to enact a comprehensive civil rights measure that would go a long way toward toppling discriminatory racial barriers and moving unruly demonstrations off the streets. Identifying the issue as essentially a moral one "as old as the Scriptures and . . . as clear as the American Constitution," he repeated the question that blacks had been raising for years as to "whether all Americans are to be afforded equal rights and equal opportunities, [and] whether we are going to treat our fellow

Americans as we want to be treated."[16] Kennedy's answer was a bill to desegregate public accommodations, authorize the Justice Department to file school-desegregation litigation, allow the national government to withhold funds from federally-assisted programs that operated discriminatorily, and create a Community Relations Service to mediate racial disputes. Although these proposals were more extensive than ever before, Kennedy hesitated to request the establishment of an agency to challenge job bias for fear of further angering southern lawmakers. Nevertheless, liberal legislators succeeded in adding a provision for a permanent Equal Employment Opportunity Commission.[17]

Proponents of the bill waged an intensive lobbying effort on its behalf. The chief executive summoned to the White House business, civic, and religious leaders to rally their support. While the president maneuvered quietly in the Oval Office, civil rights activists dramatically mobilized their forces at a massive demonstration in the nation's capital. Fearing that such a mammoth gathering would "create an atmosphere of intimidation" for uncommitted congressmen, Kennedy had urged black leaders not to hold it. Once assured by the architects of the March on Washington of their peaceful intentions and willingness to forego acts of civil disobedience, Kennedy swung his approval behind the idea. The subsequent rally at the Lincoln Memorial on 28 August attracted nearly a quarter of a million people and much favorable publicity. In a dignified manner, it spotlighted the interracial vision of brotherhood that had characterized the early year of the struggle for civil rights. Eloquently reciting his dream of freedom and justice for all, Martin Luther King, in the words of the historian Harvard Sitkoff, "transformed an amiable effort at lobbying Congress into a scintillating historic event."[18] Nevertheless, neither the rhetoric of the popular president nor that of the charismatic civil rights leader was sufficient to secure passage of the bill. On 22 November the measure was still tied up in the House of Representatives.

The assassination of John F. Kennedy did not kill hope for enactment of the bill, and the battle for the proposal went on without him. Despite his limitations as a presidential advocate of civil rights, Kennedy had inspired youthful idealism in pursuit of racial justice. Even his critics acknowledge that there was greater progress in civil rights because Kennedy rather than Richard Nixon had been elected to the White House in 1960. Yet the civil rights movement had preceded Kennedy and would persist beyond his death. Indeed, the president could never quite catch up to the advancing civil rights forces and the demands they made, although he was getting closer when he died.[19]

Kennedy's successor took up where he had left off. A southerner from Texas, Lyndon Johnson had broken away from the segregationist positions taken by fellow politicians from the region. By the time he reached the White House, he displayed a moral fervor for civil rights that exceeded Kennedy's. Immediately upon taking office, President Johnson urged Congress to write the slain chief executive's epitaph by enacting the pending civil rights measure. A nation's grief alone, however, could not break the legislative logjam. After some eight months of painstaking efforts by the administration and its liberal allies on Capitol Hill, a bipartisan coalition finally overcame southern opposition to put through the law that President Johnson signed on 2 July 1964.

The successful outcome represented a stunning triumph for the principle of equal opportunity and the liberal faith in a color-blind society. Emphasizing integration, the 1964 law sought to foster the movement of African Americans into the mainstream of economic and civic life by tearing down the most pernicious obstacles standing in their path. The lengthy debate on the bill reinforced the viewpoint that once the stigma of race was removed black citizens would be judged by virtue of their talents and abilities. Having maintained white supremacy throughout their history, southern opponents of the measure wanted assurance that racial classifications would not be imposed to benefit blacks. In response, the bill's supporters stressed that all individuals must be treated equally before the law regardless of race. Whether relating to school desegregation or job discrimination, the prevailing attitude could be described as favoring racial neutrality. Expressing this position Hubert Humphrey, the Senate floor manager of the legislation, acknowledged that the proponents were not seeking to achieve "racial balance" through "preferential treatment" or quotas.[20] Despite this sentiment the question had yet to be settled whether the federal government had to ignore racial considerations in fashioning remedies to remove the effects of past bias in education and employment.

Although victorious, the civil rights movement increasingly suffered from dissension within its ranks. During the summer of 1964 civil rights workers who gathered in Mississippi to promote voter registration wound up feuding among themselves and with the federal government. Racial and political concerns accounted for this friction that produced a growing strain between white and black fieldworkers. Many of the seven hundred college student volunteers who participated in the Freedom Summer came from white middle-class backgrounds and were better educated than their black compatriots from the South. Members of SNCC, the militant group in the forefront of the campaign, complained about white paternalism and questioned the commitment of college students who would return to their comfortable northern campuses after the summer. "Look at these fly-by-night freedom fighters bossing everybody around," a SNCC worker declared. Making matters worse, sexual relations between black males and white women aroused the ire of black females who considered their rivals "neurotic whites who sought to ease their guilt by permitting blacks to exploit them sexually and financially." Even the murder of three civil rights workers, two of whom were white, did not hold in check the burgeoning racial resentments.[21]

The rising anti-white feelings of black activists also extended toward their liberal allies in Washington. The Kennedy and Johnson administrations raised great expectations that remained unfulfilled, and the gap between promise and reality added to the physical and psychological pain inflicted upon civil rights workers in the South. The issue of federal protection of voter registration canvassers reflected this problem. The Kennedy Justice Department had encouraged civil rights organizations to undertake suffrage drives and had led them to believe that the government would provide protection. Justice Department officials did try to carry out their obligation but within narrow bounds. They preferred the cumbersome process of litigation and the use of Federal Bureau of Investigation agents as neutral observers rather than the deployment of federal marshals and the assignment of the FBI to an active role in combating racial harassment. Although the federal government retained the authority to intervene in local affairs when constitutional guarantees were threatened, it hesitated to do so for fear of creating a national police force. In contrast, civil rights groups argued that the Kennedy-Johnson regimes refused to act more forcefully for political reasons and accused them of holding back because they did not desire to alienate influential southern officials. Civil rights activists insisted that, having encouraged them in the first place, the federal government had a moral duty to ensure their safety. As the killings, beatings, and intimidation mounted, so did black disillusionment with white liberals.[22]

The abortive attempt of the Mississippi Freedom Democratic Party (MFDP) to gain recognition at the Democratic National Convention in 1964 accentuated the difficulties. Emerging from grassroots organizational efforts during Freedom Summer, the MFDP challenged the exclusionary racist practices of the regular state Democratic party and sought to replace it as the representative of the national party. Although the predominantly black Freedom Democrats made a strong moral case at the convention, and many thought a valid legal argument as well, President Johnson orchestrated a compromise that left them bitter. They were denied status as the official delegation from Mississippi, but two members of the group, one white and one black, were selected to sit as honored guests of the convention. Branding this a "back of the bus" sell-out, the MFDP was particularly unhappy with what it saw as white paternalism in naming the delegates to represent it.[23] Angry with a solution that elevated political over moral and even legal considerations, many of the black activists returned to the South with ever-increasing suspicions about alliances with white liberals.

These hostilities did not keep the interracial coalition from achieving one of its greatest triumphs. Behind the controversies over federal protection and seating the MFDP loomed the suffrage issue. By 1965 the imposition of literacy tests and poll taxes, reinforced by the application of physical and economic intimidation, had resulted in only 35 percent of eligible blacks signing up to vote. The Mississippi Freedom Summer had amply demonstrated the tenacity of southern officials in reinforcing these obstacles. Following enactment of the 1964 Civil Rights Law, President Johnson turned his attention to the suffrage problem and instructed the Justice Department to prepare legislative proposals for the next congressional session. The chief executive believed strongly in the right to vote, and he thought that once southern blacks were permitted to cast their ballots "many other breakthroughs would follow and they would follow as a consequence of the black man's own legitimate power as an American, not as a gift from the white man."[24]

Civil rights leaders also shared this premise. For several years SNCC fieldworkers had been operating a voter registration drive in Dallas County, Alabama, an area with a black population majority but virtually no black voters. Headquartered in the county seat of Selma, the civil rights group had met with much resistance and scant success. The recalcitrance of local officials, especially Sheriff Jim Clark, made Selma a prime target for provoking a confrontation to publicize the plight of disfranchised blacks. With this in mind, in January 1965 Martin Luther King spearheaded a series of demonstrations in Dallas County to focus attention on the system of oppression that treated blacks as second-class citizens. These protest activities yielded the expected, if regrettable, results. Peaceful marchers were met with arrest, demonstrators were beaten by law enforcement agents, and a sympathetic white minister from the North was bludgeoned to death on a city street. The climax came with a march scheduled to proceed from Selma to Montgomery. Hardly had the civil rights crusaders ventured beyond the outskirts of the city when a club-wielding sheriff's posse and mounted state troopers charged into their ranks and brutally beat them back. This bloody performance did not go unnoticed as television cameras vividly recorded the event for viewers across the nation.

There was no more concerned spectator than the president. Greatly disturbed by the behavior of Alabama officials and pressed for a speedy response by civil rights leaders, Johnson fully marshalled the resources at his disposal to safeguard the demonstrators who still intended to march to Montgomery. Furthermore, in a nationally televised address to a joint session of Congress, the chief executive passionately urged lawmakers to demolish the barriers to black enfranchisement. The African American "has called upon us to make good the promise of America," Johnson reminded his audience. "And who among us can say that we would have made the same progress were it not for his persistent bravery and faith in American democracy."[25]

Following these stirring remarks, the journey from Selma to Montgomery finally concluded, and Congress swiftly prescribed a powerful remedy to treat voting ills in the South. The bill President Johnson signed into law on 6 August 1965, suspended for five years the operation of literacy tests in states and counties where less than 50 percent of the adult population was registered or had voted in the 1964 presidential election. This formula covered the jurisdictions with the most severe suffrage abuses—Alabama, Georgia, Louisiana, Mississippi, South Carolina, Virginia, and parts of North Carolina.[26] The law also empowered the Attorney General of the United States to authorize federal examiners to enroll qualified applicants in these areas. In the future local officials had to submit all changes in electoral procedures to the Justice Department or the federal district court in Washington, D.C., before they could go into effect. Until a covered state proved that it had not sanctioned racial discrimination in voting for five years, the act would remain in force. In addition Congress instructed the Justice Department to initiate a suit challenging the constitutionality of the poll tax, and within a year the financial levy had been outlawed by the courts.

The Voting Rights Act not only provided a strong measure for expanding the suffrage, but it also offered important lessons for attacking racial discrimination in general. The law dealt with the current condition of black enfranchisement by recognizing its roots in the past. Moreover, it aimed to correct patterns of racial bias against persecuted groups rather than rectify specific instances of discrimination suffered by individuals. Accordingly, a statistical formula was devised that automatically presumed the existence of racial bigotry and authorized the government to overcome the consequences of previously harmful practices. It did so through the concept of "freezing." The statute acknowledged that enrollment procedures historically had favored whites and ordered that prospective black registrants merely have to meet the same permissive standards operating to the advantage of whites in the past. In effect this meant the suspension of literacy tests, and because most whites were already on the rolls, the statute provided the majority of black adults with a chance to join them.[27] Within four years approximately 60 percent of eligible blacks had registered to vote in the covered states, and the newly enfranchised helped elect over 265 black public officials, an impressive gain from only a few years earlier when successful black candidates were extremely rare.[28]

In another important way, the Johnson administration had articulated the necessity of taking positive steps to destroy the remnants of racial injustice. In an eloquent commencement address at Howard University in June 1965, the president had asserted: "We seek not just freedom but opportunity—not just legal equality but human equality—not just equality as a right and theory, but equality as a fact and as a result." He recognized that changes in the law alone did not place blacks at the same starting line with whites in the race for material success. Equality of opportunity was restricted for African Americans as long as they competed with whites who benefited from the economic, political, and social advantages accumulated through centuries of racial supremacy. The chief executive realized the magnitude of the problem, which he likened to "converting a crippled person into a four minute miler."[29]

Having steered two monumental civil rights bills into law, President Johnson sought to explore new directions toward achieving full equality. For this purpose he convened a White House Conference on Civil Rights that met in Washington in early June 1966. This gathering of government officials, businessmen, liberal academics, and civic, religious, and black leaders spent two days discussing programs designed to implement the rights blacks had only so recently obtained.[30]

By 1966 the national consensus that the president had previously counted on was quickly eroding. Outwardly, the conference of some 2500 delegates came off without a hitch. The representatives produced a hundred–page document, *To Fulfill These Rights*, calling for legislation to ban racial discrimination in housing and the administration of criminal justice, and they also suggested increased federal spending to improve the quality of housing and education. Despite agreement on these proposals, the meeting revealed deep fissures within the civil rights coalition. The tensions that had been building since the 1964 Freedom Summer rose to the surface. Some of the participants attacked the Johnson administration for failing to do more to protect civil rights workers in the South; others questioned the traditional emphasis on integration and expressed their belief in the need to control the levers of economic and political power within black communities; and a few condemned the president's escalation of the war in Vietnam as a racist and imperialist policy. In fact the divisive nature of these issues had become evident even before the meeting had begun, when SNCC decided to boycott the conference. Several months earlier the organization had issued a statement condemning the United States for waging a "murderous policy of aggression in Vietnam."[31] Within a year Martin Luther King, the most popular black leader in the country, loudly denounced Johnson's widening of the Southeast Asian hostilities.

Meanwhile, the warring tensions within black souls and the civil rights movement erupted dramatically during James Meredith's march through Mississippi. In June 1966 the first black graduate of the University of Mississippi undertook a 265–mile pilgrimage to challenge fear and encourage black voter registration. Shortly after starting out, Meredith was ambushed and wounded by a white sniper. While he recovered the march continued under the leadership of SCLC, SNCC, and CORE. Along the route Stokely Carmichael, the newly elected chairman of SNCC and a veteran of civil rights protest in the South, seized the opportunity to call for black solidarity and active resistance to oppression. He wanted the trek through Mississippi to "deemphasize white participation" and "highlight the need for independent black political units." The SNCC leader urged black Mississippians to secure power for themselves and not to "beg the white man for anything [they] deserve." In one electrifying moment, Carmichael issued a clarion call for a new departure in the civil rights movement. "The only way we gonna stop them white men from whippin' us," he shouted to a rally, "is to take over. We been saying freedom for six years and we ain't got nothin'. What we gonna start saying is Black Power."[32]

This black power doctrine was forged out of personal experience, the model of the African liberation struggle, and the idea of cultural pluralism. Borrowing from each, Carmichael advocated black separatism over assimilation, retaliatory violence over passive suffering, and group power over individual rights. SNCC fieldworkers had come to scorn nonviolence and integration as psychologically debilitating in light of their savage treatment by southern racists and the paternalism they found in white liberals. In seeking freedom from mental and physical oppression, Carmichael urged black communities, like African colonies, to throw off the yoke of white imperialism and achieve "self-determination." Although speaking in revolutionary terms, including calling for the overthrow of capitalism, Carmichael also presented his ideas within a traditional conceptual framework. "For each new ethnic group," he asserted in classic textbook fashion, "the route to social and political integration into America's pluralistic society has been through organization of their own institutions with which to represent their communal needs within the larger society."[33] However disparate the various parts of this ideological amalgam may have been, they added up to a powerful longing of an oppressed minority for acceptance as both blacks and Americans.

Not all blacks responded favorably to Carmichael's message. Martin Luther King believed the slogan of "black power" was an unfortunate choice of words, sounding too inflammatory and suggesting "wrong connotations." He accepted Carmichael's contention that other ethnic groups had advanced by mobilizing their economic and political resources and that blacks "must work to build racial pride and refute the notion that black is evil and ugly." But, King asserted, the black power phrase gave "the impression that we are talking about black domination rather than black equality."[34] Unlike the leaders of SNCC and CORE, Dr. King refused to believe that promotion of a healthy black consciousness depended on excluding white liberals from the struggle for racial justice.

As King feared the positive aspects of black power were lost on most whites. This was especially true in the wake of the bloody urban riots sweeping the North during the mid-1960s. The reasons for the uprisings were complex, but in general black northerners sought to gain what the American Dream had promised but the ghettos lacked—decent housing, jobs, and personal security. Justifiably proud of the accomplishments of the civil rights movement in the South, blacks in the North were letting government officials know that all the legal rights they had long possessed still had not brought them economic and political power. Although Carmichael and his associates were not responsible for the spontaneous outburst of violence consuming cities throughout the country, their bellicose rhetoric fanned the flames of racial discord. After a riot broke out in Cleveland, Carmichael declared: "When you talk about black power, you talk of building a movement that will smash everything western civilization has created."[35]

Such menacing words together with the ghetto violence frightened whites at a time when the national consensus in favor of black advancement was already beginning to crack. Even before the riots became a prominent feature of the urban landscape, signs of a white backlash had emerged. Convinced that the major aims of the civil rights struggle had been achieved by mid-decade, many whites failed to appreciate the sources of enduring black frustration, favored a halt to further demonstrations, and considered as ungrateful those who continued to agitate.[36] No one played on the anxieties of whites better than did George Wallace. Having whipped up the antagonism of southerners against desegregation, the Alabama governor transported his racist messages to the North where they received a favorable reception from whites who feared that black progress came at their expense. Wallace exploited class as well as racial tensions. He appealed to blue collar workers and denounced "left-wing theoreticians, briefcase totin' bureaucrats, ivory tower guideline writers and pointy headed professors" for thumbing their noses at them.[37] The racial uprisings of the late sixties added fuel to Wallace's political ambitions. Running in the Democratic presidential primaries in 1964, Wallace surprised his opponents by showing well in three northern states before withdrawing from contention; four years later, campaigning on an independent party ticket, he captured 13.5 percent of the popular vote for president in the November general election.

During that period the more intently the Johnson administration championed the goals of the civil rights movement, even those deemed most temperate, the further it angered whites unhappy with the accelerated pace of the black liberation struggle. In 1966 a well-informed presidential aide noted "that it would have been hard to pass the emancipation proclamation in the atmosphere prevailing this summer."[38] Rather than retreating, Johnson charted a moderate position between denouncing the perpetrators of violence and expressing concern for the continuing plight of blacks and offering legislative proposals to relieve it. Despite the sting of the white backlash, for two years the administration fought to obtain omnibus civil rights legislation directed at housing discrimination and bias in the criminal justice system, issues affecting both the North and the South.

Operating in an explosive political environment, lawmakers had violence very much on their minds. Civil rights supporters condemned the ghetto uprisings, but they tried to turn them to their advantage. By passing the proposed civil rights legislation, they hoped to show blacks that they could resolve their legitimate grievances in a peaceful and orderly way. A leading House Republican, William McCulloch of Ohio, suggested that the omnibus civil rights measure would succeed "in moving the struggle for equal rights and equal opportunities from the streets into the polling places and into the courts." The blade of violence cut both ways as a debating weapon. Opponents of the bill scoffed at the contention that the passage of additional legislation would bring a cease fire on racial battlegrounds. They pointed out that the ghetto rebellions had grown in number following enactment of strong civil rights laws in 1964 and 1965. Horace Kornegay, a North Carolina Democrat, spoke for many of his colleagues in noting that the "more Civil Rights bills the congress passes, the worse race relations become in the country."[39]

In 1968 a renewed round of violence helped break the legislative log-jam. The White House had been working very closely with civil rights groups, especially the NAACP, to forge a bipartisan coalition behind the pending bill. Their hard work paid off as Senator Everett Dirksen of Illinois, the Republican Minority Leader, swung his support behind a compromise measure endorsed by the administration. The last legislative hurdle had not yet been cleared when, in early April, Martin Luther King was assassi-nated, and a wave of urban disorders swept the nation. The precise impact of King's murder and the ensuing riots is difficult to calculate, but these events provided the final push for passage of the bill. As a sign of the times, not only did the lawmakers approve the civil rights package, but they also adopted tough antiriot measures.[40]

This hard-earned victory crowned Johnson's extraordinary accomplish-ments in obtaining civil rights legislation. Three times in five years the president and his allies had cracked barriers to racial equality that had existed for a century. The 1968 triumph was particularly rewarding be-cause it came against considerable odds at a time when public support for racial reform had ebbed and the civil rights movement was torn by faction-alism. Although the chief executive's last years in the White House were marred by strife, Johnson's presidency constituted the high point of the Second Reconstruction. The Great Society had extended civil and political equality to southern blacks, helping them to shatter Jim Crow.

As Johnson retired from office, this phase of the civil rights struggle came to an end. The laws placed on the books, as magnificent as they were, focused on equal rights and scarcely touched the vital issues of the distri-bution of economic and political power. Indeed, many white liberals be-lieved that the federal government's obligation ceased once the legal obstacles of racial discrimination had been destroyed. With these impedi-ments removed, it remained for blacks to take advantage of the opportuni-ties that awaited them and strive for success according to their individual abilities. However, the chance to buy a cup of coffee at a lunch counter or obtain housing in the suburbs meant little to black residents of inner city ghettos or rural plantations who could not afford a decent standard of liv-ing. In the long run, the right to vote might ease the burdens of poverty, but in the meantime blacks still had difficulty electing officials of their own race who best represented their interests.

In moving to the next stage of the civil rights struggle, blacks raised a fresh storm of controversy. In demanding affirmative action to improve their condition, African Americans upset traditional standards of equality. Since race had been used for centuries to victimize them, blacks now argued that they would not be able to overcome the pervasive effects of past discrimination without the legal and political systems taking race into account, but this time in their favor. A rigid racial caste system had kept most blacks far behind whites in gaining a fair share of status, wealth, and power, and they would never be able to close the distance without special treatment. In public education this would require busing to ensure integration and quality schooling; in employment and admission to universities and professional schools it meant the establishment of quotas and the active recruitment of qualified minorities to fill them; and in political participation it involved the elimination of procedures that diluted the black vote. Wherever applied, affirmative action was defended by blacks as a reasonable means of compensating them for prior wrongs and the most effective way of obtaining significant results within their lifetimes. Otherwise, they believed, additional generations of African Americans would be sacrificed to the ravages of discrimination.

The Johnson administration shaped these ideas into policies. In his Howard University address in 1965, the president declared that affirmative steps must be taken to close the economic gap between blacks and whites in order to achieve "equality as a fact." Later that year he backed up his words by issuing an executive order requiring federal contractors actively to recruit and hire qualified minority job seekers. Subsequently, in 1968 the Department of Labor instructed major contractors to adopt a "written affirmative action compliance program" that included "the development of specific goals and time-tables for the prompt achievement of full and equal employment opportunity."[41] Thus, in developing affirmative action criteria, the Johnson regime began defining equal opportunity, not according to some legal abstraction, but by the actual results that were produced.

This approach generated a great deal of opposition. Many whites who had once joined blacks in challenging segregation concluded that affirmative action would lead to preferential treatment, the establishment of flexible goals would turn into the imposition of rigid quotas, and the attempt to promote proportional representation would undermine the egalitarian concept of a color-blind society. They argued that racially sensitive solutions practiced "discrimination in reverse" against whites and offended the meritocratic principle that each individual be judged by his or her qualifications. They attacked the notion that blacks were entitled to special consideration because of their membership in a racial group and contended that charges of discrimination be examined on an individual basis. Proponents of this point of view, termed "neoconservatives," condemned affirmative action for resulting in "an increasing consciousness of the significance of group membership, an increasing divisiveness on the basis of race, color, and national origin, and a spreading resentment among disfavored groups against the favored groups."[42]

The affirmative action issue polarized relations between blacks and white ethnic minorities. Jews who had risen high into the ranks of the academic, legal, and medical professions felt threatened by the assault on meritocracy. After all, they remembered that quotas had long been set to keep them out of graduate and professional schools, and they feared that in the guise of benign goals a new version of the quota system would again restrict their access to positions of prestige. Members of other immigrant groups had also experienced the pain of discrimination in struggling for upward mobility. Comfortably entrenched in civil service jobs and gaining rewards from union seniority, Irish, Italian, and Polish Americans were troubled by policies that appeared to take away some of their hard-earned advantages, redistribute them among blacks, and diminish the prospects of continued success for their children.

Ironically, the black emphasis on racial pride during the latter half of the 1960s stimulated a heightened consciousness among the members of these other ethnic groups, leading to both an increased awareness of their own heritage and a greater sense of their own grievances. As with black nationalism, the new ethnic chauvinism had positive and negative aspects. "Experiencing an appreciation for ethnic values, family loyalty, and neighborhood solidarity," historian Richard Polenberg has written, the ethnic reawakening "suggested that only when people were comfortable with their own backgrounds would they be socially and psychologically whole."[43] On the darker side, however, growing ethnic identification reinforced the political animosities of the white backlash and fueled anti-black sentiments by promoting the virtues of "turf and territoriality." Pulled apart by ethnic and racial factionalism, the descendants of black slaves and white immigrants nonetheless shared a common concern about assimilating into American culture without losing their cultural uniqueness.

Despite these deep divisions, the federal government plunged ahead with affirmative action. The main force behind implementing this policy came not from the president, as it had during the Johnson administration, but from the Supreme Court and Congress. In fact, the election of Richard Nixon in 1968 brought to the White House a chief executive who had conducted a campaign that appealed mainly to the racial frustrations of disgruntled whites. Though he attempted to redirect racial policies in a manner that pleased the "silent majority" of whites in the North and South, he found his options narrowed by a judiciary and national legislature still support-ive of black equality.

The chief executive faced his stiffest challenge in the field of education. He backed the "freedom of choice" plans that the southern states had de-signed to comply with the technicalities of desegregation without produc-ing much in the way of integrated schools. Such had been the case in New Kent County, Virginia, where freedom of choice left 85 percent of black pupils in segregated facilities. In 1968 fourteen years after Brown, the Su-preme Court ruled that it would no longer tolerate delay. The justices charged school boards operating dual educational systems with "the affirmative duty to take whatever steps might be necessary to convert to a unitary system in which racial discrimination would be eliminated root and branch."[44] The court sanctioned the use of statistics to assess the discriminatory impact of educational assignments and ordered that race be taken into account to promote integration. One legal commentator concluded: "The Constitu-tion was, indeed, becoming color conscious as well as color blind."[45]

Nixon did not wait long to make his intentions perfectly clear. After a fierce bureaucratic battle between White House practitioners of a "south-ern strategy" and civil rights enforcement officials in the Department of Health, Education and Welfare, the administration decided to ask the judi-ciary to postpone a desegregation plan for Mississippi that was scheduled to go into effect in the fall of 1969. For the first time since Brown, the federal government and civil rights advocates squared off against each other on opposite sides of school desegregation litigation. When the Supreme Court heard the case, it delivered a sharp rebuke against the White House–sponsored procrastination. Emphasizing the need for less deliberation and more speed in completing the integration process, the high tribunal under-scored "the obligation of every school district . . . to terminate dual school systems, at once and to operate now and hereafter only unitary schools."[46]

The explosive issue of busing also came under judicial scrutiny. The use of buses to transport students to school had been a commonplace fea-ture of American education. Students from scattered rural areas rode buses to commute to centrally-located schools as did handicapped and excep-tional children who participated in special education programs. In the South black and white pupils had customarily traveled on buses to attend segre-gated schools, frequently passing a nearby school that was closed to them because of their skin color. Few whites had registered complaints over these traditional forms of busing; they did raise a howl, however, against busing for the purpose of achieving school desegregation. Given the judicial man-date to integrate immediately, local school boards in the South had little choice but to introduce busing and reassign pupils on the basis of race. The Charlotte-Mecklenburg County Board of Education in North Carolina had devised an innovative plan for its sprawling 550 square-mile district containing over one hundred schools and eighty-four thousand students. On 20 April 1971, the Supreme Court gave its qualified endorsement to busing as a remedy in such school systems that had previously practiced segregation by law. The court refrained from approving "racial balance or mixing" as a constitutional right, but it upheld "the use of mathematical ratios . . . [as] a starting point . . . rather than inflexible requirement."[47]

Most Americans accepted busing for traditional purposes and most favored the principle of desegregation, but the overwhelming majority disapproved of busing to promote integration. Even blacks were split over the issue. They expressed reservations about extensive busing mainly because they usually bore most of the travel burden; however, they tended to support busing to a far greater extent than did whites. A 1972 survey revealed that when asked whether they favored busing if it was *essential* for desegregation, 71 percent of blacks replied in the affirmative compared to 43 percent of whites.[48] Both groups agreed that quality education was their main concern, but they differed over how to achieve it. Blacks took pride in their schools for the contributions they had made in developing leaders and preserving cultural traditions. Nevertheless, they recognized that, within the context of a racist society, separate education had never been equal nor was it likely to become so in the near future. In contrast most whites felt that busing would harm their children's education by placing them in inferior ghetto schools, and they argued that the compulsory transportation of pupils was self-defeating because it led to "white flight" from the cities to the suburbs where there were few blacks available for integration.[49]

The Nixon administration championed the sentiment of the white majority and tried to roll back the buses. "I do not believe that busing to achieve racial balance is in the interests of better education," the president declared following the Charolotte-Mecklenburg County ruling, and he urged Congress to call a halt to further busing.[50] In 1972 Nixon proposed legislation that barred courts from ordering the transfer of elementary school pupils beyond the closest or next closest schools to their neighborhood. The bill passed the House but failed in the Senate, a pattern that was repeated throughout the Nixon years. What Nixon could not accomplish through legislation, however, he achieved through executive action. Under his regime federal agencies responsible for school desegregation eschewed the busing remedy and concentrated instead on reducing instances of racial discrimination within schools and equalizing funding between existing segregated schools. In effect the administration operated on the premise that separate schools did not necessarily have to provide unequal educational opportunities.[51]

Civil rights leaders strongly disagreed. They interpreted Nixon's actions as part of a drive to halt racial equality. Clarence Mitchell, the chief Washington lobbyist of the NAACP, called the foes of busing "the same people who are against equal treatment in all aspects of American life." In a similar vein, Vernon Jordan, Executive Director of the National Urban League, accused the Nixon administration of grossly distorting the facts in portraying massive busing as a means of achieving "racial balance." Rather, Jordan argued, "busing, as ordered by the courts and other government bodies, takes place for only one reason—to desegregate segregated schools."[52] Although unable to stop the executive branch from discarding busing remedies, civil rights groups kept sufficient pressure on Congress to defeat proposed constitutional amendments for ending court-ordered busing.

The opponents of busing were more successful in the North than in the South. In many of the industrialized areas of the Northeast and Midwest the post–World War II exodus of whites from the cities to the surrounding suburbs had left most blacks behind in the urban ghettos to attend increasingly segregated schools. In the mid-1970s the city of Detroit, viewing the problem from a metropolitan perspective, came up with a workable plan to integrate its schools by transporting students across municipal boundary lines into adjacent school districts. In this case the Supreme Court, although previously approving busing within the confines of northern cities that had been guilty of officially practicing racial discrimination, greatly restricted its possible extension to surrounding suburban jurisdictions. Only if it could be proven that segregated educational patterns had resulted from intentional government action in both city and suburb, the justices ruled in *Milliken v. Bradley*, was metropolitan-wide busing across school districts permissible.[53] In practice this decision ensured that the North and the South switched positions as the most segregated regions of the country. In 1976, 47.1 percent of black students attended schools in the South with a white majority compared to 42.5 percent of blacks who did so in the North.[54] Although the schools in Dixie had to balance their student populations by race, most of those in the North were allowed to maintain a dual system of education. And in those urban areas such as Boston where the demography of the inner city permitted busing as a legal remedy for segregation, the attempt to transport students produced a violent response from whites who saw their neighborhoods under siege.[55]

Like school busing the expansion of the black suffrage also raised questions about race-conscious policies. After 1965 the Voting Rights Act had evolved from a measure primarily concerned with dismantling the formal barriers to voter registration to one that challenged dilution of black ballots. In this category were such devices as gerrymandering, multi-member districts and at-large elections, and annexation of predominantly white territory adjacent to majority black areas. In a landmark opinion in 1969, the Supreme Court declared that the Voting Rights Act "was aimed at the subtle as well as the obvious" and broadly interpreted the right to vote to mean "all action necessary to make a vote effective."[56]

Civil rights advocates were delighted with this line of reasoning. They argued that Congress had anticipated that the southern states would devise new techniques to restrict black voting. Though the legislators could not have foreseen the exact shape these subterfuges would take, they had written the preclearance requirement (Section 5) into the Voting Rights Law to challenge biased practices as they arose. Furthermore, a few years of exercising the ballot had not erased the results of a century of disfranchisement, and civil rights supporters pointed out that continued federal vigilance was necessary. Howard Glickstein, the Staff Director of the United States Commission on Civil Rights, explained in 1971: "The Voting Rights Act was designed to provide a protective umbrella under which a viable black political tradition could begin to grow . . . [and should] be kept constantly in place until black political participation in the South develops strong roots."[57] Consequently, the 1965 law was conceived less as a means of combating registration problems and more as a tool for extending to blacks an opportunity to make their ballots count more fully. Increasingly, suffragists evaluated the success of the law by the number of blacks who won election and calculated the remaining distance to racial equality by the gap between the percentage of black officeholders and the proportion of blacks in the population.

This expansive view of enfranchisement did not go unchallenged. Justice John Marshall Harlan issued a vigorous dissent from the Supreme Court bench. He accused the majority of his colleagues of requiring a "revolutionary innovation in American government." Maintaining that in adopting the Voting Rights Act lawmakers had intended only to curtail "those techniques that prevented Negroes from voting at all," Harlan asserted that "Congress did not attempt to restructure state government" by altering the form of elections.[58] This opinion was shared by the White House. Attempting to carry out his southern strategy, President Nixon asked Congress to soften the potent enforcement features of the 1965 law and extend application of the act throughout the country. In doing so the Republican administration would be removing the regional stigma from the South and weakening implementation of the statute where it was most needed. Other critics cared less about the burdens the South had to shoulder for its past misdeeds and more about the consequences to the principle of equality of individual opportunity resulting from the new emphasis on getting blacks elected. They asked what had happened to the original civil rights goal of the color-blind society and wondered whether "group power, not individual worth is made the measure of political equality." Neoconservatives warned that the judicial redefinition of the Voting Rights Act "envisions blacks as a permanent group apart [and] . . . assumes that there is no escape from race."[59]

Congress was not prepared to agree that the day of racial neutrality had arrived and that blacks no longer were worthy of special protection to compete equally with whites for political office. On three occasions, in 1970, 1975, and 1982, lawmakers renewed the vital provisions of the Voting Rights Law and even expanded its guarantees to language minorities. Although the legislators refused to make proportional representation the constitutional benchmark for judging black political equality, they made it easier for blacks to prove that the rules of the electoral game had been stacked against them.[60] The consensus behind continued enfranchisement has been stronger than that on any other civil rights issue. Bipartisan and national, the legislative coalition in its favor attracted a majority of Democrats and Republicans and, more surprisingly, southerners as well as northerners. In contrast to the divisive racial conflicts generated by busing, a congressional observer remarked, "Everyone is for letting a guy have his full right to vote."[61]

Granting language minorities the special guarantees of the Voting Rights Act reflected the belief that non-English-speaking groups were also being deprived of equal treatment under the law. In 1975 the legislators decided that English-language requirements had disfranchised foreign-speaking citizens, and they provided relief for them, as they had for blacks, in the conduct of elections. A year earlier the Supreme Court had reached a similar verdict concerning education. In *Lau v. Nichols*, the high tribunal ruled that school districts had to take "affirmative steps" to provide instruction to non-English-speaking students in their native tongue. This opinion challenged the traditional American assumption that immigrants should learn the language of their adopted homeland, and instead it upheld bilingualism. The selection of these minority groups for compensatory action did little to soothe the antagonistic feelings of other ethnic-Americans whose ancestors had struggled to learn English several generations before without any preferential treatment.[62]

Much more controversial than the suffrage, programs that provided for special treatment of blacks in employment and higher education aroused as much white indignation as did busing. Perhaps more than any other form of affirmative action, racial goals and quotas in hiring and university admissions directly pitted the interests of blacks against those of whites. In an economy that had not yet reached full employment, the stiff competition for better-paying jobs meant that programs seeking to advance blacks would come at the expense of whites. The same was true for entry into professional schools were spaces were limited and qualified applicants were plentiful. The recessionary spiral of the 1970s and the coming of age of the postwar baby boom generation exacerbated the struggle for the limited positions available. While the economy had flourished in the 1960s, many whites could afford to take a generous attitude toward black civil rights goals, but with the harder times of the next decade, they preached the virtues of a neo-Social Darwinism. Having gained their legal right to equality, blacks were told to forget their previous history of enslavement and discrimination, prove themselves meritorious, and make it on their own without government favor or else the rewards of progress would come to an end.[63]

Even the staunchest defenders of this position nonetheless admitted that employers should make a positive effort to hire qualified minorities. A 1972 survey showed that 82 percent of whites opposed giving blacks a job promotion over an equally qualified white, but it also revealed that 77 percent favored the establishment of job training programs for blacks. Most respondents distinguished between "legitimate" compensatory action programs that helped disadvantaged minority groups compete on an equal basis and "unfair" preferential treatment that enhanced the opportunities of one group over another. The *New Republic* refused to endorse the kind of affirmative action that "guaranteed advancement for the members of a particular group" but supported policies ensuring "talented individuals, from every social group, have a chance to shine."[64]

Initially, the federal government had recognized the need for affirmative action and compensatory treatment of disadvantaged minority job applicants and workers. Although the civil rights movement had brought steady economic gains for blacks, by the late 1960s the income of African American families was 60 percent that of whites, a figure that had grown slightly from approximately 53 percent in 1954. Prohibitions against discriminatory hiring did not guarantee jobs for blacks who, because of past bias, were less successful than whites in meeting employment criteria. In many instances scores of standardized tests were used to measure job qualifications, and this worked to the detriment of blacks, many of whom were victims of an inferior education. The Johnson administration had sought to relieve the persistent imbalance in the employment market by ordering federal contractors to establish affirmative hiring programs for minorities.

This approach continued during the Nixon administration, which applied it to unions as well as employers. The "Philadelphia Plan" required construction workers' unions employed on federal projects to sign up a fixed percentage of black apprentices who would subsequently be admitted to the union. Moreover, in 1971 the Supreme Court delivered a strong endorsement of affirmative action. In *Griggs v. Duke Power Company*, the justices ruled that "neutral" employment tests were not valid if they maintained the effects of prior discriminatory employment practices. They placed the onus on employers to prove that an employment exam that operated to exclude blacks was related to job performance. Thus, the *Griggs* doctrine focused on the enduring results of previous discrimination and presumed them to exist when blacks fell short of holding jobs in rough proportion to their percentage of the general population.[65]

By the mid-1970s, the Supreme Court began to retreat from this position. President Nixon had been able to turn the court in a more conservative direction. The four judges he appointed, led by Chief Justice Warren Burger, helped sound the retreat from the liberal positions taken by the Warren Court during the previous decades. In the *Griggs* case, the judiciary had based its opinion on a positive interpretation of the 1964 Civil Rights Act. When the justices examined the Equal Protection Clause of the Constitution in dealing with similar controversies over standardized employment tests, however, they found the requirements for proving discrimination to be more stringent. The high tribunal judged as constitutionally valid the administration of a federal civil service exam for Washington, D.C., police officers that blacks failed at a rate four times greater than did whites. The justices ruled that such examination standards could be nullified only if they had been adopted for a "discriminatory purpose." This opinion marked a setback for affirmative action programs because it was much harder for minorities to demonstrate a biased intent behind a law than to show its actual discriminatory effects.[66]

The Court struck another blow to affirmative action in the *Bakke* case. At issue was the special program of admission to the University of California Medical School at Davis that set aside sixteen of a hundred places for entering minority students. In 1973 Alan Bakke, a thirty-four year-old aerospace engineer with a burning desire to become a physician, unsuccessfully competed for one of the eighty-four openings available to white applicants. Bakke had been turned down by other institutions because he was considered to be over the traditional age for a beginning medical student. He was not alone in feeling the pain of rejection as 42,155 applicants competed for 15,774 seats in medical schools throughout the nation. Apparently Bakke was willing to accept the customary reasons for failing to obtain one of the scarce spots—receiving lower scores on competitive entrance tests or the matter of his age. Bakke, a Vietnam veteran, did not seem to mind the preferential consideration that many institutions accorded former G.I.s. He would not leave unchallenged, however, a system that on the basis of race prevented him from competing for a fixed number of positions.[67]

In suing the Board of Regents of the University of California, Bakke sought only his admission into medical school; nevertheless, the litigation afforded the judiciary a chance to examine what limits the constitutional guarantee of equal protection of the law placed on race-conscious remedies. Those who expected the high bench to settle the affirmative action issue conclusively were sorely disappointed. Rather than presenting a united front, the badly-divided justices could agree on little else than that Bakke should receive his coveted admission. Justice Lewis Powell cast his vote with the majority of five to declare the Davis program unconstitutional because it reserved a fixed number of places based on a racial classification. Having spoken against the use of quotas, Powell then joined a different majority of five to approve a university's flexibility in considering a prospective applicant's race in order to assemble a diverse student body. Although Justice Powell provided a legal opening through which affirmative action programs could continue to exist, he attacked the basic assumption upon which they functioned. The Justice decried the notion of "benign" quotas that did not stigmatize the white majority and expressed his belief that restrictive racial categories would force "innocent persons . . . to bear the burdens of redressing grievances not of their making." Pointing out the racial and ethnic tensions that were sharpened when members of one group were preferred over another, he refused to hold individual whites to blame for the racial injustices of the past.[68]

Consequently, it remained for a minority of four to defend in full force the principle of compensatory treatment. Justice Thurgood Marshall, who had represented the black plaintiffs in the *Brown* case, spoke most fervently about the historical justification for singling out blacks for special consideration. He challenged those who suggested that African Americans were just another ethnic group that had faced prejudice and must overcome it in the same fashion of hard work and individual effort. "The experience of Negroes in America has been different in kind, not just in degree, from that of other ethnic groups," Marshall declared. "The dreams of America as the great melting pot has not been realized for the Negro; because of his skin color he never even made it into the pot." His colleague, Justice Harry Blackmun, summed up the practical lesson that centuries of racial discrimination had taught: "In order to get beyond racism, we must first take account of race."[69]

As the United States moved into the final quarter of the twentieth century it appeared very little inclined to heed this message. The Supreme Court that two decades before had paved the way toward establishing racial equality hesitated to go much further. In a 1979 decision, it upheld an affirmative action plan that the United Steelworkers of America and Kaiser Aluminum and Chemical Corporation adopted voluntarily to provide blacks with 50 percent of the available spaces in a craft training project regardless of whether they had less seniority than whites. In a 1984 case, however, the high tribunal declared that the Memphis Fire Department could not suspend its seniority rules by laying off whites in order to protect recently-hired blacks with fewer years of employment. Benjamin L. Hooks, Executive Secretary of the NAACP, charged that the opinion ignored the historical pattern of blacks being the "last hired and first fired" and was blind to "the reality that such discriminatory practices have had and continue to have upon excluded groups."[70]

Nor did civil rights activists find imaginative leadership in occupants of the White House after Kennedy and Johnson. Nixon and his successor, Gerald Ford, responded with either outspoken opposition to or grudging acceptance of civil rights measures. More sympathetic than his Republican predecessors, Jimmy Carter, a Georgia Democrat, was nonetheless limited in his accomplishments. Though pleased with the transformation that the civil rights movement had brought to his native South, Carter was either unwilling or unable to direct his presidential resources to carry on those changes. Carter's Justice Department had taken the affirmative action side in the *Bakke* case, but in a manner so hesitant that civil rights groups came away confused and dismayed.[71] Still, Carter tried to boost the black cause when he could, whereas Ronald Reagan deliberately attempted to contain it. A spokesman for the forces of conservatism that equated affirmative action with reverse discrimination, Reagan called a virtual moratorium on implementing race-sensitive programs. His administration considered racial classifications "morally wrong" and intolerable in any form, and re-

163

laxed minority hiring guidelines for federal contractors, argued in the courts against employment quotas, and restructured the United States Commission on Civil Rights to reflect these views.[72] Although civil rights supporters fought against this retrenchment, they did so from a weakened position. The struggles of the late 1960s and early 1970s had cost them support from many of their former allies who felt threatened by the new definition of equality.

To a large degree, the controversy over whether or not blacks merited special treatment revolved around differing perceptions of minority progress. Most whites apparently believed that the main goals of the civil rights movement had been secured, and they resisted new measures that went beyond granting equal rights under the law to all citizens. A 1977 Harris survey revealed that only 33 percent of whites thought that racial discrimination persisted and 55 percent agreed that blacks were pressing "too fast" for equality.[73] Most blacks, however, felt that their struggle to reap a fair share of the rewards of first-class citizenship was yet to be completed. Without programs to remove the vestiges of racism, they saw little hope for entering the mainstream of American life. An exchange between Justice Marshall and Alan Bakke's lawyer during the oral argument before the Supreme Court underscored the affirmative action conflict. "You are arguing about keeping somebody out and the other side is arguing about getting somebody in?" Marshall questioned the attorney, who succinctly replied: "That's right."[74]

The intense feelings that arose from the increasing racial polarization obscured a realistic assessment of the black condition in America. The statistical indicators displayed a complicated picture that makes easy generalizations risky. Whether measuring socioeconomic or political factors, the data suggested the tremendous gains achieved by blacks since 1960. A much greater percentage of black students than ever before were completing high school, and there was little difference between the percentage of high school graduates of each race who went on to college. In addition a majority of African Americans had moved into the electorate from disfranchisement, thousands of successful black candidates were holding office throughout the country, and in 1984 a black challenger made a serious bid for the Democratic Party's presidential nomination. Despite these important strides forward, blacks had not caught up to whites either educationally or politically. Their rate of graduation from college was lower than that of whites, and most blacks in 1980 attended two-year rather than four-year institutions of higher learning. Furthermore, on the average, the voter registration and turn-out figures for blacks lagged behind those for whites and the percent-age of black elected officials trailed considerably behind the proportion of blacks in the total population.[75]

Civil rights advocates had assumed that equal educational and political opportunities would relieve the economic plight of blacks. Despite notable improvements, their hopes have not been fully realized, as shown in Table 1. By 1980 a significant proportion of black families had joined the middle class and one-third of black workers were employed in white-collar jobs as professionals, managers, and clerical workers. However, the bulk of the black population remained far less upwardly mobile. In 1980 black families lived on incomes averaging 58 percent of those earned by whites, only a slight improvement from two decades earlier. Although many blacks had advanced into professional ranks, blacks still were underrepresented in better paying white-collar jobs and overrepresented in lower income positions. More ominously, during the period between 1960 and 1980, the black unemployment rate consistently was double that of whites and had reached depression-era levels by the late 1970s. Approximately 30 percent of all blacks lived below the poverty line compared with 10 percent of whites. Economists attributed this dire condition to the leap in female-headed households among blacks from nearly 24 percent in 1965 to 40 percent in 1980, and they pointed out that approximately two-thirds of impoverished black families had females at their head.[76]

To some observers black educational and political attainments along with the enlargement of the black middle class meant that race had ceased to be a significant factor in explaining continuing inequalities. They explained the gaps that remained between blacks and whites as stemming more from the working of the economic marketplace than from racial discrimination. With the decline of Jim Crow barriers, the proponents of this viewpoint asserted, blacks were held back from advancing for the same reasons that blocked other low income groups from getting ahead: unsteady economic growth and structural changes in the modern industrial state. Accordingly, technology and automation were supposed to have had an impact on black and white job seekers and workers alike, and it was generally argued that affirmative action could do little to remedy their problems.[77] In fact by introducing the element of race such programs split potential allies who might otherwise have joined together in fighting shared economic battles.

This analysis was certainly correct in highlighting the class dimension of inequality in the United States, but it unfortunately minimized the en-

Table I
Black Economic Status, 1964-1980

	1964-1965	1975-1976	1980
Black family income versus white family income	56.0[a]	62.0[a]	58.0[b]
Black unemployment	9.6[c]	13.9[c]	13.1[d]
Black families before poverty line	—	27.1[e]	28.9[e]
Female-headed black household	23.7[f]	37.0[f]	40.0[f]
Female-headed black households before poverty line	—	50.1[e]	49.4[e]
Black families earning under $5000	19.5[g]	17.7[h]	20.7[h]
Black families earning $35,000-49,999	3.8[g]	6.1[h]	7.7[h]

a. Dorothy K. Newman, *Protest, Politics, and Prosperity: Black Americans and White Institutions, 1940–1975* (New York, 1978), 269.

b. Harrell R. Rodgers, Jr., "Fair Employment Laws for Minorities: An Evaluation of Federal Implementation," in Charles S. Bullock III and Charles M. Lamb, eds., *Implementation of Civil Rights Policy* (Monterey, Calif., 1984), 105.

c. Newman, *Protest, Politics, and Prosperity,* 64.

d. *Economic Report of the President* (Washington, D.C., 1984), 259. The poverty line was devised by the federal government in 1969.

e. *Economic Report of the President,* 262.

f. Harvard Sitkoff, *The Struggle for Black Equality, 1954–1980* (New York, 1981), 235.

g. United States Department of Commerce, Bureau of the Census, *Statistical Abstract of the United States, 1984* (Washington, D.C., 1983), 459. The earliest figures are for 1967.

h. *Statistical Abstract of the United States, 1984,* 459.

during sources of racial discrimination. One cannot easily separate race from class in an economic system reflecting long-standing discrimination against African Americans. Individual acts of racism have diminished substantially, but biases remain embedded in societal institutions. Such concepts as meritocracy might have worked to ensure equality of opportunity in a color-blind nation, but in practice they operated to reinforce the injustices inherited from the past. If blacks are to continue to make progress toward real equality, white Americans must recognize the ongoing significance of race and take affirmative measures to reverse the effects of discrimination. To the extent that this is tried, the country will continue to move toward closing the gap between its democratic promise and reality.

THE FINAL YEARS OF THE SECOND RECONSTRUCTION

In the seventeen years since this essay first appeared, the country has continued to struggle over the meaning of racial equality. The constitutional, political, and ideological issues that tore it apart in 1986 still divide the nation and remain unsettled. Led by the Reagan administration, its judicial appointees, and conservative strategists, including blacks as well as whites, the permissible uses of affirmative action have narrowed considerably. The courts have generally rejected the concept of institutional racism and have overturned broad remedies to help African Americans overcome the legacy of past discrimination. Instead the judiciary has ruled individuals must prove that they themselves have been subject to racial bias and the government has sought specific and limited relief for the problem. As applied to employment, school desegregation, and electoral politics, this doctrine threatens the further expansion of the African American quest for racial equality in fact as well as in promise.

President Ronald Reagan led the assault against affirmative action, which he considered reverse discrimination. The chief executive opposed the construction of race-conscious programs because he charged that they sought to end one form of discrimination against blacks by replacing it with another against white males. Upon entering the White House in 1981, Reagan seized the opportunity to turn back two decades of civil rights enforcement. His appointment of William Bradford Reynolds as assistant attorney general for civil rights and Clarence Thomas as director of the Equal Employment Opportunity Commission signaled this shift in policy. Along with Reagan, they believed that the civil rights laws and judicial rulings of the 1950s and 1960s had only endorsed desegregation and were not designed to impose integration or extend preferences to African Americans because of their past experiences with racial discrimination. To do so, these conservatives argued, would violate the color-blind language of the Constitution as well as the intentions of the framers of the civil rights acts, who had stipulated that they did not mean to sanction racial goals or quotas as public policy. The president's men contended that a combination of aggressive federal bureaucrats and misguided judges had stood non-discriminatory civil rights statutes on their heads and devised programs that did the opposite of what had been intended.[78]

While Reagan attempted to change the political culture that had supported the goals of the civil rights movement, he also worked to stock the federal judiciary with appointees who reflected his conservative viewpoint. Not only did he select a large number of ideological soul mates to the lower federal courts, but he also tilted the balance on the Supreme Court rightward by elevating William Rehnquist to chief justice and appointing Sandra Day O'Connor, Antonin Scalia and Anthony Kennedy. By 1989, after Reagan had retired and was succeeded by his vice-president, George H. W. Bush, the conservative appointments began to pay large dividends. Two decisions in 1989 struck serious blows to affirmative action. In *Wards Cove Packing Company v. Atonio,* the court moved away from the *Griggs* decision concerning the standard of proof needed to show racial discrimination in employment. It shifted the burden of proof from employers to employees. Plaintiffs charging racial bias could no longer rely on statistics of numerical imbalance in the work force to prove discrimination; rather, they had to provide evidence that a "specific employment practice" illegitimately harmed minority employment.[79]

That same year, in *City of Richmond v. J.A. Croson* the high tribunal severely limited the power of municipal governments to award a fixed percentage of contracts to minority-owned firms. Richmond, Virginia, in which blacks constituted 50 percent of the population but minority businessmen received only 1 percent of city contracts, had set aside 30 percent of its contracts to go to minority enterprises. Speaking for a narrowly divided Supreme Court, Justice Sandra Day O'Connor ruled that all race-conscious programs would be judged strictly on whether they proved that discrimination actually resulted from current practices rather than past societal discrimination. Along with *Wards Cove*, this case established a high burden of proof on plaintiffs who challenged discriminatory employment patterns, especially those resulting from previous racialist policies embedded into the system of hiring and promotion.[80]

The momentum in the courts to retard affirmative action that had built up during the Reagan and Bush regimes carried over into the administration of Bill Clinton. Unlike his Republican predecessors, the Democratic Clinton garnered a large share of African American votes and favored affirmative action. He called for a national dialogue on race and appointed the distinguished historian John Hope Franklin to head a commission to conduct it. Nevertheless, Clinton could not stop the Supreme Court from continuing to erode affirmative action. The conservative position had been bolstered by Bush's appointment of Clarence Thomas in 1991, an African American whose right-wing ideology repudiated that of the court's first black justice Thurgood Marshall, whom he replaced. In 1995, Justice Sandra Day O'Connor, speaking for a slim 5-4 majority, declared that "all racial classifications [are] inherently suspect and presumably invalid." *Adarand Constructors v. Pena* concerned minority "set asides" in federal contracts, and O'Connor ruled that affirmative action programs based on race were constitutional only if they were "narrowly tailored measures that further compelling government interests."[81] The application of this standard of "strict scrutiny" made it very difficult for the government to sustain its affirmative action programs. Proclaiming "lets mend it, not end it," Clinton instructed his aides to develop guidelines that were sufficiently racial neutral to pass constitutional muster and satisfy the court. Thus, by the end of the Clinton administration, affirmative action measures with respect to government business opportunities were not dead, only wounded.

A similar situation existed in higher education. The 1993 ruling in the case of *Hopwood v. State of Texas* virtually overruled the *Bakke* decision. The 5th U.S. Circuit Court of Appeals upheld the claim of four white students that they had been refused admission to the University of Texas because of racial preferences extended to supposedly less-qualified black and Hispanic applicants. The judiciary declared that race was not a valid means of achieving diversity at the law school campus or eliminating the effects of past discrimination by those other than the law school itself. The Supreme Court refused to hear this case on appeal, which in effect banned affirmative action in the 5th Circuit states of Texas, Louisiana, and Mississippi.[82]

As of 2002, the Supreme Court has refused to decide whether the *Bakke* precedent still holds. The state of affairs has become extremely murky because of contradictory opinions in various federal appellate courts. In 2000, 9th Circuit judges, covering Alaska, Arizona, Hawaii, Idaho, Montana, Nevada, Oregon, and Washington, concluded that race could be used as one of many factors to achieve a more diverse student body at the University of Washington. Similar opinions prevailed for both undergraduate and law school admissions at the University of Michigan.[83] In contrast, the 11th Circuit Court of Appeals (Georgia, Alabama, and Florida) decided the University of Georgia's affirmative action program that awarded bonus points to applicants on the basis of racial diversity was unconstitutional.[84] On June 23, 2003, the Supreme Court finally spoke. The court upheld the use of race as a factor in promoting educational diversity as long as a university did not consider it in a "mechanical way." As a result, the justices approved the University of Michigan's Law School affirmative action plan for operating in a "holistic way," while rejecting Michigan's undergraduate plan for too rigidly taking race into account. Thus, by a narrow margin, affirmative action prevailed, but administrators still have to proceed cautiously (*New York Times*, June 24, 2003).

Opponents of affirmative action have not relied exclusively on the courts. In 1996, led by California Republican Governor Pete Wilson and University of California Regent Ward Connerly, an African American conservative, the voters of the Golden State passed Proposition 209. In the name of guaranteeing civil rights, the measure outlawed racial preferences. The effect on minority attendance at state universities was mixed. At the flagship UCLA and Berkeley campuses, minority enrollment decreased and minority law school and medical school admissions plummeted at the three University of California law schools. However, minority admissions increased at less prestigious campuses throughout the university system.[85]

Florida achieved a similar result with a twist. In 2000, the Sunshine State replaced affirmative action with a "percentage" plan that guarantees admission to one of the state universities based on student ranking in high school graduating classes. The "One Florida" plan assures college admissions to all high school students ranked in the top 20 percent of their class—except the University of Florida, which picks its entering class from the top 10 percent of the graduating class. In the first year, the racial and ethnic diversity of the freshman class stayed roughly the same at all campuses except the flagship University of Florida, where the enrollment of black freshman fell by 44 percent. In 2002, minorities in the freshman class increased system-wide. Blacks made up 8 percent and Latinos 12 percent of the total freshman class.[86] In effect, Florida and California have created a two-tier level of admissions, but by removing overt racial criteria and increasing minority admissions at a variety of state campuses, they provide the likely alternative to race-based affirmative action that will pass constitutional muster.

Also related to education, the busing controversy that gripped American politics in the 1970s and 1980s has largely disappeared. Lawsuits in Charlotte and Boston in the late 1990s released these cities from court-mandated busing, as did judicial rulings in other cities. One would have expected from these decisions that desegregation finally had been achieved, but this was hardly the case. In 2002, the proportion of the nation's black students attending predominantly minority schools reached slightly over 54 percent, while the percentage of whites enrolled in schools with a majority of members of their own race hovered around 80. Since 1980, the percentage of black students in majority-white schools has dropped from 44 to fewer than 31.[87] Nevertheless, because African American children had shouldered the burden of busing, for the most part their parents were not sorry to see busing cease.

African Americans fared somewhat better in integrating the electoral arena than they did the schools. A series of cases in the 1990s limited the application of race-conscious remedies for electoral representation, but they did not wipe them out completely. In *Shaw v. Reno*, the Supreme Court held that North Carolina had acted unconstitutionally in designing a majority-black congressional district with such a bizarre shape that it could have only resulted from racial motivations. Speaking for the court, Justice O'Connor decried the attempt to construct this predominantly black district as a form of "apartheid" by separating white and black voters. Similarly, the court struck down "majority-minority" districts in Georgia and Texas. However, the judiciary did not altogether eliminate race as a legitimate factor in legislative districting. In 2001, the court ruled that race was not an improper consideration as long as it was not the "dominant and controlling" one. The case involved the same district that North Carolina had tried to redraw several times, and on this occasion, in a five to four opinion, Justice Stephen Breyer, a Clinton appointee, contended that the Democratic political affiliation of African Americans rather than race was the predominant concern in the minds of the Tar Heel legislators who created the challenged district.[88]

The attacks against affirmative action redistricting have turned the guarantee of equal protection upside down by substituting it as a safeguard for whites at the expense of blacks. Judicial opponents, with Clarence Thomas firmly among them, conveniently ignore the fact that white legislators traditionally have drawn districts to ensure white candidates a greater opportunity than blacks to win elections. However, when lawmakers attempt to increase the chances of African Americans to make their votes count more effectively for their own candidates, they have had their efforts overturned for taking race into consideration. The justices reached this conclusion because to them race only means black or Latino, not white. If a majority-black district elects an African American representative, then race is suspect; yet if a majority-white district chooses a white candidate, the court assumes that some characteristic other than race controls the outcome.[89]

Despite limitations placed on legislative redistricting by the court, the number of African American elected officials has continued to grow. Over 80 percent of the members of the Congressional Black Caucus (thirty-three of thirty-nine) have been elected since 1990. For the first time, in the year 2000, the number of African American officials elected nationally jumped to over nine thousand. The most impressive gains occurred in Georgia, Louisiana, Mississippi, South Carolina, and Texas. Indeed, Mississippi, the state that had the lowest number of black adults registered to vote in 1965, had the highest number of black elected officials (897) of any state in the nation.[90] The next major hurdle for the civil rights forces is to convince Congress to renew the special provisions of the Voting Rights Act when they expire in 2007. These sections, which passed in 1965 and have been approved three times since, will allow the federal government to continue to monitor and disallow discriminatory changes in electoral laws. Without these special provisions the Voting Rights Act would remain on the books, but its strength would be greatly diminished.

Despite gains at the polls, African Americans have yet to catch up to whites economically. The 2000 Census Report shows that the median income for blacks was $29,470, while whites earned $46,305. Approximately 22.7 percent of African Americans lived in poverty, nearly double the national rate of 11.7 percent, while only 7.8 percent of non-Hispanic whites lived in poverty. Poverty rates were the highest in the South where African Americans make up 54.6 percent of the population.[91]

African Americans also lagged behind educationally. In 1999, almost twice as many whites received a bachelor's degree (28 percent) as did blacks (15 percent). Among blacks, more women than men earned at least a bachelor's degree—16 percent as opposed to 14 percent. For whites, this was reversed—more men received at least a bachelor's degree (31 percent) than women (25 percent).[92] The figures for African American men reflect a tragic reality experienced particularly by black youth and young adults. African Americans have a six times greater chance of going to prison during their lifetime than whites and can expect to serve longer sentences for the same offenses. More than 28 percent of African American men can expect to be incarcerated over their lifetime, while whites only have a 4 percent chance of imprisonment. In 1996, African Americans represented 30 percent of all convicted federal offenders despite the fact that they made up only 13 percent of the population. In the decade between 1985 and 1995 the percentage of African Americans under correctional supervision increased 81 percent.[93]

These gloomy statistics mask some notable progress. The persistence of poverty disproportionately burdening African Americans stands alongside the growth of the black middle class and its success stories in business, entertainment, and the professions. It is a dramatically changed United States that has two African Americans in the highest foreign policy positions of government—Colin Powell as Secretary of State and Condoleeza Rice as National Security Advisor. In an age when celebrities dominate the media and advertising, no one has greater crossover appeal to whites and blacks alike than the basketball star Michael Jordan and the golfer Tiger Woods. Yet singular achievements do not add up to the acquisition of economic equality for African Americans as a group. It is true that in sustaining itself for the past forty years, the Second Reconstruction has long outlasted the first. However, this record will provide little solace for African Americans and the nation as a whole if the expansion of equal economic access and political representation is cut short before it has been fulfilled.

PART FOUR

FROM THE BOTTOM UP

FLORIDA'S LITTLE SCOTTSBORO

The residents of Lake County, Florida, awoke on the morning of July 16, 1949, to a drama that was hauntingly familiar and yet disturbingly different. Word passed quickly through the area of small towns and rural communities that before dawn on this summer Sunday a white woman had been attacked and raped by four black men near Groveland. In the past, such crimes had stirred lynch mobs into acts of vengeance, and this occasion proved no exception. However, in this instance, blood-thirsty vigilantes did not succeed in rendering summary punishment, but they partially achieved their objectives through lawful means. Although lynching diminished in influence in the post–World War II South, public officials, responding to social and political pressures, accomplished the same goals in a legally-sanctioned fashion.

Following the war, black veterans who returned home found the Jim Crow South virtually unchanged. They encountered hostile whites determined to preserve the rigid system of racial oppression. Despite the elimination of the white primary by the Supreme Court in 1944, southern politicians applied literacy tests, poll taxes, and other devices to keep blacks disfranchised. These official forms of discrimination were reinforced by private acts or threats of violence. In 1946, senator Theodore Bilbo of Mississippi encouraged his "red blooded" constituents to prevent blacks from voting by paying them a visit "the night before the election."[1] During the first half of 1949, the Southern Regional Council reported 108 cases "in which southern private citizens and public officials attempted to usurp the functions of our legal institutions."[2]

Florida also faced a stiff challenge to its defense of the racial status quo. Led by the state NAACP and local civic groups, black Floridians launched an assault on the edifices of discrimination. After the defeat of the white primary, Harry T. Moore formed the Florida Progressive Voters League to encourage blacks to register. Between 1947 and 1950, the number of blacks enrolled on the suffrage lists swelled from 49,000 to over 116,000. Moore also served as president of the state conference of NAACP branches, and he initiated judicial action to equalize the salaries of underpaid black school teachers with those of whites. For his activities, he and his wife were fired from their teaching positions in Brevard County.[3] In 1949, Moore turned his attention to the Groveland rape case, an episode that put Florida racial justice on trial before the nation and the world.

Nestled in the center of citrus and lake country in mid-Florida, Groveland became a home for blacks almost immediately after its establishment in 1910. Whites living in nearby Mascotte decided that they did not want blacks in their community, although they did want them sufficiently close at hand to work in the groves. Because citrus tended to be a seasonal occupation, blacks were encouraged to develop small farms to feed their families during the off season. Many of Groveland's blacks resided in an area called Stuckey's Still where several owned their own homes. This measure of independence was tolerated, even supported by grove owners, as long as blacks remembered that when it came time to pick the fruit or fertilize the trees, they returned to the groves. This condition of dependency existed for many years and required little violence or intimidation to enforce successfully.[4]

Following World War II, however, a number of young blacks returning home from military service were less acquiescent to this labor system. The threat to racial traditions in the community did not escape the attention of owners who worked closely with county sheriffs to dissuade returning veterans from creating unrest. In 1945, the Workers Defense League, a group closely aligned with the Socialist party, accused the sheriff's office in Lake County of actively supporting peonage in the orange groves. Thus, when Walter Irvin and Samuel Shepherd returned to Groveland from the military and seemed reluctant to work in the citrus industry, Sheriff Willis McCall reportedly told them to remove their uniforms and take their places in the groves where they belonged.[5]

A forty-year-old Lake County native, McCall liked to boast that he had received his education "mostly in the University of Hard Knocks." He had prospered in the dairy business, served as the county inspector of fruit, and built a network of supporters who helped him win the sheriff's post in 1944. Once in office, McCall clashed with labor union organizers and civil rights groups and blamed communists for stirring up trouble among black work-ers. In 1946, he personally chased a union representative out of the county.[6] McCall had no use for an "uppity nigger" like Sammy Shepherd, the son of an independent farmer who had become embroiled in a series of altercations with his white neighbors. Since 1943, Sammy's father, Henry Shepherd, had diligently worked his farm which he had reclaimed from swampland. He had come into periodic conflict with whites who let their cows graze on his property and trample his crops. He put up fences to protect his land, only to have them torn down. The Shepherds belonged to the small group of black families that had raised their standard of living during the war. When the younger Shepherd returned home from military service and declined to seek employment with the citrus growers, whites were reported to grumble "that it was time now that somebody put both Henry and Sammy in their places."[7]

Soon afterward Sammy Shepherd and his army buddy, Walter Irvin, found themselves in the midst of a racial maelstrom which neither would be able to escape. Together for two hitches in the military, during their second enlistment they had served a prison sentence for "misappropria-tion of government property" and subsequently were discharged dishonor-ably from the army.[8] This trouble behind them, they returned to their homes in Lake County to find that another shared ordeal was just about to begin.

In the early morning hours of July 16, 1949, Irvin and Shepherd, along with two other black men, Charles Greenlee and Ernest Thomas, stood accused of kidnapping and raping Mrs. Norma Padgett and assaulting her husband, Willie. Padgett told the police he and his wife had left a dance and that his car had stalled on the road as he was turning around. Although the four blacks initially had stopped to offer assistance, Padgett claimed that they soon turned on him, beat him, and drove off with his wife. Greenlee, Shepherd, and Irvin were arrested within hours of the incident. For over a week, Thomas eluded a posse led by McCall and three other sheriffs before being shot and killed in the woods of Taylor County, nearly two hundred miles northwest of where the search began.[9]

As news of the rape spread through the town and into Lake County, a caravan of over two hundred cars carrying five hundred to six hundred men descended on Groveland during the evening of July 17. Unable to lo-cate the defendants in the town jail, they drove to the county seat in Tavares. The mob gathered at the jail and demanded the release of the three prison-ers. But Sheriff McCall persuaded the mob that the men had been transferred to the state penitentiary, even though he had them hidden in the jail. The mob seemed satisfied after Padgett's husband and her father inspected the facility, and McCall promised that justice would be served. "This is a. crucial moment that could cause a crisis here and throughout the state," the sheriff admonished the crowd. "Let's let the law handle this calmly."[10]

Unable to get their hands on the accused but still eager to exact retribution, the caravan returned to Groveland where it set fire to black homes and shot into them. Apparently local black families had realized the impending danger and had departed with the assistance of several white residents. The following day, a mob from Mascotte waylaid cars on the highway outside of Groveland in hope of intercepting any local black, but they went home frustrated. Responding to pleas from the NAACP and local black residents, Governor Fuller Warren, an opponent of the Ku Klux Klan, sent in the National Guard. Arriving on Tuesday, the eighteenth, and leaving the following Sunday, the militia gradually restored order, though most black homes had been seriously damaged by this time. The house and property of Samuel Shepherd's father had been singled out by the mob and virtually destroyed.[11]

Why some white residents assisted blacks while others sought revenge remains uncertain. Perhaps the more prosperous local whites feared that violence against blacks would hurt business. "The Negroes are a vital part of our economy," a Groveland merchant declared. "They spend a great percent of the money in local stores. They are badly needed by farmers and growers."[12] Though others may have been aware of the value of blacks as customers and laborers, they thought it more important to take action to keep blacks subservient. By resorting to violence and making an example of the accused rapists, whites who resented the economic strides some blacks had made were issuing a warning to "other Negroes [to] stay in line." With racial barriers under attack throughout the South, whites felt extremely anxious and were inclined to preserve their supremacy through violent means if necessary. The presence of many out-of-state license plates among the automobiles transporting the mob members around the county demonstrated the widespread concern over perceived threats to white control of race relations.[13]

The image of the black rapist had long provoked the wrath of white mobs. In placing white women on a protected pedestal to keep them out of reach of "black beasts," white males also kept their wives, sisters, and daughters in a separate and unequal sphere. "White women," Jacqueline Dowd Hall has written, "were the forbidden fruit, the untouchable property, the ultimate symbol of white male power."[14] Chivalry, the code of honor that meant paternalistic rather than equal treatment for southern women, guaranteed swift retribution against blacks who were suspected of violating the purity of white womanhood. A Lake County resident explained the motivation of the frenzied mobs which burned black homes: "They had to protect their wives, or they couldn't leave them alone at night."[15]

Though the paternalistic ethos lived on, since the 1930s, lynching as a response to rape had declined. This was largely due to the educational campaigns of organizations such as the NAACP and the Association of Southern Women for the Prevention of Lynching, both with active Florida branches.[16] Increasingly, whites expected the judicial process to achieve those ends once gained through private acts of terror. Lake County residents reflected this new emphasis on legal revenge. The female editor of the *Mount Dora Topic* reminded the journal's readers that the honor of the rape victim "will be avenged in a well-conducted court of law, and if the facts are straight and a guilty verdict is returned—revenge will be accomplished by a more frightening and awful means than a mob has at its command." Another newspaper summed up the more ambiguous sentiments of many people in the area: "We'll wait and see what the law does, and if the law doesn't do right, we'll do it."[17]

Prior to Groveland, the infamous Scottsboro case had shown that "due process of law" in southern courts might operate less savagely than vigilante actions for blacks charged with interracial rape, but it did not insure them justice. In March 1931, nine young black men, out of work and drifting through the South, allegedly raped two white women aboard a train passing through the small Alabama town of Scottsboro. A white mob assembled shortly after the arrest of the nine youths, but a lynching was averted by the sheriff. Nevertheless, the trial was conducted in an hysterical and highly charged atmosphere, and the defendants were found guilty on very questionable evidence. The Communist party and the NAACP took up the cause of the "Scottsboro Boys," and over a period of twenty years managed to win several landmark opinions from the Supreme Court and eventually obtain their release from prison.[18]

In May 1950, the last of the Scottsboro defendants walked out of jail, an outcome that seemed to suggest the South had taken a step forward, however shaky. The case also revealed the limits of southern justice, for it had taken two reversals by the Supreme Court, widespread public condemnation of the trials, and considerable self-doubt in Alabama before the defendants were able to escape the death penalty. If the case had not captured national headlines, eight of the nine men almost certainly would have been executed. Had the South and southern justice, then, truly moved forward with the Scottsboro case? Groveland, Florida's "Little Scottsboro" provided some answers to that question.

Shortly after the charges were filed against the four Groveland defendants on July 17, the president of the Orlando branch of the NAACP telephoned the national office to request legal assistance. Franklin Williams, a young attorney on the Legal Defense Fund staff, answered the phone and said he would fly down the next day. Upon arriving in Orlando, Williams began to hear evidence suggesting that the case was highly suspect. From a meeting with Irvin, Shepherd, and Greenlee he learned that despite the sheriff's announcement that the accused had admitted their guilt, they had been badly beaten by the deputies until they had agreed to confess. Their story was corroborated when an examination completed by Williams several days after their arrest revealed numerous cuts and bruises all over their bodies. The three men said they had been hung from pipes along the ceiling and cut glass had been scattered on the floor. Whenever they moved, their feet were cut by the glass. They were also beaten with clubs around the chest and head. The journalist Stetson Kennedy claimed that Jefferson Elliott, Governor Warren's special investigator, told him that it was evident from the wounds and scars on Greenlee, Irvin, and Shepherd "that they had been 'beaten around the clock.'" Even so, Irvin had refused to admit his guilt.[19]

Further investigation by Williams disclosed other problems with the prosecution's case. While Irvin and Shepherd were good friends and acquaintances of Thomas, they did not know Greenlee, who had arrived in Groveland from Gainesville only hours before the rape. Thomas apparently had brought Greenlee to town to help him with his bolita (gambling) activities. Rumors persisted in the black community that Thomas had pocketed some bolita receipts rather than turn them over to his reputed boss, Henry Singleton, a local black. These charges were never substantiated, but Sheriff McCall regarded Thomas as a troublemaker who needed disciplining.[20]

Perhaps even more disturbing, Williams and many black residents doubted that Norma Padgett had been raped. Only seventeen-years-old, she and her husband had been married for a brief period of time when she returned home to her parents because her husband had beaten her. Padgett had been warned by his in-laws not to hit Norma again. On the evening of July 15, Padgett had persuaded his estranged wife to attend a dance with him in an attempt to reconcile their differences. On the way to the event, Padgett bought a bottle of liquor which he and his brother-in-law subsequently consumed. Following the dance, the Padgetts planned to have dinner near Groveland but changed their minds. Instead, Padgett turned the car around to take his wife home, but what happened after that remains a mystery. Padgett claimed his car stalled because of a weak battery, and four blacks stopped their car to offer assistance. According to his own testimony, he was assaulted by the men who then kidnapped and raped his wife. Norma Padgett was next seen early the following morning standing near a restaurant on the outskirts of Groveland, where she was spotted by the restaurant owner's son. He gave her a ride into town, and he noted that she did not appear unusually concerned or upset and did not mention being raped. Willie Padgett had in the meantime started his car which he drove to a filling station in Leesburg where he told attendant Curtis Hunter that he had been assaulted and his wife kidnapped.[21]

183

Norma did not claim that she had been raped until she encountered her husband and a deputy sheriff who were out searching for her. Willie took his wife aside, spoke alone with her for several minutes, and then she told her story. Franklin Williams speculated that the Padgetts had fabricated this tale on the spot to protect Willie. He guessed that following the dance, Willie had beaten Norma for refusing to grant him his "matrimonial rights," and subsequently he implored his wife to claim she had been raped by blacks or her family would take revenge upon him.[22]

When Norma and Willie Padgett first saw Greenlee, who had been arrested at a gasoline station during the early morning hours for vagrancy, they did not implicate him. In fact, they disagree whether he was one of the culprits. Willie Padgett did, however, identify Shepherd and Irvin as he accompanied sheriff's deputies to Irvin's home and the home of Shepherd's brother. He also contended that the car owned by Shepherd's brother was the one used in the crime.[23]

The Circuit Court judge and county attorney quickly assembled a grand jury to hear the charges. In a move calculated to show that the defendants could receive a fair trial, Lake County Attorney Jesse W. Hunter impaneled a black resident on the jury. According to the local paper, he was "the first ever to serve on a Lake County Grand Jury." Emotions ran very high in the county, however, and it was not likely that any black could exercise much independence of judgement. On the day before the grand jury convened, the *Orlando Morning Sentinel*, the largest newspaper in central Florida, ran a front page cartoon depicting a row of four electric chairs with the headline, "The Supreme Penalty," and the caption, "No Compromise!" Not surprisingly, the jury ruled quickly and unanimously that there was sufficient basis for indicting the three men.[24]

When the grand jury met, Franklin Williams, who lacked a license to practice in Florida, had yet to find a Florida attorney to defend Shepherd,

Irvin, and Greenlee. He had hoped to find a white lawyer from the area to improve their chances of receiving a fair hearing. Williams approached Spessard Holland, Jr., the son of Florida's United States Senator, who had represented some black migrant workers in peonage cases. Though sympathetic, Holland declined, explaining: "My wife is a typical flower of southern womanhood and this is a rape case and I can't take it."[25] Instead, Williams secured the services of Alex Akerman, Jr., of Orlando, who had recently completed a term as the only Republican in the state legislature. Akerman chose his assistants—Joseph E. Price, Jr., and Horace Hill, a black attorney from Daytona Beach—to help with the defense.[26]

A trial date was set for August 29, but Akerman asked for a month's extension because he had just been hired and had not had ample time to prepare a defense. Circuit Judge Truman G. Futch, a native of Lake County, refused his request, contending that Williams had been involved in the case since July. Futch also commented that since Akerman was convinced of his clients' innocence, he must have sufficient evidence to go to trial. Futch did agree, however, to delay the trial for three days.[27]

When the trial opened, Akerman petitioned for a change of venue, arguing that a fair trial in Lake County was impossible because of the negative publicity surrounding the case. But the mayor of Tavares, E.I. Burleigh, and a black insurance agent, F.L. Hampton, testified that race relations in Lake County were "the best in Florida." Akerman also moved to quash the indictments because blacks had been systematically excluded from grand juries in Lake County for twenty-five years, arguing that the one black who had been placed on the grand jury was there "for the sole purpose of creating the impression of compliance with the 14th Amendment." The voting rolls showed that there were 802 blacks in the county, but only one had ever been called to serve on a grand jury. Futch reject both appeals, ruling that the first motion did not comply with the laws of Florida and that no evidence had been introduced that suggested a fair trial could not be held in Lake County. Futch denied Akerman's second motion, pointing to the presence of a black on the grand jury as a fair and lawful impaneling of this jury.[28]

Testimony began on the third day of the trial with Norma Padgett taking the stand as the state's star witness. She repeated her story as she had reported it to the county attorney's office. After the four kidnapped her, she asserted, they drove her to a small road off the highway and took turns raping her. She then recalled, "They asked me if I wanted them to take me to town, and I told them I'd rather walk." This seemed like a curious question from four blacks, three of whom resided in Groveland, after they had just finished raping a white woman. Charles Greenlee later testified that if he had known a white woman had been raped he would have left the county immediately. The four released Norma in a field, and she swore she hid in the woods until daylight.[29]

Willie Padgett followed his wife to the stand and repeated the same testimony. He also declared that the blacks who had overpowered him were driving a 1941 or 1946 Mercury with a prefix number on the license plate that indicated it was from Lake County. As had his wife, he identified the three black defendants and the deceased as the men who had kidnapped and raped Norma. Padgett also stated they stole his wallet which contained a driver's license and twenty dollars.[30]

Besides the Padgett's testimony, that provided by Deputy Sheriff James L. Yates proved most crucial to the state's case. According to Yates, footprints and tire prints left at the scene of the crime were directly traceable to Irvin and the car owned by Shepherd's brother. The prosecution presented plaster casts that Yates supposedly had made at the crime scene and later matched to Irvin's shoes and the Mercury sedan. When Akerman asked Yates where he learned to make plaster moldings, the deputy replied that he had been doing it for years. A handkerchief that belonged to Norma had also been found by Yates, and according to his testimony the lint on it was similar to that discovered in the rear of the Mercury and on Mrs. Padgett's dress.[31]

The state rested its case following Yates's testimony. Significantly, it had not introduced any medical evidence to show that Norma had been raped. Nor did it introduce the confessions of Greenlee and Shepherd. County Attorney Jesse Hunter believed that he could win a conviction without the confessions, and that they would damage the state's case on appeal because the defense could produce evidence showing the defendants had been beaten.[32] At the same time, the defense did not attempt to break down Mrs. Padgett's story of the rape or introduce medical evidence to refute it. As Akerman recalled, cross-examination "had to be handled delicately—you couldn't have gotten anywhere by roughing her up."[33] Given the inflammatory nature of the rape charge, defense counsel thought it prudent not to arouse further sympathy for Norma.

All three men accused of the rape testified on their own behalf. Shepherd and Irvin recounted their trip to Orlando on the evening of the crime and told of their visit to a series of bars. Both testified that they had not seen Norma and Willie Padgett that evening, nor did they know Greenlee. Shepherd's brother testified that he had let Sammy borrow his car and that when the younger Shepherd returned it, he was not nervous nor did he act as if he were trying to hide something.[34] Greenlee admitted that he had been arrested in the early morning hours, just prior to the rape, at a closed gasoline station in Groveland. He said he had journeyed from Gainesville because his mother cried constantly over the death of his two sisters who were run over by a train. Greenlee added that he had not known the Padgetts or his fellow defendants.[35]

Despite the defense team's efforts to show that Greenlee could not have been at the scene of the rape when it occurred, and the testimony of all three about their innocence, the jury returned a guilty verdict only ninety minutes after it had been charged by the judge. Irvin and Shepherd were sentenced to death, but the jury recommended mercy for the sixteen-year-old Greenlee, presumably because of his youth. Franklin Williams remarked that the trial had "all the characteristics of a dime store novel. . . . A perfect frameup." The *Mount Dora Topic* vigorously disagreed and declared that the "county can well be proud of the conduct of its officers of the law, its prosecutor and its judge from the start to the finish of the Groveland Story."[36]

The defense immediately filed an appeal to the Florida Supreme Court amidst rumors of a federal inquiry. In response to a series of articles written by Ted Poston, a black reporter covering the trial for the *New York Post*, United States Attorney General J. Howard McGrath ordered an investigation into the charges that the three defendants had been tortured while in custody. A surgeon and a dentist had examined the trio at Raiford State Prison and reported that all showed signs of brutal beatings. The investigation collapsed, however, when United States District Attorney Herbert Phillips of Tampa, inexplicably refused to call either doctor. With the case against the sheriff and his deputies resting on the unsupported testimony of the defendants, the federal grand jury dismissed the charges.[37]

In this instance, as well as others, the federal government proved less than helpful. Although President Harry Truman had committed his administration to advancing the cause of civil rights, the Justice Department exercised restraint in prosecuting criminal cases involving racial discrimination. With considerable justification, federal lawyers believed they could not win such litigation before southern white juries which were not inclined to convict their neighbors for violating black civil rights. The Justice Department might instruct the FBI to investigate thoroughly "whether or not a violation of federal criminal law was committed," but the bureau did not accord these matters a high priority.[38] Its director, J. Edgar Hoover, did not share much sympathy with the civil rights cause, and he was reluctant to assign the needed manpower to cases with little likelihood of success. Moreover, because the agency depended on the cooperation of local law enforcement officials in investigating what they judged to be their primary concerns, such as bank robberies and stolen cars, it was usually cautious in taking action that might upset indigenous racial customs. This approach drew criticism from civil rights groups. The NAACP could not understand how the FBI had "maintained a world-wide reputation for great efficiency in the investigation, apprehension, and successful prosecution of the cleverest criminals in history," but it was "unable to cope with violent criminal action by bigoted, prejudiced Americans against Negro Americans."[39]

187

Though federal agencies failed to shed fresh light on the Groveland case, a crusading and unusually progressive Florida newspaper did. In April 1950, the *St. Petersburg Times* published an investigative series demonstrating that it was physically impossible for Charles Greenlee to have been at the scene of the crime. Indeed, he had been arrested nineteen miles away during the time the assault allegedly occurred. The article also raised a number of questions about the fairness of the trial and the charges against Shepherd and Irvin. In the second of three articles, the reporter, Norman Bunin, observed that all the jurors were aware of the pre-trial publicity surrounding the case and had read about the confessions of the defendants. The reporter also painstakingly traced the steps of Irvin and Shepherd during the evening of the rape. They were last seen at Club 436 in Altamonte Springs after midnight according to two witnesses. Irvin and Shepherd claimed they started for home around 12:30 A.M. and drove directly to Groveland, a trip of nearly forty miles and a considerable distance from the place where the assault was said to have occurred. Both men testified that they never drove near the area of the rape, although, in contrast to Greenlee, they would have had sufficient time to have done so. The *Times* did report that on a tape recording provided by Sheriff Willis McCall, Greenlee acknowledged that all four had committed rape. Yet when asked about the confession while in prison, Greenlee charged that McCall had taken him into his office, held a gun to his head, and told him what to say. At various points in the "confession," McCall turned off the recording machine and gave Greenlee instructions on how to proceed.[40]

These revelations had no influence on the Florida Supreme Court, however, when it heard the appeal. The litigation involved only Shepherd and Irvin because their counsel feared that if Greenlee was also granted a new trial, a white jury might sentence him to death this time. Yet on the long shot that Shepherd and Irvin were subsequently acquitted, the attorneys could seek to reopen Greenlee's case. Akerman based the appeal on five conditions: widespread publicity which prejudiced the case; lack of sufficient time to prepare an adequate defense; cruel and illegal treatment of the prisoners; failure of the state to prove its case; and absence of blacks on the jury. Three months later, the state justices found no reason to overturn the conviction, writing that "all legal rights of the appellants were ably and thoroughly presented in the lower court." Though acknowledging strained race relations had existed in Lake County as a result of the crime, the justices asserted that "our study of the record reflects the view that harmony and good will and friendly relations continuously existed between the white and colored races in all other sections of Lake County." In concluding, the court found that "the inflamed public sentiment was against the crime . . . rather than [the] defendants' race" and that there was no evidence of any intentional discrimination against blacks in the selection of persons for jury duty.[41]

Less than one year later, the United States Supreme Court unanimously overturned the convictions of Shepherd and Irvin. In a blistering opinion delivered by Robert Jackson, the justices called the pre-trial publicity "one of the best examples of one of the worst menaces to American justice." Jackson found numerous examples of prejudicial influences outside the trial courtroom that warranted a change of venue, including the *Orlando Sentinel* political cartoon picturing the row of four electric chairs and its report of the alleged confessions of the defendants. Noting that neither the county attorney nor the sheriff had ever repudiated the confessions, Jackson observed that prospective jurors all assumed them to be true. He added that such confessions either did not exist or they were "obtained under circumstances which made [them] inadmissible." A majority of the seven justices were also prepared to overturn the verdict because no blacks had been included on the jury. But as Justice Jackson pointed out, even if blacks had been allowed to serve on the jury, the pre-trial publicity prevented the defendants from obtaining a fair hearing, and he did not see "how any Negro on the jury would have dared to cause a disagreement or acquittal."[42]

Lake County officials denounced the court's decision, and Sheriff McCall commented that "the mere fact that mercy was recommended for Greenlee is proof that the jury was fair and impartial." Despite the court's pronouncement, County Attorney Jesse Hunter did not believe that the merits of his case had been weakened, and he was eager to retry it and obtain another conviction. A former school teacher, railroad mail clerk, and self-taught lawyer, the seventy-year-old Hunter was a folksy character with a cracker barrel wit, whose participation in this celebrated legal affair would climax what had been a very popular public career.[43]

In November 1951, while the defense submitted a petition for a new trial site and also sought to disqualify Hunter as prosecuting attorney, Sheriff McCall went to Raiford State Prison to transfer Irvin and Shepherd to Tavares for the pre-trail hearing. Transporting both prisoners in his automobile, McCall followed Deputy Yates's patrol car to the county seat. While driving along a back road near his home town of Umatilla, McCall complained to his prisoners that his right front tire was low on air. He also alleged later that Irvin had asked to go to the bathroom. As a result, McCall said he pulled to the side of the road to let Irvin relieve himself, but first instructed Irvin and Shepherd to get out and change the tire, though they remained handcuffed together. When McCall opened the door, he claimed that Shepherd hit him with a flashlight. Freeing himself from Shepherd's attack, McCall pulled his gun and shot both prisoners, killing Shepherd. According to this version, Deputy Sheriff Yates went into town after checking on McCall and returned with Hunter and several others. To their surprise, they discovered that Irvin was still alive.[44]

Despite two serious bullet wounds, Irvin survived and told his lawyers a substantially different story from McCall's. He claimed under oath that after McCall pulled his car over to the side of the road he ordered the prisoners from the car and without provocation shot Shepherd and then shot him in the upper right chest. Irvin pretended to be dead and heard McCall mutter, "I got rid of them; killed the sons of bitches." He then called Yates on his car radio and informed him that the two had "tried to jump me and I did a good job." When Yates arrived he turned his flashlight on Irvin who had opened his eyes. "That son of a bitch is not dead, let's kill him," Yates shouted. When he snapped the trigger, the revolver misfired. He and McCall examined the gun almost nonchalantly in the automobile headlights, apparently exchanged weapons and Yates turned and shot Irvin in the neck.[45]

If McCall now chose to practice vigilante justice, why had he saved the two from a lynch mob earlier? Initially McCall may have felt confident that the accused would be sentenced to death, especially after he had extracted confessions from them. Perhaps he believed that a lynching would tarnish his record. When the United States Supreme Court overturned the case, however, McCall probably began to have second thoughts. Having promised the lynch mob and local residents that justice would be done, McCall possibly decided on the road to Tavares that the circumstances were convenient for him to take summary action. Mabel Norris Reese, editor of the *Mount Dora Topic* and a strong supporter of McCall prior to the shooting, also claimed that the fruit growers were anxious for the issue to be settled because their black workers were becoming afraid to go to work as the trial approached. McCall may have thought that his action would return the county more quickly to normal.[46]

A coroner's inquest into the death of Shepherd and the wounding of Irvin exonerated McCall, praising him for "acting in the line of duty." The

NAACP denounced the verdict and called on Governor Fuller Warren to order the arrest or at least the suspension of McCall. A special investigator appointed by Warren concluded that McCall did not use "maximum precaution" in transporting his prisoners, but he found no evidence of criminal wrongdoing.[47] Accordingly, Judge Truman Futch dismissed the grand jury that had been called after the coroner's inquest. Nevertheless, this inquiry left many questions unresolved. Why had McCall driven the prisoners at night along an out-of-the-way back road instead of along the main highway? Why did the sheriff transport Irvin and Shepherd alone in his car? Why did McCall have to use deadly force against two men who were handcuffed together? An FBI probe of this shooting never revealed the answers to these questions, and Sheriff McCall was never indicted on federal charges.

Despite Judge Futch's decision to clear McCall, for the first time a number of people began to question whether justice was being served. Mabel Norris Reese doubted the sheriff's version of the shooting and began re-examining the evidence in the first trial. She deplored the "black mark etched on the night of November 6 by the gun of a man who lost his head."[48] Reese also discovered that Jesse Hunter had developed some misgivings about the case. Before Irvin's retrial, Hunter offered the defendant a life sentence if he would acknowledge his complicity in the rape. Akerman and Thurgood Marshall, a future United States Supreme Court Justice, who had replaced Franklin Williams as chief counsel, discussed Hunter's offer with Irvin, but he insisted on his innocence and refused to negotiate with the county attorney.[49]

The shooting not only embarrassed some of Lake County's leading citizens but the United States as well. McCall's brand of justice sparked an international incident at the height of the Cold War. Andrei Vishinsky, the chief Soviet delegate to the United Nations, declared that the United States "had a nerve talking about human rights and upbraiding other nations while Negroes were shot down by an officer of law while in custody." Though not unmindful of the lack of freedom in the Soviet Union, the NAACP picked up its line of argument. "Samuel Shepherd is not better off for this American hypocrisy," the organization asserted, "nor are his fifteen million fellow Americans who happen not to be white."[50]

The glare of such unfavorable publicity prompted a shift in the course of the litigation. In December 1951, Judge Futch approved a motion by the defense to move the location of the trial from Lake County. It was rescheduled for Marion County, a curious choice because the sheriff there had been murdered the previous spring by a young black.[51]

Before the new trial could begin, another act of violence cast a bloody stain on Florida race relations. On Christmas Eve 1951, dynamite blasted the house of Harry T. Moore, the NAACP statewide coordinator, killing him and mortally wounding his wife. Moore had been active in raising funds for the Groveland defendants, and following the shooting of Shepherd and Irvin, he had led a campaign urging Governor Warren to remove McCall from office.[52] The NAACP believed his "death fits into the pattern of terror which has centered around the town of Groveland . . . and advertises to the world that though we preach democracy abroad we cannot practice it at home."[53] Despite a reward for capture of the killers and an FBI investigation, the murderers were never apprehended.[54]

This latest outrage, however, did not keep Irvin from his scheduled court appointment. Recovered enough from his wounds to stand trial on February 13, 1952, Irvin watched as his defense council sought a change of venue and introduced the results of an Elmo Roper survey showing that residents of Marion County were prejudiced against the defendant. In contrast, Hunter was able to convince Judge Futch that the public opinion poll had attempted to deceive people who were questioned and therefore was biased and unreliable. Futch also refused to suppress the introduction of Irvin's clothes as evidence, notwithstanding charges by the defense that they had been seized illegally. Mrs. Delilah Irvin, Walter's mother, told Judge Futch that Deputy Yates had said he was coming for "that black Nigger boy's clothes," and later warned her that "there may not be no trial."[55]

The second trial produced a few surprises. The prosecution's case relied heavily on the testimony of the Padgetts and Yates as it had the first time, but the defense added two new witnesses to its presentation. The first, Herman V. Bennett, a former law enforcement official for the federal government, stated that the plaster cast of footprints made by Deputy Yates was not produced while Irvin was wearing the shoes. The witness pointed out to the jury that footprints would normally be concave if somebody made them while standing on a soft spot, but they would be convex, as these were, if made from an empty shoe. Attorney Hunter could not shake the testimony, but he did note that this witness was being paid by the defense counsel. The other key witness for the defense was Lawrence Burtoft, the first person to encounter Norma Padgett walking along the road. As he approached her to offer assistance, she called "Good Morning" and asked if she could get a ride to town. Burtoft stated that she seemed calm and unruffled. As he drove her toward town, Mrs. Padgett told Burtoft that "she had been abducted by four Negroes, and said she could not identify them." He added that "she made no complaint of having been attacked." During the cross-examination, Burtoft declared he had brought this to Hunter's attention during the first trial and had been subpoenaed as a witness, but Hunter never asked him to testify. Irvin once again testified in his own behalf and maintained his innocence.[56]

During the 1960s, information came to light in another rape case that raised serious doubts about the veracity of Yates's testimony. In circumstances very similar to the Groveland case, Lake County deputies had manufactured a plaster molding of a shoe print which Yates insisted had been taken at the scene of the crime. Testimony revealed, however, that the shoe print had been made by Yates in the sheriff's office.[57]

But these revelations were yet to come, and despite the questions raised by the testimony of Bennett and Burtoft, the Marion County jury deliberated only an hour and a half before finding Irvin guilty and recommending a death sentence. The defense immediately filed an appeal, arguing that numerous errors in the trial and especially the unlawful search and seizure of Irvin's clothes warranted overturning the verdict. The appeal stood pending before the United States Supreme Court for a year until January 1954, when the Court declined to rehear it.[58]

With Irvin facing the death penalty in November, his lawyers petitioned Governor Charley Johns for clemency. Some white Floridians also joined the campaign to spare Irvin's life. On its editorial page, the *St. Petersburg Times* noted the doubts that surrounded the conviction of Irvin and declared: "Both compassion and calm judgement argue for his sentence to be changed to life imprisonment."[59] The Reverend Ben Wyland of the United Churches of St. Petersburg agreed, as did Jesse Hunter, the prosecutor who had won the conviction in the first place.[60] Nevertheless, Johns, an outspoken segregationist, denied the petition. The NAACP, however, won a stay from the United States Supreme Court just two days before the scheduled execution.

A change in governors finally saved Irvin. As a result of the election in November 1954, LeRoy Collins, a moderate on racial issues, replaced Johns and asked his assistant, Bill Harris, to re-examine the case. Harris found numerous errors in the investigation of the crime. In his report to Collins, Harris emphasized the questionable nature of the plaster cast moldings that Deputy Yates had produced at the first trial. He observed that Yates had testified he did not understand what "integrity of footprints" meant, and several hours had passed before he made a set of plaster casts. He had also waited several hours before making moldings of the tire tracks. Harris went on to raise questions about the entire inquiry conducted by state and county officials. He noted that no effort was ever made by the state to explain what had happened to Willie Padgett's wallet or Norma's perfume which remained missing since the morning of the rape. Unexplainedly, the prosecution also failed to introduce medical testimony establishing conclusively that rape had occurred. On the basis of Harris's investigation, Governor Collins commuted Walter Irvin's sentence to life imprisonment, informing the State Pardon Board that Irvin's guilt had not been established "in an absolute and conclusive manner."[61]

Collins's decision was angrily denounced by Lake County officials. Judge Futch was so upset that he ordered a grand jury investigation of the commutation proceedings. Collins refused to participate in the hearing. The jurors' report charged that the governor had mistakenly reached the wrong conclusions, but it exonerated him of malfeasance. Feelings still remained high in the county, however. In February 1956, Collins and his wife took part in a parade in Eustis, Florida, when Norma Padgett, escorted by two of McCall's deputies, approached his car. She yelled at the governor, "You're the one who let off the nigger that raped me. Would you have done that if it had been your wife?"[62]

Norma Padgett was not alone in expressing her indignation against Collins. Sheriff McCall left no doubt about how he felt, viewing the commutation as a threat to the preservation of law and order. He admonished that in the future "all a negro criminal would need to do would be pick out some innocent helpless white woman as a target to satisfy his ravishing sexual desires, keep his mouth shut, proclaim his innocence and let the NAACP furnish the money and lawyers and beat the rap."[63] Seconding the sheriff's opinion, Herbert S. Phillips predicted the governor's action would produce dire consequences. In his capacity as United States district attorney in 1950, Phillips had failed to obtain an indictment from a federal grand jury investigating McCall for beating the Groveland prisoners in his custody. His sympathies apparently rested with the sheriff rather than the defendants. Six years later in retirement, he called Collins's handling of the case "a victory for the National Association for the Advancement of Colored People [that] is bound to encourage lynchings in rape cases."[64]

These warnings notwithstanding, the Groveland case gradually drifted from public view in the late 1950s, with the accused staying behind bars despite widespread doubt about their guilt. Greenlee was not paroled until 1962, and Irvin remained incarcerated until 1968 when he was paroled by Claude Kirk, Florida's first Republican governor in the twentieth century. After his release, Greenlee left the state and never returned, settling in Tennessee. Irvin moved to Miami but returned to Lake County for a visit in 1970, and died there of an apparent heart attack. Meanwhile, Sheriff Willis

193

McCall continued in office despite the death of three black prisoners in his jail and numerous charges of corruption and abuse of office against him and his deputies. After Governor Reubin Askew suspended McCall for kicking a black prisoner to death, he resigned in 1973.[65]

Like its predecessor in Scottsboro, Groveland was a "tragedy of the American South." In both instances, alleged rapes of white women by blacks occurred amidst circumstances that raised serious questions about their guilt and about the fairness of the southern judicial system. Despite the intervening war years and the precedent of the Alabama case, the four black Floridians were presumed guilty once a white woman had identified them. The interval between Scottsboro and Groveland did not diminish the white southern response to allegations of rape. The crime remained an emotionally charged one. Clearly, the accusation of rape by a white woman against a black man carried a special burden that could not be readily dismissed. The protection of southern white womanhood justified racial control. However questionable in specific cases, the word and sexual morality of southern daughters were considered equally pure. The fear of rape and the threat of menacing blacks provided a potent rationale for keeping all Negroes in their subordinate place.[66]

Without outside intervention, the situation for the surviving Groveland defendants would have been even worse. The NAACP waged a national fundraising campaign to conduct the defense and assigned some of its best legal talent to plead the case. Along with the Workers Defense League, it gathered information and testimony and extensively publicized the plight of the defendants. Though unsuccessful in the trial courtroom, the NAACP managed to convince the United States Supreme Court to overturn the original verdict. When the second trial failed to change the outcome, the NAACP persuaded the high tribunal to issue a stay of execution. However, the civil rights organization was less successful in getting the executive branch in Washington to act forcefully. In response to NAACP protests, the Justice Department and the FBI investigated the violence against the black prisoners and against Harry T. Moore, but they were unwilling or unable to press charges.

Left on its own, the state of Florida would have quickly electrocuted Irvin and Shepherd. Neither all-white juries nor state supreme court justices hesitated to conclude that the defendants had been proven guilty beyond a reasonable doubt. Similarly, when called upon to judge the actions of Sheriff McCall, a coroner's jury consisting of Lake County residents cleared him of wrongfully killing one prisoner in his custody and seriously wounding another. In the end, only the governor could and did spare Irvin's life. Convinced that too many questions remained unanswered, LeRoy Collins issued a reprieve. Nevertheless, it had taken appeals to two governors to gain the reprieve and even Collins acted cautiously. In announcing his decision, the governor emphasized that he was not bowing to outside pressure, and considering it politically expedient, he denounced the NAACP's handling of the case.[67]

Like most areas confronting racial conflicts in the postwar South, Lake County intended to preserve white supremacy legally or otherwise. The old order of lynching may have passed, but as one reporter observed after the second Groveland trial, the "rope and faggot is giving way to the even more deadly and unobtrusive deputations of one or two persons, who do the job with less notoriety and greater impunity."[68] The social changes and ideological battles surrounding World War II and the Cold War made little difference to the Lake County officials charged with trying the Groveland case. Attacks by black men upon white women, or even the suspicion of such assaults, could not be tolerated or second guessed. To do so would pose a challenge to the traditional assumptions governing race relations in the postwar South, assumptions that remained little changed as Florida prosecuted the Groveland case.

INVESTIGATIONS AND
MASSIVE RESISTANCE

Law has played a central role in structuring race relations in the United States. Though violent confrontation accompanied the civil rights struggle, the most significant battles were fought in courthouses and legislatures as well as in the streets. Segregationists resorted to violence and intimidation, but they were as likely to respond to civil rights demands by shaping the law to their own ends. In firm control of political and judicial power, white leaders in the South fashioned new statutes to forestall integration. Passage of such legislation and its interpretation in the courts was challenged by civil rights organizations and sometimes defeated; yet white southern politicians did succeed in managing the legal system to reduce the pace of racial change.

Southern politicos defended their efforts to maintain white supremacy on democratic grounds, in the name of majority rule. Following the pathbreaking *Brown v. Board of Education* ruling in 1954, Governor LeRoy Collins of Florida championed continued racial separation by invoking the principals of the Declaration of Independence. "The feeling for segregation is so deep rooted," Collins remarked, "that proposals to abandon such violate the 'consent of the governed' . . . which is essential in our democratic society to give substance and strength to law."[1] This majoritarian emphasis virtually ignored the concept of minority rights, except when applied to state prerogatives. According to white leaders, the Tenth Amendment to the federal Constitution, reserving undelegated powers to the states, took precedence over the nine articles of the Bill of Rights relating to individual freedoms. Southern leaders viewed their society in organic terms in which the interests and values of communities and the state merged together in a common bond and paternalistic whites took care of blacks. The emphasis was on conformity rather than dissent. As the historian Numan Bartley pointed out, southerners designed their political theory for the "promotion of social and ideological orthodoxy."[2]

Southern segregationists used laws as a preservative instrument; nonetheless, many civil rights proponents considered the legal system a powerful tool for social change. Since 1909 the National Association for the Advancement of Colored People (NAACP) had employed a case-by-case approach to obtain equality for blacks. Seeking the rights guaranteed to all Americans within the framework of the Constitution, the NAACP specifically sought redress under the Fourteenth and Fifteenth amendments. In pursuing this goal, the NAACP operated according to the traditional ground rules of the American legal system, fighting for reformist ends by conventional means. "By no manner of speaking," one of its officials asserted, "can remedy so sought be called acting in irresponsible haste or proceeding in an extreme manner."[3]

White southerners did not agree. During the post–World War II era of McCarthyism, enemies of the NAACP equated it with the Communist party. Nationwide the cold war's anti-Communist enthusiasts questioned the patriotism of labor, liberal, and civil liberties groups that advocated progressive social change of any type. Distinctions between subversion and radicalism, Stalinism and New Deal liberalism, security and loyalty, were blurred in an atmosphere of political hysteria. In the South, where labor and liberal groups were scarce, the NAACP with its tightly organized network of branches provided a convenient target for conservatives. The organization's opponents defended segregation as 100 percent American and denounced the NAACP as an alien conspiracy. They claimed that the association was directed by outsiders from its New York City "Kremlin" with the intent of undermining the southern way of life by brainwashing contented Negroes to persuade them to revolt.

In the sense that civil rights organizations were working to overthrow the system of white supremacy, segregationists were correct in perceiving the NAACP as a threat.[4] However, they were wrong in considering the national association a front for Communism. Like other liberal groups opposed to Stalin's brand of left-wing authoritarianism, the NAACP purged Communists from its ranks in the postwar years. In 1950 the national convention of the NAACP adopted a resolution condemning Communism and provided machinery to expel suspected Communists from membership. In cooperation with other anti-Communist liberal and labor groups, NAACP officials composed a blacklist of Communist-tainted organizations for their branches to avoid and distributed dossiers on party activists to lessen the danger of infiltration. Nor surprisingly, this internal housecleaning won the official endorsement of the FBI's J. Edgar Hoover and the House Committee on Un-American Activities (HUAC).[5] Despite these commendations, the NAACP could never secure a clean bill of health in the South so long as it continued challenging Jim Crow.

Following the *Brown* decision, southern states combated the NAACP, which they considered a subversive organization. Starting from the premise that the national association conspired to violate the duly established laws of segregation, they attempted to restrict its ability to function. Alabama prosecuted the NAACP for failing to register as an out-of-state corporation and waged a relentless battle to require the group to turn over its membership list. Given the hostile, anti-civil rights climate, such public exposure would endanger current members and make it difficult to recruit new ones. Registration laws to obtain the records of the NAACP were popular in many states, as were those aimed at preventing the organization from sponsoring litigation, the lifeblood of its program. South Carolina went so far as to bar NAACP members from public employment, and Louisiana prohibited teachers from advocating integration of the schools. A number of states also created investigation committees aimed officially at uncovering some kind of wrongdoing by the NAACP but actually intended to intimidate the association through the glare of unfavorable publicity. Indeed, the purpose of these varied measures was to criminalize the activities of the NAACP, stigmatize its followers, and minimize political dissent.[6]

Florida joined the counterattack against integration and its proponents. A gerrymandered state legislature, in which a majority of lawmakers were elected by less than 15 percent of the population, passed an interposition resolution nullifying the controversial *Brown* opinion. Extreme segregationist proposals were tempered by the gubernatorial leadership of LeRoy Collins, a moderate who preferred to "meet the segregation problem in a peaceful and lawful manner . . . [and] not engage in defiance of constituted authority nor in agitation of furor and disorder."[7] His opposition to interposition and his successful support of the Pupil Placement Act, which permitted school segregation for reasons other than race, reflected his cautiously measured approach to the matter. Yet on one issue the governor and the legislature agreed: the NAACP was providing "irresponsible leadership" in stirring up racial turmoil.[8]

In 1956 the lawmakers acted directly to hamper the premier civil rights organization in the state. Prodded by Charley Johns, an outspoken proponent of segregation, a special session of the assembly formed an interim committee to investigate groups that endangered "the well being and orderly pursuit of . . . personal and business activities by the majority of the citizens of the state."[9] Though the measure did not single out the NAACP by name, its sponsors aimed their sights on the association, which they charged with disturbing the racial peace and violating segregation laws. At the same time, the Florida Legislative Investigation Committee (FLIC), with a one-year authorization, gave moderates an opportunity to explore less radical ways of fighting the integrationist forces.[10] Seeking to undermine the NAACP, they made common cause with conservatives in their belief that the group was an enemy of the state and that its "true purpose . . . is Communist inspired," as well as incorporating a "definite desire for financial gain."[11] Collins may have entertained doubts about the necessity of such a committee to supplement his preferred Pupil Placement Act, but he did not veto the FLIC bill, allowing it to become law without his signature.[12]

As the chief target of this legislation, the NAACP prepared to protect itself. Having learned from its experiences in Alabama, the association requested its Florida affiliates to place their crucial membership lists out of reach of state investigators. As soon as the committee was established in August 1956, the Florida State Conference of NAACP Branches dispatched several of its lawyers to visit every chapter around the state "for the purpose of inspecting records and gathering membership" files. Association officials believed that this material would be protected by the attorney-client privilege of confidentiality, but to be on the safe side they packed up the records and shipped them to NAACP headquarters in New York City. Then they steeled themselves "for the onslaught."[13]

The attack came early the following year when the committee decided to hold public hearings. The seven-member committee contained four representatives from the house and three from the senate, including Charley Johns. Balanced with lawmakers from northern and southern sections, rural and urban areas, the group was chaired by Representative Henry Land of Orlando, who had a reputation as a racial moderate. To direct its probe, the committee employed Mark Hawes, a criminal attorney from Tampa, who had most recently prosecuted participants in the Tallahassee bus boycott. Meeting in February and March 1957, the FLIC conducted inquiries in Tallahassee and Miami, where it subpoenaed NAACP officials to answer questions about the workings of their association. The committee denied that it intended to engage in a witch-hunt and insisted that it was merely trying to uncover those organizations breaking the laws of the state.[14]

The committee searched for ways in which the NAACP might have behaved improperly and focused its spotlight on the organization's role in handling lawsuits. Hawes questioned a series of witnesses to find out the connection between the NAACP and the attempted desegregation of buses in Tallahassee, the University of Florida Law School, and public schools throughout the state. The committee counsel sought to prove that, contrary to the code of ethics of the state bar association, the NAACP solicited litigants to file integration cases, financed their way through the courts, and directed them by its own attorneys without the specific authorization of all the plaintiffs.[15] NAACP lawyers adamantly denied these allegations and swore that "contrary to popular belief, we don't go out looking for plaintiffs. In fact, we have more volunteers than we can think of using."[16]

The NAACP aroused suspicion about its practices by refusing to release its records. As had his counterparts in other southern states, Hawes tried to obtain the files in hope of casting doubt on the organization's activities and exposing the names of local members to unfavorable community sentiment. His quest for the documents led him and the committee to Miami and one of the most active NAACP chapters in the state. He and the committee learned from Ruth Perry, the secretary of the local branch and of the state conference of branches, that she had turned over her files to Grattan E. Graves, Jr., an NAACP attorney from Miami and part of the team of lawyers that gathered branch records throughout Florida. Called to testify on February 25, Graves revealed that under instruction from the national office, he had sent the records to the NAACP's headquarters in New York. Both Graves and Perry agreed to the committee's request to try to have the desired material returned. This effort proved fruitless, and the executive secretary of the NAACP, Roy Wilkins, declined to disclose membership lists and other confidential information "because of reprisals visited upon those whose names have become known."[17]

This dispute underscored the negative publicity the hearings brought the NAACP. The civil rights group could take scant pleasure in the fact that the FLIC had also spent several days probing into white extremist groups such as the Citizens' Council. Investigating the NAACP alongside the Citizens' Council had the effect of reinforcing the image of the association as a lawbreaking, radical organization. Its shipment of records outside the state only heightened this impression. The *Tampa Tribune* concluded that the inquiry "has brought substantial discredit to the [NAACP]" and condemned the association's "defiance of a duly constituted arm of the Commonwealth."[18]

Shortly after the hearings adjourned, the NAACP faced a fresh challenge from the legislature. In April members of the investigation committee introduced into each chamber a package of five bills aimed at undermining the NAACP. The measures resembled those adopted by other southern states: three of them made it illegal to solicit lawsuits, prohibited attorneys employed by an association from representing individual members of the group, and barred individuals or organizations not party to litigation from financing or participating in a lawsuit. Another proposal required all groups that tended "to destroy the peace, tranquility and good order" of a community to register with and submit annual membership and financial records to the secretary of state. If laws such as these had been on the books, one of their sponsors declared, "most of our schools suits would have been dismissed."[19] The remaining measure extended the life of the FLIC for two years.

201

Despite considerable interest in these bills, only the one to renew the investigation committee passed. The antibarratry and registration measures, approved unanimously by the senate, went down to defeat in the house, where lawmakers feared that their broad wording might adversely affect other business, social, and fraternal organizations. Apparently the FLIC provision posed no similar problem to the representatives, for it passed overwhelmingly, with only one dissenting vote. The committee offered a familiar vehicle for proceeding against desegregation, and at the same time the legislators significantly expanded the committee's scope. They instructed its members to examine the influence of Communism in provoking racial agitation, a subject that had been virtually ignored during the previous hearings.[20] Even Collins, whose support for the committee had been cool, declared that extending its term "may have some merit because its conduct has been praiseworthy."[21]

Lawmakers thought the committee a more acceptable way of restricting the NAACP than adopting complicated legislation whose side effects might be harmful. They justified the extension measure as an appropriate response to the "great abuse of the judicial processes of the courts in Florida," presumably with the NAACP's civil rights litigation in mind.[22]

Defeat of the antibarratry package did not free the NAACP from continuing challenges to its legal practices. In the wake of the hearings, the FLIC's counsel, Mark Hawes, concluded that the NAACP's activities were "contrary to the spirit and letter of the canons of ethics and general laws governing the practice of law in Florida."[23] Consequently, in September 1957, he sent the transcript of the testimony to the Florida Bar Association to determine whether the NAACP had violated rules governing the conduct of attorneys. Early the next year a preliminary investigation concluded that five leading NAACP lawyers in Florida had acted unprofessionally in handling school-desegregation litigation.[24] Despite this finding, the bar association eventually cleared the civil rights counselors. In "unalterable" disagreements with the "precepts of the NAACP," its leaders nonetheless tried to approach the issue dispassionately and decided that no unethical conduct by the individual lawyers had taken place.[25] Most likely they preferred that the legislature and its investigative committee deal directly with the NAACP, rather than dragging themselves publicly into the controversy.

The FLIC was more than willing to oblige, especially with Senator Charley Johns installed as its new chair. An arch-segregationist and a foe of Collins's brand of racial moderation, Johns wielded the weapon of anti-Communism against the NAACP. Before launching a new round of hearings in February 1958, he announced that the committee had in its possession "information regarding Communistic activities in several phases of life in Florida."[26] Borrowing a page out of Joseph McCarthy's book, he brought J.B. Matthews, a former aide to the Wisconsin senator, to testify at Tallahassee. Matthews, who several years earlier had been forced to resign from McCarthy's subcommittee for accusing Protestant clergy of being an integral part of the Communist apparatus, informed Johns and his colleagues that the Communists had been "directly involved in every major race incident of the past few years." He also encouraged the committee to pick up the trail of the NAACP, which, he said, "for the past thirty years . . . has been a prime target of Communist penetration."[27]

Johns did not need much encouragement, and at the end of February he took the committee to Miami to demonstrate that the "Communist Party and the NAACP are tied up together in Florida."[28] The committee's investigators had done their homework and produced two witnesses who admitted having once belonged to both the Communist party and the NAACP. Their testimony, however, proved less than conclusive. Neither informant currently was an NAACP member, and though one could recall seeing some of his Communist comrades at association meetings, his memory was vague concerning the details of these encounters. Nor did the committee find out more from questioning a left-wing lawyer who had defended NAACP clients in the past but had severed his connection with the organization around 1954 to avoid embarrassing it with his progressive affiliations.[29]

Having learned nothing about any present link between the NAACP and Communism, the FLIC subpoenaed officials of the civil rights group to testify, along with alleged functionaries of the Communist party in Florida. The association came prepared. It had checked out the informants and the accused Communists and concluded that "either they were not members [of the NAACP] in the past or if so are not currently active." To safeguard its membership roster and other records from inspection by the committee, the Miami chapter of the NAACP placed all its files in the hands of its president, Father Theodore R. Gibson, the rector of Christ Episcopal Church.[30] In addition, the branch officers decided not to respond to questions related to individual membership in their organization. Ruth Perry explained that to answer such questions would be "an invasion of my rights to due process of law and freedom of speech and association" guaranteed by the First and Fourteenth amendments. She further denied that the NAACP was infested with Communists.[31]

Perry's testimony sparked fireworks. Perhaps because she was a white woman fighting for black equality, she triggered an angry reaction from committee members. Representative W.C. "Cliff" Herrell of Dade County, Perry's home county, called her performance a "disgrace" and declared her "not fit to be a citizen of Florida." Mrs. Perry, the granddaughter of South Carolina slaveholders, also received a tongue-lashing from Representative J.B. Hopkins of Pensacola for attempting "to hoodwink and deceive the people of Florida."[32] Denying they were engaged in a witch-hunt, the interrogators wondered why the NAACP refused to cooperate if it had nothing to hide. These sharp words did not shake Perry's resolve. Although she found the experience "harrowing," she refused to comply, in the belief that her constitutional rights were at stake.[33]

Gibson and the rest of his NAACP colleagues also refused to answer questions about suspected Communist members in their organization. Gibson conveyed his disdain most emphatically when, following the attack on Perry, he declined to testify, called the committee a "star chamber . . . disqualified . . . to sit as an objective fact-finding body," and dramatically walked out of the hearing room.[34] Joining Gibson in his beliefs was Reverend Edward T. Graham, a former officer of the Miami chapter, who maintained membership in the association as well as in the American Civil Liberties Union (ACLU). He and Gibson were the city's most prominent black ministers actively fighting for civil rights. Graham had tried unsuccessfully to obtain a court order blocking the hearings, and when forced to appear, he would not tell the committee whether he currently belonged to the NAACP. "I have the right to peaceably assemble and to lawfully work for my ideals," he declared to his inquisitors.[35]

Whereas Gibson, Graham, and their colleagues cited the First and Fourteenth amendments to justify their silence, the alleged Communists who were called to testify took the Fifth Amendment in addition to the other two constitutional provisions.[36] The difference was crucial, because the NAACP based its position on freedom of speech and association and not on the right to invoke the privilege against self-incrimination. However, this distinction was often lost on a public that during the 1950s had come to equate failure to testify before investigation committees with an implied admission of guilt. Mark Hawes reinforced this impression by asserting: "It is significant that the NAACP chose to resort to identical tactics used by the Communist Party to fight these hearings."[37] Collins did little to dispel this view. He refused to comment on how the committee was conducting its investigation under Johns, answering instead that the "public will hold them [sic] accountable and responsible for their actions."[38]

Actually it would be up to the courts rather than public opinion to determine the future of the so-called Johns Committee and the NAACP. After the panel obtained a decree from a state circuit judge ordering the defiant witnesses to testify under threat of a contempt citation, the case was appealed to the Florida Supreme Court. The legal questions involved the clash between a state legislative committee that sought to compel testimony as part of an official investigation and individuals who claimed the right to associate freely without fear of reprisal. When did the right to privacy of members of a group give way to the state's right to safeguard its internal security from the widely recognized menace of Communism? Though the NAACP engaged in political dissent in an open and lawful manner, could a southern state government that considered the civil rights cause obnoxious restrain the organization in a fashion that might be deemed permissible? In short, could state authorities wield the hammer of anti-Communism to club the NAACP into submission?

In answering these questions, the Florida judiciary had some recent precedents for guidance. Under the leadership of Chief Justice Earl Warren, the U.S. Supreme Court had ruled on the separate issues of legislative probes of Communism and the associational privacy of the NAACP. In a series of cases in 1956 and 1957, the high tribunal reined in HUAC to check it from misusing congressional investigatory power "to expose for the sake of exposure"; restricted a similar agency in New Hampshire from forcing a witness to testify because its statutory authorization was too vague and imprecise; and struck down a Pennsylvania antisedition law on the ground that it had been superseded by federal legislation.[39]

While limiting the scope of governmental activities in the area of loyalty and security, the Supreme Court also impeded Alabama from forcing the NAACP to disclose its membership rosters. The state had attempted to obtain NAACP records through its law requiring foreign corporations to register. Weighing the ability of the civil rights group to operate in a hostile climate if the names of its members were revealed against the state's concern for regulating outside enterprises, the unanimous Court declared that the state "has fallen short of showing a controlling justification for the deterrent effect on the free enjoyment of the right to associate which disclosure of the membership lists is likely to have."[40]

These pronouncements seemed to buttress the NAACP's position in Florida. Led by Robert Carter, the NAACP's general counsel, and Grattan Graves, Jr., the Miami attorney who was also a party to the suit, the civil rights plaintiffs petitioned the state supreme court to set aside the order against them. To coerce them to testify and produce membership records, their attorneys argued, violated their freedom of association protected by the First Amendment and incorporated into the due-process clause of the Fourteenth Amendment. They insisted that the FLIC had not satisfied the standard, established in the Alabama case, that permitted the state to interfere with their constitutionally protected rights only by proving its interest to be dominant and compelling. The committee had not met this standard, the NAACP claimed, because the statute creating it was loosely worded and its announced purpose of examining Communist penetration bore no reasonable relationship to the NAACP, which neither allowed Communist members nor sanctioned violence. The attorneys emphasized that the exposure of the names of the rank and file to public scrutiny would have a chilling effect on freedom of association in a state where NAACP members constituted "a weak and unpopular minority."[41]

The appellant witnesses reinforced their position with the Supreme Court's rulings on the scope of legislative inquiries and state antisubversion laws. Based on the HUAC case, *Watkins v. United States*, they contended that the FLIC had not shown "with unmistakable clarity the precise relationship between the questions propounded and the inquiry authorized." Without such specificity, the committee had embarked on a "fishing expedition," conducted a "mock trial," and treated such witnesses as Ruth Perry in a "highly prejudicial" way. Had communist infiltration, rather than public humiliation, been the real purpose of the hearing, the lawmakers would have focused on the association's demonstrated activities and not on the names of its members.[42] In addition, relying on *Pennsylvania v. Nelson*, the petitioners claimed that federal laws against subversion had preempted the field and blocked state lawmakers from investigating a subject on which they had no constitutional authority to legislate.[43]

The committee's counsel, Mark Hawes, denied that these decisions supported the NAACP's position in this instance. He contended that *Alabama* did not prohibit a state from compelling testimony and obtaining membership files so long as it proved a substantial need. Hawes claimed that Florida had shown ample reason for its attempt to discover "the degree to which . . . known Communists . . . have penetrated, infiltrated, and influenced the actions of the Miami Branch of the NAACP."[44]

The FLIC attorney flatly disputed that the issue involved race or attempts to avert desegregation. He asked the court whether or not a sovereign state could take measures to protect itself from the Communist menace. *Pennsylvania v. Nelson* did not keep Florida from conducting investigations on the subject because Article V of the U.S. Constitution empowered states to initiate proceedings to amend the governing document. Hawes suggested that Florida's legislature might use the information obtained from the hearings to overcome the effects of the *Nelson* decision through the prescribed constitutional revision. Furthermore, he dismissed the charge that the committee had conducted its inquiry irresponsibly or with prejudice by pointing out that it had also investigated white-supremacist groups. Having discounted any hint of bias, Hawes could not resist insinuating that the NAACP's "false accusations . . . [were] a typically Communist tactic of resistance to investigation."[45]

The Florida Supreme Court fundamentally agreed with Hawes's arguments. Speaking for a unanimous bench, on December 19, 1958, Justice Campbell Thornal reaffirmed that legislatures had the power to conduct investigations toward a valid objective but warned against "exercising it . . . sadistically . . . as a media to hunt witches." He concluded that the FLIC had acted properly and praised Johns for clearly informing witnesses about the subject of the inquiry, thus enabling them to determine the pertinency of the questions posed. With respect to the manner in which the committee allegedly mistreated the appellants, particularly Perry, Thornal asserted that confronted by "defiant and recalcitrant witnesses," the panel exhibited "a degree of patience and composure customarily demanded only of judicial officers."[46]

In reaching its opinion, the tribunal distinguished this case from recent Supreme Court opinions. Thornal denied that *Pennsylvania v. Nelson* prevented a state from coping "with purely internal problems," protecting the "welfare of its people," and acquiring information that might "set in motion the amending procedure" of the U.S. Constitution. In contrast to the situation in *Alabama*, Thornal found that Florida had sufficiently demonstrated a compelling reason to obtain the names of NAACP members, whereas the civil rights groups had failed to prove that the "identification of members would have a deterrent effect on freedom of association."[47]

Convinced that the committee had acted correctly and that the NAACP would suffer no stigma by cooperating with the agency, the state high court

issued a decree tailored to fashion a delicate balance between the competing interests of the litigants. In a masterful stroke of judicial decision making, Thornal held that the FLIC was entitled to secure the information it
demanded, though he granted the NAACP nominal protection of its privacy. He ordered the witnesses to answer the disputed questions about
Communists in the organization, "based upon . . . reference to available
membership lists." This procedure allowed the civil rights officials to keep
the records in their possession but forced them to reveal whether persons
named by the committee as Communists were on the lists. The court found
no evidence that merely by answering such questions would NAACP adherents suffer from guilt by association, "contrary to their own protestations
of absolute innocence."[48]

The NAACP appealed this decision to the U.S. Supreme Court, which on
June 22, 1959, refused to grant a review. Though the justices did not publish
their reasons, most likely they refrained from considering the case because it
had not yet reached a final judgment. They expected the petitioners to go back
before the committee, refuse to cooperate once again, and be held in contempt. At that stage of punishment, the high bench would probably hear the
case.[49] Whatever might happen in the future, the NAACP felt "very discouraged and frustrated." Ruth Perry lamented that the Johns Committee was "convinced now that the Supreme Court thinks we are all Red down here."[50]

Her concern proved well founded. Revived by the legislature in 1959,
the FLIC convened hearings in Tallahassee on November 4 and 5. Charley
Johns remained a member of the panel, and his successor as chair, Representative Cliff Herrell, proved no less willing to pursue Communists. Herrell
had clashed with Perry at the hearing the previous year, and he took pre-
cautionary measures to assure that the committee met its constitutional
obligations of fairness. He opened the inquiry by carefully reading a statement explaining the committee's desire to examine Communist penetration of organizations dealing with race relations and admonished against
drawing an inference that a subpoenaed witness was a likely Communist.[51]

Having established the basis for the pertinency of their forthcoming
questions and disavowed any feelings of bias, the legislators first summoned
several white Floridians they suspected of belonging to the Communist
party in the state. After listening to their refusal to answer any questions,
the panel called its chief investigator to the stand. R.J. Strickland informed
the group about what it presumably already knew: fourteen people, including the recalcitrant witnesses, were Communists who had attended NAACP
meetings in Miami. However, a subsequent witness, Arlington Sands, a self-
confessed former Communist who had once belonged the NAACP but

207

had not been active since the late 1940s, cast some doubt on Strickland's evidence. Although Sands had been a source for much of that information, he publicly disputed the investigator's claim that he had personally encountered most of the accused Communists at NAACP meetings.[52]

Only the NAACP officers could confirm whether the persons named by the committee belonged to the Miami branch. This they refused to do. The association's representatives had no objection to testifying whether they recalled seeing an individual, designated as a Communist, at NAACP meetings or whether they recognized such persons as members of the group. However, they declined to check their memories against the membership lists, which Gibson held exclusively in his possession. "If people who join our organization discover that we are going to disclose their identity in the organization," the Miami chapter president told the committee, "that is a sure way that our organization would be wrecked." Instead, Gibson willingly answered questions about individuals the committee identified as Communists, though he denied knowing any of them as NAACP members. Nor did any of the remaining branch officials recognize the suspected subversives. In addition, Reverend Edward Graham, who was not an NAACP official, refused to reply whether he was a member of the civil rights group for fear that it would jeopardize "his right to privacy."[53]

The NAACP witnesses had walked a thin line in their appearance before the FLIC. Their commitment to free speech and association did not prevent them from answering questions about individuals named as Communists. After all, their organization had taken a strong stand in purging Communists from its ranks. They complied with the judicial order to respond to the committee's questioning, but they refused to follow the court's decree to have membership rolls available for consultation. It was one thing to discuss possible members of the Communist party, an organization that they agreed was illegitimate, and another to expose their own lawful association to public inspection.[54]

The FLIC refused to accept the NAACP's reasoning and initiated contempt proceedings against Gibson, as official custodian of the files, and Graham, for declining to answer questions about his membership in the association. Despite a court order instructing them to testify on April 5, 1960, the two civil rights activists once again defied the committee. The following month, Circuit Judge W. May Walker of Leon County (Tallahassee) held a hearing on the violation of his decree. Though a parade of witnesses testified that membership in the NAACP had declined and its officials had been threatened since the beginning of the investigation committee hearings in 1957, the judge did not find the evidence believable and ruled against the defendants. Even if he had discovered the necessary "substantial risk of deterrent effect," Walker held that the interest of Florida in investigating Communist subversion was "so grave, pressing and compelling" as to override the rights of Gibson and Graham.[55] Ordered to appear before the committee on July 27, they refused to acquiesce in its demand for information. As a result, Walker found them in contempt and levied twelve-hundred-dollar fines and six-month prison sentences.[56]

Both appealed to the state supreme court. Gibson's counsel, Robert Carter, argued that his client saw no distinction between taking the membership list to the committee for reference and turning it over to the panel. As far as he was concerned the results would be the same: fear and intimidation of present and prospective NAACP members and supporters. Together with Graham's ACLU attorneys, Howard Dixon and Tobias Simon, Carter claimed that Florida had to do more than suggest that alleged communists were associated with the NAACP; rather, the state had to prove "that the activities of the organization are subversive or tend to be subversive."[57] This it had not done, except to charge that some Communists might have belonged to the Miami branch before 1950. The civil rights counselors also pointed out that the U.S. Supreme Court had recently overthrown an attempt by Little Rock, Arkansas, to force disclosure of NAACP membership rolls as an otherwise legitimate function of its municipal licensing and taxing authority. As in that case, they contended, governmental officials in Florida had failed to prove that their need for information outweighed the "demonstrated deterrent effects upon the witnesses."[58]

The opposing counsel applied a different standard to address the constitutional question. Mark Hawes asserted that to subordinate the rights of witnesses all the state had to do was "exhibit a legitimate . . . interest in the subject matter of the investigation" and ask questions that were pertinent to obtaining the desired information. In contrast to the circumstances in the Little Rock case, Hawes found a sufficient connection between the FLIC's inquiry into Communism and the agency's effort to identify specific NAACP members. Besides, he claimed that the witnesses had produced insufficient evidence to show the harm in testifying.[59]

On December 30 the state supreme court upheld the verdict for Gibson but not Graham. On behalf of a unanimous bench, Justice Thornal asserted that the custodian of the NAACP records had to consult them to authenticate his testimony. He declared that this procedure did not have a deterrent effect on "legitimate and good faith members of the NAACP" because their names would not be exposed to public disclosure. As for the alleged Communists, they were "not entitled to the same associational privacy." However, in a surprising opinion with respect to the question of Graham's membership in the NAACP, the justice could not discern the committee's dominant interest in obtaining a response. Thornal argued that the FLIC had not specifically linked Graham to any Communist affiliation, it could obtain the relevant information about subversive infiltration of the NAACP from Gibson, and its efforts could lead to reprisals against the witness for admitting that he belonged to an "organization perfectly legitimate but allegedly unpopular in the community."[60]

The tribunal's companion decisions complicated the situation for the NAACP. In reaching different outcomes, the state judges appeared to follow the kind of balancing process that the U.S. Supreme Court had sanctioned in weighing governmental power against the rights of individuals. In the face of adverse consequences, a person did not have to testify about membership in the NAACP, whereas an authorized NAACP official could not refuse if the state demonstrated an appropriate interest in the answer. To win a reversal for Gibson, his lawyers would have to show convincingly that the lower court's ruling did not adequately safeguard the constitutional rights of innocent NAACP members or the group as a whole. If they failed, other southern states, so far blocked in their attempts at exposure, would most likely succeed in eliciting the names of NAACP members under the guise of uncovering Communists. "The Gibson case," Roy Wilkins declared, "is of strategic importance to the survival of the civil rights movement in Florida and the entire southeast."[61]

The prospects of victory appeared mixed. From 1959 to 1961 the Supreme Court moved in opposite directions in cases involving southern efforts to hamstring the NAACP and governmental attempts to extend the scope of investigations into Communism. In the former area, the Court struck down an Arkansas statute that required public school teachers to file an annual list of all organizations they had belonged to during the past five years. The high bench ruled that although a state could inquire into the competence of its teachers, on this occasion its methods were too sweeping and infringed upon personal liberties. The Court reached a similar conclusion in voiding a Louisiana law calling for out-of-state associations to submit their membership rosters along with affidavits swearing that their officers were not Communists.[62] In contrast, the tribunal enlarged the range of legislative discretion in probing Communist affiliations and narrowed the options of witnesses who stood behind the shield of the First Amendment to keep from testifying. In three cases involving HUAC and one concerning an investigative panel in New Hampshire, the justices ruled that the government's interest in self preservation outweighed the individual's right in associational privacy.[63]

After the Court agreed to hear the Gibson case in the fall of 1961, NAACP attorneys had to convince the justices to reconcile the competing lines of precedent in favor of their civil rights cause. In light of recent decisions upholding HUAC's broad sway in questioning alleged Communists. Robert Carter and his associates dropped their previous argument that the Florida statute creating the FLIC was "unconstitutionally vague and inexplicit."[64] Instead they attempted to prove that the committee had failed to show a "nexus" between Communist activities and the NAACP. Without such a concrete demonstration, they argued, the interest of the state in obtaining information about subversion failed to justify the deterrence to Gibson's freedom of association resulting from compulsory disclosure.

On this basis, they distinguished Gibson's case from the HUAC rulings. Because Gibson himself was not accused of being a Communist and his organization did not have any relationship with Communist activities, the FLIC did not have sufficient reason to invade his right of privacy. Carter reviewed the NAACP's history of anti-Communism and pointed out that the committee's main informer, Arlington Sands, had failed to identify suspected Communists as NAACP members. Thus the committee lacked the requisite probable cause for believing that Gibson had any valid testimony to offer and could not compel him to respond. "Undoubtedly, a mere assertion that a subordinating interest exists or a mere statement that the committee has 'knowledge' that subversives are infiltrating the organization," Carter maintained, "does not constitute justification for intrusion" on personal liberties.[65]

Because there was no tangible evidence to connect Communism with the civil rights group, NAACP lawyers insisted that Gibson should not be forced to divulge the names of the organization's members even under the carefully drawn guidelines adopted by the Florida Supreme Court. Carter argued that it made no different whether the NAACP branch president handed over the entire membership list or merely checked it to confirm the identity of particular members. Under either circumstance subversion would be linked with the NAACP and aspersions would be cast on an innocent organization. By bringing into doubt the loyalty of the group, public disclosure would generate reprisals against current members and scare off prospects from joining.[66]

Naturally, Mark Hawes reached the opposite conclusion. He failed to comprehend how the "disclosure of membership of a person shown to be a member of the Communist Party would work . . . [a] deterrent effect upon loyal and patriotic members of the organization." Only acknowledged subversives would suffer, and they had no constitutional guarantee to remain anonymous. Besides, the FLIC counsel denied the claim that the committee had not sufficiently linked the NAACP with Communist activities. His brief pointed out that the committee's chief investigator had introduced evidence of Communist infiltration, and the civil rights group admitted in its 1950 resolution that Communist penetration was a serious problem. He assured the Court that the FLIC harbored no desire to expose the NAACP to reprisals and noted that the panel had been evenhanded in investigating white segregationists as well as civil rights groups.[67]

These contending arguments underscored the dilemma faced by the Court. This case fell between the pro-NAACP rulings on one hand and the anti-Communist decisions on the other. Because a majority of five justices had come to favor a broad interpretation of investigative power, the civil libertarians on the bench worried about the outcome here. One of Chief Justice Warren's law clerks admitted that the current case was weaker than those in Alabama and Arkansas because the Miami chapter president had not been coerced to turn over the entire membership rolls to the committee. Moreover, the NAACP's assertion of a right to protect its members was "somewhat feeble in view of the fact that . . . [Gibson] indicated he would willingly testify from his own memory as to" the identity of possible Communists. Most likely mirroring the chief justice's thinking, the aide believed nonetheless that the lower court's ruling should be reversed or every southern state would seize the opportunity to harass the NAACP under the banner of anti-Communism.[68]

However, the liberals initially did not have the votes. With Felix Frankfurter and John Marshall Harlan in the lead, the Court split five to four in support of the FLIC's position. On March 13, 1962, Harlan circulated to his brethren the draft of a majority opinion affirming the lower court decision. He argued that to pass constitutional muster a legislative committee, "in pursuit of an otherwise legitimate state or federal inquiry, must act responsibly and not irrationally." To obtain information from a witness, a committee did not have to prove "probable cause" in meeting the same high standards as it would in securing a search warrant under the Fourth Amendment. Accordingly, after examining the record, Harlan concluded that the FLIC acted reasonably. To hold differently, he declared, would mean granting preferential treatment to the NAACP and freeing Gibson from responding "to a legitimate official inquiry with the same degree of responsibility that is demanded of officials of other organizations."[69]

A stroke of fate saved Gibson. Frankfurter became seriously ill in April 1962, and his absence from participation in the deliberations held up final disposition. Without Frankfurter, the justices deadlocked at four apiece. The delay caused by his illness forced the Court to schedule the suit for reargument the following term. In the meantime, Frankfurter retired in August, and Arthur Goldberg took his seat.[70]

This personnel change produced a majority of five behind the NAACP. Speaking for his brethren on March 25, 1963, Goldberg asserted that before the legislative committee could infringe upon First Amendment rights it had to demonstrate a direct connection between the NAACP and subversive activities. He demanded a higher standard of proof than in previous cases involving accused Communists, because in this instance the NAACP was "a concededly legitimate and nonsubversive organization." Goldberg's review of the record found the evidence linking the NAACP and Communism "indirect, less than unequivocal, and mostly hearsay." Thus, the committee's demand for disclosure threatened the "constitutionally enshrined rights of free speech, expression, and association" of an unpopular but innocent group.[71]

Goldberg occupied the middle ground between the absolutist and minimalist approaches toward civil liberties. Representing the former, Hugo Black and William O. Douglas agreed with the result but issued separate concurring opinions. They insisted that the Bill of Rights protected individuals and groups in associating with non-Communists as well as Communists, and they denied that the principle of innocence by association, as enunciated by Goldberg, was any more constitutionally valid than was guilt by association. "One man's privacy," Douglas asserted, "may not be voided because of another's perversity."[72] In sharp contrast, Harlan delivered a dissenting opinion that criticized the majority for distinguishing between a government's power to investigate "Communist infiltration of organizations and Communist activity by organizations." Neither could he fathom the difference between Gibson's willingness to testify from memory and his refusal to verify his recollection by consulting the membership records. Nor could the justice understand how the Court, in searching for a nexus, could require "an investigating agency to prove in advance the very things it is trying to find out."[73]

The majority ruling conferred on so-called innocent organizations an associational right to privacy guaranteed by the Constitution. The NAACP may have been viewed by white southerners as on a par with Communism, but the Supreme Court disagreed. The majority of the justices apparently recognized, without explicitly stating so, that the FLIC probe was part of a larger program to discredit a respected civil rights group.[74] Though members of illegitimate Communist or Communist-infiltrated groups presumably did not share the constitutional protection afforded to those in lawful ones, the high tribunal's decision also made it more difficult for legislative committees to investigate them. The judiciary would continue to balance governmental and individual interests in each case; however, as a consequence of *Gibson*, associational privacy would be assigned a higher priority than investigative rights, "especially where prospects for legislation are slight and the political overtones are obvious."[75]

The *Gibson* decision effectively stifled Florida's legislative probe of the NAACP. A verdict unfavorable to Gibson would have signaled the go-ahead for the FLIC to resume its anti-civil rights efforts. As late as 1961, while the case was still pending, Charley Johns chaired hearings to search for Communist influence in the burgeoning racial protest across the state. The inquiry focused on the activities of the Southern Conference Education Fund, a group cited as a Communist front by HUAC, and the Johns Committee managed to link it to the NAACP in absentia.[76] The *Gibson* opinion brought an end to further committee efforts to investigate the NAACP, and public support for such attempts waned. The *Miami Herald* called Gibson's victory "just," and the *Miami News* agreed that it was "strongly in the American tradition."[77] Within two years, the legislature allowed its investigative agency to expire.

The impact of the FLIC on the NAACP cannot be measured precisely. Undoubtedly, the FLIC struggle and the uncertainty of its outcome took a toll on NAACP energies and finances; time and money spent challenging the committee could have been used elsewhere for the frontal assault on racial discrimination. Civil rights activists suffered reprisals and had to live constantly with the possibility of intimidation. As a result, membership in the organization temporarily declined, and the group found it difficult to sign up new recruits.[78] However, the NAACP outlasted its nemesis, and unlike its counterparts in Alabama and Louisiana, the association did not cease functioning in Florida while the judicial conflict dragged on. It continued to file lawsuits attacking segregated education and public facilities, and in 1960 its youth councils led successful sit-in demonstrations against Jim Crow lunch counters throughout the state. By that time the drop in membership had been reversed, and the association promoted the *Gibson* case to stimulate interest in its cause. Rather than breaking the NAACP, the FLIC battles bolstered the esprit de corps of civil rights advocates and, as Ruth Perry put it, generated a "new faith in the rightness of our cause."[79]

The NAACP survived for several reasons. The segregationists were not as solidly united in Florida as they were in other states of the region. Traditional southern racial values were voiced by rural and small-town lawmakers from north Florida, whose influence was inflated in a malapportioned legislature. Yet growing urbanization in the southern half of the state and the declining percentage of blacks in the population tended to lessen the intensity of racial obstructionism, without eliminating it.[80] As in neighboring states, Florida legislators enacted an interposition resolution and a pupil-assignment law to deter integration, but they failed to pass massive resistance bills that closed public schools and shut down the operation of the NAACP. Though racial moderates accepted the validity of the FLIC, they did so without enthusiasm and worried about Charley John's direction of the panel. They preferred to follow the lead of Governor LeRoy Collins and avoid extremist positions that might impede efforts to promote economic development of the Sunshine State. Still, the committee might have accomplished its mission against the NAACP if not for the outside intervention of the federal judiciary. Despite their differences, Florida's political leaders joined together in shaping the legal system to maintain segregation as long as possible and to diminish the NAACP's opposition. The state's highest tribunal sanctioned that effort, leaving only the U.S. Supreme Court to block it. The *Gibson* opinion assured that the investigative agency had no legitimate way of getting at the civil rights group.

Moreover, the NAACP withstood the constitutional barrage because it commanded the overwhelming allegiance of blacks in the state. While awaiting the final stamp of judicial approval, the association preserved its leadership of the civil rights movement in Florida. The NAACP had a tightly knit network of chapters, and officials such as Father Gibson won the admiration of black Floridians by keeping up the pressure for first-class citizenship on a variety of fronts and by refusing to be intimidated by state officials. Not only did they petition the courts to gain their rights, but they adapted their techniques to provide just enough militancy to satisfy the masses of blacks. Notwithstanding the presence in the state of more activist groups, such as the Congress of Racial Equality and the Southern Christian Leadership Conference, the NAACP retained its preeminence in the field.[81]

The triumph of the NAACP in *Gibson* guaranteed its freedom of association; however, it did not immediately dismantle the structure of discrimination that kept blacks separate and unequal. For all of its dangers, the FLIC was not the greatest obstacle to racial change in the Sunshine State. Its limitations stemmed in part from the ability of the NAACP to tie up the panel in court. The main hurdle to school desegregation, which had spawned the legislative counterattack in the first place, remained the "lawful" statutes on the books permitting the state to circumvent the Supreme Court's 1954 ruling. Until the high tribunal, backed by the legislative and executive power of the federal government, took appropriate action in the late 1960s, the legal roadblocks constructed by Florida to enforce segregation remained intact.

Still, the defeat of the FLIC meant that, as Justice Goldberg noted, constitutional freedoms "are protected not only against heavy-handed frontal attack, but also from being stifled by more subtle governmental interference."[82] Gibson's victory helped ensure that the NAACP would be around to press its unfinished business to a successful conclusion. In the end, its attorneys demonstrated that conservative rules of law could be shaped for progressive ends.

FROM SIT-IN TO RACE RIOT

Much of the literature concerning the civil rights movement and race relations in the South has concentrated on their explosive nature. Journalists and scholars alike have been fascinated with confrontation and crisis resolution. Montgomery, Little Rock, New Orleans, Greenwood, Birmingham, Saint Augustine, and Selma dot a civil rights road map as signposts of heroic struggles. The turbulent battles fought in such places generated enough publicity to shape a national consensus supporting passage of five civil rights acts in the decade and a half after *Brown v. the Board of Education*. Studies of race relations during this era also follow the headlines, particularly those that attracted national attention for a prolonged period. Often left unrecorded are the sagas of southern communities which labored to resolve racial conflicts calmly and out of the limelight. In such a fashion, they often hoped to cast an image as part of the progressive "New South."

In examining racial policy-making on the local level, attention has been focused on civic elites, particularly on businessmen who influenced the political process either formally through participation in public agencies or informally by virtue of the deference they commanded from elected officials. Social scientists have discovered that the character of controlling elites determined the quality of race relations in troubled southern cities. Influential whites, such as those in New Orleans and Saint Augustine during the 1960s, derived their social standing from old family backgrounds rather than from recently acquired wealth. Committed to a traditional ethic, they scorned the efforts to promote new economic growth, and they usually abstained from providing leadership to avert racial crises that might scare away potential outside investors in their city's financial development. In contrast, in Atlanta, Houston, and Miami, elites composed of nouveau riche and recent arrivals espoused a progressive ideology. Welcoming new industry and culture, they had a stake in thwarting racial turmoil that might damage prospects for their city's booming future. Hence, modernizing elites threw their considerable influence on the side of racial moderation.[1]

However, business leaders who chose to identify with the brand of the "New South" did not automatically become unrestrained advocates of racial egalitarianism. C. Vann Woodward, drawing upon his vast historical insight, in the early 1960s warned that a previous generation of "New South" promoters had fostered segregation and disfranchisement in the first place as a means of luring capitalists with a "contented and docile" labor supply. Subsequent empirical research has demonstrated that although modern apostles of the "New South" lent a hand in dismantling some of the discriminatory barriers erected by their predecessors during the Age of Redemption, they accepted "only enough moderation as [was] necessary to oppose extreme measures such as violence."[2] Furthermore, white elites chose conciliation, especially with respect to school desegregation, as a useful tool for implementing alterations in racial behavior patterns in the slow, orderly, and piecemeal manner. In this light, moderation can be seen as a strategy adopted by influential whites to maintain their social control over biracial community affairs.

Models of race relations must further take into account the role of black leadership. Without the rise and acceptance of direct-action protest to replace the old style of accommodation, the contemporary version of the "New South" would have departed little from its post–Civil War prototype. In southern municipalities two kinds of strategies helped blacks to achieve first-class citizenship. After demonstrators had dramatically challenged practices of segregation and discrimination, respected blacks, sympathetic with the protesters' demands and recognized as responsible spokesmen, steered a moderate course to resolve specific problems without violent conflict. Thus, the push for racial equality in the urban "New South" was initiated by militant protest and was subsequently moderated by the responses of white and black elites.[3] Tampa, Florida, a self-proclaimed "New South" city, provides fertile but unexplored ground for testing these generalizations about changes in race relations.

On February 29, 1960, the afternoon temperature in Tampa climbed to seventy-seven degrees under bright, sunny skies, highlighting the kind of winter day that delighted the Chamber of Commerce. The splendid weather, however, was slightly marred by a peaceful sit-in by blacks at Woolworth's lunch counter. Seven years later, on June 11, 1967, the thermometer soared to ninety-four degrees, ushering in another long, hot muggy summer. In the twilight hours when the day should have grown cooler, it turned unusually torrid and uncomfortable for Tampans as a riot erupted in the black ghetto. Different in many respects, these two events produced a consistent response: the exercise of moderation to remedy racial ills. From 1960 through 1967, community leaders prescribed cooperation and the soothing power of rational persuasion to check extremism and end discrimination. The cure did not heal all the wounds inflicted by racism, but the treatment allowed Tampa in 1967 to reduce the fever of civil disorder.

Straddled upon the banks of the meandering Hillsborough River and tucked against a bay whose waters empty into the Gulf of Mexico on Florida's west coast, Tampa in 1960 was in the midst of an economic boom reminiscent of that of the 1920s. Since 1950, the population of the city had doubled to approximately 275,000 residents, 47,000 of whom were black; over four hundred companies had moved into the area adding $25 million to annual payrolls; and along with its sister cities across the bay, Saint Petersburg and Clearwater, Tampa had risen in the ratings as a national sales market. Presiding over this economic advance was a new breed of businessmen— bankers, industrialists, and merchants—many of whom had migrated to the Suncoast after World War II. "Ten years ago," the Tampa *Tribune* recalled in 1960, "Tampa was just a cigar factory with a port. Today we have all sorts of new industry—and the town has woken up." A Chamber of Commerce official gloated that the city's growth had "reached snowball dimensions—we wouldn't stop it if we wanted to." Prospects for the future appeared bright. Plans for renovation of the downtown section, urban renewal, construction of a state university campus, and extension of two interstate highways through the city tickled a newspaper reporter who gleefully noted that the "Associated Press won't even have to tack 'Fla.' onto Tampa in the datelines of dispatches. People all over the United States will know Tampa is in Florida."[4]

There were other changes on the horizon in 1960. Although Tampa followed the color line faithfully in maintaining Jim Crow, preparations were being made within the segment of its population that was 17 percent black to assault the walls of segregation. In the vanguard were officials of black fraternal and labor associations, the NAACP, and the Young Adults for Progressive Action, a nonpartisan organization composed mainly of black teachers and professionals. Most of them were under forty years old and had received degrees from southern black colleges; some had served in the armed forces during World War II or the Korean War; nearly all had spent time outside of the South; and a majority were either self-employed, worked for a black-owned enterprise, or taught in the school system. The Florida field director for the NAACP, one of its principal attorneys in the "Sunshine State," and the president of the State's Conference of Branches all lived in Tampa, a circumstance guaranteeing that civil rights' concerns would be voiced. Part of the black bourgeoisie, they considered racial separation in or exclusion from public accommodations as an affront to their dignity and a deprivation of their rights as tax-paying citizens. "Segregation has proved itself a badge of inferiority," the *Florida Sentinel-Bulletin*, a black, biweekly newspaper, protested.[5] Furthermore, Negro leaders stressed that full equality depended upon obtaining jobs previously denied on the basis of race.

As with their white counterparts, black leaders welcomed the economic changes coming to Tampa and used them as the basis of arguments for breaking down racial barriers. C. Blythe Andrews, Sr., publisher of the *Florida Sentinel-Bulletin*, endorsed the trend toward industrialization as a "noble idea." However, his support was conditioned on the premise that blacks be given equal opportunity to obtain skilled jobs. "When the Negro is paid more in wages," Andrews asserted in the language that businessmen best understood, "the cash registers of the merchants . . . 'will run hot.'" Blacks also pointed out that while increased employment opportunities improved profits, racial discrimination reduced them. In the early sixties, the president of the local NAACP chapter reminded white civic leaders who looked forward to the expansion of Tampa's tourist trade "that millions of dollars are being lost . . . because organizations are refusing to meet in cities where racial segregation practices limit the use of facilities to Negroes."[6]

To facilitate contacts between black and white elites, in the fall of 1959 Mayor Julian Lane had created a twelve-member interracial advisory committee. At the time, the NAACP had pending in the courts a school desegregation suit against Hillsborough County, and it was preparing litigation to challenge the policy of barring Negroes from visiting Tampa's main recreational attraction. Lane created the committee to encourage racial conciliation and to foster a peaceful environment that would boost civic plans for conversion of the "Cigar City" into a major economic and cultural center in the New South. The six black appointees included respected business, labor, and religious leaders, as well as the president of the Florida NAACP, Rev. A. Leon Lowry. Among the six recruited from the white community were several businessmen, a minister, and one of Tampa's most prominent attorneys, Cody Fowler, who served as chairman. Fowler had been president of the American Bar Association in the early fifties, had provided legal counsel for the Tampa Chamber of Commerce, and was head of a rapidly growing savings and loan association.[7] Convinced that Florida could not avoid integration for very long, he wanted the committee to pave the way for changes to occur slowly and bloodlessly, controlled by common sense instead of emotionalism. Several of the white and Negro members had already cooperated on another venture, the construction of Progress Village for black homeowners displaced by urban renewal. "When men of good will sit down together to attack a common problem," the *Tampa Times* correctly summed up the attitude of all the committeemen, "the likelihood of an acceptable solution being reached is greatly enhanced."[8]

The white committeemen defined their primary mission as encouraging equal opportunity rather than imposing racial integration. "We must give to the Negroes," Cody Fowler remarked, "the rights to which they are entitled . . . the elimination of the practices which make them feel inferior." However, Fowler also noted that "Negroes [are] Negroes and will remain Negroes, and that whites are whites and will remain whites. They must be made to realize that the whites have a right to choose their own friends and those with whom they wish to associate. They must develop their own society, just as . . . other races have done." Nevertheless, white moderates recognized that degrading Jim Crow conditions would not long survive militant black challenges; thus they sought to minimize the possibilities of violence and repression. After all, the pragmatic Fowler pointed out, "the white population must realize . . . that . . . [millions of] Negroes cannot be kept under police surveillance."[9]

The views of the black members complemented those of their white colleagues. Although strongly endorsing integration, Negro leaders preferred to achieve it without inflaming racial passions. Holding these beliefs, Blythe Andrews, Sr., denounced the policy of segregation that "makes possible a dual system of inferior schools; encourages the provision of inadequate and often filthy eating places for Negroes . . . breeds slum housing . . . encourages inequalities of facilities in the areas of parks, swimming pools, and recreation centers." At the same time Andrews cautioned that while "we are grasping for our legal rights and better job opportunities, it is well and vitally important that we tarry long enough to teach our people that if we wish to be accepted as first class citizens, we must first act like first class citizens."[10] Whatever yardstick was used to measure racial advancement, both blacks and whites on the committee agreed that progress should come on a step-by-step basis without arousing bitter animosities.

Demonstrations to integrate Tampa's department store lunch counters furnished a major test of the committee's ability to defuse potentially explosive racial conflicts. Inspired by sit-in protests in Greensboro, North Carolina, in early February, 1960, Clarence Fort, a twenty-year-old barber and president of the NAACP Youth Council, made arrangements to bring similar activities to Tampa. He questioned why blacks were refused service at a lunch counter, but were invited to purchase items in the rest of the store. Intending to demonstrate against this injustice, young Fort planned with older NAACP officials to conduct a direct-action drive. Well briefed by Robert Saunders, the association's state field director, and accompanied by Lowry, on February 29, Fort and about fifty black high school students tried twice to integrate the lunch counter at Woolworth's downtown store. Denied service in each instance, the protesters quietly sat on the counter stools for nearly two hours until closing time when they departed.[11]

The next day, racial tempers flared briefly. Approximately one hundred black youths, not associated with the NAACP, marched for two hours through the downtown area, where they were refused service at nine stores. At one location, the Greyhound bus terminal restaurant, a well publicized fracas erupted between a black protester and an unsympathetic white customer. In addition, newspapers disclosed that the apparent leader of the second day's efforts had a lengthy juvenile police record. Upset by the unfavorable publicity, the NAACP quickly repudiated the "rebels" and moved to reassert its control. The following afternoon on March 2, Clarence Fort returned with approximately eighty Negroes wearing identification tags with the inscription "I am an American, Youth Council, NAACP" and staged an orderly but unsuccessful half-hour sit-in at the Woolworth and Kress stores.[12]

Neither white nor black opinion-shapers wanted a violent confrontation. The *Tribune* warned that "demonstrations of this kind rub against the thinly covered nerves of racial feeling, as a wind-tossed tree branch scrapes against a high tension wire," and while the editors of the *Florida Sentinel-Bulletin* cheered the young people on, they also cautioned their elders "to restrain and police the rowdy of our race and demonstrate that we can handle an ugly situation—without violence."[13] Significantly, the police were not called upon to evict the demonstrators, and the only arrests, resulting from the incident at the Greyhound station, involved a black and a white. Throughout the three days, law enforcement officials were conspicuously evident on the scene and preserved order in an evenhanded manner.[14] After unknown assailants fired several shots into the Lowry's home in the early morning hours of March 13, the *Tribune* pleaded: "If Florida is to preserve good race relations, if it is to continue to enjoy peace and prosperity . . . then people in the middle must make their influence felt."[15]

In the meantime, the Biracial Committee prepared to mediate the dispute. The day after the attack on his home, Lowry invited representatives of the Merchants Association "to discuss intelligently and sensibly the present situation." In extending this request, Lowry also alerted the merchants that what "has been custom must now be changed, if you expect Negroes to continue to patronize your establishments."[16] Aware that a black boycott was a possibility, store managers also worried about losing white customers if they integrated their lunch counters. Nevertheless, under pressure from the mayor and the Biracial Committee to work out an agreement, the Merchants Association, led by its executive vice-president Colby Armstrong, promised to participate in conferences to study how other cities approached the problem and to present recommendations. As a gesture of good faith, the NAACP declared a moratorium on sit-ins in order "to give the bi-racial committee a chance to solve racial problems in Tampa."[17]

Negotiations took place on both the municipal and state levels. Near the end of March, Governor LeRoy Collins lived up to his reputation as a racial moderate by appointing a state biracial committee to settle the lunch counter issue fairly and harmoniously. Two of the six men selected came from Tampa and also sat on the city's biracial advisory board: Cody Fowler and Perry Harvey, Sr., president of the black longshoremen's union local. Throughout the spring and summer, the statewide commission chaired by Fowler met privately with Florida businessmen, urging them to adopt a new racial posture or suffer the consequences that prolonged resistance would bring. In typically cool-headed fashion, the Tampa attorney admonished that an "objective look at Little Rock will show us that such policies mean economic deterioration of a very substantial kind. It is our belief that thoughtful people do not want such a damaging effect on Florida's bright future."[18]

Fowler also delivered this message to Tampa. After several months of unpublicized sessions, the mayor's committee and the Merchants Association hatched a plan to desegregate lunch counters. The chain-store operators apparently had received word from their national headquarters to reach any accord acceptable to the local community. They listened carefully to reports that cities in Texas and North Carolina had integrated lunch counters without a loss in white trade. Convinced that the same pattern could prevail in Tampa, the merchants agreed to serve pairs of carefully selected black young adults on a prearranged date without prior public notice. By acting uniformly to drop the eating restrictions, the managers prepared to lessen the chance that any one of their stores would be singled out for reprisals by angry whites. They instructed waitresses to treat Negroes courteously, and those who balked were given the day off. The committee tried to reduce the possibility of racial tension even further by scheduling black couples to patronize the stores when few white diners would be present. In addition, Negro committeemen advised black participants to conform to norms of proper middle-class behavior. Calling for an exertion of internal discipline, Blythe Andrews admonished that as "a race, we must show ourselves worthy of integrated service at the lunch counters."[19] Finally, on September 14, pairs of decorous Negroes were served at eighteen establishments without fanfare according to the carefully developed plan.[20]

Civic and business leaders interpreted this episode as a victory for moderation. Compared with Jacksonville, which had refused to form a biracial committee and had recently suffered through bloody clashes, Tampa voluntarily had talked over its difficulties until a calm settlement was reached between the races. "As long as men of reason and good will can sit down together," the *Tribune* boasted, "there is no racial problem which can't be diffused before it bursts into violence." Lowry commended businessmen "for their sensible attitude and realistic approach to problems." In this case, arbitration had succeeded because the position of stores in accepting blacks as shoppers but not as diners made little economic or moral sense. "A few years hence," the *Tribune* predicted correctly, "many citizens will look back at the yellowing headlines and wonder what the fuss was all about."[21]

Over the next six and one-half years the Biracial Committee implemented the "Tampa Technique," and segregation gradually disappeared while equal opportunity increased slightly with relatively little strife. The city quietly abandoned segregation in public buildings and facilities such as beaches, parks, and swimming pools. Although racial barriers fell at movie theaters, most hotels, and the annual Gasparilla Day Parade, most restaurants and bowling alleys did not open their doors to blacks until the passage of the 1964 Civil Rights Act. Even after the enactment of this landmark statute, hospitals continued to admit patients only on a segregated basis. When NAACP officials complained to Washington, the Biracial Committee intervened and persuaded the hospitals to operate in a nondiscriminatory fashion. At the same time, Tampa also phased out the existence of Clara Frye Hospital, a decrepit and neglected public institution for blacks.[22] Meanwhile the committee broke new ground along the employment front. In 1963 it had joined the Merchants Association, the Young Adults for Progressive Action, the Urban League, and the NAACP in setting up a retail training program involving eighteen department stores. Threatened boycotts and sporadic picketing marked some of these accomplishments, but in general black activists agreed to curtail their demonstrations and accept mediation. This happened largely because some of those associated with the protest groups sat as committee members alongside business and civic leaders whom they trusted.[23]

The Merchants Association's workshop provided a typical example of decision making involving blacks, businessmen, and white civic leaders. In late October, 1962, the Young Adults for Progressive Action (YAPA) informed Colby Armstrong of its intention to institute "selective buying practices" against retail stores that followed "outdated traditions in not employing Negroes in other than menial positions." Led by James Hammond, an electrical contractor and civil rights activist instrumental in bringing about the integration of Tampa's municipal beach, the YAPA already had used the boycott as a weapon for obtaining job opportunities. Throughout the first eight months of 1961, members of the group had picketed a downtown grocery store heavily patronized by blacks "until Negroes are hired in all capacities." Halted by a court injunction in September, the boycott cost the grocery approximately $125,000. In the fall of 1962, when Hammond contacted the Merchants Association, he couched his demands in conciliatory language. Thus, he wrote Armstrong that the YAPA hoped to settle the issue through "peaceful negotiation" and keep the "city free from racial tension."[24]

With the Christmas shopping season approaching, Armstrong sought to avert the threatened boycott. He assured Hammond that the merchants desired an "amicable settlement," and the YAPA leader agreed to postpone the demonstration. At the time, Hammond served with Armstrong on the Biracial Committee; reflecting the philosophy of that group he had "no particular desire to disrupt the community, if our demands for employment can be met in a less spectacular fashion." In response to Hammond's olive branch offering, the Merchants Association created an Equal Job Opportunities Committee. For the first six months of 1963, Armstrong and representatives of Tampa's largest chain department stores conferred with Hammond, officials of the Urban League and the NAACP, and Perry Harvey, Sr., of the Biracial Committee. In April, twelve firms agreed to start interviewing black applicants and set September 9 as a target date for hiring at least one Negro at each store. Armstrong had cautioned that the process would be slow: "[We] at the present time are not interested in having one hundred or two hundred Negro persons apply for jobs at the same time, because certainly they are not all going to be hired. There is not going to be any great influx of colored employees." Furthermore, the Merchants Association insisted on giving the plan little publicity, because it did not want "to arouse extremists."[25] The merchants did not have to worry about being stampeded by black applicants, because not enough Negroes were recruited who could pass the standardized written tests given to prospective employees by the retailers

Determined to fulfill its commitment to meet the September deadline, the Merchants Association decided to set up job-training workshops on a carefully monitored basis. To this end, the Equal Job Opportunities Committee instructed the Urban League to place in the *Florida Sentinel-Bulletin* an advertisement requesting applications for a variety of white-color positions. After the announcement appeared on June 22, some 125 blacks responded promptly. From this group, 30 were selected to take a four-week course in "Basic Retail Salesmanship" scheduled to begin on July 16. In addition, 18 stores agreed to hire some of the black participants who successfully completed the training.[26]

In the meantime, racial confrontation in the city nearly halted the initiation of the program. On June 20, the NAACP Youth Council organized a march in front of two of the largest downtown movie theaters, protesting their policy of excluding blacks. Chanting freedom songs and carrying placards with such slogans as MY BROTHER DIED IN KOREA–SO AMERICA COULD BE FREE, fifty black and white youths of high school and college age spent four hours picketing under the hot afternoon sun. The demonstrators apparently chose to march because they believed that the Biracial Committee was moving too slowly in eliminating segregation. In its customary manner, the committee had been negotiating quietly and behind the scenes with the theater operators. However, it did not keep the NAACP informed of the progress of the deliberations, and the youth leaders were dissatisfied. Thus, the decision to take to the streets was designed as a protest against the biracial establishment as well as the cinemas.[27]

The demonstration, although conducted peacefully, upset civic leaders. Aware of the increasing level of racial confrontation in other parts of Florida and throughout the South, Mayor Lane called the NAACP's action "a mistake" that could "inflame more trouble." Lowry, whose influence within the NAACP was declining as his participation in the Biracial Committee grew, asserted that he was "very disappointed," preferring "to see integration of Tampa business facilities done . . . through negotiations rather than demonstrations." After meeting with Mayor Lane, Cody Fowler, and the Biracial Committee on June 21, the NAACP Youth Council leaders and their adult advisors consented to cease picketing in order to give city officials "sufficient time to adjust certain problems in employment and entertainment."[28] In the midst of delicate discussions over the job program, Colby Armstrong warned Jim Hammond "that if the type of trouble over the theatres . . . starts up again, I am certain you will not receive the full cooperation that we want to give."[29] With calm ensured, the Merchants Association soon began its workshop, and shortly after, the Biracial Committee persuaded the movie houses to admit blacks.

Throughout these difficulties, progressive business leaders supported moderation to avoid bloody clashes that might attract unfavorable national attention and bring intervention by the federal government. They considered the Biracial Committee an excellent instrument for regulating the pace of desegregation in a systematic manner and for retaining control of racial policy in the hands of Tampans. Thus, the Chamber of Commerce "appreciated the fine work" of the mayor's advisory board, while at the same time it went on record in opposition to federal civil rights legislation.[30]

After passage of the national Civil Rights Act of 1964, Tampa officials established a new agency to improve the mechanism for resolving conflicts locally. In order to develop a "planned progressive program of nondiscrimination and equal opportunity for all [that] will give to this community an environment of good race relations and an area where industry and business growth will have an opportunity to move forward," Tampa created a Commission of Community Relations (CCR). The Biracial Committee had functioned without statutory authority as an informal, part-time group; in November, 1964, the city officially established the CCR with a full-time administrator, James A. Hammond. Leader of the Young Adults for Progressive Action and once arrested for participating in a civil rights demonstration at a drive-in movie theater, the thirty-five-year-old electrical contractor was a shrewd choice. Respected by blacks for his activism, he had also impressed whites by his willingness to discuss volatile issues around the bargaining table. "We would rather see Hammond stepping on a toe here and there," the *Sentinel-Bulletin* commented, "than to see him . . . launching demonstrations and boycotts . . . [that] do damage to the good name of Tampa which has enjoyed . . . the best race relations in the South."[31] Under his tenure, the CCR labored as a complaint bureau and as an initiator of innovative programs in compensatory preschool education and job training.

The creation of the CCR and the selection of Hammond to lead it heightened black aspirations of achieving economic and civil equality quickly. When the gap between expectation and reality continued to remain large, some civil rights leaders blamed the CCR. The NAACP applauded lunch counter and "twenty dollar a day hotel" desegregation, but charged that racial discrimination could "still be rigidly enforced through use of economic sanction." Guided by Robert Gilder, an outspoken black business executive, in 1965 the NAACP lambasted local government officials for perpetuating racial bias in public housing, municipal hospitals, and civil service employment, while spending "large sums of money on . . . a Commission . . . which . . . serves as a window dressing to give the City the appearance of having done a good job in the area of race relations." Unhappy with this situation, Gilder and the NAACP occasionally petitioned federal agencies to investigate the operation of Tampa's public facilities for violations of civil rights statutes. Nevertheless, despite such strident criticism by the NAACP, it usually chose to cooperate with Hammond and to give the CCR a chance to settle issues voluntarily and tranquilly at the local level before appealing to Washington or resorting to direct-action demonstrations. "Tampa enjoys wholesome race relations," the *Sentinel-Bulletin* proclaimed, stating the opinion of biracial leaders in mid-1966. "The lines of communication are kept open, and any problem can be solved without fanfare within a reasonable time."[32]

By 1967, biracial cooperation and vigilance on the part of the NAACP had achieved many of the goals of the civil rights movement without "angry polarization," but beneath the tranquil surface lay embers of discontent ready for a spark to ignite them. Segregation was officially dead, but discrimination persisted in subtle and powerful forms. With respect to municipal employment, civil service examinations obstructed blacks from obtaining all but the most menial jobs; and, those who did get hired often found that they were passed over for promotion by less experienced whites.[33]

Conditions were only slightly better in the private sector. Many firms paid lip service to the goal of hiring black employees, but maintained that they could not find enough Negroes who could pass the educational requirements for employment. Most businessmen did little more than call upon the public schools to upgrade their standards to satisfy the manpower needs of free enterprise. However, a shortage of skilled labor was not the sole barrier blocking advancement. Even when adult blacks had "a marketable skill and job openings are available," Jim Hammond insisted, "the person meets 'employer resistance,' and therefore does not get the job." The CCR administrator acknowledged that unskilled Negro labor posed a serious handicap, but he emphasized "on-the-job training and getting employers to cooperate in hiring these persons . . . rather than on testing of educational background." The Merchants Association, which had done more than any other business group along lines sketched by Hammond, nevertheless admitted: "Our resulting efforts are pathetic."[34]

On another front, most adult blacks were registered to vote; yet, there were no elected black officials and only a handful of Negroes received government posts. Much of the difficulty stemmed from the use of multimember districts and at-large electoral procedures. A small fraction of Tampa's voters, blacks found it impossible to gain enough white backing outside of their residential districts to win political races. Black electors sometimes swung the outcome of close political contests, but more frequently they failed to take advantage of the potential strength indicated by their high registration figures. The problem of voter apathy was a complex one, and in Tampa a contributing factor was the absence of an effective, independent, political organization to educate and mobilize Negroes. Aware of this deficiency, the *Sentinel-Bulletin* repeatedly urged blacks to participate at the polls in order to achieve first-class citizenship. "We should walk proudly," the newspaper cajoled, "much like dedicated soldiers . . . and cast our ballot for our total freedom."[35]

229

In the area of education, moderates deliberately slowed down the rate of desegregation without violating the letter of the law. In 1960, faced with litigation by the NAACP, Hillsborough County School Superintendent J. Crockett Farnell had informed civic leaders of their choices: "token integration, mass integration, or the closing of the public schools." The first option was the favored one and became official policy in 1962 after a federal district judge ordered desegregation on a grade-a-year basis starting with the elementary schools. The *Tribune*, reflecting the attitude of influential Tampans, did not interpret the court's decision as ushering in a "social revolution" and cautioned against adopting massive resistance.[36] Hence, school officials with the support of business, civic, and religious leaders permitted Negroes to attend institutions with white pupils who lived inside the same attendance zone. Educational policy-makers did not panic, because they realized that residential segregation patterns would severely limit the scope of integration within the framework of the neighborhood school concept. The Tampa *Times* in 1962 correctly predicted that Hillsborough County would "be able to pick its way along a difficult path and achieve the goal of racial accord."[37] Thus by 1967, the moderate course had succeeded both in preserving peace and in confining integration to less than one-half the system's schools.

Inadequate low-cost housing, a shortage of recreational facilities, the poor quality of police protection, and discrimination by white merchants in the ghetto completed the list of grievances. These complaints had reached alarming proportions by the end of 1966. Addressing local businessmen, the *Sentinel-Bulletin* noted that recent riots in the North "were really consumer revolts by the poor against exploitation in the marketplace in their neighborhoods." The newspaper warned white retailers to take corrective measures or face the consequences brought by "the winds of trouble and destruction."

Already feeling the heat from the simmering racial cauldron, a prominent black attorney admonished the CCR that Tampa stood "on the threshold of the same riots that took place in Cleveland, Atlanta, and other cities."[38]

In the meantime, these danger signals did not go unnoticed by the CCR. In August, 1966, Hammond reported the "need for establishing necessary rapport and lines of communication with the youth element in our community."[39] Following up this suggestion, the administrator began visiting poolrooms and bars to hear directly the grievances of the most economically impoverished blacks. In the fall of 1966, as racial tensions mounted in West Tampa, the CCR staff subdued passions by persuading white merchants to hire blacks for other than servile duties. The biracial group also convinced General Telephone Company to institute an affirmative action project to train and hire fifty-seven blacks for a variety of occupations. With the beginning of the new year, Hammond endeavored to win approval for expanding the CCR's personnel to include an industrial advisor, a job developer, and a vocational consultant. Endorsing this proposal, Cody Fowler remarked that the amount of money sought "is not so high when you consider what the cost of trouble here would be."[40] The city agreed to the request.

Despite these well-intended efforts, on Sunday, June 11, 1967, a major riot exploded in the black section adjacent to the downtown business district. Triggered by a white policeman's fatal shooting of an unarmed black robbery suspect, the disorder followed recent incidents involving charges of police brutality. Rioting first broke out in an area where over half of the families had an income under $3,000; the unemployment rate for black males was 10 percent, a figure double that for whites; 60 percent of the housing units were deteriorating or were dilapidated; and the median number of school years completed was 7.7.[41]

The civil rights struggles in Tampa, as elsewhere, had the paradoxical effect of both raising black expectations of full equality and intensifying the sense of disillusionment and despair. While official obstacles to integration crumbled, the races nevertheless remained segregated and unequal. Five months before racial violence erupted, the usually optimistic *Sentinel-Bulletin* grumbled: "Integration means nothing to the Negro if he is cast into the 'mainstream' without a job; into 'community affairs' if his family is starving in a rundown neighborhood. The word 'integration' has definite political and Jim Crow overtones to the Negro when already stiff qualifications are purposely set upward to deprive [him of] a job."[42] The violence in the ghetto was a form of spontaneous protest that publicized complaints neglected within conventional political channels. Moreover, it suggested that a shift was taking place away from the traditional civil rights goal of equal access and toward demands for a redistribution of economic and political power. For many black Tampans the legal victories of the 1960s did not convert into sufficient economic rewards. According to a report presented to the Biracial Committee less than a year before the riot, the "gains . . . are middle class advantages, the average Negro still remains untrained, unemployed, and unthought of." The *Sentinel-Bulletin*, which had scarcely missed an opportunity to praise Tampa's biracialism, admitted after the riot: "We have tended to support flowery talk about things getting better for a few."[43]

231

Nevertheless, in coping with the civil disruption, Tampa relied heavily on the channels of interracial communication built up over the years. Through four nights of burning, looting, and rock tossing, influential blacks and whites cooperated to restore order. The CCR dispatched Jim Hammond and his staff into the riot zone, where they joined popular community leaders to try to "keep the cool." It took several days to overcome the hostility of angry young rioters who voiced suspicion of the "cats who get respect downtown but not with their own people." Finally on Wednesday morning, after round-the-clock meetings, Hammond and other peacemakers convinced law enforcement authorities to withdraw their troops and allow black youth squads to patrol the strife-ridden neighborhoods. Assembled into paramilitary units, wearing white helmets, and accompanied by adult Negro advisors, young blacks, including a few who had previously participated in the rioting, labored successfully to contain additional violence. They were particularly helpful in pacifying blacks outraged by an official exoneration of the policeman whose fatal shot originally had sparked the disturbance. By Thursday, June 15, as a result of tireless negotiations and alert vigilance on the part of the CCR staff, government officials, the "white hat" youths, and black civic leaders, the riot had ended.[44]

The costs of the riot were considerable. Although no one was killed, sixteen people received injuries. Estimated economic losses ranged in amount from $100,000 to over $1,000,000, and the city spent about $75,000 in overtime pay for police and firemen in addition to the money required to process and prosecute the 111 individuals arrested during the disturbances. Furthermore, the upheaval wounded the pride of smug city fathers who thought race relations were so good that "it couldn't happen here."[45] Colby Armstrong reminded them: "Local business is most affected by local civil unrest and the terrible cost of wasted human resources. We are soberly reflecting upon the unpleasant national publicity of June 1967, recognizing belatedly that it CAN happen in our city also."[46]

Before the smoke cleared, soul-searching had begun. While acknowledging that the riots had hurt the city's economy and record of racial harmony, Tampans searched for ways of relieving sources of black indignation. "Both in fairness and self protection," the *Tribune* argued, "the community must strive to correct conditions which create justifiable resentment and give incendiaries a handy torch."[47] To work as trouble-shooters at the grassroots level, the city hired five of the "white hats." In addition, money poured into the ghetto for recreational activities. The CCR and the Merchants Association organized another series of employment workshops and managed to line up some four hundred jobs for those who participated. At the same time, General Telephone Company invested three thousand dollars in a second job-training course. By the end of the year, the CCR, the Merchants Association, and the Chamber of Commerce had obtained a sixty-thousand-dollar matching grant from the William Donner Foundation to create a Young Adult Council. According to this plan, groups of fifty youths would be given an accelerated academic education along with on-the-job training for three months. Exhorting businessmen to raise their share of the funds, the president of the Chamber of Commerce justified the contribution on the basis of "hard cold business facts."[48] The CCR was also designing a similar project to cover civil service jobs.

In shaping their responses, Tampa's businessmen encouraged local initiative and voluntarism. The Merchants Association and Chamber of Commerce pointed out "the fallacy of dependency upon the state and national revenue as the panacea of all our community ills." The Donner Foundation conceived its grant as an "excellent opportunity to mount a program under private and local control contrasted with Washingtonian bureaucracy." However, businessmen lacked the dedication necessary to sustain an intensive drive to remove the vestiges of employment discrimination. Rhetoric outdistanced commitment, and Tampa business leaders soon retreated from implementing their lofty pledges uttered in the wake of the disorders. After an initial flurry of financial contributions to match the Donner Foundation grant, donations trickled off and never reached more than one-third of the expected amount. By the end of the decade, the experiment was scrapped.[49]

Nevertheless, Tampa maintained a favorable image and salvaged a victory from a disastrous uprising. In November, 1967, the city gained national recognition for its work in race relations in general and curbing the riots in particular, when the CCR and Biracial Committee won a public service award of one thousand dollars bestowed annually by the Lane Bryant Corporation in New York City. In accepting the prize, Leon Lowry, chairman of CCR, emphasized the key principles behind seven years of biracialism in Tampa: "To keep our city moving forward in wholesome racial relations is our objective. To keep violence and rioting away from our city is our sworn duty." Such policies, the *Tribune* commented enthusiastically, paid "high dividends in our community."[50]

From sit-in to race riot, Tampa's civic and business elites endorsed racial moderation. They preferred rational persuasion, voluntarism, and gradualism, instead of coercion, repression, and confrontation. A progressive Biracial Committee was certain that customs were about to change and sought to encourage an orderly and peaceful transition. Cooperation came from merchants and businessmen who calculated that ugly racial incidents did not make good dollars and cents. Little Rock, Birmingham, Jacksonville, and Saint Augustine offered vivid lessons for Chamber of Commerce and Merchants Association officials. "What new industry," the *Tribune* wondered in the early sixties, "would decide to go into a city which seethes with murderous racial conflict?"[51] Furthermore, the successful performance of the "Tampa Technique" owed much to the nature of black leadership, which blended militancy with restraint. Civil rights forces occasionally took to the streets and appealed to the federal government to redress grievances, but they usually chose to settle disputes locally around the conference table or quietly in the courts. This process did not benefit everybody, as it barely touched the lives of blacks trapped inside the poverty of slums after a century of educational and economic deprivation. Although from 1960 through 1967, the civil rights movement stormed the legal barricades of segregation, it had only begun to attack the unofficial remnants of racism still embedded in economic, social, and political institutions. As one assault gave way to another in Tampa, the Commission of Community Relations aptly remarked: "The end has not been reached, nor the beginning of the end, but perhaps the end of the beginning."[52] Moderation had provided a practical tool wielded by civic elites pushing for economic modernization with a minimum of political and social disruption.

PART FIVE

NEW PATHS OF EXPLORATION

ROCK 'N' ROLL, THE PAYOLA SCANDAL, AND THE POLITICAL CULTURE OF CIVIL RIGHTS

On February 1, 1960, students in Greensboro, North Carolina sat-in at a Woolworth's lunch counter in a demonstration much heralded in the annals of civil rights history. This momentous confrontation with racial segregation invigorated the African American freedom struggle and would substantially change the lives of blacks and whites ˙ throughout the South and the United States. A week later, on February 8, a seemingly unrelated event occurred in Washington, D.C. On that day, a committee of the House of Representatives convened public hearings on the subject of payola in the broadcasting industry, a practice that involved illicit payments to get music aired on radio and television programs.

Contemporary coverage of each made no mention of the other, and on the surface it was hard to see the connections. Yet the struggle for racial change, which inspired the sit-ins, also helped shape seemingly nonracial issues such as business ethics in broadcasting. In this case, rock 'n' roll, a musical form that traced its origins to African Americans, became a surrogate target for opponents of civil rights in the South and for those who feared increasing black cultural influence over American youth throughout the country. The increased visibility of the black freedom movement, marked by the Supreme Court's 1954 ruling in *Brown v. Board of Education*, the 1955 Montgomery bus boycott, and the 1957 Little Rock school integration crisis, encouraged supporters and critics alike to find racial dimensions in political arenas not usually considered under the category of civil rights. Heightened racial agitation produced a highly charged atmosphere and the political and cultural fallout from these explosive issues landed in unexpected places.

The payola scandal of 1959–60 was also part and parcel of the political culture of investigation that characterized the 1950s. Congressional committees served as the main vehicle for inquiry, and the new medium of television brought the drama of confrontation between scolding lawmakers and defensive witnesses into millions of homes. Though the need for corrective legislation provided the rationale for these inquiries, the impulse toward exposure and demonization drove them forward. Anticommunist inquisitions by the House Committee on Un-American Activities, Wisconsin Senator Joseph R. McCarthy, and Senator James Eastland of Mississippi have drawn the greatest attention from historians, furnishing textbook representations of the political tensions of the postwar period. Their importance notwithstanding, they formed only part of a larger structure of popular investigation. These included inquiries led by Tennessee Senator Estes Kefauver into organized crime and juvenile delinquency, John McClellan of Arkansas and John F. Kennedy of Massachusetts into labor racketeering, and Arkansas Representative Oren Harris into television quiz shows.[1]

Within the context of this culture of investigation, narrow economic rivalries and broad social tensions fueled the payola inquiry. Initially, charges of fraudulent payments for air play on radio stations arose out of a power struggle between two competing agencies inside the business. The internal conflict between the American Society of Composers, Authors, and Publishers (ASCAP) and Broadcast Music International (BMI) over control of publishing and performance royalties escalated into an attack by the more tradition-oriented ASCAP on BMI-associated rock 'n' roll music.

What started out as an internecine economic battle, however, soon took on the trappings of race. Following the landmark *Brown* decision, southern segregationists embarked on a campaign of massive resistance to racial equality that included attacks on black-inspired rock 'n' roll. Joining them were northerners who believed that rock 'n' roll, identified with working-class black and white youths, eroded middle-class values and standards of sexual conduct, thereby threatening the morality of their sons and, more importantly, their daughters. Congressional probes of payola gave voice to the economic and aesthetic complaints of music-business professionals as well as to fears over the erosion of racial and class boundaries by middle-class parents and their congressional representatives. The fact that the payola investigation did not continue as a significant component in the struggle over racial equality was a consequence not of the retreat by white politicians and their constituents, but rather of mass mobilization of black youths and their white allies, which shifted the battle from Congress and radio stations to the streets of America.

The practice of payola did not suddenly spring up with the appearance of rock 'n' roll; it had a history as long as commercial, popular music. *Variety*, the music trade newspaper which first coined the term payola, reported in 1914 that vaudeville singers "tell the publisher what they want to sing, how much a week they must have for singing the song or songs, and if not receiving a stipulated weekly salary, think nothing of asking for an advance."[2] Although the shape of the music business changed over the next several decades, undisclosed commercial transactions for performances remained a constant. The growth of radio in the 1920s and 1930s brought live broadcasts and the possibility of reaching millions of listeners in a single sitting. Given this potentially wider audience, popular bandleaders commanded higher payments than had their vaudevillian predecessors.[3]

In the 1950s, the cast of characters changed, but payola persisted. The development and widespread appeal of television altered the character of radio. Live broadcasts of musical concerts virtually disappeared and programs of recorded music replaced them. Disk jockeys took over from bandleaders as maestros of musical selections. The decade also witnessed a proliferation of small, independent record companies that competed with the six majors (Columbia, Capitol, Decca, RCA, MGM, and Mercury) for air play. The advent of 45 rpm single records, whose sale price was much cheaper than 33 and 1/3 longer-playing albums, inflated the number of records in circulation, increasing competition even further. Disk jockeys stood as gatekeepers in choosing songs from the burgeoning supply of records sent to the stations. What *Variety* called the "time-dishonored standard operating procedure in the music business," payola, now centered on payments from record companies and their distributors to disk jockeys.[4]

Throughout its considerable history, payola had spawned campaigns, largely unsuccessful, against it. For all the criticism it generated, payola was not a crime. No federal statute outlawed the practice, and the closest it came to a criminal offense appeared in state commercial bribery laws.[5] The main effort to combat payola came from elements within the music business. Spearheaded by *Variety* in 1916, the Music Publishers' Protective Association was formed "to promote and foster clean and free competition among music publishers by eradicating the evil custom of paying tribute or gratuities to singers or musicians."[6]

In the early 1950s when the issue resurfaced amidst the postwar obsession with moral decline and the growing prospects for racial change, *Variety* again led the campaign. In July, 1954, the trade newspaper launched a series of editorials condemning the practice. The editors declared, "the music biz payola had reached ridiculous and dangerous proportions," and concluded "it's about time it was curbed." Speaking for the denizens of "Tin

Pan Alley" in New York City, where established music publishers and songwriters congregated, they raised a concern that would be repeated frequently in the years to come. "Private side-changing chicanery," as *Variety* referred to payola, lowered the quality of songs and decreased the likelihood that truly talented stars would get heard.[7]

The trade paper left little doubt about its taste in music. In February, 1955, *Variety* issued a "Warning to the Music Business." Upset over the growing popularity of songs with sexually-suggestive "leer-ics," the paper called for the industry to impose some self-restraint or face unwanted federal regulation. Their real target was rock 'n' roll, which had burst on the scene during the previous few years and appealed almost exclusively to young people. Considering rock 'n' roll a "raw musical idiom ... [that] smelled] up the environment," *Variety* condemned its "hug" and "squeeze" lyrics for "attempting a total breakdown of all reticences about sex."[8] These comments reflected the disdain traditional segments of the music business and the adult public held for rock 'n' roll; opponents assumed that such inferior music could push its way into the marketplace only through the connivance of payola.

Historians do not dispute the existence of payola, but its significance lies in its political linkage with rock 'n' roll and race. Rather than simply an objectionable business practice of interest mainly within the recording and broadcasting industries, payola became, for a short time, a heated subject of public debate. It involved more than private morality and individual greed and moved beyond the pages of trade paper whistle blowing. Following the *Brown* decision, the Supreme Court's clarion call for racial equality, payola became a topic for public scrutiny because it coincided with growing anxiety about the nation's youth and racial minorities. The association of rock 'n' roll with these two groups turned the music from just another in a long line of popular, juvenile fads into a subject of intense national inquiry.

The behavior of teenagers had already aroused serious apprehension. "Never in our 180-year history," *Collier's* remarked in 1957, "has the United States been so aware of—or confused about—its teenagers."[9] The political response to this concern had already appeared in congressional hearings. In 1955, Senator Estes Kefauver, who had earlier investigated adult criminals, convened a legislative inquiry into the causes of juvenile delinquency. James Gilbert, the leading historian of this subject, concluded that "the delinquency hearings, the attack on youth culture, the crusade to censor culture expressed a deep malaise at what was emerging during the 1950s: a vastly different order of social, sexual, and cultural practices."[10] The perceived erosion of parental authority had serious implications for the vitality of the nuclear family during the Cold War period when domestic har-·mony was considered the first line of defense against Communism.[11]

The Kefauver Committee underscored the extent to which rock 'n' roll had become contested ground between parents and their teenage offspring. Worse than its lack of aesthetics and professionalism, rock, according to its critics was spreading antisocial, working-class values among America's youth. The words of the songs, even when they were cleaned up for popular radio consumption, combined with the throbbing sounds and pulsating performers, opened the way for sexual expression deemed unacceptable in polite society. Even if the emergent music did not turn unsuspecting middle-class youngsters into depraved delinquents, it might lead them down that path. As Jeff Greenfield, a New York City teenager in the mid-1950s, re-marked, rock 'n' roll spread the message "that our bodies were our own Joy Machines." Afraid that this was indeed the case, parents sought to curtail "the sounds of pain and joy now flooding the airwaves, infecting the bodies of their children."[12]

Middle-class worries over the unwanted influences of rock 'n' roll were not confined to whites. Members of the black bourgeoisie also expressed their distaste. When asked by a seventeen-year-old in 1958 whether it was sinful to play rock 'n' roll, the civil rights leader and pastor Dr. Martin Luther King, Jr., replied, that whether it was a sin or not, rock music "often plunges men's minds into degrading and immoral depths." In a similar vein, a col-umnist in the New York *Amsterdam News,* had earlier attacked the music as "smut" and "tripe" and proclaimed that African Americans themselves should not listen to lyrics that "projected the idea that all Negro women longed for was barnyard-type romance."[13]

As the commentary in the *Amsterdam News* suggests, class concerns intersected with those of gender. The heightened sexuality of rock 'n' roll both lyrically and musically was seen as posing a particular threat to young girls. According to middle-class social norms, adolescent females were pri-marily mothers-in-waiting, preparing themselves for marriage, raising chil-dren, and safeguarding the virtues of the nuclear family. Virginity was next to godliness, and sex was reserved for marriage. As moral caretakers of the home, wives and daughters were seen as strengthening the nation by com-bating evil conspiracies designed to undermine it. During the Cold War, communism stood at the top of the list of enemies, but any assault on pu-bescent, female chastity was seen as subversive.[14]

Rock 'n' roll was regarded as posing such a threat. According to Jeff Greenfield, the "honking tenor sax and the vibrating electric guitar and the insistent drum beat," were considered by his parents' generation as "fearful engines of immorality, driving daughters to strange dance steps and God knows what else."[15] Although adults usually found the wild gyrations of the performers and the raucous quality of the sound distasteful if not unfathomable, they were just as alarmed by the slow music, known as doo wop. Teenage dance shows on television gave adults a peek at the possible dangers as they watched young couples clutch each other trying to get as close as possible on the dance floor. "If you were a parent at home watching your daughter," a disk jockey admitted, "watching a guy all over a girl, you figure, 'Is this what my daughter does at record hops?'"[16]

Whether young female rock 'n' rollers saw themselves as subverting the moral order is debatable. Charlotte Grieg contends that the music transformed "all the conventional ideas of love, romance and marriage ... into visions of a steamy teenage paradise throbbing with erotic and sexual desire" which undermined adult notions of responsibility and domesticity."[17] Yet throughout the fifties most of the songs that teenage girls listened to had less to say about consummating sex than about longing for the boy of their dreams and marrying him. Nor did rock 'n' roll overturn the double standard that distinguished "good girls" from "bad girls." Nevertheless, it did allow many young women to experience a forbidden sexual energy that their elders found dangerous. If not exactly revolutionary, the music allowed teenagers, girls and boys, to express themselves in a language and style removed from their parents' tight control.[18]

This mixture of class and gender fears occasioned powerful anxieties about rock 'n' roll and teen culture, but the addition of race proved explosive. The term "rock 'n' roll" had evolved out of the rhythm and blues lyrical expression for sexual intercourse. As long as rhythm and blues remained "race music," separated from the popular tunes white audiences listened to, it aroused only minimal concern within the non-black community. But when it began to enter the musical mainstream as rock 'n' roll, which appealed largely to white youths, it alarmed the guardians of teenage morality. *Variety* undertook its crusade against sexually-suggestive "leer-ics" with great urgency because rhythm and blues was no longer "restricted to special places and out and out barrelhouses." Transformed into rock 'n' roll, it had broken out of the segregated confines of black venues and appeared "as standard popular music for general consumption, including consumption by teenagers."[19]

Rock 'n' roll gave white teenagers the rare opportunity to come into cultural contact with African Americans in a nation that was still racially segregated. Particularly in the South, Jim Crow maintained a rigid wall to keep whites and black apart. Dixie's laws could keep schools and public accommodations racially restricted but not the public air waves. Radio stations targeted for blacks picked up a sizable white audience, some twenty to thirty percent of overall listeners.[20] In the privacy of their own rooms young southern whites turned on their radios to hear the forbidden sounds of rhythm and blues or they took their portable transistor radios, which had just become available in the early 1950s, to gathering places for teens, away from their parents' watchful eyes. One white youth recalled that he loved to listen to the music on black-oriented stations "whenever and wherever I could.... I loved to dance to it. That got me into trouble with my parents and the schools, because we were not allowed to listen to this music openly." Some of the bolder youths attended live performances with blacks, and in spite of efforts to keep them apart, the excitement of the music frequently pulled them side by side in the aisles or on the dance floor.[21]

Moreover, white teen icons such as Elvis Presley stepped over the racial divide by incorporating the sounds and styles of African American music into his act. A Mississippian who achieved stardom in Memphis, Presley readily acknowledged his debt to blacks. "Colored folks have been singing and playing this music for more years'n anybody knows," the twenty-one-year-old Presley explained in 1956, "They played it in the shanties all 'round Tupelo, Mississippi, where I got it from them, and nobody paid 'tention till I goose it up."[22] Nelson George has written that the "young Presley came closer than any other rock 'n' roll star to capturing the swaggering sexuality projected by many Rhythm and Blues vocalists."[23]

In the North and West where *de facto* segregation and more subtly constructed patterns of racism kept blacks and whites apart, rock 'n' roll likewise exerted the centripetal force that pulled teenagers of both races together. Colorful white radio disk jockeys such as Alan "Moondog" Freed in Cleveland and New York City, George "Hound Dog" Lorenz in Buffalo, and Hunter Hancock and Johnny Otis in Los Angeles exposed their predominantly white teenage listeners to black rhythm and blues and rock 'n' roll artists. Not only did they feature the original records of black performers over versions covered by white artists, but they talked in the hip street vernacular of the singers. As in the South, their live concerts and dances drew an interracial crowd, throwing together white and black youths who would otherwise have remained in their own neighborhoods. More than in any other setting in America at that time, these gatherings permitted teenagers to step over racial and class boundaries in defiance of their elders.[24]

Rock 'n' roll served as a musical backdrop to the black freedom struggle that was breaking onto the national scene during the 1950s. Some have discerned a direct connection between the rise of rock 'n' roll and racial change. A singer for the Platters, Harvey Weinger, looking back on that period remarked: "Because of our music, white kids ventured into black areas. They had a sense of fair play long before the civil rights movement." Herbie Cox of the Cleftones seconded this view, asserting that rock 'n' roll "disk jockeys and record distributors were doing more for integration than *Brown v. the Topeka Board of Education.*"[25] The journalist Robert Palmer perceived rock 'n' roll as the cultural component of the black freedom struggle. "It's no mere accident of history," Palmer argues, "that Rosa Parks's refusal to move to the back of a segregated Alabama bus ... occurred during the brief pop-music ascendancy of performers like Chuck Berry and Little Richard, black men whose very sound and sign communicated their refusal to respond to the racists' traditional 'C'mere, boy'"[26]

Without doubt rock 'n' roll contributed to changing patterns of racial and cultural interaction, but its impact should not be exaggerated. Because white youths listened to black-inspired music or attended concerts with African Americans did not mean that they shed the racial prejudices of their families and neighborhoods. The sensuality of the rhythms that attracted many white teens also served to reinforce stereotypical notions of black male and female sexuality, views that white society had historically used to demonize African Americans. Besides, most white kids listened to rock 'n' roll within the confines of racially segregated environments—homes, social clubs, schools, and cars—without venturing into close proximity to blacks.[27] Moreover, although rock 'n' roll energized young people and cast them in opposition to dominant styles, the teenagers who became the vanguard of the civil rights movement in places such as Little Rock and Greensboro owed their inspiration less to avant-garde music and more to their churches, youth groups, and other community organizations.

Nevertheless, opponents of racial change considered rock 'n' roll as subversive. In the wake of the Supreme Court's ruling in *Brown*, segregationist watchdogs saw an increasing need to guard the South's white youth from all forms of race mixing. Schools occupied the primary political battleground because they offered the most likely space for white and black students to interact. But the war for racial purity did not end at the schoolhouse door. As the commercial marketplace, including the entertainment industry, directed more of its efforts toward gaining a share of rising teenage spending, segregationists turned their attention to youth culture. They perceived danger as coming from many directions—television, radio, motion pictures—and considered the national media, in the words of the *Shreveport Journal,* as "one of the South's greatest foes in its fight to maintain racial segregation."[28] The greatest threat came from images and sounds that might lure white and black youngsters together.

Hostility to rock 'n' roll became part of the agenda for southern white massive resistance. In addition to other efforts to preserve segregation and disfranchisement, White Citizens Councils, a slightly more moderate counterpart of the Ku Klux Klan, campaigned against rock 'n' roll. In 1956, Asa Carter, the head of the North Alabama White Citizens Council, called rock "the basic, heavy-beat music of Negroes." Allowed to go unchecked, he feared nothing less than the collapse of "the entire moral structure ... the white man has built through his devotion to God." He and his followers did not consider their concern farfetched as they saw that "white girls and boys were turned to the level of animal" by the sensuous music.[29] In a racialized society rapidly coming under assault from the civil rights movement, music that promoted social intercourse also aggravated fears of miscegenation.[30]

Carter and segregationists like him contended that the proliferation of rock 'n' roll had not occurred naturally; how could it given their view of the music's inherent worthlessness? Rather, they saw it as part of a sinister plot designed by integrationist groups such as the National Association for the Advancement of Colored People (NAACP) to contribute to the "moral degradation of children."[31] The *Brown* decision and rock 'n' roll were just two sides of the same integrationist coin and segregationists responded to both by trying to beat them back.

Racism was not confined to the South, and similar assumptions guided opponents of rock 'n' roll in the North. The thrust of the attack above the Mason-Dixon line was not so much to preserve the system of Jim Crow but to combat anxieties over the spread of juvenile delinquency which the Kefauver Committee had publicized. In 1957, Senator John F. Kennedy, a Massachusetts Democrat, read into the *Congressional Record* an article from *Newsday*, a Long Island, New York newspaper, connecting rock 'n' roll with the designs of broadcasters, record companies, and music publishers to foist decadent music on an unsuspecting public. Nonetheless, the language used to link rock with the behavior of antisocial youths was couched in the same racial stereotypes. *Music Journal* asserted that the "jungle rhythms" of rock incited juvenile offenders into "orgies of sex and violence" just as its forerunners did for the "savages." The New York *Daily News* derided the obscene lyrics set to "primitive jungle-beat rhythms." A week before Asa Carter traced rock 'n' roll's penetration of the South to the NAACP, a New England psychiatrist disparaged the music as "cannibalistic and tribalistic." Similarly, a Catholic clergyman from Boston denounced the sexually-suggestive lyrics for inflaming youths "like jungle tom-toms readying warriors for battle."[32]

As targets of this criticism, African Americans generally recognized the racial animus behind attacks on rock 'n' roll. Although they too expressed dismay at the use of inappropriate lyrics aimed at youngsters and did not always find the music to their liking, many black adults softened in their reactions to the music as they witnessed the growing campaign against the civil rights movement. As massive resistance swung into high gear in 1956, black commentators perceptively drew the connection between the South's efforts to defend segregation and to smear black-derived music. A writer for the New York *Amsterdam News* suggested "that the hate rock 'n' roll seems to inspire in some of its critics stems solely from the fact that Negro musicians predominate in the field, originated it, and are making the loot out of it." Even more forcefully, the *Pittsburgh Courier* editorialized that the war against rock 'n' roll constituted "an indirect attack against Negroes, of course, because they invented rock 'n' roll (as they did all other distinctive U.S. music), and because it has so captivated the younger generation of whites that they are breaking down dance floors and gutting night clubs here and abroad.[33] A matter of racial pride, many black adults came to consider the harsh denunciation of rock 'n' roll as an attempt to demean the contributions made by African Americans to American popular culture.

Although race and rock 'n' roll set the stage for the congressional investigation of payola, the immediate stimulus for the probe grew out of an internal struggle for power in the music business. Until 1940, ASCAP controlled the licensing of performance rights and the collection of royalties due its members from any place music was sold or played. Locked in a bitter dispute with ASCAP over higher fees, in 1941, radio broadcasters transformed BMI, which they had created two years earlier, into a rival performance licensing group. For the next two decades, ASCAP sought to destroy BMI as a competitor through lawsuits and congressional action.[34]

In 1953, ASCAP songwriters filed a $150 million antitrust case charging BMI with engaging in monopolistic practices. They argued that because broadcasters operated BMI, they had a special interest in playing music licensed by their own organization to the detriment of songs contained in the ASCAP catalogue. In fact, radio stations contracted with both ASCAP and BMI and entered into standard financial arrangements with each. Indeed, ASCAP had continued to profit since the formation of BMI, its income nearly quadrupling to $25 million between 1939 and 1956. By the mid 1950s, the older organization still licensed 85 percent of the music heard on radio and 75 percent of the songs distributed on record albums, which accounted for the largest proportion of sales in the record business. Nevertheless, BMI made significant inroads on the older organization's share of the market. Until 1955, ASCAP-licensed songs dominated the popular music charts and particularly the tunes ranked in the top ten of the highly regarded *Billboard* magazine listing. However, by the late 1950s, BMI-recorded hits appeared more frequently than those of ASCAP in the coveted top ten rankings.[35]

Rock 'n' roll became the outlet for much of ASCAP's discontent. Major recording studios could adapt to changing tastes by signing up rock 'n' roll performers. RCA did so in 1956, buying Elvis Presley's contract from Sun Records, one of the many independent companies providing unwelcome competition for the major firms. Tin Pan Alley songwriters, however, found it much more difficult to pen tunes for the changing youth-oriented market. Those who had crafted hits in the past for Broadway shows and Hollywood movies had little inclination to shift their efforts to a musical form that they despised and considered professionally inferior. In 1959, *Billboard* wrote that "many frustrated music men—out of step with current song and recording trends ... sigh for the good old days."[36] Believing that payola spawned rock, songwriters of traditional music attacked the former in hope of curtailing the latter. The fact that BMI firms published most rock 'n' roll songs stoked the fires of ASCAP's fury.

As ASCAP's lawsuit against BMI dragged on through the courts during the 1950s without success, the organization turned to Congress to press its case. In 1956, ASCAP received a sympathetic reception from the House Judiciary Committee, which held extensive hearings on the subject of broadcasting monopolies. The support provided by Emanuel Celler, the committee chairman, shows that outside of the South's massive resistance campaign, race operated in a more subtle fashion. On the one hand, Celler, a liberal representative from Brooklyn, was a staunch supporter of black advancement and a leader of the successful effort to pass civil rights legislation in 1957. At the same time, the congressman did not have much appreciation for rock 'n' roll. The music had a place in the culture because, as he explained patronizingly, it had given "great impetus to talent, especially among the colored people: it's a natural expression of their emotions and feelings."[37] This attitude did not keep Celler from fighting against legal segregation and disfranchisement, but it did line him up on the same side as those who viewed black-derived rock 'n' roll as inferior music.[38]

Despite a lengthy inquiry into the dispute and clear sympathy with ASCAP's position, nothing came out of the Celler Committee deliberations.[39]

The Senate then took up the issue. George Smathers of Florida embraced ASCAP's cause as the South continued to combat school desegregation and attempts of blacks to register to vote. Shortly before passage of the Civil Rights Act of 1957, Smathers introduced a bill to force broadcast stations to divest themselves from BMI or lose their licenses from the Federal Communications Commission (FCC). The Senate Committee on Interstate and Foreign Commerce held hearings on the Smathers measure beginning in March, 1958.[40]

Chaired by John Pastore of Rhode Island, like Celler, a liberal Democrat, the investigation traveled over familiar terrain. ASCAP supporters argued that without sponsorship of BMI and the constant plugging of disk jockeys, rock 'n' roll would have collapsed. Perhaps the most vivid testimony of this sort was articulated by Vance Packard, who had been hired as an expert witness by the Songwriters Protective Association, whose membership overlapped with that of ASCAP. A popular magazine writer and author of a best-selling book exposing the practices of advertisers in manipulating the public's taste for consumer goods, Packard charged that many of the social problems that affected Americans stemmed from the techniques of "hidden persuasion" perfected by Madison Avenue. He warned the committee that the nation was becoming increasingly "standardized, homogenized, hypnotized, and sterilized," and was losing such core values "as respect for the dignity of the individual, freedom from conformity, and freedom of choice."[41] The notion of hidden persuaders fit in with prevailing perceptions—whether applied to communist infiltration, juvenile delinquency, labor racketeering, or civil rights protest—that clandestine forces rigged the country's institutions and sapped their moral strength.

Packard applied the same analysis to explain the teenage infatuation with rock 'n' roll. Tracing it to the hidden hand of broadcasting corruption, he argued that the kind of music BMI mainly handled could not have possibly become successful unless the broadcasters themselves had pushed it upon the public. Like other critics of rock 'n' roll, Packard disparaged its racial antecedents. "Inspired by what had been called race music modified to stir the animal instinct in modern teenagers," Packard informed Pastore,"its chief characteristics now are a heavy, unrelenting beat and a raw, savage tone." Music of this inferior sort, he suggested, could not have gained commercial success without the manipulation of juvenile tastes by unscrupulous disk jockeys under the sway of payola.[42] This notion of conspiratorial machination had far reaching implications. For example, it reinforced the thinking of southern white segregationists who believed that outside civil rights agitators were conniving to upset time-honored Jim Crow practices in their region.

Packard's views did not go unchallenged. BMI supporters pointed out that far from engaging in a conspiracy to undermine American standards of decency, the appeal of rock 'n' roll vindicated faith in democracy by demonstrating that people could choose what they wanted to hear. The testimony of individuals not associated with rock 'n' roll proved most effective. The distinguished opera star Robert Merrill doubted that rock tunes harmed "the spiritual and emotional health of young people," and seriously questioned whether the problems attributed to teenagers "would disappear if our youngsters were exposed exclusively to Puccini and never to Presley."[43] Another witness took exception with Packard's characterization of rock 'n' roll as lowlife music. The wife of Nat King Cole testified on behalf of her husband who was out on tour. Although her husband sang a different style of music, Maria Ellington Cole presented a spirited defense of rock 'n' roll as "authentic music ... [that] must stand or fall on its own merits." In a blunt rejoinder to opponents who denigrated rock as race music, she proudly noted that "just as country music grew up as the folk music of people in the hills of Tennessee and in the West, so did race music grow as a part of the folk music of American Negroes."[44]

After listening to the evidence over several months, Pastore and his committee decided not to intrude legislatively in what was essentially an economic battle between ASCAP and BMI. The Rhode Island senator was not convinced that BMI engaged in a conspiracy to deceive the public into accepting rock 'n' roll and dismissed the notion that divorcing BMI from broadcasters would mean "the end of all rock 'n' roll." Hardly a fan of the music, he nevertheless tolerated it as part of "a fashion and a fad that appeals to young people," including his fourteen-year-old daughter (who, he admitted with chagrin, liked the Coasters' hit "Yakety Yak"). To join in a battle to destroy rock 'n' roll and what it stood for culturally, smelled to Pastore like a form of dreaded censorship and "thought control."[45]

As ASCAP continued to scuffle with BMI in the courts and to heap scorn upon rock 'n' roll, hearings into television quiz show improprieties unexpectedly launched a full-blown congressional inquiry into payola. In 1959, the House Legislative Oversight Subcommittee, chaired by Representative Oren Harris, an Arkansas Democrat, conducted a highly publicized investigation into a scandal that had been brewing for several years. In the 1950s, quiz and other game shows had made the transition from radio to television and attracted huge audiences. Programs such as the

"$64,000 Question" and "Twenty-One" awarded big cash prizes to contestants who competed to furnish information usually buried in the pages of encyclopedias. Producers of these shows heightened the level of their authenticity by keeping the participants in isolation booths and delivering the questions under armed guard. However, the facade of honesty collapsed when a few disgruntled contestants admitted that they had been coached and that the outcome of these televised matches of brain power were rigged. After a grand jury in New York City, where most of these programs originated, gathered considerable evidence of deception, Congress took up the matter.[46]

The quiz show scandal riveted public attention on Washington. It provided the Democratic majority in Congress with an opportunity to look ahead to the presidential campaign in 1960 and build a case that under the Republican Administration of Dwight Eisenhower a climate of moral decay had set in. Already in 1958, the Legislative Oversight Subcommittee had probed federal regulatory commissions and uncovered influence peddling between federal regulatory agencies and Sherman Adams, Eisenhower's closest advisor, who was forced to resign. Planning his race for the presidency, Senator John F. Kennedy exploited the public disillusionment these scandals produced. A close friend of George Smathers and a moderate on civil rights, Kennedy was courting key southern Democrats to support his nomination for the presidency. Yet his strategy aimed beyond the South. Richard N. Goodwin, a staff lawyer on the Oversight Subcommittee during the quiz show probe, explained that the Massachusetts senator had "an intuitive belief that his fellow citizens were dissatisfied, that they expected more from their society and themselves, that they wanted to 'Get America Moving Again.'"[47]

The quiz show revelations reinforced the notion that the United States had lost its moral compass, and Charles Van Doren became a symbol of this concern. An English instructor at Columbia University and the son of a prominent professor there, Van Doren had achieved victory on "Twenty One" through a combination of his own intelligence and the back stage manipulation of the show's producers. Until he admitted his guilt in testimony before the Legislative Oversight Subcommittee in 1959, the thirty-three-year-old academic was viewed as a worthy role model for youth to follow.[48] In contrast to rock stars whose performances aroused teenagers into an emotional frenzy, Van Doren offered his cool intellect as an attractive alternative. Adults embraced him as the counter-Elvis, "a new kind of T.V. idol of all things, an egghead ... whom many a grateful parent regards as T.V.'s own health-restoring antidote to Presley."[49] His fall from grace before the House Committee removed Van Doren as a useful weapon in the generational culture wars. Deeply disturbed over the moral implications of Van Doren's behavior, in 1959, the writer John Steinbeck rued: "on all levels [society] is rigged. A creeping all-pervading nerve gas of immorality . . . starts in the nursery and does not stop before it reaches the highest offices, both corporate and governmental."[50]

The quiz show scandal also prompted lawmakers to mount another investigation into manipulation and deception in broadcasting and the music business. The Harris Committee thus turned its attention to payola as another example of the dangers lurking in the "rigged society." Indeed, ASCAP and its allies regarded the quiz show hearings as benefiting their continuing efforts to hamstring BMI. At the end of that investigation, in November, 1959, Burton Lane, the president of the American Guild of Authors and Composers and a longstanding antagonist of BMI, informed the Legislative Oversight Subcommittee that the evidence it had uncovered with respect to quiz show fraud had "a counterpart in the promotion of music." He told lawmakers that commercial bribery in the form of payola "has become a prime factor in determining what music is played on many broadcast programs and what musical records the public is surreptitiously induced to buy."[51] Lane had leveled these charges without success many times before to Congress, the Federal Communications Commission, and the Federal Trade Commission. This time, however, he received a more favorable response. By the end of the year, the Oversight Subcommittee's preliminary inquiry revealed that payola was "rampant" and both the FCC and the FTC initiated their own probes.[52] In the wake of the widespread attention garnered by the quiz show hearings and in anticipation of the 1960 elections, lawmakers found the time right to tackle the century-old practice of payola.

Racial motives influenced some key congressmen. Representative Oren Harris of Arkansas, chair of the Legislative Oversight Subcommittee, lined up with his southern colleagues in opposition to civil rights legislation. In 1950, he had served on the steering group that helped defeat passage of a bill establishing a Fair Employment Practice Committee (FEPC), a measure designed to check racial bias. Harris did not see it that way. According to the Arkansas congressman, "just as discrimination should not be practiced as affecting minorities, neither should the minorities arbitrarily control our political institutions against the best interest and real desires of the majority."[53] Harris and his colleagues painted a dire if distorted picture of the FEPC acquiring "unlimited authority, the most far reaching powers [over] the business and economic life of this country ever given throughout our entire history."[54]

Throughout the rest of the decade, Harris's anxieties about federal involvement to promote civil rights only increased. In 1956, he signed his name to a manifesto of 101 southern congressional lawmakers challenging the legitimacy of the Supreme Court's desegregation decree in *Brown*. The following year, President Eisenhower vividly displayed Washington's commitment to the enforcement of federal court orders by sending troops into Little Rock, Arkansas. During the confrontation, Harris staunchly defended the segregationist stand taken by Governor Orval Faubus and distanced himself from any attempt to hammer out a peaceful compromise. "Stunned beyond expression" by Eisenhower's action, the congressman "deeply resented it, [and] thought it was unnecessary and unwarranted."[55]

To Harris and other proponents of massive resistance, the payola investigation offered an opportunity to check integrationist advances not only politically but culturally. Harris endorsed the views of the *American Nationalist*, an extreme right-wing publication originating in southern California, which claimed that "Negroes have been raised to stardom and adulation as a result of the fictitious popularity of rock 'n' roll music—popularly purchased through payola." Raising the specter of miscegenation, this pro-segregationist and anti-rock tract recoiled over "teenage daughters ... squealing and drooling over Negroidal crooners."[56] Harris fully agreed with these sentiments, and he replied to his hometown constituent who sent him the material: "I have the same views as you do on such distasteful propaganda to integrate the races." Vowing to make "every effort in opposition, either by legislation or Executive action," Harris assured his correspondent that his committee "would not shirk in any way or overlook" the subject of payola, and he did not consider its racial angle "too hot to handle."[57]

Actually, the white southern counteroffensive of massive resistance had already slowed down the civil rights momentum building after *Brown* and the Montgomery Bus Boycott, especially at the grassroots level. Throughout most of the deep South, school desegregation made almost no progress, and bus boycotts expanded to very few southern cities. Although Martin Luther King, Jr., established the Southern Christian Leadership Conference in 1957, an organization designed to mobilize nonviolent, direct action, protests, the group made little headway in promoting mass demonstrations or placing blacks on the voter rolls. In fact, the pace of black voter registration, which had grown steadily since World War II, leveled off far short of enfranchising a majority of black adults by the end of the 1950s.[58] Nevertheless, the persistent gap between actual civil rights breakthroughs and continued white domination only slightly moderated southern fears of losing control over fundamental racial matters.

Whatever the realities of the civil rights situation, Harris felt much more strongly about containing racial equality than he did about stamping out corruption in broadcasting. In the mid-1950s, the Arkansas congressman had received a 25 percent interest in KRBB, a television station in his home town of El Dorado. He paid a token amount of $500 for the investment and signed a promissory note for the much larger figure of $4,500, which the station never asked him to repay. In 1958, the FCC granted KRBB permission to expand its power output to a level the commission had denied before Harris became part owner. When the chief investigator for Harris's own Legislative Oversight Committee leaked the details of this story to the press, the congressman sold his interest in the station and at the same time fired the whistle blower.[59] His own questionable behavior did not stop Harris from chairing investigations of unethical conduct relating to the FCC and FTC as well as television quiz shows; nor would it keep him from probing payola. In light of the enormous public drama surrounding the downfall of Charles Van Doren, it made good political sense for the committee to carry its probe in the related direction of the rigging of records for broadcast.

Most if not all of the nine legislators who sat on Harris's Legislative Oversight Committee had a dim view of the quality of rock 'n' roll; however, this did not mean, that race was foremost in all their minds.[60] No one paid greater attention to the proceedings than did John Moss, a California Democrat. Born a Mormon, Moss had ceased practicing the religion because of the church's "strong pattern of racial discrimination." Before entering politics, he owned a small appliance store, and his business outlook shaped his attitude toward payola. It did not matter that payola was frequently used by small, independent record companies to outmaneuver the giant firms. To Moss, payola constituted commercial bribery, which he identified with the kind of activity big business used to undermine competition. A believer in free enterprise in the Populist and Progressive tradition, he favored governmental regulation to oversee "powerful interests that thwart opportunity and competition." His commitment to openness also emerged in Moss's sponsorship of freedom of information legislation to minimize government secretiveness.[61] As for rock 'n' roll, Moss did not exhibit much of an open mind and expressed the typical reaction of his colleagues: hearing it played on the radio his response was "to snap the thing off, as quickly as possible." He complained that his own teenage children listened to this "trash" because disk jockeys pushed it on them.[62]

Some legislative action to curb payola appeared certain. The Eisenhower Administration joined the chorus condemning the practice. Already stung by the scandal involving one of his closest aides, Sherman Adams, the Republican president sought to recapture higher moral ground. Following the public brouhaha over television quiz show deception, Eisenhower instructed Attorney General William Rogers to investigate the problem of fraud in broadcasting and report back to him.[63] Rogers issued his findings at the close of 1959, declaring there was "evidence of widespread corruption and lack of the personal integrity which is so essential to the fabric of American life." He proposed legislation to make the receipt of payola by station personnel a federal criminal offense.[64]

The Eisenhower Administration had hoped to get out in front of the Democratically-controlled Legislative Oversight subcommittee, but Harris did not intend to relinquish the spotlight in a presidential election year. Harris did not need much additional incentive to turn up the political heat on the Eisenhower regime. The military intervention in Little Rock and the Republican administration's successful sponsorship of civil rights legislation in 1957 had irked the Arkansas congressman. Opening on February 8, 1960, the hearings confirmed what the trade press and industry insiders had known about for years—the widespread existence of payola. The Harris Committee paraded a lineup of witnesses consisting mainly of disk jockeys and record company executives and distributors. Most witnesses did not deny their part in the acceptance of gifts, but they adamantly rejected the notion that these payments affected their play selection.[65] According to this defense, at the very most disk jockeys took payments not to dictate what they played but to advise record companies on what kind of tunes would appeal to their listeners. Actually, the under-the-table gratuities did not ensure that a deejay could turn a particular record into a hit, but they did guarantee that of the hundreds of free records the radio station received each week, those furnished by companies dispensing payola would make it to the top of the pile for the disk jockey's review and increase the potential for air play.[66]

Congressional inquisitors remained unconvinced by the denials. Influenced by Vance Packard's warnings of "hidden persuaders," they believed that consumers did not have a free choice and were more likely to have their desires shaped by advertisers and product merchandisers. In particular, they considered a teenage audience even more vulnerable to manipulation than adults. Harris asserted from the outset that "the quality of broadcast programs declines when the choice of program materials is made, not in the public interest, but in the interest of those who are willing to pay to obtain exposure of their records." Without payola, he declared, "we probably would not have a lot of stuff that the American people have had to listen to."[67]

The bad "stuff" undoubtedly referred to rock 'n' roll. Record spinners who accepted gifts but who did not play rock 'n' roll escaped committee censure. A Boston deejay admitted receiving Christmas gifts from record distributors, but he continued to play "the type of music that an adult audience would enjoy ... not ... the raucous kind of sound that I had always associated payola with." Another disk jockey in the same city, Stan Richards, passed muster from the lawmakers by denouncing rock 'n' roll as "junk music" that he refused to play. According to *Billboard* reporter Mildred Hall, who observed the hearing closely, such condemnations "won approving congressional smiles in each instance."[68]

Indeed, in condemning rock 'n' roll and underscoring its connection to payola, disk jockeys who came clean received praise from the committee. This public process of denunciation resembled the role that ex-Communists played in the McCarthy era in providing justification for controversial investigations into unpopular political beliefs. The culture of investigation contained a ritual of forgiveness and redemption for those who cooperated, allowing them to receive the blessing of the committee. For example, Chairman Harris applauded Richards at the conclusion of his testimony, noting that while he had once engaged in "pathetic" conduct as a disk jockey, his presentation had proven him to be a "good fellow" entitled to continue his career.[69]

Rock 'n' roll remained a focus of the deliberations, as it had in the Pastore hearings two years earlier, but this time the ASCAP-BMI war had shifted to another battleground. After its supporters had helped initiate the investigation with their complaints to the legislative committee, ASCAP turned its attention to the executive branch. Following the fallout from the quiz show scandal and Attorney General Rogers's recommendation for more vigorous federal regulation, ASCAP officials took their case against payola and BMI to the FCC and FTC.[70] Without the congressional spotlight on the ASCAP-BMI conflict, much of the discussion shifted away from private rivalries in the music business and centered on the decline in standards of public morality.[71]

In contrast with the often stated ties between rock 'n' roll and the decline of public morality, race had a muted presence during the congressional probe. Unlike the situation in previous hearings, witnesses did not publicly refer to rock 'n' roll in racially coded terms, for example, as "jungle" music arousing "savage" passions. The disappearance of such rhetoric, however, did not mean that racial fears had subsided. Rather it reflected two changes in the cultural and political environment. First rock 'n' roll music had become considerably whiter. The hard, raunchy edge of the original music turned softer as record companies, always sensitive to bad publicity, responded to the concerted attacks on suggestive lyrics. Black pioneers, such as Chuck Berry and Little Richard, passed from the scene, as had the white rocker Jerry Lee Lewis, who lost public favor, after marrying his thirteen-year-old cousin. Moreover, the most popular of them all, Elvis Presley, had gone into the Army and returned as a toned-down balladeer and Hollywood movie star. From an alleged fomenter of juvenile delinquency, the black-inspired Presley had assumed the identity of a patriotic ex-GI and all-American boy.[72] In their places the rock scene attracted less threatening white crooners who seemed more cuddly than menacing.

Second, while rock 'n' roll had functioned as a convenient symbol of racial anxieties in the 1950s, by 1960 the civil rights movement offered a more tangible target for racist attacks. White supremacists in the South had more direct problems facing them than "race music."

Beginning in late 1959 and erupting in February 1960, they had to face a resurgent freedom struggle invigorated by African American high school and college students who challenged racial inequality through sit-ins, freedom rides, and other forms of direct-action protest. Whatever notion segregationists may have had that in destroying rock 'n' roll they could frustrate racial reform paled beside the visible threat posed by young black protesters and their white allies. In the heightened atmosphere of racial agitation that accompanied this new phase of the civil rights struggle, anti-rock and anti-payola crusades lost much of their significance compared with the bruising battles that took place in cities and towns throughout America.

Besides, in the latter part of the 1950s, southern state governments directly launched their own investigations into subversive influence within the civil rights movement. Primarily targeting the NAACP in Florida and Louisiana, state legislative investigation committees attempted to link the civil rights group with Communist infiltration. For a time, Alabama managed to ban the NAACP from operating within its borders. In the wake of *Brown*, Mississippi created the State Sovereignty Commission which monitored civil rights activists, planted informers within their ranks, and collaborated with local law enforcement agencies to harass them. Thus, on the state level, committees such as these mirrored the legislative culture of investigation in Washington, D.C. that in the 1950s sustained an array of inquisitorial forays into the "rigged society."[73]

While race moved to the background of the payola hearings at the same time as it moved into the foreground of politics and social change, it still cast a shadow over the congressional investigation. The racial connotations of rock 'n' roll, and hence their association with the black freedom

struggle, played themselves out in the opposing fates of the two most prominent disk jockeys in the business: Dick Clark and Alan Freed. The "whiten-
ing" of rock and its movement into the musical mainstream, which had
lessened somewhat the hysterical opposition to it, helps explain how Clark
emerged relatively unscathed from the hearings. In contrast, Freed, who
represented the early and less acceptable black-oriented version of the music,
fared much worse.

In August 1957, when Dick Clark became host of *American Bandstand*,
the nationally televised teenage dance show on the ABC network, the twenty-
seven-year-old Syracuse University graduate with a degree in advertising
was not yet a decade past his own teenage years. Clark considered himself
more a businessman than a rock 'n' roll enthusiast, and his own musical
tastes ran along the lines of Glen Miller. Convinced that if he could successfully market rock 'n' roll to a broad teenage audience, Clark looked forward
to making "a good deal of money."[74]

Clark packaged himself as an understanding mediator between adult
society and the mysterious world of teenagers. Publishing an advice manual
for teenagers, Clark pressed them on the need to understand their parents,
who "have a strange way of being right most of the time."[75] Moreover, he
sought to tone down the controversial aspects of rock 'n' roll. He insisted
that the kids on his program conform to a dress code, because "it made the
show acceptable to adults." He came across as a "friend, adviser, older
brother or young parent," the kind of man a teenage boy aspired to become
and a teenage girl looked for in a husband. He domesticated the wilder
features of rock 'n' roll and consciously posed no threat to traditional family values. The music did not have to turn girls wild, it could also tame
them. He encouraged young housewives, many of them not too far removed
from their teenage years, "to roll up the ironing board and join us when
you can."[76] He largely achieved his goal. Describing the participants on
American Bandstand as an "attractive group of youngsters," the stately *New
York Times*, approvingly noted the absence of any "motorcycle jackets and
hardly a sideburn in the crowd."[77]

Furthermore, Clark built his popularity on whiteness. Although he featured black performers on *Bandstand*, he strictly adhered to the network
broadcasting policy of not stirring the racial brew. The dance party impre-
sario did make an overture to bring black youths into his studio audience
when he went on the air throughout the nation in 1957, but their presence
was exceedingly thin and hardly visible in front of the cameras. As with
rock 'n' roll, he approached racial matters in a careful and practical manner. Acknowledging that he was not an "integrationist or pioneer," Clark

broke the color barrier, however modestly, not out of any moral conviction but because he could "see it was going to happen, and there was no sense not doing it."[78] Nevertheless, African Americans remained largely invisible on his show. A black teenager from Philadelphia, where the show originated, complained: "When we have attempted to attend *[Bandstand]* ... we've been given the run-around by officials of the show. And if a few of us manage to get inside, we're discouraged from dancing on the floor."[79]

However, it is too simple to dismiss Dick Clark as a racist. An impressive number of black performers first appeared on national television on *American Bandstand,* including Chuck Berry, Sam Cooke, Little Anthony and the Imperials, the Chantels, the Coasters, and Jackie Wilson. Clark also took many of them along with a group of white stars on integrated bus caravans touring the South.[80] Nevertheless, what Clark did best was not to promote African American culture or foster social integration but to help absorb black music into a popular format dominated by whites. He certainly did not discriminate against black performers and even helped some in their careers, but he was much more closely associated both in public perception and in reality with young white heartthrobs such as Frankie Avalon, Fabian, Bobby Rydell, and Bobbie Vinton. Clark acknowledged that he owed a great deal to the African American community for supplying the source of the music, but given his enormous popularity, he was more responsible than anyone else for refashioning that legacy into a whiter product.[81] At a time when African Americans were beginning to win battles in the courts, in Congress, in the schools of Little Rock, and on the streets of a few cities such as Montgomery, Alabama, Clark's orchestration of rock roll lessened some of its perceived threat to white racial and cultural hegemony.

Clark's efforts stand in sharp contrast to those of Alan Freed, who appeared to challenge the racial status quo already under assault from the incipient civil rights movement. Whereas Clark appeared to represent "middle America, nice, a white-bread face," as one record company executive put it, "Freed was gruff, a street man, New York rock 'n' roll, tough."[82] Eight years older than Clark, Freed first made his reputation in Cleveland before he moved on to New York City in 1954. Though he did not coin the label rock 'n' roll, he popularized it in concerts and on his frenetically-paced radio shows, complete with sound effects, jive talk, and shouts of joy. If Clark appeared cool, calm, and collected if somewhat stiff and detached from the teenagers and their music, Freed acted just the opposite and got caught up in the energy and excitement of the programs he produced.[83]

At the heart of Freed's unique style was his association with the black roots of rock 'n' roll. Freed's "Big Beat" concerts, starting in Cleveland in

March 1952, showcased black performers and attracted largely African American audiences. Even as he increasingly attracted white fans, he insisted on playing the original recordings of rock songs by black artists. He considered the cover versions record companies put out by white artists as "anti-Negro." He served as a transmission belt for black-oriented rock seeping into the lives of white teenagers, and this made him dangerous to many. He reported receiving "batches of poison-pen letters calling me a 'nigger-lover.'"[84]

His association with blacks got him in trouble. When violence erupted outside one of his Big Beat concerts in Boston in 1958, his detractors blamed the attacks on black hoodlums, a charge that could not be substantiated. Nevertheless, local authorities indicted Freed for inciting a riot and his New York City radio station cut him loose.[85] The self-proclaimed "King of Rock 'n' Roll" also had his own dance party television program canceled by WABC in New York City the year before because of an incident with racial overtones. While *American Bandstand* managed to keep a low profile when it came to blacks, Freed's show spotlighted one of his vocal guests, Frankie Lymon of the Teenagers, dancing with a white girl in the audience. Distributed throughout the country, the show caused a furor in the South, and in 1957, the network dropped it.[86]

Freed was far from perfect. He was brash and arrogant, employed an agent with connections to organized crime, drank alcohol too heavily, and lived a lavish life style that he supported in part with elaborate gifts from record companies that he explained away as consulting fees. His affinity for black talent did not prevent Freed from cutting himself in on the songwriting credits of Chuck Berry's "Maybeline" and the Moonglows' "Sincerely" and receiving royalties from their successes.[87]

However, as Freed steadfastly maintained his commitment to black performers and became a target of those who attacked rock 'n' roll with racist smears, he gained even greater admiration among African Americans. The singer Jackie Wilson explained Freed's esteem among black entertainers: "Looking at it from an economic standpoint, I can say that because of him, hundreds of Negro musicians, singers, and arrangers got work." When Freed became a prime focus of the payola probe, the *Pittsburgh Courier* wondered if the investigations were "being used as a means of destroying the music that millions of teenagers have come to regard as their own."[88]

The payola scandal destroyed what was left of Freed's downwardly spiraling career. Even before the hearings commenced, Freed had lost jobs on both radio and television. Having moved from WINS to WABC after the Boston incident, Freed was asked by the latter station to sign an affidavit swearing that he had never taken payola. He refused, calling the demand "an insult to my reputation." Nevertheless, the flamboyant deejay hurt his own case by issuing characteristically flippant remarks. "A man said to me," Freed commented, "'if somebody sent you a Cadillac, would you send it back'? I said, 'It depends on the color.'" By way of clarification, Freed told reporters that he never accepted money in advance to play a record, "but if anybody wanted to thank him for playing a tune, he saw nothing wrong in accepting a gift."[89]

In contrast, Dick Clark held onto his lucrative job hosting *American Bandstand*. Employed by ABC, the parent company that owned Freed's New York City station, Clark did not have to sign the same kind of affidavit as did his fellow deejay. Instead, network executives permitted the Philadelphia broadcaster to fashion his own document that allowed him greater flexibility in denying that he had engaged in improper activities. Defining payola narrowly—the receipt of payments in exchange for playing a particular record—Clark asserted that he had never engaged in it. Yet Clark had to pay a price to keep his position. Heavily involved in an extensive array of enterprises including music publishing, marketing, manufacturing, and artist representation, Clark had to divest himself of these holdings to satisfy ABC's demand that he avoid any conflict of interest. This arrangement infuriated Freed, who howled that given the chance he could have truthfully signed the same statement as did Clark."[90]

Typically, Freed did not exit quietly. Griping that if he were "going to be a scapegoat" then Clark should "be one too," Freed got his wish. He even cooperated with the Harris Committee by appearing in executive session. Under the rules of the House this would keep him from incriminating himself with respect to other judicial action, but it also allowed him to help the committee build a case against Clark. On April 25, 1960, Freed testified in closed session that although he had been on the payroll of several record companies, he had never taken "a dime to play a record. I'd be a fool to. I'd be giving up control of my program."[91] He also criticized ABC officials for favoring Clark, a conclusion that the committee had also reached.

Indeed, Clark and not Freed became the primary target of the Harris committee's inquiry. To Washington lawmakers, even those as racially sensitive as the Arkansas chairman, rock 'n' roll was harmful whether the records were spun by Freed or Clark. The Philadelphian, however, provided the legislators with the opportunity to make headlines by exposing a star as bright as Charles Van Doren.[92] For those who believed in the continuing danger of a rigged society, Clark offered a shining example. He might appear clean-cut and virtuous on the outside, but the committee intended to show him as corrupt and deceitful on the inside.

Harris's staff had not uncovered much evidence that Clark had accepted payola, narrowly defined as "play for pay." Rather committee investigators discovered that Clark profited from holdings in a network of enterprises related to the music he aired on his program. The popular image of a shadowy individual greasing the palm of a greedy disk jockey with payments did not fit Clark's operation. Through various companies in which he had invested, the proprietor of *American Bandstand* "played records he had an interest in more frequently than those with no interest." A statistical breakdown of his program selections revealed that he played the records he had a stake in earlier and longer.[93] Thus, *Billboard* concluded, the nation's premier disk jockey derived royalties from "every possible source of revenue in the music industry, from copyright to distribution. "[94] Congressman Moss coined the word "Clarkola" to describe the Philadelphian's unique variation on the subject under investigation.[95] On this basis, the *New York Post* entertainment columnist Earl Wilson asserted that "Dick's on the edge of a precipice—and could easily be pushed off."[96]

These dire predictions notwithstanding, Clark turned in a virtuoso performance, one that saved his career, setting him apart from both Freed and Van Doren. Unlike Freed who presented his story behind closed doors in executive session, giving the appearance that he had something to hide, Clark faced the committee in open session on April 29 and May 2, with reporters and cameras recording his testimony. He proved that serving as a pitchman for rock 'n' roll hardly made him an anti-establishment figure. Although he defended the music he played as a wholesome, recreational outlet for teenagers, he came across more as a shrewd businessman than a diehard fan of rock 'n' roll. Pressed about his financial interests in thirty-three different companies that stood to gain from the popularity of *American Bandstand*, he explained his motive as trying to ensure his economic future by diversifying investments in "the recording, publishing, manufacturing [and] distribution fields." At most, he pleaded guilty with an explanation: "I would note that until the committee's activities, no one had really pointed out the inconsistency of performing records and owning an interest in record and music companies," a standard practice in the music industry. Besides, having sold off his outside musical holdings in agreement with ABC, Clark argued that the issue of improper influence had become moot.[97]

Despite the damaging evidence against him and his obvious tiptoeing around the meaning of the practice of payola, incredibly Clark walked away

261

from the hearings with his reputation intact. The skepticism many committee members voiced about the deejay's questionable business arrangements did not have much depth. He proved neither a serious threat to traditional American values nor to the civil rights concerns of southern white lawmakers. Chairman Harris spoke for most of his colleagues before dismissing Clark when he said: "You have given us a different light on the use of the broadcast media that has been presented to us by the admitted payola people.... You have been very helpful to the committee in the consideration of its responsibility. And I want to compliment you for that." Later when Clark wrote Harris privately to thank him for his "kind consideration," the Arkansas representative replied: "I was pleased to have the privilege of knowing you. I thought you gave a very good account of yourself."[98] Rather than coming off as the "Baby Face Nelson of the music business," Clark performed before the committee in a polished, courteous manner that distinguished him from the popular image of the sordid disk jockey on the take. A fellow of great charm who continued to receive the firm backing of his network employer ABC, Clark was never in as much danger as he had anticipated. How could he have been? As he later recalled, the chief counsel for the committee, Robert Lishman, during a lunch break brought up his teenage son to Clark to get his autograph and have a picture snapped with him.[99]

Alan Freed did not fare as well. He was the anti-Clark, who fostered an image of the untamed, rebellious, and dark (racially and socially) sides of rock 'n' roll. No parent would want him to marry their daughter. If adults could consider Clark the likeable boy next door, they had no room for Freed in their neighborhood. Freed's cooperation with the Harris committee did not spare him from an indictment for commercial bribery by a grand jury in New York City. Whereas Clark's subsequent career has thrived for nearly four decades, after the hearings Freed accepted a plea bargain of a $500 fine and a suspended six-month jail sentence. He bounced around from job to job for a few years until his death from kidney failure in 1965.[100]

The final outcome of the Harris investigation produced mixed results. After Congress passed an anti-payola bill, President Eisenhower signed it into law on September 13, 1960. The legislation required any station employee who accepted a payment for broadcasting material or the person making the payment to report it first to the station management. Failure to comply constituted a crime with a penalty of a year in jail and a $10,000 fine.[101]

Passage of the law may have given lawmakers an election-year victory to bring home to their constituents, but it did not kill payola. Endemic to the music business, the practice continued in even more clandestine form. At the end of the year, *Billboard* reported that the law had merely driven payola further underground. According to a survey conducted by the trade journal, the majority of disk jockeys believed that the payola investigation "was more of a political football than a practical cleanup." Music journalist Ralph Gleason observed that payola was "still alive and well" and that non-traceable cash payments had replaced checks as the standard fare of conducting surreptitious business dealings.[102] Nevertheless, with the Justice Department, FCC, and the Internal Revenue Service as an increased threat to those who dispensed or accepted illegal payments, payola no longer flourished as it had in the 1950s."[103]

After building throughout the 1950s, the anti-payola campaign reached its peak in 1960. The timing mirrored a number of features of the decade's political culture. Consistent with the myriad investigations into communism, organized crime, juvenile delinquency, and television quiz show fraud, the payola probe sought to expose the dangers to an unsuspecting public, especially among American youth, that came from the manipulation of their musical choices. Genuine payola and real deception certainly existed in the music business, as it had for most of the century, but during the 1950s the subject became a serious political issue because it conformed to the popular view that conspiratorial elements were operating to produce a rigged society. In this context, payola became the "hidden persuader" that produced an inferior and decadent brand of music undermining the nation's cultural strength and vitality. The drive against payola—"musical McCarthyism" as one contemporary disparagingly called it[104]—smeared rock 'n' roll with sinister influences and conveyed multiple fears related to youth, discipline, economic competition, race, and the Cold War. Some involved concerns over the decline of public morality and national purpose in an era of hostile relations with the Soviet Union; others grew out of a power struggle between professional associations in the music field. Moreover, rock 'n' roll and payola mirrored the growing presence of the civil rights movement and racial confrontation on the American political landscape.

In the years after *Brown v. Board of Education*, rock 'n' roll served as a symbolic target for those worried about the wrenching racial changes looming on the horizon. These fears accelerated with tangible examples of black protest such as the Montgomery bus boycott and the desegregation of Central High School in Little Rock. Yet for most of the half decade following *Brown*, civil rights efforts were scattered, non-confrontational, and confined largely to Congress and the courts. This changed dramatically in 1960 with the rise of student activism and the sit-ins. The pace of black protest heightened as did awareness of direct attacks on the racial status quo. Those upset by the changes that the black freedom struggle promised to bring had more palpable areas for concern than rock 'n' roll now furnished. Thus, by 1960, a chief threat to white supremacy came not from the musical transmission of black popular culture, but from the mobilization of a mass movement of blacks and their white allies. Although rock 'n' roll continued to provide the soundtrack for young activists in the struggle, it drifted away from the center of the contest for black advancement in the South and the nation. During the 1960s, payola persisted in the music industry and rock 'n' roll transformed itself into a more powerful product even as their value as political and cultural signifiers of racial tensions diminished."[105]

WOMEN, CIVIL RIGHTS,
AND BLACK LIBERATION

It is impossible to write about the civil rights movement without recognizing the centrality of women. Two pioneering events associated with the launching of the movement, *Brown v. Board of Education* in 1954 and the Montgomery, Alabama, bus boycott in 1955, drew women to the forefront. Linda Brown, an elementary school student from Topeka, Kansas, lent her name to the landmark suit resulting in the Supreme Court's proclamation against racially segregated public schools. A year later, Rosa Parks, a middle-aged seamstress and respected community activist in Montgomery, refused to abide by the city's segregationist policy and give up her seat to a white man on a crowded bus, thereby precipitating a successful year-long boycott. Yet hardly had Brown and Parks appeared on the scene than the focus of the movement shifted to men. The Reverend Martin Luther King, Jr., a newcomer to Montgomery in 1955 and far less involved in civil rights activities than Mrs. Parks, quickly vaulted to the center of attention as the foremost leader of the civil rights struggle, a position he never relinquished. Whether they were ministers or secular leaders of civil rights organizations, men commanded the bulk of the publicity devoted to coverage of the freedom struggle. Occasionally, women such as Rosa Parks gained notice, but they were long the exceptions to the male-dominated portrayal of the civil rights movement.

The paradox of women's importance to the black freedom movement and their relative invisibility in discussions of it requires explanation. Traditionally, historical narratives have been driven by political events occurring on a grand, nationwide scale. Groups that lobbied Congress, brought cases before the Supreme Court, and met with presidents stood out as movers and shakers. The major organizations that fit this description—the National Association for the

Advancement of Colored People (NAACP), the National Urban League, the Southern Christian Leadership Conference (SCLC), the Congress of Racial Equality (CORE), and the Student Nonviolent Coordinating Committee (SNCC)—were all led by men during the peak of the movement. The media, especially television, which developed as the main source of news during the 1950s and 1960s, focused the spotlight on men. This hardly comes as a surprise because during the postwar era affairs of state and matters of weighty public policy were seen as resting predominantly in male hands. Cameras recorded demonstrations in which women participated in significant numbers, but the male heads of the preeminent civil rights groups served as spokesmen for the protests and, in turn, attracted most of the limelight. Women such as Rosa Parks gained visibility when their actions sparked demonstrations that attracted national coverage, but then faded into the background as male leaders such as Dr. King presented black demands to a national audience.

Despite outward appearances, however, women played critical roles in securing first-class citizenship for African Americans. The key to understanding the contributions of black women rests in distinguishing between types of leadership. Males occupied formal leadership positions, as gendered divisions of labor common to mixed-sex organizations thrust men into the most visible roles in dealing with public officials. Because churches furnished the staging areas for mobilizing many black communities, ministers undertook primary responsibility for voicing their congregants' demands. Male pastors who participated actively in the movement exhibited the paternalistic, self-confident style of leadership that they were familiar with in running their ministries. The Reverend King's SCLC, an alliance of male ministers, operated in this fashion. The style proved unacceptable to Ella Baker, an experienced activist who served as its executive director. Baker, neither a minister nor a man, bristled from the male chauvinism she experienced in running the organization. One of the few women who held a senior position in a major civil rights group, Baker represented an alternative brand of leadership, one that reflected the experiences of women. She recognized that top-down leadership, whether in the form of ministerial-led associations or in hierarchical, secular groups like the NAACP, marginalized the efforts of women and relegated them mainly to secretarial and clerical positions. She advocated, instead, decision making that did not depend on either charismatic or bureaucratic authority; rather, Baker wanted people in local communities, women and men, to define their own goals and develop solutions to achieve them. In these day-to-day grassroots activities, women typically excelled. Black women formed the backbone of community life; their voluntary labor kept the churches functioning during the week and filled on Sundays, and their network of social clubs and interactions extended lines of communication throughout the community to bring black people of different classes and social standing together in times of crisis.

As Charles Payne observed with respect to the movement in the Mississippi Delta, "men led, but women organized."[1] Women not only sustained the community through religious and social activities, they also nurtured the civil rights struggle in their familial roles as wives and mothers. Without the sources of support they provided, the movement would never have gotten off the ground. Because the struggle relied on young people as plaintiffs in education cases and as marchers in demonstrations, women had enormous influence in shaping their children's decision to join the cause. It took great courage and faith to put their daughters' and sons' lives in jeopardy in the face of often brutal white resistance. Both inside and outside the home, women played an essential part in building the foundation for the movement to flourish. Depicting women as organizers, however, does not do justice to the leadership they exhibited. They did not usually hold official titles or follow formal job descriptions, but operating behind the scenes in routine, often gendered ways, women functioned as "bridge leaders." According to Belinda Robnett, who coined this term, women in the civil rights movement served as intermediaries between local communities, where their power was greatest, and regional and national civil rights agencies, where their access was much more limited.

In the last decade, scholarship on the civil rights movement has begun to explore the significance of women in the struggle against white supremacy. As historians moved away from studying macro-politics, they have highlighted how ordinary women and men gave meaning to their lives in the face of modernizing forces that undermine community: centralization, bureaucratization, and globalization. With respect to African Americans, this has meant detailed case studies of the various ways southern blacks reacted to racism. As scholars probed into local conditions, they increasingly discovered the importance of women as agents of change. Most of these women did not leave personal papers for historians to use in resurrecting their experiences, but oral histories have now opened to view the lives of people who were neglected. At the same time, a younger generation has reshaped the field of women's history, extending coverage beyond white women in the Northeast, the earlier focus of attention, to include women of color, especially in the South and Southwest. This trend has particularly stimulated interest in African American women and their participation in the civil rights struggle.

African American women's historians have shown that women's involvement in the civil rights era followed a much longer trajectory in anti-racist campaigns. Paula Giddings and Deborah Gray White separately have traced the intimate relationship between black women and racial advancement. With segregation, disfranchisement, and lynching in the ascendancy by 1900, black women seized opportunities to rise out of the nadir of oppression. Ida B. Wells, a brilliant newspaper editor and propagandist, spoke out vigorously against lynching and derided the supposed manliness of "civilized" whites for engaging in such beastly and cowardly behavior. Along with white women such as Mary White Ovington and black and white men, she helped organize the NAACP in 1909. The disfranchisement of black men in the South at the turn of the century placed them on a par with their black sisters who had yet to obtain suffrage. Turning this situation into something hopeful, African American women, North and South, sought to improve their communities by working together to raise standards of education, social service, and public health. The majority of women who were politically active did not join protest organizations such as the NAACP, but expressed their desire for progress through women's clubs. Mary Church Terrell's National Association of Colored Women (NACW), formed in 1896, adopted as its motto: "Lifting As We Climb." This racial uplift ideology depended on women as the guardians of moral purity to lead the way in improving the social and cultural conditions of all African Americans.

The passage of the Nineteenth Amendment in 1920 gave southern black women the right to vote in principle, but in practice they remained disfranchised along with their black brothers. Nevertheless, women remained in the vanguard of racial uplift. In the 1930s, the National Council of Negro Women (NCNW), led by Mary McLeod Bethune, proclaimed itself the "Voice of Negro Womanhood." It used interest group politics to pressure Franklin D. Roosevelt's New Deal to extend greater access and economic benefits to African Americans, the group hardest hit by the Great Depression. Bethune wielded formal power from her appointment as a high-ranking official of the National Youth Administration and informally from her close association with Eleanor Roosevelt, the president's wife. Both the NACW and the NCNW were composed primarily of middle-class women. Working-class black women found greater representation in the United Negro Improvement Association, the black nationalist movement of Marcus Garvey and his wife Amy Jacques-Garvey, which flourished in the 1920s. In the next decade, the International Ladies' Auxiliary of the Brotherhood of Sleeping Car Porters supported trade unionism and consumer cooperatives. In their roles as wives and mothers, its members strove to promote union activities among their husbands and to feed their families more economically through the formation of consumer cooperatives. All of these groups faced the common dilemma of having to balance issues of race, gender, and class. As Deborah White has shown, African American women bore a very heavy load in defending themselves against racism, sexism, and economic discrimination, while at the same time maintaining racial solidarity with men.

By World War II, whatever progress black women had achieved fell short of restoring freedom to African Americans. In the literature on the civil rights movement, World War II has gained recognition for jumpstarting the modern black freedom struggle. The anti-racist ideology inherent in fighting a war against Nazism furnished African Americans with a potent weapon to explode the United States' smug claim of practicing democracy at home. Pursuing victory abroad as well as within the nation's shores, blacks intensified their campaigns for desegregation of the military, equal employment opportunities, and expansion of the right to vote. Spurred on by growing wartime expectations, the NAACP, the premier civil rights organization of this period, saw its membership skyrocket, and A. Philip Randolph and Bayard Rustin first devised such tactics as mass marches and freedom rides that would be implemented with great success in the 1960s. Moreover, the participation of black men in the military, albeit under segregation, created a group of veterans who returned home after the war intent on asserting constitutional rights that had long been denied them and gaining a fair share of the economic rewards the American Dream promised. In communities throughout the South, many ex-GIs took the lead in mounting court cases and conducting voter registration drives. Community development through moral and economic uplift had paved the way, but it would take direct political pressure to achieve "Freedom Now."

Connecting the rise of the civil rights movement to World War II further increased the focus on men as soldiers and veterans. How, then, do we explain why women played key roles from the outset of the postwar black liberation struggle? If, as this chapter argues, women have had a long history of participation and leadership in black emancipation efforts, why have their contributions in the years immediately after 1945 been neglected, in contrast to those of men? The answer lies in the reconstruction of memory in the light of contemporary concerns. For instance, standing alongside male veterans and ministers, black women helped wage voter registration campaigns in the South, spurred on by the Supreme Court's outlawing of the white primary in 1944. Two years later, black women in Atlanta organized their communities and signed up previously disfranchised citizens in record numbers. The actual history, much of which was recognized at the time, is replete with women's involvement. However, as African Americans in Atlanta succeeded in electing mainly black men to office over the next three decades, culminating in the triumph of Maynard Jackson as mayor in 1973, the pioneering role of women faded from public memory. Instead, the official narrative of racial progress featured exclusively the black men who rose to power through the mobilization of African American voters. Consequently, as Kathryn L. Nasstrom has effectively argued, black women who had been the "centerpiece" in first organizing their community around suffrage campaigns "slipped from the prominent place [they] . . . formerly had in assessments of the voter registration drives, and with it the fortunes of women slipped as well."[2]

Despite the historical amnesia, it must be emphasized that World War II did encourage women to renew their struggle for first-class citizenship. Inspired by the wartime rhetoric of equality, some 4,000 black women managed to gain admission into the Women's Army Corps and other branches of the military. Moreover, the war whet the appetite of black women for continued progress. Having profited from the greater availability of jobs during the war, many African American women desired to hold onto them in peacetime. As Paula Giddings noted, the postwar period witnessed a rising percentage of black women college graduates and professionals and their entry into the middle class. As their educational and economic achievements escalated, African American women heightened their expectations of attaining the political and constitutional rights that marked full citizenship. Not surprisingly, young women and girls, like Linda Brown, were prominent among the students who took the lead in desegregating southern schools. Reflecting the rising number of black women attending college, Autherine Lucy briefly desegregated the University of Alabama and Vivian Malone made it permanent, while Charlayne Hunter did the same at the University of Georgia.

Other factors besides the war left women poised to seek civil rights. With the NAACP directing strategy in the early postwar period, education topped its legal agenda. Since the end of slavery, education had assumed enormous importance for African Americans. As moral guardians of the family, black mothers remained primarily responsible for getting their children safely to school. As Joanne Meyerowitz has shown, the traditional demands of motherhood could result in unconventional consequences in the 1950s. Thus, black women became very visible on civil rights battlefields as they stood behind their daughters and sons who sought admission to previously segregated schools.

Furthermore, black women—married and single—who worked outside the home at a higher rate than white women experienced other frustrations of racial discrimination. From early in the century, they constituted a large share of the passengers on public transportation and encountered rude treatment and arbitrarily enforced segregation rules. As Giddings pointed out, "there had always been a tinderbox quality to the ill treatment of Black women on pubic conveyances."[3] Not only did women who worked in menial jobs in white sections of their communities experience the harshness of racism, but so had more prominent black women such as turn-of-the-century journalist Ida B. Wells and the North Carolina educator Charlotte Hawkins Brown. With expectations rising for racial equality after World War II, it was only a matter of time before women trained their sights on public transportation to express their grievances.

Montgomery, Alabama, provided the opportunity. If there has been one woman identified with the civil rights movement among the crowd of prominent men, it is Rosa Parks. Despite this recognition, Parks's involvement has been shrouded in myth. Portrayed as returning home from work as a department store seamstress and just too tired to relinquish her bus seat to a white man, Parks appears as a single individual who just happened to ignite spontaneously a history-making boycott. This narrative is constructed in a way that allows the story to reach its true significance only when Dr. King and his fellow ministers take control of the protests. The boycott and the conventional account of it assume added importance because Montgomery marks the opening salvo of the modern civil rights movement, and its portrayal has reinforced the distorted image that men led and women quickly disappeared into the background. Hence it is vital to get the Montgomery chronicle straight. First, Mrs. Parks did not casually get caught up in some larger historical whirlwind. She had been an officer of the local chapter of the NAACP, and as far back as World War II had challenged the actions of biased bus drivers. Earlier in 1955, Parks had received training from the Highlander Folk School in Tennessee, a civil rights movement center that offered intensive interracial sessions in community organizing. Her refusal to give up her seat may have been spontaneous insofar as she had not planned it in advance; but it more accurately reflected Parks's personal history as a longtime civil rights activist.

Not only was Mrs. Parks other than an unwitting agent of a social revolution, but the initial success of the boycott owed a great deal to Montgomery's other women. Since the late 1940s, a group of middle-class and professional women had laid the basis for challenging bus discrimination. In the early 1950s, the Women's Political Council petitioned the Montgomery city government to hire African American bus drivers for routes in black neighborhoods, discipline discourteous white drivers, and ease inflexible restrictions on seating arrangements. Buoyed by the decision in *Brown*, the Council eagerly waited for a test case to fulfill its demands. Mrs. Parks provided it, and the Council possessed the organization to spring into action. One of its leaders, Jo Ann Gibson Robinson, an English teacher at the local black college, engineered the printing and distribution of 50,000 leaflets that informed blacks of the planned boycott and the mass meeting that would be held to launch it. Once the boycott began, Robinson remained active in the newly formed Montgomery Improvement Association, headed by the Reverend King. Moreover, women not only walked and carpooled to work, but they filled the church pews at the rallies that sustained the morale of the boycotters. The episode of the *Eyes on the Prize* documentary television series that deals with Montgomery graphically shows that although ministers orated from the pulpits, women provided the energy that infused these meetings through their singing and affirmations of support.

In addition to public conveyances, schools offered a vehicle for women's leadership. Three years after Mrs. Parks's protest, Little Rock, Arkansas, sorely tested the resolve of African Americans seeking equal, desegregated education for their children. In 1957, armed with a federal court order requiring Central High School to admit nine black students, the NAACP sought compliance. Daisy Bates, the chapter president, took charge of the teenagers attempting to break through the racial barricades. Bates was not a newcomer to civil rights activism. Together with her husband L.C., she edited the local black newspaper and investigated racial injustices, which resulted in white hostility and economic reprisals. Of the nine students, six were young women, and one of them, Elizabeth Eckford, became the poster girl for the harrowing experience. On the first day of trying to attend Central, she found herself alone surrounded by a howling mob of whites attempting to deny her entry. Photographers captured her strength and courage as she remained calm and finally managed, with the help of a couple of sympathetic white bystanders, to make her way to safety. In the end, President Dwight Eisenhower had to send in federal troops and order the Alabama National Guard to protect the Little Rock Nine. Melba Patillo Beals, one of the students, has poignantly written of the experience. She credits her mother and especially her grandmother for providing the encouragement to sustain her through an extremely difficult year, one in which the state militia did little to restrain the often brutal physical and psychological harassment blacks faced inside the school.

In both Montgomery and Little Rock, as would be true in subsequent situations, black activists portrayed themselves as adhering to the highest standards of middle-class respectability. The ideology of white supremacy had included at its core negative sexual stereotypes of African Americans, male and female. Black men were looked upon as bestial, potential rapists, and women were viewed as promiscuous Jezebels eager to give up their bodies for pleasure. The racial uplift philosophy embraced by black club women throughout the century sought to counter these negative images by replacing them with bourgeois notions of morality, sexuality, and cleanliness, which they hoped would prove African Americans worthy of citizenship. However, racial uplift ideology, although frequently conveying conservative connotations, was flexible enough to carry over to the liberationist goals of the civil rights movement. Thus Rosa Parks and Daisy Bates garnered favorable publicity from all but the most diehard segregationists because they clearly maintained standards of decency and respectability that challenged racist stereotypes of African American women. This can be seen most vividly from still photographs and documentary film footage of the movement in the late 1950s and 1960s that captured images of black women protesters neatly dressed in skirts and blouses and black men in jackets and ties. Wearing their best churchgoing attire, they highlighted the intimate connection between presenting a favorable image of moral correctness and obtaining racial equality.

Indeed, the most solidly middle-class civil rights organization, the NAACP, attracted a number of strong black women to leadership positions. In the 1940s, Ella Baker served as director of branches and set up youth councils. Though she left the association because its hierarchical form of leadership conflicted with her more democratic approach, Baker had accomplished a good deal by spearheading the NAACP's postwar surge in growth. Ruby Hurley, a Washington, DC, activist, replaced Baker as youth council director and in the 1950s was appointed to direct the Southeast region, the site of the most important battles of the civil rights era. During this period, the NAACP's legal team included Constance Baker Morley, who litigated cases in school desegregation hot spots in the South. She later was appointed to the federal bench. What still needs to be written is an analysis of how a top-down, male-centered organization like the NAACP succeeded in utilizing the talents of so many impressive women.

Furthermore, it is generally forgotten that older, gender-based groups

273

like the NCNW adapted their programs to meet the challenges of the civil rights era. Dorothy Height, who led the organization following Bethune, created the Wednesdays in Mississippi project, which dispatched interracial teams of women from the state to promote school desegregation and voting rights. Height also helped organize the historic 1963 March on Washington, and though she did not address the crowd, she sat on the platform alongside the most prominent male leaders. While recognizing the importance of the foremothers of the civil rights movement, it is also noteworthy to remember that even at the national level, prominent women such as Height have not received proper acknowledgment for their contributions, with most of the credit still bestowed upon men.

Few of the women who threw themselves into the black freedom struggle considered themselves feminists, because their concerns primarily centered around the advancement of their race rather than their sex. Yet it is difficult to separate gender from race. It is fair to say that as male civil rights activists were motivated by the need to exert their manhood, female activists pursuing racial equality sought to validate their womanhood. In her description of the late nineteen-century activist Maggie Lena Walker of Richmond, Virginia, as a "womanist," who viewed race and gender as intimately connected to her personal identity and political commitment, Elsa Barkley Brown has furnished a term that aptly applies to many African American women in the civil rights era. Throughout its long history, the black liberation struggle has not been so much a campaign for individual freedom as it has for collective emancipation. By exerting their womanhood and manhood, black women and men attempted to resist racially embedded, white supremacist notions of their sexual depravity.

Though some black women throughout the twentieth century identified themselves as feminists, they, too, combined struggles for woman's rights with the battle for racial equality. At the same time, although white women have been more closely identified with campaigns for gender equity than racial justice, there were important exceptions. Indeed, the history of white women in the civil rights movement generally remains as unfamiliar as that of black women. The earliest efforts during the first third of the twentieth century centered on campaigns against lynching, though the southern white women who led them did not attack racial segregation directly. Jessie Daniel Ames of Texas, as Jacquelyn Dowd Hall has demonstrated, opposed lynching because it placed southern white women on a hollow pedestal that really kept them subservient to men. Along with black anti-lynching advocates, Ames and her organization, the Association of Southern Women for the Prevention of Lynching, demolished the excuse that murderous retribution was necessary to protect white women from savage black rapists. Marshaling evidence that most lynchings did not involve charges of rape, Ames and her associates argued that women did not need safeguarding through violent reprisals, and in making this argument they helped breach the boundaries of paternalism that operated to reinforce the racial and sexual hegemony of white males.

275

As lynchings began to decline by the late 1930s, the focus of white women's racial activism was aimed more at class than gender concerns. The economic crisis of the Great Depression, which hit the South hardest, underscored the necessity of bringing relief to the poor, white and black alike. The foremost group advocating economic and racial justice was the Southern Conference for Human Welfare (SCHW). Bringing together labor organizers, Communists, African American activists, and white liberals and moderates, in the late 1930s and 1940s the SCHW campaigned for economic reforms and defied norms of racial segregation. The Conference had the support of Eleanor Roosevelt, and one of its leading proponents was Virginia Foster Durr. The daughter of a respected family from Montgomery, Durr moved easily in New Deal liberal circles. She worked tirelessly to reduce the influence of conservative white southern politicians in the Democratic Party, and to this end she helped organize as an offshoot of the SCHW the National Committee to Abolish the Poll Tax. Durr believed that the elimination of this franchise requirement would extend the suffrage to poor whites as well as blacks who might then join together and rescue the Democratic Party from the control of southern oligarchs. In 1948, Durr lined up behind the Progressive Party candidacy of Henry A. Wallace and ran for the U.S. Senate in Virginia. Though neither won, their campaigns addressed integrated crowds and appealed for black votes. In 1955, Durr and her husband Clifford, an attorney, were among the first to come to the assistance of their friend Rosa Parks after her arrest in Montgomery. Along with the Durrs, Anne and Carl Braden of Louisville, Kentucky, agitated for racial and economic justice, and their efforts yielded antagonism from powerful southern politicians who sought to smear them as subversives.

In Virginia Durr and Anne Braden, a younger generation of white, college-educated, southern women found role models. Like their black counterparts, many white women gained inspiration for joining the struggle from their religious values. In her book, *Personal Politics* (1980), Sara Evans writes that although "southern Protestantism in the 1950s was in general as segregated and racist as the rest of southern society, it also nourished elements of egalitarian idealism." Anne Braden recalled that her childhood church had first taught her "that all men are One," a lesson that reinforced her activism throughout her life.[4] As more young women began to enroll on college campuses in the 1950s, some of them fell under the influence of campus ministers expounding Christian existentialism, whose principles of authenticity and personal witness provided a radical critique of mainstream America and southern racism. Typical of this group was Sandra "Casey" Cason. Attending the University of Texas at Austin as an undergraduate in the late 1950s, Cason became active in the YWCA and the Faith and Life Community, which advocated leading one's life according to principles of brotherhood and respect for others, commitments that were taken seriously. She met like-minded women and men, and Cason's experiences in these groups turned her from "'a lively bobby soxer' into one of the principal leaders of the interracial movement in Austin."[5] Black women such as Ella Baker and Dorothy Height, who worked with the YWCA on interracial projects, mentored Cason and other young whites. From Texas, Cason went on to become one of the most important southern white female staff members of SNCC. After marrying fellow activist Tom Hayden, one of the founders of the Students for a Democratic Society, she continued to work with other women from similar backgrounds, including Mary King, Dorothy Dawson, Joan Browning, and Constance Curry.

Radical Christianity alone does not explain the growing participation of young women in the civil rights movement of the 1950s and 1960s. Deborah Schultz has recently explored women from Jewish backgrounds who flocked to the black freedom struggle. Blacks and Jews historically had an uneasy relationship. Although common objects of discrimination, they frequently clashed in the mundane affairs of daily life. As Jews assimilated into American culture and achieved success as shopkeepers, merchants, and landlords, they came into conflict with blacks and were seen by them as no different than other exploitive whites. Expressions of black anti-Semitism stood side by side with those of Jewish racism. Nevertheless, among the leadership class, blacks and Jews often cooperated in battling discrimination that affected members of both groups. Jews had been among the founders of the NAACP and provided influential lawyers to represent the national association in winning early victories before the Supreme Court. Individual Jews provided financial contributions to fund civil rights activities, and Jewish organizations cooperated in lobbying for civil rights legislation. In similar fashion as young Christian women with a finely honed religious consciousness, college-education Jewish women also turned to the civil rights movement to bear witness to their moral principles. However, ethnicity more than religious devotion shaped Jewish women's identities as activists. Women who went South in the 1960s to work in the movement, including Dottie Miller Zellner and Elaine DeLott Baker, tended to come from secular Jewish homes; some, like Zellner, had parents who had been Communists. But as Schultz has argued, Whatever their personal background, these young women inherited a "Jewish moral framework about social justice."[6] In addition, they had grown up at a time when American Jews were first trying to make some sense of the Holocaust, and at a basic level these young activists absorbed the lesson that an oppressed people had to "fight back" against racial injustice or perish.

However important their stories, white women and men, Christian and Jewish alike, played a secondary role to that of blacks in leading the movement. The student sit-ins of 1960 galvanized a new generation behind the freedom movement and gave African American women increased opportunities for leadership. Diane Nash, a Fisk University undergraduate, and Ruby Doris Smith Robinson of Spelman College helped direct protests against segregated facilities in Nashville, Tennessee, and Atlanta, Georgia, respectively. In April 1960, along with over one hundred veterans of the fledgling sit-in movement, Nash joined in the creation of SNCC (Robinson entered the group the next year). In May 1961, when the freedom rides stalled in the wake of violence in Birmingham, Alabama, Nash made certain that SNCC members boarded buses to continue the trip. Robinson heeded her call and was one of over three hundred riders jailed in Mississippi. Nash and her husband, James Bevel, moved on to work for SCLC and were instrumental in paving the way for Dr. King to conduct his famous march from Selma to Montgomery in 1965. That same year, Robinson won election as executive secretary of SNCC.

More than any major civil rights group, SNCC fostered women's participation and leadership. In great measure this was a result of the influence of Ella Baker, who encouraged the young organization to remain independent of existing civil rights associations. Baker's conception of leadership as group centered and her view of decision making as an outgrowth of participatory democracy appealed to women. Middle-class, educated women like Nash found it easier to make their voices heard in this kind of political atmosphere and to gain respect for their ideas. The grassroots organizing tactics that SNCC preferred further enhanced the position of women in the group. Women proved adept at organizing projects in the rural South that depended on dealing patiently with local people and winning their trust. They displayed similar courage as men in bearing personal witness to racism in the most hostile areas. As a democratic, nonhierarchical organization, SNCC provided many spaces for black and white women staff to display their leadership skills. Nevertheless, traditional gender norms did not automatically disappear within SNCC (its slogan was "A Band of *Brothers*, A Circle of Trust" [emphasis added]), and with the brief exception of Ruby Doris Smith Robinson, men held the top titled positions. However, as much as possible within the larger male-dominated culture, SNCC women shared leadership responsibilities with men.

Women also gained significant influence within other civil rights organizations. The leadership positions wielded in the NAACP by women such as Ruby Hurley and Daisy Bates have been noted earlier. At the grassroots level, this also included the campaigns that Modjeska Simkins undertook for the South Carolina Conference of the NAACP. In planning strategy, raising money to finance school desegregation cases, and distributing food and clothing to the needy, Simkins came to be considered a "mother-benefactress" by those she assisted.[7]

Next to the NAACP, the SCLC had the tightest organizational structure, whose hierarchical chain of command led directly to the Reverend King. Eschewing group-centered for charismatic leadership, King and his fellow ministers made it impossible, as Ella Baker had discovered, for women to gain equal authority with men. Nevertheless, strong women did make powerful contributions to the Conference. As mentioned earlier, Diane Nash Bevel was one, Septima P. Clark was another. A teacher in the Charleston, South Carolina, public schools in the 1950s, Clark participated in the YWCA and NAACP and attended leadership training workshops at the Highlander Folk School. After losing her teaching job because of her civil rights activities, Clark was hired by Highlander as educational director, where in 1955, she encountered Rosa Parks. She also worked closely with Baker, and in 1961, the SCLC employed her to supervise workshops on citizenship training and literacy, using innovative techniques that placed nontraditional teachers, recruited from the community, in charge of preparing people to vote.

CORE, which in many ways shared SNCC's approach to organizing in the deep South, also attracted strong women. In her classic autobiography, Anne Moody describes her journey from a racially stifling hometown in Mississippi to her recruitment by CORE to participate in some of the most dangerous civil rights battles in the Magnolia State. In the local villages and towns that Moody and the other movement women ventured into, they routinely connected with black women who offered them their homes for shelter and their kitchens for meals, thus exposing their families to grave risk. Not only providers of daily sustenance, these local women, affectionately called "Mamas," were at the very heart of civil rights activities and opened doors in their communities that outsiders could not otherwise have entered. Moreover, they furnished vivid examples of independence and courage for young black and white women in the movement to emulate.

Of all the local women, Fannie Lou Hamer perhaps best represents the ability of the civil rights movement to identify and cultivate grassroots female leadership. Her story has been well told in two biographies by Chana Kai Lee and Kay Mills. A timekeeper on a plantation in Ruleville, Mississippi, Hamer became a SNCC staff worker. She lost her job because of her civil rights efforts, but unlike most local women, she gained national fame. A founder of the Mississippi Freedom Democratic Party in 1964, she traveled to the National Democratic Party Convention in Atlantic City, New Jersey, to win recognition and seats for its delegates as replacements for representatives of the white supremacist state party organization. In the plain-spoken, folksy style that reflected her lack of education and poor background, she delivered a widely publicized indictment of white racism in Mississippi and a stirring account as to how it had brutalized her personally. When national party leaders at the behest of President Lyndon Johnson offered a token compromise of representation, Mrs. Hamer forcefully rallied her fellow delegates to reject it. Although Mississippi insurgents did not achieve their immediate demand for seating, the national party instituted nondiscriminatory guidelines that guaranteed Mississippi reformers, including Hamer, seats at the Democratic nominating convention in 1968.

As biographies of key movement women have appeared in the past decade, giving greater visibility to many of the heroines of the struggle, they caution us not to treat these women as one-dimensional figures. Because these activists had not previously received the acclaim they deserved, in bringing them out of obscurity it is tempting to romanticize them. The autobiography of Anne Moody, published in 1968, should make readers aware that black female activists, especially those who lived their entire lives in the South, carried on the struggle at great personal sacrifice. Chana Lee's 1999 biography of Hamer makes this point abundantly clear. Lee poignantly reveals Hamer's distress concerning her grandmother who, like numerous southern black women, was sexually molested by white men. Hamer suffered the pain of an unwanted sterilization procedure while she was in the hospital for an operation for an unrelated stomach ailment, the results of which prevented her from becoming a birth mother. In revering Mrs. Hamer's strength and courage, we forget the physical disabilities she endured on a daily basis and the depression she suffered in the years before her death in 1977. Lee suggests the toll her public life exacted on her husband and family, which was a particularly difficult situation for women who were expected to make domestic affairs their top priority. Many women saw their marriages and personal relationships buckle under the pressure of participating in a stressful and time-consuming political and social revolution.

Despite plentiful evidence of the egalitarian treatment of women in organizations like SNCC, a protracted historical debate has raged about the presence and impact of sexism within the movement. The debate has focused on SNCC because it had the reputation as the most hospitable civil rights group for women's activism. In *Personal Politics*, Sara Evans described the complaint of white women in SNCC that they received second-class treatment within the organization. This incipient feminist consciousness erupted at a SNCC gathering in Waveland, Mississippi, in late 1964 as the group sought to reassess its place in the civil rights movement. An anonymous memo circulated at the retreat and authored by two veteran white staff members, Mary King and Casey Hayden, listed their grievances. Why is it in SNCC, the memo asked, "that women who are competent, qualified, and experienced, are automatically assigned to the 'female' kinds of jobs such as typing, desk work, telephone work, filing, library work, cooking, and the assistant kind of administrative work but rarely the 'executive' kind?"[8] Moreover, at a party to unwind after hours of intense discussions, Stokely Carmichael, who the following year would take over as chair of SNCC, jokingly referred to the anonymous manifesto: "The only position for women in SNCC is prone."[9] Carmichael's flippant remark became widely quoted in budding feminist circles and amounted to something of an opening salvo in the emerging women's liberation struggle.

In the wake of Evans's study, most scholars initially accepted the interpretation that women experienced sexism within SNCC and the gap between the group's egalitarian ideals and its practices encouraged the growth of feminism. However, recent scholarship and the publication of several autobiographies of SNCC women have presented a different and more complicated explanation of the memo in particular, and SNCC's attitude toward women in general. It is important to explain the context in which the Waveland Conference was held. It came a few months after the exceedingly stressful Freedom Summer, and SNCC was undergoing an identity crisis. Controversies flared over whether the group should continue to tolerate its hyperdemocratic, loose organizational structure or adopt a more centralized, structured framework. Challenges surfaced as to the extent that white people should participate in a black-centered struggle, especially as many blacks in the organization were beginning to embrace racial nationalism. For many, the influx of northerners during Freedom Summer, most but not all of whom were white, and their desire to continue on staff raised questions about the ability of the organization to remain true to its original principles, including nonviolence and integration. Ironically, the authors of the memo, Hayden and King, despite what appears to be very plain language describing SNCC's sexist character, have claimed that this impression is false. Both have argued that they did not target sexism per se in their 1964 statement, but they were really troubled by the possibility that SNCC would renounce its participatory democratic principles and move toward top-down leadership. Because women in SNCC had flourished within a decentralized structure, Hayden and King asserted they were mainly concerned that women would lose out in the proposed reorganization.

Black women did not join the challenge mounted by SNCC's white women and deny that sexism was a problem for them. They have pointed out that black women worked side by side with men and ran their own field projects in the South. The election of Ruby Doris Smith Robinson as SNCC's executive secretary in 1965 further attests to the acceptance of a strong black woman to occupy one of the two main leadership posts in the organization. In fact, functioning equally with black men, as Cynthia Washington, a SNCC staffer put it, black women were placed "in some category other than female."[10] One result, however, was that white women, who occupied more traditional feminine roles than African American women, often became more suitable for dating by black men, which fostered resentment by black women.

Although King and Hayden's retrospective comments place the issue in larger perspective, they fail to explain the specific complaints against the treatment of women that were presented in 1964. A more complete answer lies in consideration of race rather than gender as the primary explanation of SNCC's attitudes. The sharpest difference in treatment of black and white women occurred during Freedom Summer. Northern white women flocked to the South ready to jump into the fray. Intelligent, strong-minded, and courageous women, nevertheless they had little first-hand experience of southern culture and customs. Intent on openly showing their contempt for racism, some of them flaunted norms against interracial dating without fully realizing the danger they posed to black men. Fannie Lou Hamer, whose commitment to integration remained steadfast, nevertheless sharply criticized white women for acting as if race did not matter in Mississippi. Worried that violation of racial taboos would get black men killed, Mrs. Hamer complained that if young white women continued to hang around black men in full public view and "can't obey the rules, call their mothers and tell them to send their sons instead!"[11] Concern over appearances and the threat to the safety of black men, more than explicitly sexist attitudes, resulted in confining white women volunteers to the kind of traditional female work catalogued by Hayden and King in their provocative memo. Despite the criticism she has received for highlighting SNCC's sexism, Evans recognized that the problem for white women was not just a male/female one, and in this vein she quotes an African American female SNCC staff member: "It was a race problem rather than a woman's problem."[12] In the final analysis, the legacy of SNCC's influence on women may be mixed, but as the leading authority on African American women and the civil rights movement, Belinda Robnett, has concluded: "While SNCC was not completely successful, women were not subjugated to, nor were their contributions predefined by, men."[13]

Moreover, the story of black women's relationship to racial and gender justice movements continues to evolve. In later years, after the heyday of the civil rights movements passed, many black women recognized that in showing solidarity with African American men, they had diminished the extent to which gender concerns affected them. Yet the brand of feminism they defined and displayed was affected by several considerations. In the late 1960s and 1970s, second-wave feminism, itself shaped and stimulated by the civil rights movement, began to embrace race and class issues that were important to black women. The rise of Black Power and Black Nationalism, with their displays of acute masculinity, raised the consciousness of black female activists to the sexist side of the struggle to achieve equality. Such political radicals as Angela Davis, Black Panthers Elaine Brown and Kathleen Cleaver, and writers Alice Walker and Toni Morrison have all expressed the view that sexism cannot be ignored if black women and men intend to free themselves, their families, and communities from racial, economic, and gender discrimination. By the early 1970s, a number of women with long experience in civil rights founded the National Black Feminist Organization. Others continued to emphasize womanist perspectives, but focused greater attention on the specific concerns of African American women.

In the forty years since the height of the civil rights movement, scholars have produced a rich literature on the people, communities, and organizations that helped reconstruct the South and the nation along more egalitarian lines. Not until the last decade or so have women gained recognition for the central contributions they made. More remains to be explored as researchers move from the first tier of notable female activists to those unsung women whose participation and leadership were so embedded in the daily struggle that they have been hard to distinguish from the movement itself. In the process of further disentangling women's diverse roles, researchers are beginning to pay greater attention to the operation of gendered norms within the civil rights movement. So far we have mostly had a women's history tacked onto a men's history of civil rights, which emphasizes the contributions of each sex rather than the complicated relationship between the two. Future studies should reveal that in the long battle against racism, black men were not merely seeking to exert their manhood, nor were black women their womanhood, but together they sought to affirm their race consciousness and personhood.

NOTES

INTRODUCTION

1. Steven F. Lawson, *Black Ballots: Voting Rights in the South, 1944–1969*. (Revised Edition, Lanham, MD,1999); *In Pursuit of Power: Southern Blacks and Electoral Politics, 1965–1982*. (New York: 1985); *Running for Freedom: Civil Rights and Black Politics in America, Since 1941*. (Second Edition, New York, 1997); Steven F. Lawson and Charles Payne, *Debating the Civil Rights Movement 1945–1968*. (Lanham, MD, 1998.)

FREEDOM THEN, FREEDOM NOW

1. Sundiata K. Cha-Jua, "Mississippi Burning: The Burning of Black Self-Activity," *Radical History Review*, 45 (1989): 125–36. In addition to *Eyes on the Prize*, a production of Henry Hampton and Blackside, Inc., see also the documentary film by Jo Ann Grant, *Fundi: The Story of Ella Baker* (New York: First Run Films, 1981). For a companion volume to the former, see Juan Williams, *Eyes on the Prize: America's Civil Rights Years, 1954–1965* (New York, 1987).

2. Robert L. Zangrando, "Manuscript Sources for Twentieth-Century Civil Rights Research," *Journal of American History*, 74 (1987): 243–51. Carl M. Brauer, *John F. Kennedy and the Second Reconstruction* (New York, 1977); August Meier and Elliot Rudwick, *CORE: A Study in the Civil Rights Movement, 1942–1968* (New York, 1973); Robert Frederick Burk, *The Eisenhower Administration and Civil Rights* (Knoxville, Tenn., 1984); Harris Wofford, *Of Kennedy and Kings: Making Sense of the Sixties* (New York, 1980); Steven F. Lawson, *Black Ballots: Voting Rights in the South, 1944–1969* (New York, 1976); Thomas R. Peake, *Keeping the Dream Alive: A History of the Southern Christian Leadership Conference from King to the 1980s* (New York, 1987); James Farmer, *Lay Bare the Heart: An Autobiography of the Civil Rights Movement* (New York, 1985).

3. Kim Lacy Rogers, "Oral History and the History of the Civil Rights Movement," *Journal of American History*, 75 (1988): 567–76. The Civil Rights Documentation Project in the Moreland Springarn Collection at Howard University was the exception.

4. Clayborne Carson, "Civil Rights Reform and the Black Freedom Struggle," in Charles W. Eagles, ed., *The Civil Rights Movement in America* (Jackson, Miss., 1986), 23, 27.

5. William E. Leuchtenburg, "The Pertinence of Political History: Reflections on the Significance of the State in America," *Journal of American History*, 73 (December 986): 585–600.

6. The volumes in this collection have different titles. Hereafter, the series will be cited as Garrow Series (GS).

7. Although they contain useful information and firsthand accounts, James H. Laue, *Direct Action and Desegregation, 1960–1962* (GS 15), and Martin Oppenheimer, *The Sit-In Movement of 1960* (GS 16), both written in the early 1960s, read more like the sociological dissertations they are than polished works of history. Joan Turner Beifuss, *At the River I Stand: Memphis, the 1968 Strike, and Martin Luther King*, was originally self-published by the author in 1985 but did not receive a wide circulation. Aimee Isgrig Horton's study of the Highlander Folk School, originally written in 1971, has been supplanted by John M. Glen, *Highlander: No Ordinary School, 1932–1962* (Lexington, Ky., 1988).

8. For a comprehensive bibliography, see Clayborne Carson, *A Guide to Research on Martin Luther King, Jr., and the Modern Black Freedom Struggle* (Stanford, Calif., 1989).

9. For some intriguing suggestions regarding future directions for civil rights historiography, see William H. Harris, "Trends and Needs in Afro-American Historiography," in Darlene Clark Hine, ed., *The State of Afro-American History* (Baton Rouge, La., 1986), 152.

10. The most significant recent studies include David J. Garrow, *Bearing the Cross: Martin Luther King, Jr. and the Southern Christian Leadership Conference* (New York, 1986); Taylor Branch, *Parting the Waters: America in the King Years, 1954–1963* (New York, 1988); and "A Round Table: Martin Luther King, Jr.," *Journal of American History*, 74 (1987): 436–81. These authors built on valuable works by Lawrence D. Reddick, *Crusader without Violence: A Biography of Martin Luther King, Jr.* (New York, 1959); Lerone Bennett, Jr., *What Manner of Man: A Biography of Martin Luther King, Jr.* (Chicago, 1968); David L. Lewis, *King: A Biography* (Urbana, Ill., 1978); Stephen B. Oates, *Let the Trumpet Sound: The Life of Martin Luther King, Jr.* (New York, 1982); and Adam Fairclough, *"To Redeem the Soul of America": The Southern Christian Leadership Conference and Martin Luther King, Jr.* (Athens, Ga., 1987); see also Peter J. Albert and Ronald Hoffman, *We Shall Overcome: Martin Luther King, Jr., and the Black Freedom Struggle* (New York, 1990).

11. David J. Garrow, "From Reform to Revolutionary," in David J. Garrow, ed., *Martin Luther King, Jr.: Civil Rights Leader, Theologian, Orator* (Brooklyn, N. Y., 1989), 2: 435 (GS 2).

12. See Richard Hammer, "The Life and Death of Martin Luther King," in Garrow, *Martin Luther King, Jr.*, 2: 465–78, for an early presentation (1968) of this construction.

13. Martin Luther King, Jr., *Stride toward Freedom* (New York, 1958); Stephen B. Oates, "The Intellectual Odyssey of Martin Luther King," in Garrow, *Martin Luther King, Jr.*, 3: 301–20 (GS 3); Ira G. Zepp, Jr., *The Social Vision of Martin Luther King, Jr.*, David J. Garrow, ed (Brooklyn, 1989) (GS 18); James H. Cone, "Martin Luther King, Jr., Black Theology—Black Church," in Garrow, *Martin Luther King, Jr.*, 1:

285

203–14 (GS 1). For King's impact on white churches, see James F. Findlay, "Religion and Politics in the Sixties: The Churches and the Civil Rights Act of 1964," *Journal of American History*, 77 (1990): 69–70.

14. Paul R. Garber, "King Was a Black Theologian," in Garrow, *Martin Luther King, Jr.*, 2: 404. For other examples, see Lewis V. Baldwin, "Martin Luther King, Jr., the Black Church, and the Black Messianic Vision," Ibid., 1: 1–16; Cone, "Martin Luther King, Jr., Black Theology—Black Church," 1: 203–14; Robert M. Franklin, Jr., "An Ethic of Hope: The Moral Thought of Martin Luther King, Jr.," Ibid., 2: 349–59; James P. Hanigan, "Martin Luther King, Jr.,: The Images of a Man," Ibid., 2: 479–506; C. Eric Lincoln, "Martin Luther King, the Magnificent Intruder," Ibid., 3: 611–22; James H. Smylie, "On Jesus, Pharaohs, and the Chosen People: Martin Luther King as Biblical Interpreter and Humanist," Ibid., 3: 839–56.

15. Baldwin, "Martin Luther King, Jr.," 1: 7.

16. Cone, "Martin Luther King, Jr., "Black Theology—Black Church," 1: 207.

17. August Meier, "On the Role of Martin Luther King," in Garrow, *Martin Luther King, Jr.*, 3: 635–42.

18. Keith D. Miller, "Martin Luther King, Jr. Borrows a Revolution: Argument, Audience and Implications of a Secondhand Universe," in Garrow, *Martin Luther King, Jr.*, 3: 643–59. Miller viewed King's borrowing of "major themes, literary quotations and other homiletic commonplaces" in a positive light, because it allowed the civil rights leader to communicate with whites in the tried and tested language they understood. Revelations about plagiarism in his doctoral dissertation underscore the problem of disentangling King's ideas from those of his sources. The most promising way of examining this issue appears to be looking at King's writings as derived from the oral traditions of the black church in which, according to Miller, words were not defined as commodities. See David J. Garrow, "Martin Luther King, Jr.: Borrowing Trouble," *Washington Post*, National Weekly Edition (November 26–December 2, 1990): 25.

19. J. Pious Barber quoted in Garrow, *Bearing the Cross*, 43.

20. Vincent Gordon Harding, "King and the Future of America," *Journal of American History*, 74 (1987): 473.

21. Winifred Breines, "Whose New Left?" *Journal of American History*, 75 (September 1988): 528–45.

22. In addition to the Garrow Series volume, *Chicago* 1966 (GS 11), see Alan B. Anderson and George W. Pickering, *Confronting the Color Line: The Broken Promise of the Civil Rights Movement in Chicago* (Athens, Ga., 1986). On the FBI, see Kenneth O'Reilly, *"Racial Matters": The FBI's Secret File on Black America, 1960–1972* (New York, 1989); and David J. Garrow, *The FBI and Martin Luther King, Jr.,: From "Solo" to Memphis* (New York, 1981).

23. Adam Fairclough, "Was Martin Luther King a Marxist?" in Garrow, *Martin Luther King, Jr.*, 1: 301–09; J. Mills Thornton, "Commentary," in Eagles, ed., *Civil Rights Movement*, 150.

24. James H. Cone, "Martin Luther King, Jr., and the Third World," *Journal of American History*, 74 (1987): 456.

25. Aldon D. Morris, *The Origins of the Civil Rights Movement: Black Communities Organizing for Change* (New York, 1984), 51–52, 148–49; Jo Ann Gibson Robinson, *The Montgomery Bus Boycott and the Women Who Started It: The Memoir of Jo Ann Gibson Robinson*, David J. Garrow, ed. (Knoxville, Tenn., 1987).

26. Robin D. G. Kelley, *Hammer and Hoe: Alabama Communists during the Great*

Depression (Chapel Hill, N. C., 1990); Robert Korstad and Nelson Lichtenstein, "Opportunities Found and Lost: Labor, Radicals, and the Early Civil Rights Movement," *Journal of American History*, 75 (December 1988): 786–811; Karen Sacks, *Caring by the Hour: Women, Work, and Organizing at Duke Medical Center* (Urbana, Ill., 1988, chap. 2. See also Gerald Horne, *Communist Front: The Civil Rights Congress*, 1946–1956 (East Rutherford, N. J., 1988).

27. A comprehensive history of the NAACP remains to be written. In the meantime, see Charles Flint Kellogg, NAACP (Baltimore, Md., 1967); Roy Wilkins with Tom Mathews, *Standing Fast* (New York, 1982); Richard Kluger, *Simple Justice* (New York, 1975); Mark V. Tushnet, *The NAACP's Legal Strategy against Segregated Education*, 1925–1950 (Chapel Hill, N. C., 1987); B. Joyce Ross, *J. E. Spingarn and the Rise of the NAACP, 1911–1939* (New York, 1972); Gilbert Ware, William Hastie: *Grace under Pressure* (New York, 1984); Genna Rae McNeil, *Groundwork: Charles Hamilton Houston and the Struggle for Civil Rights* (Philadelphia, 1983); and Robert L. Zangrando, *The NAACP Crusade against Lynching, 1909–1950* (Philadelphia, 1980).

28. Charles U. Smith and Lewis M. Killian, "The Tallahassee Bus Protest," in David J. Garrow, ed., *We Shall Overcome: The Civil Rights Movement in the United States in the 1950s and 1960s* (Brooklyn, N. Y., 1989), 3: 1017–39 (GS 6).

29. August Meier and Elliot Rudwick, "The Origins of Nonviolent Direct Action in Afro-American Protest: A Note on Historical Discontinuities," in Garrow, *We Shall Overcome*, 3: 908.

30. However, once an innovative tactic appeared, it spread in waves to other nearby locales; see Carl R. Graves, "The Right to Be Served: Oklahoma City's Lunch Counter Sit-ins, 1958–1964," in Garrow, *We Shall Overcome*, 1: 283–97 (GS 4).

31. William H. Chafe, *Civilities and Civil Rights: Greensboro, North Carolina, and the Black Struggle for Freedom* (New York, 1981); see also Robert J. Norrell, *Reaping the Whirlwind: The Civil Rights Movement in Tuskegee* (New York, 1985).

32. Branch, *Parting the Waters*, chap. 1.

33. Aldon D. Morris, "Black Southern Sit-In Movement: An Analysis of Internal Organization," in Garrow, *We Shall Overcome*, 3: 953; see also Morris, *Origins of the Civil Rights Movement*; Doug McAdam, *Political Process and the Development of Black Insurgency* (Chicago, 1982).

34. Lewis M. Killian, "Organization, Rationality and Spontaneity in the Civil Rights Movement," in Garrow, *We Shall Overcome*, 2: 513, 514 (GS 5).

35. Irwin Klibaner, *Conscience of a Troubled South: The Southern Conference Educational Fund, 1946–1966*, David J. Garrow, ed. (Brooklyn, N. Y., 1989) (GS 14); Aimee Isgrig Horton, *The Highlander Folk School: A History of Its Major Programs, 1932–1961*, David J. Garrow, ed. (Brooklyn, 1989) (GS 12). See also Thomas A. Krueger, *And Promises to Keep: The Southern Conference for Human Welfare, 1938–1948* (Nashville, Tenn., 1967).

36. David M. Chalmers, *Hooded Americanism: The History of the Ku Klux Klan* (New York, 1981); Neil McMillen, *The Citizens' Council: Organized Resistance to the Second Reconstruction, 1954–1964* (Urbana, Ill., 1971); Numan V. Bartley, *The Rise of Massive Resistance* (Baton Rouge, La., 1974).

37. J. Mills Thornton, "Challenge and Response in the Montgomery Bus Boycott of 1955–1956," in David J. Garrow, ed., *The Walking City: The Montgomery Bus Boycott, 1955–1956* (Brooklyn, N. Y., 1989), 323–79 (GS 7); David R. Colburn, *Racial Change and Community Crisis: St. Augustine Florida, 1877–1980* (New York, 1985); Elizabeth Jacoway and David R. Colburn, *Southern Businessmen and Desegregation*

287

(Baton Rouge, La., 1982); Stephen L. Longenecker, *Selma's Peacemaker: Ralph Smeltzer and Civil Rights Mediation* (Philadelphia, 1987).

38. On this theme, see Neil R. McMillen, *Dark Journey: Black Mississippians in the Age of Jim Crow* (Urbana, Ill., 1989).

39. Glenn T. Eskew, "The Alabama Christian Movement for Human Rights and the Birmingham Struggle for Civil Rights, 1956–1963"; and Lee E. Bains, Jr., "Birmingham 1963: Confrontation over Civil Rights," both in David J. Garrow, ed., *Birmingham, Alabama 1956–1963: The Black Struggle for Civil Rights* (Brooklyn, N. Y., 1989), 3–114 and 151–289 (GS 8) respectively.

40. Jack L. Walker, "The Functions of Disunity: Negro Leadership in a Southern City," in David J. Garrow, ed., *Atlanta, Georgia, 1960–1961: Sit-Ins and Student Activism* (Brooklyn, N. Y., 1989), 17–29 (GS 9). On cleavages in Mississippi, see John Dittmer, "The Politics of the Mississippi Movement," in Eagles, *Civil Rights Movement*, 65–93; and John R. Salter, Jr., *Jackson, Mississippi: An American Chronicle of Struggle and Schism* (Hicksville, N. Y., 1979). For contrasting views about cooperation and conflict in the movement, see Nancy J. Weiss, "Creative Tensions in the Leadership of the Civil Rights Movement," and David J. Garrow, "Commentary," in Eagles, *Civil Rights Movement*, 59–64.

41. One important contribution in this area is Darlene Clark Hine, ed., *Black Women in the United States*, vol. 16 of Vicki L. Crawford, Jacqueline Rouse, and Barbara Woods, eds., *Women in the Civil Rights Movement: Trailblazers and Torchbearers* (Brooklyn, N. Y., 1990).

42. Steven M. Millner, "The Montgomery Bus Boycott: A Case Study in the Emergence and Career of a Social Movement," in Garrow, *Walking City*, 485, 579; Robinson, Montgomery Bus Boycott. For studies of women in other locales, see Paula Giddings, *When and Where I Enter: The Impact of Black Women on Race and Sex in America* (New York, 1984); Charles Payne, "Ella Baker and Models of Social Change," *Signs*, 14 (1989): 885–99; Daisy Bates, *The Long Shadow of Little Rock: A Memoir* (Fayetteville, Ark., 1987); Anne Moody, *Coming of Age in Mississippi* (New York, 1968); and Cynthia Stokes Brown, ed., *Ready from Within: Septima Clark and the Civil Rights Movement* (Navarro, Calif., 1986).

43. King, *Freedom Song*, 460. Sara Evans's arguments appear in her *Personal Politics: The Roots of Women's Liberation in the Civil Rights Movement and the New Left* (New York, 1980).

44. Evans herself suggested that black and white women in SNCC had different perceptions of their roles and situations within the organization. She quoted Jean Wiley, a black member: "If white women had a problem in SNCC it was not just a male/woman problem . . . it was also a black woman/white woman problem. It was a race problem rather than a woman's problem"; Evans, *Personal Politics*, 81. See also Martha Norman, "Brightly Shining Lights: SNCC and the Woman Question," paper presented at Southern Historical Association meeting, Lexington, Kentucky, November 10, 1989.

45. Sacks, *Caring by the Hour*, 119–21, 138–41. See also Charles Payne, "Men Led, But Women Organized: Movement Participation of Women in the Mississippi Delta," in Crawford, Rouse, and Woods, *Women in the Civil Rights Movement*, 1–11.

46. John A. Ricks, "'De Lawd' Descends and Is Crucified: Martin Luther King, Jr. in Albany, Georgia," in Garrow, *We Shall Overcome*, 3: 985–96.

47. Howard Zinn, SNCC: *The New Abolitionist* (Boston, 1964); Clayborne Carson, *SNCC and the Black Awakening of the 1960s* (Cambridge, Mass., 1981); James Forman,

The Making of Black Revolutionaries (New York, 1972); Cleveland Sellers with Robert Terrell, The River of No Return: The Autobiography of a Black Militant and the Life and Death of SNCC (New York, 1973); Mary King, Freedom Song: A Personal Story of the 1960s Civil Rights Movement (New York, 1987); and Doug McAdam, Freedom Summer (New York, 1988).

48. Emily Stoper, The Student Nonviolent Coordinating Committee: The Growth of Radicalism in a Civil Rights Organization, David J. Garrow, ed. (Brooklyn, N. Y., 1989), 100 (GS 17). The inability of SNCC to handle new recruits who did not share its early experiences and camaraderie resembles the problems of the Students for a Democratic Society, as discussed by Jim Miller, "Democracy Is in the Streets": From Port Huron to the Siege of Chicago (New York, 1987).

49. Openheimer, Sit-In Movement, 15; David Goldfield, Black, White, and Southern: Race Relations and Southern Culture 1940 to the Present (Baton Rouge, La., 1990), discusses those elements of black and white southern culture that he found made the resolution of civil rights demands possible. William H. Chafe, "The End of One Struggle, the Beginning of Another," and J. Mills Thornton, "Commentary," both in Eagles, Civil Rights Movement in America, 127–55, contrast the communitarian and individualistic values in American political culture. King was a master at shaping his oratory to conform to the language of American values; see James H. Cone, "The Theology of Martin Luther King, Jr.," in Garrow, Martin Luther King, Jr., 1: 215–33.

50. Joyce Ladner, "What Black Power Means to Negroes in Mississippi," in August Meier, ed., The Transformation of Activism (Chicago, 1970), 131–54.

51. Carson, "Civil Rights Reform and the Black Freedom Struggle," 28.

52. For two recent syntheses on the movement, see Robert Weisbrot, Freedom Bound: A History of America's Civil Rights Movement (New York, 1989); and Steven F. Lawson, Running for Freedom: Civil Rights and Black Politics since 1941 (New York, 1991). See also Harvard Sitkoff, The Struggle for Black Equality 1954–1980 (New York, 1981); and Manning Marable, Race, Reform and Rebellion: The Second Reconstruction in Black America, 1945–1982 (Jackson, Miss., 1984).

53. J. L. Chestnut, Jr., and Julia Cass, Black in Selma (New York, 1990); Ralph David Abernathy, And the Walls Came Tumbling Down (New York, 1989); Denton L. Watson, Lion in the Lobby: Clarence Mitchell, Jr.'s Struggle for the Passage of Civil Rights Laws (New York, 1990); Frank R. Parker, Black Votes Count: Political Empowerment in Mississippi after 1965 (Chapel Hill, N. C., 1990); Hugh Davis Graham, The Civil Rights Era: Origins and Development of National Policy (New York, 1989); Nancy J. Weiss, Whitney M. Young, Jr. and the Struggle for Civil Rights (Princeton, N. J., 1989); Stephen J. Whitfield, A Death in the Delta: The Story of Emmett Till (New York, 1988).

54. John Dittmer is working on Mississippi, Adam Fairclough on Louisiana, and Raymond Gavins on North Carolina. Robert Korstad is finishing a study on the labor antecedents of the civil rights movement in North Carolina. Robert L. Harris, Jr., is completing a study on the United Nations and the black freedom struggle.

55. John Dittmer, Local People: The Struggle for Civil Rights in Mississippi (Urbana, Illinois, 1994); Charles Payne, I've Got the Light of Freedom: The Organizing Tradition and the Mississippi Freedom Struggle (Berkeley, Calif., 1995).

56. For a fuller discussion of this problem see Steven F. Lawson and Charles Payne, Debating the Civil Rights Movement, 1945-1968 (Lanham, Md., 1998). Mills Thornton has recently published a monumental work completing several decades

of research on Selma, Montgomery, and Birmingham, Alabama in which he finds the key to understanding the timing and location of the movement in municipal politics, thereby emphasizing a localistic approach. See J. Mills Thornton, III, *Dividing Lines: Municipal Politics and the Struggle for Civil Rights in Montgomery, Birmingham, and Selma* (Tuscaloosa, Ala: University of Alabama Press, 2002).

57. Mary L. Dudziak, *Cold War Politics* (Princeton, 2002); Thomas Borstelmann, *The Cold War and the Color Line* (Cambridge, Mass., 2001); Michael L. Krenn *Black Diplomacy: African Americans and the State Department, 1945-1969*, (Armonk, N.Y., 1999); Penny M. Von Eschen, *Race Against Empire: Black Americans and Anticolonialism, 1937-1957* (Ithaca, N.Y., 1997); Brenda Gayle Plummer, *Rising Wind: Black Americans and U.S. Foreign Affairs, 1935-1960* (Chapel Hill, 1996).

58. Patricia Sullivan, *Days of Hope: Race and Democracy in the New Deal Era* (Chapel Hill, 1996); Michael Honey, *Southern Labor and Black Civil Rights* (Chicago, 1993).

59. For a nuanced, longitudinal study of this problem, see Timothy Minchin, *The Color of Work: The Struggle for Civil Rights in the Southern Paper Industry, 1945-1980* (Chapel Hill, 2001). See also, Minchin, *Hiring the Black Worker: The Racial Integration of the Southern Textile Industry, 1960-1980* (Chapel Hill, 1999).

60. Peter Lau, "Freedom Road Territory: The Politics of Civil Rights Struggle in South Carolina During the Jim Crow Era," (unpublished doctoral dissertation, Rutgers University, 2002); Alan Brinkley, *The End of Reform: New Deal Liberalism in Recession and War* (New York, 1995).

61. Timothy N. Thurber, *The Politics of Equality: Hubert H. Humphrey and the African American Freedom Struggle* (New York, 1999).

62. Adam Fairclough, *Race and Democracy: The Civil Rights Struggle in Louisiana, 1915-1972* (Athens, Ga., 1995) and *Better Day Coming: Blacks and Equality, 1890-2000* (NY, 2001); Kavern Verney, *Black Civil Rights in America* (London, 2000).

63. Glenn T. Eskew, *But for Birmingham: The Local and National Movements in the Civil Rights Struggle* (Chapel Hill, 1997).

64. Jervis Anderson, *Bayard Rustin: Troubles I've Seen* (New York, 1997); Daniel Levine, *Bayard Rustin and the Civil Rights Movement* (New Brunswick, N.J., 2000); John D'Emilio, *Lost Prophet: The Life and Times of Bayard Rustin* (New York: Free Press, 2003); Joanne Grant, *Ella Baker: Freedom Bound* (New York, 1998); Barbara Ransby, *Running Against the Storm: Ella J. Baker and the Black Radical Tradition*. Chapel Hill: University of North Carolina Press, 2003. Eric Burner, *And Gently He Shall Lead Them: Robert Parris Moses and Civil Rights in Mississippi* (New York, 1994); Cynthia Griggs Fleming, *Soon We Will Not Cry: The Liberation of Ruby Doris Smith Robinson* (Lanham, Md.,1998); Marjorie L. White and Andrew M. Manis, *Birmingham Revolutionaries: Fred Shuttlesworth and the Alabama Christian Movement for Human* Rights (Macon, Ga., 2000); Andrew M. Manis, *A Fire You Can't Put Out: The Civil Rights Life of Birmingham's Reverend Fred Shuttlesworth* (Tuscaloosa, Alabama, 1999); Ben Green, *Before His Time: The Untold Story of Harry T. Moore, America's First Civil Rights Martyr* (New York, 1999). See "Select Bibliography" at the conclusion of this volume.

65. Timothy B. Tyson, *Radio Free Dixie: Robert F. Williams and the Roots of Black Power* (Chapel Hill, 2000).

66. Chana Kai Lee, *For Freedom's Sake: The Life of Fannie Lou Hamer* (Champaign, IL, 1999).

67. Charles Eagles, *Outside Agitator: Jon Daniels and the Civil Rights Movement in Alabama* (Chapel Hill, 1993); Mary Stanton, *From Selma to Sorrow: The Life and*

Death of Viola Liuzzo (Athens, Ga., 2001). On white liberals see David L. Chappell, *Inside Agitators: White Southerners in the Civil Rights Movement* (Baltimore, 1994) and John Egerton, *Speak Now Against the Day: The Generation Before the Civil Rights Movement in the South* (Chapel Hill, 1994). On Wallace, Dan T. Carter, *The Politics of Rage: George Wallace, the Origins of the New Conservatism, and the Transformation of American Politics* (Baton Rouge, 2000) and Stephan Lesher, *George Wallace: American Populist* (Reading, Mass., 1994); on Faubus, see Roy Reed, *Faubus: The Life and Times of an American Prodigal* (Fayetteville, Arkansas, 1997). See also Jacquelyn Dowd Hall, "Broadening Our View of the Civil Rights Movement," *The Chronicle of Higher Education*, XLVII(July 27, 2001): section 2, B7-B11.

291

68. Peter J. Ling and Sharon Monteith, eds., *Gender in the Civil Rights Movement* (New York, 1999); Belinda Robnett, *How Long? How Long? African American Women in the Struggle for Civil Rights* (New York, 1997). On Motley see Constance Baker Motley, *Equal Justice Under Law: an Autobiography* (New York, 1998).

69. See Elaine Brown, *A Taste of Power: A Black Woman's Story* (New York, 1992).

70. John Howard, *Men Like That: A Southern Queer History* (Chicago, 1999); William H. Chafe, *Never Stop Running: Allard Lowenstein and the Struggle to Save American Liberalism* (New York, 1993); Stacy Braukman, "Nothing Else Matters but Sex: Cold War Narratives of Deviance and the Search for Lesbian Teachers in Florida, 1959-1963," *Feminist Studies* 27(Fall 2001): 553-75.

71. Brian Ward, *Just My Soul Responding: Rhythm and Blues, Black Consciousness and Race Relation* (Berkeley, 1998)

72. Justin Lorts is currently writing a doctoral dissertation at Rutgers University on black comedy and the freedom struggle. See also Barbara Dianne Savage, *Broadcasting Freedom: Radio, War, and the Politics of Race, 1938-1948* (Chapel Hill, 1999); Suzanne Smith, *Dancing in the Streets: Motown and the Cultural Politics of Detroit* (Cambridge, Mass., 1999); William L. Van Deburg, *New Day in Babylon: The Black Power Movement and American Culture, 1965-1975* (Chicago, 1992).

73. The King comment appears in "The Case Against Tokenism," in James W. Washington, ed., *The Essential Writings of Martin Luther King, Jr.* (New York, 1986), pp. 107-08. For various books on religion, see "Select Bibliography" at the conclusion of this volume.

74. Michael Gardner, *Harry Truman and Civil Rights* (Carbondale, Ill., 2002); Dean J. Kotlowski, *Nixon's Civil Rights: Politics, Principle, and Policy* (Cambridge, Mass., 2001); Raymond Wolters, *Right Turn: William Bradford Reynolds, the Reagan Administration, and Black Civil Rights* (New Brunswick, N.J.: Transaction, 1996).

75. J. Morgan Kousser, *Colorblind Injustice: Minority Voting Rights and the Undoing of the Second Reconstruction* (Chapel Hill: University of North Carolina Press, 1999); James T. Patterson, *Brown v. Board of Education: A Civil Rights Milestone and Its Troubled Legacy* (New York, 2001); Michael J. Klarman, "How *Brown*, Changed Race Relations: the Backlash Thesis," *Journal of American History*, LXXXI (June 1994):81-118. For other books on school desegregation see "Select Bibliography."

76. Charles W. Eagles, "Toward New Histories of the Civil Rights Era,"*Journal of Southern History*, LXVI (November 2000): 841.

77. "Becoming Martin Luther King, Jr. —Plagiarism and Originality: A Round Table," *Journal of American History*, LXXVIII (June 1991): 11-123; Keith D. Miller, *Voice of Deliverance: The Language of Martin Luther King, Jr. and Its Sources* (New York, 1992); Richard Lischer, *The Preacher King: Martin Luther King, Jr. and the Words that Moved America* (New York, 1995); Michael Eric Dyson, *I May Not Get There With*

You: Martin Luther King, Jr. (New York, 2000); Marshall Frady, *Martin Luther King, Jr.* (New York, 2002); Peter J. Ling, *Martin Luther King, Jr.* (London, 2002).

78. Taylor Branch, *Pillar of Fire: America in the King Years, 1963-65* (N.Y.: Simon & Schuster, 1998).

79. Ling, *Martin Luther King, Jr.*, p. 5.

80. For a more critical account, see Eagles, "Toward New Histories," 840, 842ff.

EXPLORING JOHNSON'S CIVIL RIGHTS POLICY

1. Bayard Rustin Oral History Interview, Lyndon B. Johnson Library, Austin, Texas.

2. Doris Kearns, *Lyndon Johnson and the American Dream* (New York: Harper and Row, 1976), p. 391.

3. George F. Will, "Fashions in Heroes," *Newsweek* 94 (August 6, 1979): 84.

4. Bruce Miroff, "Presidential Management of Black Politics: The Johnson White House," p. 17 (ms. In the author's possession).

5. Ronald Radosh, "From Protest to Black Power: The Failure of Coalition Politics," in *The Great Society Reader: The Failure of American Liberalism,* ed. Marvin Gettleman and David Mermelstein (New York: Random House, 1967), pp. 282, 292.

6. James C. Harvey, *Black Civil Rights during the Johnson Administration* (Jackson: University of Mississippi Press, 1973), p. 225. For similar criticisms, see Pat Watters and Reese Cleghorn, *Climbing Jacob's Ladder* (New York: Harcourt, Brace, and World, 1967).

7. John Herbers, *The Lost Priority: Whatever Happened to the Civil Rights Movement in America?* (New York: Funk and Wagnall, 1970), p. 176.

8. Clarence Mitchell Oral History Interview, Johnson Library.

9. See Anthony Lewis, "The Professionals Win Out over Civil Rights," *Reporter* 22 (May 26, 1960): 26–30.

10. Monroe Billington, "Lyndon B. Johnson and Blacks: The Early Years," *Journal of Negro History* 62 (January 1977): 42.

11. Steven F. Lawson and Mark I. Gelfand, "Consensus and Civil Rights: Lyndon B. Johnson and the Black Franchise," *Prologue* 8 (Summer 1976): 66–68. Robert Caro extensively detailed LBJ's pre-presidential civil rights position. While acknowledging his personal growth, he attributes his changes to presidential ambition. Robert A. Caro, *The Years of Lyndon Johnson: Master of the Senate* (New York: Alfred A. Knopf, 2002), 873–1011.

12. Joe B. Frantz, "Opening a Curtain: the Metamorphosis of Lyndon B. Johnson," *Journal of Southern History* 45 (February 1979): 25.

13. T. Harry Williams, "Huey, Lyndon, and Southern Radicalism," *Journal of American History* 60 (September 1973): 284.

14. Leonard Baker, *The Johnson Eclipse: A President's Vice Presidency* (New York: Macmillan, 1966), ch. 4; Carl Brauer, *John F. Kennedy and the Second Reconstruction* (New York: Columbia University Press, 1977), pp. 245–46.

15. Telephone conversation of Johnson with Theodore Sorenson, June 3, 1963, transcript, pp. 12, 14, Johnson Library.

16. Ibid., pp. 4–5.

17. Additional papers of Hobart Taylor can be found at the University of Michigan. Liberals faulted Vice-President Johnson, who as president of the Senate re-

fused to give a parliamentary ruling that would have aided cloture reform. Was he acting under Kennedy's orders?

18. "Notes on Senator Johnson's remarks to Clarence Mitchell and other delegates to January 13–14, 1960, Legislative Conference on Civil Rights," box 13, Johnson Senatorial Papers, Johnson Library.

19. Tom Wicker, *JFK and LBJ: The Influence of Personality upon Politics* (Baltimore: Penguin Books, 1969), p. 176.

20. Williams, "Huey, Lyndon and Southern Radicalism," p. 287.

21. Kearns, *Lyndon Johnson*, p. 191.

22. Daniel Berman, *A Bill Becomes a Law* (London: Macmillan, 1966), Clifford M. Lytle, "The History of the Civil Rights Bill of 1964," *Journal of Negro History* 51 (October 1966): 275–296, is a superficial account by a former official of the Community Relations Service, an agency created by the act. Perhaps the best analysis of the passage of the measure appears in James Sundquist, *Politics and Policy: The Eisenhower, Kennedy, and Johnson Years* (Washington, D.C.: Brookings Institution, 1968).

23. Brauer, *John F. Kennedy*, p. 310. This view has been endorsed in Arthur M. Schlesinger, Jr., *Robert F. Kennedy and His Times* (Boston: Houghton Mifflin, 1978), pp. 644–45. In contrast, Rowland Evans and Robert Novak believe that Johnson guaranteed a stronger bill than one his predecessor might have produced. "Now fully emancipated from his Southern base, there was no need to trim his civil rights position to please Dixie. On this issue, Johnson's political imperatives as a *Southern* President foreclosed compromise, whereas Kennedy's would not have," the reporters assert in *Lyndon B. Johnson: The Exercise of Power* (New York: New American Library, 1966), p. 379.

24. Lyndon B. Johnson, *The Vantage Point* (New York: Holt, Rinehart, and Winston, 1971), pp. 58–59.

25. Eric Goldman, *The Tragedy of Lyndon Johnson* (New York: Dell, 1969), pp. 80–84. On Senator Dirksen, see Neil MacNeil, *Dirksen: Portrait of a Public Man* (New York: World Publishing, 1970). Dirksen's papers are deposited in the senator's library and congressional center in Pekin, Illinois.

26. Department of Justice, *Administrative History*, 7:53, Johnson Library.

27. Lee White to the President, April 15, 1964, Hu 2, box 2, Executive File, White House Central Files, Johnson Library. See also Stewart Udall to the president, May 7, 1964, Hu 2, box 65, Ibid., and Mike Manatos to Lawrence O'Brien, May 11, 1964, Hu 2, box 2, Ibid.

28. Hubert Humphrey Oral History Interview, Johnson Library.

29. Lee White memorandum to the files, July 6, 1964, Le Hu 2, box 2, Executive File, White House Central Files, Johnson Library.

30. On the deteriorating relations between Johnson and the black radicals after the 1964 freedom summer, see James Forman, *The Making of Black Revolutionaries* (New York: Macmillan, 1972); Hanes Walton, *Black Political Parties* (New York: Free Press, 1972); Waters and Cleghorn, *Climbing Jacob's Ladder*; and Anne Cooke Romaine, "The Mississippi Freedom Democratic Party through August 1964" (Master's thesis, University of Virginia, 1969).

31. David J. Garrow, *Protest at Selma: Martin Luther King, Jr., and the Voting Rights Act of 1965* (New Haven: Yale University Press, 1978), p. 134, Steven F. Lawson, *Black Ballots: Voting Rights in the South, 1944–1969* (New York: Columbia University Press, 1976), ch. 10. For the role of the Community Relations Service in mediat-

ing the Selma dispute, see Thomas R. Wagy, "Governor LeRoy Collins of Florida and the Selma Crisis of 1965," *Florida Historical Quarterly 57* (April 1979); 403–420. The day-to-day events in the Alabama battleground are best described in Charles E. Fager, *Selma, 1965* (New York: Charles Scribner's Sons, 1974).

32. Joseph Califano to the President, October 25, 1965, Hu 2, Confidential File, White House Central Files, Johnson Library.

33. Nicholas Katzenbach to Joseph Califano, December 12, 1965, Le Hu 2, box 65, Johnson Library.

34. For a detailed examination of one section of the proposed bill, see Thomas J. Seess, "Federal Power to Combat Private Racial Violence in the Aftermath of *Price, Guest*, and the Civil Rights Act of 1968," (Ph.D. diss., Georgetown University, 1972). The Johnson Library has conveniently placed on its shelves a large number of theses covering the Johnson era.

35. James C. Harvey, Black Civil Rights, p. 224.

36. U.S., Department of Justice, *Administrative History*, Reports on Legislation, September 2, 1966, box 26, Johnson Library.

37. Ramsey Clark, "Report of the Civil Rights Task Force," Joseph Califano Files, Johnson Library. See also the 1966 Civil Rights Task Force, "Summary Notebook," box 12, Task Force Files, Johnson Library.

38. See the records of the White House Conference on Civil Rights and Hu 2/ Mc, White House Central Files, Johnson Library for pertinent material.

39. Henry Wilson to the president, March 11, 1966, box 11, Henry Wilson Files, Johnson Library; April 28, 1966, Le Hu 2, box 65, Appointment File, Diary Backup, Johnson Library.

40. Barefoot Sanders Oral History Interview, Johnson Library.

41. Harvey, *Black Civil Rights*, p. 40. Nicholas Katzenbach disagrees with this view. He remembers "that open housing was not an important issue in the 1966 election, although everybody predicted it would be. So I think the fact that we pushed it in 1966 helped, because [members of Congress] tested it out with the public and it was really surprising. " Katzenbach Oral History Interview, Johnson Library.

42. Eric Goldman to the President, May 4, 1964, Le Hu 2, box 65, Executive File, White House Central Files, Johnson Library.

43. Harry McPherson Oral History Interview, tape 7, Johnson Library.

44. Harry McPherson to the President, September 12, 1966, box 21 (2), Harry McPherson Files, Johnson Library; Nicholas Katzenbach to McPherson, September 17, 1966, Ibid. ; McPherson to Katzenbach, September 20, 1966, Ibid. See also Harry McPherson to George Christian, August 1, 1967, Hu 2, box 6, Executive File, White House Central Files, Johnson Library.

45. Jack Valenti (?) to the president, July 27, 1964, Hu 2, box 3, Ibid.

46. Harry McPherson Oral History Interview, tape 6, Johnson Library.

47. Harry McPherson to George Christian, August 1, 1967, Hu 2, box 6, Executive File, White House Central Files, Johnson Library. With respect to traditional racial objectives, the administration pushed the omnibus civil rights measure, accepting with it an antiriot rider. Nevertheless, the White House was not enthusiastic about the provision. Joseph Califano reported that Deputy Attorney General Warren Christopher declared, "Enactment of a Federal Act runs the risk of appearing to do more than we can really accomplish—it won't prevent riots and will lead to pressures upon the Justice Department to prosecute in dubious situations, but it could be used as leverage to enact other points of your program which may be in trouble."

Joseph Califano to the president, January 29, 1968, Le/J1, box 79, Executive File, White House Central Files, Johnson Library.

48. For discussions of the Kennedy and Johnson administrations' view of the federal system and civil rights, see Burke Marshall, *Federalism and Civil Rights* (New York: Columbia University Press, 1964); Brauer, *John F. Kennedy*, ch. 4; Howard Zinn, *SNCC* (Boston: Beacon Press, 1964); Victor Navasky, *Kennedy Justice* (New York: Atheneum, 1971); and Lawson, *Black Ballots*. Students of the riots will find in the Johnson Library the records of the National Commission on Civil Disorders and the oral histories of Ramsey Clark, John McCone, Edmund Brown, and Richard Hughes. There is no oral history with George Romney, the governor of Michigan, but his papers are at the University of Michigan. Ramsey Clark recalls in his oral history that the Justice Department emphasized that in dealing with riots "local authority must act first or we're going to have garrison cities and federal police."

49. Harry McPherson to the president, March 18, 1968, box 53, Harry McPherson Files, Johnson Library.

50. Young's statement appears in his newspaper column, May 10, 1966, Hu 2, box 4, Executive File, White House Central Files, Johnson Library; Wilkins's activities are noted in Bill Moyers to the president, August 30, 1965, Hu 2, box 3, Ibid. See also Roy Wilkins's column, January 15–16, 1966, attached to a memorandum from Jack Valenti to Frank A. Clark, January 21, 1966, Hu 2, box 4, Ibid. ; and David Halberstam, "The Second Coming of Martin Luther King," *Harper's* 235 (August 1967): 40.

51. Louis Martin to Marvin Watson, August 16, 1965, NC 19/CO 312, Johnson Library. Charles Evers and Aaron Henry telegraphed the president from Mississippi: "Inasmuch as you have seen fit to send observers to Vietnam to see that 'free and democratic' elections are held, . . . it would mean much more to America and particularly 22 million Negroes if you would use your influence and call for new elections in many sections of Mississippi and send representatives to make certain Negroes and Negro candidates are assured justice and fair play in all elections" (August 30, 1967, Pl/St 24, box 53, General File, White House Central Files, Johnson Library). Harry McPherson remarked on the connection between Vietnam and the domestic war against racism: "The war in Vietnam threatened to estrange the Democratic party from the President. If he was to retain the support of the national Democrats, . . . he would have to remain liberal at home, talking less of stopping crime than of its causes" (*A Political Education* [Boston: Little, Brown, and Co., 1972], pp. 382–83).

52. Ramsey Clark Oral History Interview, Johnson Library.

53. The administration's dealings with King from Selma to Memphis are noted in the neatly indexed White House Daily Diary and Backup Files, Johnson Library. On King's role in the civil rights movement, see David Lewis, *King*, 2nd ed. (Urbana: University of Illinois Press, 1978); August Meier, "On the Role of Martin Luther King," *New Politics* 4 (Winter 1965): 52–59; Garrow, *Protest at Selma*.

54. Louis Martin to Marvin Watson, August 16, 1965, ND 19/CO 312, Johnson Library; Clifford Alexander to the president, January 7, 1966, Hu 2, box 3, Executive File, White House Central Files, Johnson Library.

55. Harry McPherson to the president, April 4, 1967, box 14, Harry McPherson Files, Johnson Library; George Christian to the president, April 8, 1967, Hu 2, box 4, Executive File, White House Central Files, Johnson Library.

56. Harry McPherson Oral History Interview, tape 7, Johnson Library.

57. Larry Temple to the president, February 14, 1968, Hu 2, box 7, Executive File, White House Central Files, Johnson Library; Ben Wattenberg to the president,

February 29, 1968, filed Douglass Cater, FG 11–8–1, Confidential File, White House Central Files, Johnson Library.

58. *Public Papers of the Presidents, Lyndon B. Johnson* (Washington, D.C.: Government Printing Office, 1965), 2: 636.

59. Harry McPherson Oral History Interview, Johnson Library. Richard Goodwin drafted the speech and his files are in the library.

60. *Public Papers*, p. 636. Daniel Patrick Moynihan was assistant secretary of labor when he wrote the report. The document was originally intended for internal use. See John W. Leslie to Frank Erwin, July 30, 1965, Hu 2, box 3, Executive File, White House, Central Files, Johnson Library; Lee White to the President, August 10, 1965, Hu 2, box 3, Ibid. ; Lee White to Bill Moyers, August 12, 1965, box 6, Lee White Files, Johnson Library.

61. Lee Rainwater and William L. Yancey, *The Moynihan Report and the Politics of Controversy* (Cambridge, Massachusetts: M. I. T. Press, 1967), p. 16.

62. Harry McPherson Oral History Interview, tape 6, Johnson Library. See also McPherson, *A Political Education*, ch. 10. On this issue the Johnson Library contains the voluminous files of the White House Conference on Civil Rights, which can be supplemented with material from the White House Central Files and the presidential aide files of Harry McPherson and Lee White. Also available are the oral histories of several conference planners and participants. In particular see the memoir of Ben Heineman, the chairman of the conference.

63. For McPherson's depiction of subsequent events, see *A Political Education*, pp. 350–52.

64. Bruce Miroff, "Presidential Management of Black Politics," p. 1.

65. Ibid, p. 17; Francis Fox Piven and Richard A. Cloward, *Poor People's Movements: Why They Succeed, How They Fail* (New York: Pantheon Books, 1977).

66. Nicholas Katzenbach to Harry McPherson, September 17, 1966, box 21, Harry McPherson Files, Johnson Library.

67. Lee White to the President, March 11, 1964, Hu 2, box 2, Executive File, White House Central Files, Johnson Library. See also Richard Goodwin to the president, May 4, 1964, Hu 2, box 2, Ibid. Goodwin explained: "A lot of this is essentially uncontrollable. It will happen no matter what the federal government does. A wave of violence, federal intervention etc. might have serious political repercussions, North and South. But we should plan for the worst, hope for the best. "

68. Gary Orfield, *The Reconstruction of Southern Education: The Schools and the 1964 Civil Rights Act* (New York: John Wiley and Sons, 1969), p. 307.

69. Federal agencies processing civil rights complaints, particularly the Departments of Justice and Health, Education and Welfare, have some material in the White House central files, federal government (FG) groupings. Other pertinent records can be found in the human rights (Hu) category divided into specific subjects, e. g., employment (Hu 2–1), education (Hu 2–5). For a subsequent study, see Hugh Davis Graham, *The Civil Rights Era: Origins and Development of National Policy* (New York: Oxford University Press, 1990).

70. Allan Wolk, *The Presidency and Black Civil Rights: Eisenhower to Nixon* (Rutherford, New Jersey: Fairleigh Dickenson University Press, 1971), p. 247.

71. Harvey, *Black Civil Rights*, p. 224. See also Herbers, *Lost Priority*, p. 176; Harrell R. Rodgers, Jr., and Charles S. Bullock, III, *Law and Social Change: Civil Rights Laws and Their Consequences* (New York: McGraw-Hill, 1972).

72. Orfield, *Reconstruction of Southern Education*, p. viii.

73. Wolk, in *The Presidency and Black Civil Rights*, charged that the "Justice Department was a useful front, perhaps appearing to liberals as an affirmative control unit of coordination. But more often than not it assumed a restraining role in its interdepartmental relations" (p. 189). This view was shared by Samuel F. Yette, a former special assistant on civil rights in the Office of Economic Opportunity. See *The Choice: the Issue of Black Extermination in America* (New York: Berkley Medallion Books, 1975), pp. 611ff. For appraisals of the Justice Department's enforcement of the Voting Rights Act, see Lawson, *Black Ballots*, pp. 329–39; Garrow, *Protest at Selma*, pp. 179–93; U.S. Commission on Civil Rights, *Political Participation* (Washington, D.C.: Government Printing Office, 1968); and L. Thorne McCarty and Russell B. Stevenson, "The Voting Rights Act of 1965: An Evaluation," *Harvard Civil Rights-Civil Liberties Review* 3 (Spring 1968): 357–411.

74. Orfield, *Reconstruction of Southern Education*, p. 307. The author also covered the politics of northern-style de facto school desegregation, concentrating on Chicago. The task of comparing enforcement of racial policies in the North and South should be undertaken. On the subject of educational desegregation, two oral histories in the Johnson Library are particularly useful: those of former Commissioners of Education Francis Keppel and Harold Howe, II.

75. James Button, *Black Violence* (Princeton: Princeton University Press, 1978), pp. 174–76. On the implications of the Button and Garrow studies, see August Meier's and Elliot Rudwick's review in the *Journal of American History* 66 (September 1979): 466.

76. This statement by Walter Tobriner was quoted in a WTOP (Washington, D.C.) radio editorial, March 10 and 11, 1965, 1117, Charles Horsky Files, Johnson Library. For a concise background of the issue see Martin F. Nolan, "The Negro Stake in Washington House Rule," *The Reporter* 35 (August 11, 1966): 18–21.

77. Charles Horsky to Larry O'Brien, October 25, 1963, 1125, Charles Horsky Files, Johnson Library. For background on this issue, see Constance McLaughlin Green, *The Secret City: A History of Race Relations in the Nation's Capitol* (Princeton: Princeton University Press, 1967).

78. Lyndon Johnson to David Carliner, November 15, 1967, FG 216, box 267, Executive File, White House Central Files, Johnson Library.

79. Robert Sherrill, *The Accidental President* (New York: Grossman Publishers, 1967), p. 196.

80. Eric Goldman, *The Tragedy of Lyndon Johnson*, p. 628.

81. The records of the Democratic National Committee during the Johnson years chart the changing fortunes of African Americans and the party of the president. Comprised mainly of newspaper clippings and pamphlets, these files in the Johnson Library contain important material documenting the work of the Special Equal Rights Committee, which sought to expand black participation in Democratic affairs.

82. Williams, "Huey, Lyndon, and Southern Radicalism," p. 292.

83. Harry McPherson Oral History Interview, tape 6, Johnson Library.

84. The Appointment File, Diary Backup contains briefing papers preparing the president for scheduled meetings. See Michael R. Beschloss, *Taking Charge: The Johnson White House Tapes, 1963–1964* (New York: Simon and Schuster, 1997).

85. Some possibilities are Justice Department lawyers John Doar and Stephen Pollak; White House counselor Clifford Alexander; Deputy Chairman of the Democratic National Committee Louis Martin; Berl Bernhard, a staff director of the U.S. Civil Rights Commission and planner of the White House Conference on Civil Rights;

Roger Wilkins, director of the Community Relations Service; Carl Rowan, a journalist and chief of the United States Information Agency; Dorothy Height, head of the National Council of Negro Women; and Charles Horsky, the District of Columbia specialist.

86. Robert C. Rooney, ed., *Equal Opportunity in the United States: A Symposium on Civil Rights* (Austin: University of Texas, 1973), p. 128.

87. Since the publication of this essay, several books on Johnson have appeared, which touch upon his civil rights activities without significantly changing the ideas in this chapter and the successive ones. See Robert Dallek, *Lone Star Rising: Lyndon Johnson and His Times, 1908–1960* (New York: Oxford University Press, 1991) and *Flawed Giant: Lyndon Johnson and His Times* (New York: Oxford University Press, 1998); Robert A. Caro, *The Years of Lyndon Johnson: Master of the Senate* (New York: Alfred A. Knopf, 2002); Bruce J. Schulman, *Lyndon B. Johnson and the American Dream: A Brief Biography with Documents* (Boston: Bedford/St. Martin's, 1998); Michael Beschloss, ed., *Reaching for Glory: Lyndon Johnson's Secret White House Tapes, 1964–1965* (New York: Simon & Schuster, 2001).

THE IMPROBABLE EMANCIPATOR

I would like to acknowledge Mark I. Gelfand as coauthor of this chapter.

1. T. Harry Williams, "Huey, Lyndon, and Southern Radicalism," *Journal of American History* 60 (Sept. 1973): 292, 293.

2. Clarence Mitchell Oral History Interview, Lyndon Baines Johnson Library (LBJL).

3. Carl Degler, *Affluence and Anxiety:1945–Present* (Glenview, Ill. 1968), p. 235. Other works commenting favorably on Johnson's accomplishments include John Herbers, *The Lost Priority: What Happened to the Civil Rights Movement in America?* (New York, 1970), John Hope Franklin, *From Slavery to Freedom* (New York, 1969), Rowland Evans and Robert Novak, *Lyndon B. Johnson: The Exercise of Power* (New York, 1966), Eric F. Goldman, *The Tragedy of Lyndon Johnson* (New York, 1968), August Meier and Elliott Rudwick, *From Plantation to Ghetto* (New York, 1970), p. 269, Benjamin Muse, *The American Negro Revolution* (Bloomington, 1968), Sig Synnestvedt, *The White Response to Black Emancipation* (New York, 1972), Harry McPherson, *A Political Education* (Boston, 1972), Allan Wolk, *The Presidency and Black Civil Rights* (Rutherford, N. J., 1971), C. Vann Woodward, *The Strange Career of Jim Crow* (Oxford, 2nd rev. ed., 1966), and James Sundquist, *Politics and Policy* (Washington, 1968).

4. Charles V. Hamilton, "Blacks and the Crisis in Political Participation," *The Public Interest* 34 (Winter 1972): 201. For other critical evaluations, see James Forman, *The Making of Black Revolutionaries* (New York, 1972), Victor Navasky, *Kennedy Justice* (New York, 1971), Pat Watters and Reese Cleghorn, *Climbing Jacob's Ladder* (New York, 1967), Ronald Radosh, "From Protest to Black Power: The Failure of Coalition Politics," in *The Great Society Reader: The Failure of American Liberalism*, ed. Marvin E. Gettleman and David Mermelstein (New York, 1967), pp. 278–293, and James C. Harvey, *Black Civil Rights During the Johnson Administration* (Jackson, Miss., 1973), pp. 224–226.

5. Lyndon B. Johnson to James H. Rowe, Mar. 15, 1949, box 1 (Civil Rights), Senatorial Papers, LBJL.

6. Johnson to Carter Wesley, Mar. 16, 1949, ibid.: Williams, "Huey, Lyndon," p. 283.

7. For an early example of northern black voters' effect on politics and civil rights, see Harvard Sitkoff, "Harry Truman and the Election of 1948: The Coming of Age of Civil Rights in American Politics," *Journal of Southern History* 37 (Nov. 1971): 597–616; and "Where Does Negro Voter Strength Lie?" *Congressional Quarterly Weekly* 14 (May 4, 1956): 491–496.

8. Quoted in Evans and Novak, *Lyndon B. Johnson*, p. 65. Before 1957 the majority leader had begun to break away from the strict southern position. He refused to endorse the "Southern Manifesto" attacking the Supreme Court's desegregation opinion.

9. George Reedy to Johnson, Dec. 3, 1956, box 7, Senatorial Papers, LBJL. For further explanation of the Johnson strategy, see Reedy to Johnson, n. d. (Ca. 1957), box 3, ibid.

10. U.S. Congress, House, *Congressional Record*, 85 (Cong., 1 sess., 1957, p. 12564.

11. For an appraisal of Johnson's leadership, see Anthony Lewis, "The Professionals Win Out Over Civil Rights," *Reporter*, May 26, 1960, pp. 27–30.

12. "Notes on Senator Johnson's remarks to Clarence Mitchell and other delegates to January 13–14, 1960, Legislative Conference on Civil Rights," box 13 (Civil Rights), Senatorial Papers, LBJL.

13. Tom Wicker, *JFK and LBJ: The Influence of Personality Upon Politics* (Baltimore, 1969), p. 176.

14. Leonard Baker, *The Johnson Eclipse: A President's Vice Presidency* (New York, 1966), p. 219 and chap. 4.

15. "Black Elected Officials in the Southern States," Nov. 1969, Voter Education Project Files, Southern Regional Council Offices, Atlanta, Ga.: U.S. Department of Commerce, *Statistical Abstract of the United States, 1970* (Washington, 1970), p. 369.

16. Lyndon B. Johnson, *The Vantage Point* (New York, 1971), p. 161.

17. Stokely Carmichael and Charles V. Hamilton, *Black Power* (New York, 1967), p. 89; Leslie Burl McLemore, "The Freedom Democratic Party and the Changing Political Status of the Negro in Mississippi" (Master's thesis, Atlanta Univ., 1965), pp. 42–44, 49, 55; Len Holt, *The Summer That Didn't End* (New York, 1965), pp. 156, 162–163. The Freedom Democrats were not interested in establishing a third party; rather they strove to gain recognition as the legitimate upholders of the Democratic standard. The MFDP was the only integrated Democratic organization in Mississippi.

18. The regular Democrats asserted that they had complied with the loyalty requirement by pledging to place Johnson's name on the ballot. Moreover, they contended that the MFDP had not conducted elections in every district throughout the state, and thus its delegates were not representative of the Mississippi Democratic Party. Paul Tillett, "National Conventions," in Milton C. Cummings, Jr., ed., *The National Election of 1964* (Washington, 1966), p. 32.

19. Noel Day to Clifford Alexander, June 9, 1954, box 5, Lee White Files, LBJL. For the view of various law professors, see U.S. Congress, House, *Congressional Record*, 88 Cong., 2 sess., 1964, p. 15645.

20. Robert F. Kennedy to Johnson, June 5, 1964, FG 135, box 1, LBJL.

21. Lee White to Johnson, June 17, 1964, Hu 2–7, box 55, ibid.

22. Burke Marshall, *Federalism and Civil Rights* (New York, 1964), p. 5.

299

23. Nicholas Katzenbach to Johnson, July 1, 1964, Hu 2, St 24, box 26, LBJL. The deputy attorney general also noted that it was hard to dispute "the group of law professors which has publicly taken issue with the statement . . . that there was no adequate legal basis for federal law enforcement in Mississippi."

24. John Lewis to Johnson, Aug. 19, 1964, Hu 2, St 24, box 27, ibid.

25. Anne C. Romaine, "The Mississippi Freedom Democratic Party Through August 1964," (Master's thesis, Univ. of Virginia, 1969), pp. 32–34; Holt, *The Summer That Didn't End*, pp. 168–169.

26. Theodore White, *The Making of the President 1964* (New York, 1965), p. 277. However, White did not think that the MFDP's legal case was too strong.

27. *New York Times*, Aug. 27, 1964; [Tampa] *Tribune*, Aug. 27, 1964.

28. Memo typed to Juanita Roberts describing the suggestion that Johnson called "a good idea," Aug. 24, 1964, Pl 1, St 24, LBJL.

29. *New York Times*, Aug. 26, 1964.

30. Charles Diggs to Elizabeth Hirshfeld, Mar. 21, 1964, box 4, MFDP Files, Martin Luther King Library Center (MLKLC).

31. Romaine, "The Mississippi Freedom Democratic Party," p. 170.

32. "Position Paper, September 20, 1964, Reasons for Rejection of Atlantic City Compromise, box 24, MFDP Files, MLKLC; "Freedom Primer No. 1: The Convention Challenge and the Freedom Vote," p. 708; "Minutes of the Executive Committee of the MFDP, September 13, 1964," box 23, ibid.

33. Carmichael and Hamilton, *Black Power*, p. 92. Nevertheless, the MFDP returned home and campaigned for the Johnson-Humphrey ticket; the regulars did not.

34. Goldman, *Tragedy*, pp. 306–309. See also [Atlanta] *Constitution*, Aug. 26, 1964.

35. Johnson, *Vantage Point*, p. 161.

36. Lee White, memo to Johnson, Nov. 18, 1964, Hu 2/mc, LBJL; White to Bill Moyers, Dec. 30, 1964, box 3, Lee White Files, ibid.

37. "Position Paper on Civil Rights," n.d., filed by Deputy Attorney General Ramsey Clark, Feb. 5, 1965, Hu 2, box 3, ibid.

38. Katzenbach to Johnson, n.d., box 3, Lee White Files, ibid. The attorney general also suggested the possibility of legislation "vesting in a federal commission the power to conduct registration for federal elections. " As a last choice, Katzenbach proposed a measure "granting to an agency of the federal government the power to assume direct control of registration for voting in both federal and state elections in any area where the percentage of potential Negro registrants actually registered is low."

39. See the testimony of Attorney General Katzenbach, U.S. Congress, House, Committee on the Judiciary, *Hearings* (Voting Rights Act of 1965), 89 Cong., 1 sess. (Washington, 1965), pp. 5ff. For an account of the mass arrests, see *New York Times*, Feb. 4, 1965.

40. *Public Papers of the Presidents of the United States: Lyndon B. Johnson* 1 (Washington, 1965): 5. In his State of the Union message Johnson declared, "I propose that we eliminate every remaining obstacle to the right to vote. " Although he did not mention any specific suggestions, he had instructed Justice Department lawyers to draft language for the constitutional amendment. The attorney general's men were also giving some thought to legislation empowering federal registrars to supervise enrollment for national elections. "Justice Department Weekly Legislative Report to Lawrence O'Brien," Jan. 11 and 18, 1965, box 8, Reports on Pending Legislation, LBJL. According to Deputy Attorney General Clark, however, when Selma erupted the Civil Rights Division was slow to respond; its attorneys did not have a

specific bill ready, and they were constantly revising their proposals to meet the public outcry that disfranchisement be eradicated once and for all. Clark, interview with Mark I. Gelfand, Sept. 14, 1973.

41. Neil MacNeil, *Dirksen: Portrait of a Public Man* (New York, 1970), p. 252; **301** *New York Times*, Jan. 24, 27, 1965.

42. *New York Times*, Feb. 10, 1965; David L. Lewis, *King: A Critical Biography* (New York, 1970), p. 269.

43. "Justice Department Status Report," Feb. 15, 1965, box 9, Reports on Pending Legislation, LBJL.

44. Quoted in *New Republic*, Mar. 20, 1965, p. 5.

45. Fred Miller to George W. Culbertson, Apr. 15, 1965, Leroy Collins MSS, University of South Florida; Leroy Collins Oral History Interview, with permission of Julia Chapman. For a slightly different version of the delicate negotiations, see Martin Luther King, Jr., "Behind the Selma March," *Saturday Review*, Apr. 3, 1965, p. 16. John Doar has recently disclaimed that any deal was worked out with King and has contended that he did not know what the minister would do until he actually halted the march in front of the Alabama state troopers. Door, interview with Mark I. Gelfand, Aug. 27, 1973.

46. Johnson, *Vantage Point*, p. 162.

47. Goldman, *Tragedy*, pp. 372–373.

48. *Public Papers*, vol. 1, pp. 196–197, 276.

49. Lewis to White, Apr. 20, 1965, box 47, SP 2–3, 1965 Hu 2–7 (Mar. 15, 1965), LBJL.

50. The biggest threat to the measure's enactment was posed not by its Dixie foes but by its northern liberal allies. At issue was how to get rid of the poll tax in state elections. Liberals wanted to abolish it by an amendment to the administration bill, but Justice Department lawyers thought a constitutional amendment was required. Fearing that the liberals' insistence on this point would mean the loss of Dirksen, whose revolutionary ardor had its limits, on the crucial cloture vote, the administration mobilized its resources to defeat the poll tax repealer. As a compromise, Johnson agreed to a provision in the bill that authorized the attorney general to test the constitutionality of the poll tax in the courts as soon as possible. In this instance, Johnson's maneuvering worked to perfection. Cloture was easily secured, and less than a year after the 1965 act went into effect the Supreme Court ruled the poll tax unconstitutional. For the administrations's courting of Dirksen, see Katzenbach to Johnson, May 21, 1965, box 2, Henry Wilson Files, LBJL.

51. Charles N. Fortenberry and F. Glenn Abney, "Mississippi: Unreconstructed and Unredeemed," in William C. Havard, ed., *The Changing Politics of the South* (Baton Rouge, 1972), p. 494.

52. U.S. Commission on Civil Rights, *Political Participation* (Washington, 1968); L. Thorne McCarty and Russell B. Stevenson, "The Voting Rights Act of 1965: An Evaluation," *Harvard Civil Rights-Civil Liberties Review* 3 (Spring 1968): 357–411.

53. *New York Times*, Dec. 5, 1965; *Wall Street Journal*, Dec. 28, 1965. The administration thought such types of activity should be undertaken by private civil rights groups.

54. U.S. Commission on Civil Rights, *Political Participation*, p. 178. The federal agency concluded, ". . . there has been little or no progress in the entry and participation by Negroes in political party affairs—the key to meaningful participation in the electoral process. "

55. Robert C. Rooney, ed., *Equal Opportunity in the United States: A Symposium on Civil Rights* (Austin, 1973), p. 164.

MIXING MODERATION WITH MILITANCY

1. Charles Evers Oral History Interview, April 3, 1974, by Joe B. Frantz, p. 13. All cited manuscripts and oral history interviews are in the Lyndon B. Johnson Library (hereafter cited as LBJL) unless otherwise noted.

2. Denton L. Watson, *Lion in the Lobby: Clarence Mitchell Jr.'s Struggle for the Passage of Civil Rights Laws* (New York: William Morrow and Company, 1990), p. 432.

3. Joseph A. Califano, Jr., *The Triumph & Tragedy of Lyndon Johnson: The White House Years* (New York: Simon and Schuster, 1991), p. 54.

4. Joseph L. Rauh Oral History Interview, August 8, 1969, by Paige Mulhollan, tape 3, p. 14.

5. As the legendary founder of the 1941 March on Washington movement, Randolph was sought out because of the personal respect he commanded, not because of his formal position as head of the Negro American Labor Council. Sometimes included under the heading of Big Six organizations was the National Council of Negro Women.

6. Harry McPherson Oral History Interview, March 24, 1969, by Thomas H. Baker, pt. 4, tape 2, p. 17; Carl T. Rowan, *Breaking Barriers: A Memoir* (Boston: Little Brown, 1991), p. 233.

7. Roy Wilkins with Tom Mathews, *Standing Fast: The Autobiography of Roy Wilkins* (New York: Viking Press, 1982), p. 311; Louis Martin Oral History Interview, May 14, 1969, by David G. McComb, p. 32; Nicholas deB. Katzenbach Oral History Interview, November 16, 1968, by Paige E. Mulhollan, tape 1, p. 29; Bayard Rustin Oral History Interview, June 30, 1969, by Thomas H. Baker, tape 2, p. 15; Robert Weaver Oral History Interview, November 19, 1968, by Joe B. Frantz, tape 3, p. 5.

8. Nancy J. Weiss quoting Robert Weaver, in *Whitney M. Young, Jr., and the Struggle for Civil Rights*, (Princeton, N.J.: Princeton University Press, 1989), p. 148.

9. James Farmer quoted in Bernard J. Firestone and Robert C. Vogt, eds., *Lyndon Baines Johnson and the Uses of Power* (New York: Greenwood, 1988), p. 177.

10. See Weiss, *Young*, p. 148. The resources of the Johnson Library can be used to document the close communication links the president maintained with civil rights leaders. The library has files of index cards containing notations of meetings and telephone conversations between Johnson and civil rights leaders as well as other prominent individuals. Arranged in alphabetical order and cross-filed by subject, this material allows a researcher to glimpse which people had access to the chief executive and from whom he sought advice. By themselves these cards, which were prepared by his secretaries during the White House years, serve mainly as a log containing no indication of the substance of the discussion. They must be consulted in conjunction with the Diary Backup Files, which provide memorandums related to scheduled and off-the-record meetings (the same does not hold true for telephone calls). Although every instance of contact was not logged, these records offer valuable clues to the pattern of presidential communication with various leaders and groups. Wilkins had fifty-nine note-card citations, followed by Young with forty-four.

11. Wilkins, *Standing Fast*, p. 307; McPherson Oral History Interview, April 9, 1969, by Thomas H. Baker, pt. 5, tape 1, p. 11. In this nationally televised speech to Congress at the height of the SCLC's voting rights campaign in Selma, Alabama, Johnson eloquently voiced the refrain of the civil rights movement, "We shall overcome."

12. George Reedy to president, November 29, 1963, Diary Backup Files, box 1 (original emphasis).

13. Weiss, *Young*, p. 145; Whitney M. Young, Jr. Oral History Interview, June 18, 1969, by Thomas H. Baker, p. 4: Wilkins, *Standing Fast*, p. 296.

303

14. Whitney Young Oral History, p. 9; (Lee White) Notes for Discussion with Martin Luther King, January 13, 1965, White House Central Files (WHCF), Whitney Young Name File, box 41. Young was offered the post of deputy director of the poverty program.

15. Whitney Young Oral History, p. 9; Weiss, *Young*, p. 105.

16. Joseph Califano to president, June 4, 1966; WHCF, Whitney Young Name File, box 41.

17. Joseph Califano to president, July 25, 1966, WHCF, EX HU 2, box 4. Just before leaving office in January 1969, Johnson bestowed on Young the Presidential Medal of Freedom, and in return Young gave the president a copy of his book, *Beyond Racism*, with the inscription: "To Lyndon B. Johnson who more than any President almost makes this book unnecessary" (Weiss, *Young*, p. 164).

18. Paula F. Pfeffer, *A. Philip Randolph, Pioneer of the Civil Rights Movement* (Baton Rouge: Louisiana State University Press, 1990), p. 272ff. For example, Randolph was selected as honorary chair of the 1966 White House Conference on Civil Rights, a contentious affair (see note 47).

19. A. Philip Randolph Oral History Interview, October 19, 1968, by Thomas H. Baker, p. 16; Lee White to president, December 5, 1963, Diary Backup Files, box 2; Hubert H. Humphrey to president, August 5, 1965, Richard Goodwin Files, box 2; Evers Oral History, p. 16; Clifford Alexander to Harry McPherson, October 3, 1966, McPherson Files, box 22.

20. James Farmer, *Lay Bare the Heart: An Autobiography of the Civil Rights Movement* (New York: Arbor House, 1985), pp. 296, 220–22.

21. First quote, George Reedy to president, December 4, 1963, Diary Backup Files, box 2; second quote, Lee White to president, December 4, 1963, Diary Backup Files, box 3.

22. James Farmer Oral History Interview, July 20, 1971, by Paige Mulhollan, tape 2, p. 4; Farmer, *Lay Bare the Heart*, p. 298; David Garrow, *Bearing the Cross: Martin Luther King, Jr., and the Southern Christian Leadership Conference* (New York: William Morrow and Company, 1986), p. 343. Johnson did not officially ask for a moratorium. See Roy Wilkins Oral History Interview, April 1, 1969, by Thomas H. Baker, p. 12; Lee White to president, August 19, 1964, WHCF EX HU 2, box 3.

23. A perusal of the diary card files notes a drop from six to five contacts.

24. Lee White to president, July 30, 1964, WHCF, James Farmer Name File, box 23. Referring to CORE, White told Johnson, "Even in the case of those organizations that feel they must not join a moratorium, they can make every effort to encourage their followers to hold their demonstrations to specific objectives and make every effort to prevent them from becoming leaderless riots with attendant looting and violence" (Lee White to president, August 19, 1964, Diary Backup Files, box 8). Farmer himself distinguished between riots, which he condemned, and peaceful protests, which he would not suspend. David H. McClain, "The Politics of Freedom: Conflicts between Lyndon Johnson and James Farmer during the 1964 President Campaign," p. 23, unpublished paper, HIS 350L, University of Texas, LBJL.

25. Lee White to president, July 30, 1964, White to Jack Valenti, August 4, 1964, both in WHCF, James Farmer Name File, box 23.

26. White told the president that "Farmer's people did their job effectively" (Lee White to president, October 22, 1964, WHCF, Farmer Name File, box 23). Farmer also helped rein in the Brooklyn chapter of CORE in its attempt to hold a disruptive "stall in" on the highways leading to the New York World's Fair in Queens. Farmer led more conventional protests against specific targets at the exposition site (McClain, "Politics of Freedom," p. 42).

27. Wilkins interceded with the president and secured a pen for Farmer. Johnson's spite was fully in evidence when he worked behind the scenes to deny Farmer a federal grant to establish an adult literacy program. Farmer, *Lay Bare the Heart*, pp. 304–5; Charles Hamilton, *Adam Clayton Powell, Jr.: The Political Biography of an American Dilemma* (New York: Atheneum, 1991), p. 397.

28. Andrew Young Oral History Interview, June 18, 1970, by Thomas H. Baker, p. 13, adds that King had a warmer relationship with President Kennedy.

29. Califano, *Triumph & Tragedy*, p. 276; Andrew Young Oral History, p. 18. King's very first meeting with President Johnson set the pattern. When the chief executive met with him on December 3, 1963, LBJ delivered the same message as he did to the other black leaders that demonstrations would upset legislative deliberations on the pending civil rights bill. At a press conference following the meeting, however, King declared his intention of renewing protests that had been suspended in the mourning period since Kennedy's death. This response irked the White House because "Dr. King had a completely different story outside than he did in (Johnson's) office about the question of demonstrations." *New York Times*, December 4, 1963, p. 1; Lee White to president, December 4, 1963, Diary Backup Files, box 2.

30. Garrow, *Bearing the Cross*, pp. 343, 350. The White House and the FBI monitored King and kept tabs on his position concerning the seating of delegates from the Mississippi Freedom Democratic Party; note, August 19, 1964, WHCF EX PL ST 24, box 81.

31. Lee White to president, March 9, 1965, Diary Backup Files, box 15.

32. Richard N. Goodwin, *Remembering America: A Voice from the Sixties* (New York: Harper and Row, 1988), p. 310.

33. Martin Oral History Interview, p. 31; Andrew Young Oral History Interview, pp. 16–17.

34. Jack Valenti to president, November 13, 1964, WHCF, Roy Wilkins Name File, box 312; Lee White to president, December 18, 1964, WHCF, Martin Luther King, Jr., Name File, box 144.

35. Lee White to president, July 23, 1965, WHCF, Martin Luther King, Jr., Name File, box 147. King met with LBJ on August 5, 1965, for what he called a "fruitful and meaningful" discussion as he relayed his concerns about racial problems in the North (Garrow, *Bearing the Cross*, p. 436).

36. Garrow, *Bearing the Cross*, p. 440.

37. Ibid, 548–49; Martin Oral History Interview, p. 31.

38. See David Garrow, *The FBI and Martin Luther King, Jr.: From "Solo" to Memphis* (New York: W. W. Norton, 1981); Califano, *Triumph & Tragedy*, p. 277; Ramsey Clark Oral History Interview, April 16, 1969, by Harry Baker, tape 4, p. 21.

39. John P. Roche, "Eyes Only," to president, April 5, 1967, WHCF, Martin Luther King, Jr., Confidential Name File, box 147.

40. Califano, *Triumph & Tragedy*, pp. 277, 218–19.

41. Weiss, *Young*, pp. 160–62.

42. Califano, *Triumph & Tragedy*, p. 218; Clifford Alexander to president, Janu-

ary 11, 1967, WHCF, Louis Martin Name File, box 127; Martin Luther King, Jr., King to Lyndon B. Johnson, July 25, 1967, Willard Wirtz to president, July 28, 1967, Harry McPherson to president, July 28, 1967, all in McPherson Files, box 31; David Garrow, "From Reformer to Revolutionary," in *Martin Luther King, Jr., and the Civil Rights Movement*, ed. David J. Garrow (Brooklyn: Carlson Publishing, 1989), pp. 427–36; Adam Fairclough, *To Redeem the Soul of America: The Southern Christian Leadership Conference and Martin Luther King, Jr.* (Athens: University of Georgia Press, 1987), p. 383.

43. Lee White to president, August 10, 1965, WHCF, EX HU 2, box 3; Lee White to president, November 2, 1965, WHCF, EX HU 2/MC, box 22, complimenting Rustin on his help in organizing the White House Conference on Civil Rights. See correspondence from Lee White to president, August 11, 12, 13, 19, 1964, WHCF, EX PL 1/St 24, box 81, on the controversy over seating the Mississippi Freedom Democratic Party; and on Vietnam, see Roche, "Eyes Only," to president, April 5, 1967, WHCF, Martin Luther King, Jr., Confidential Name File, box 147. Fairclough, *To Redeem the Soul*, pp. 23–24. Rustin did severely criticize the administration in 1966 for ignoring the $180–billion Freedom Budget proposal he devised with Randolph to promote full employment over ten years (Pfeffer, *Randolph*, pp. 287–90). Clifford Alexander to Harry McPherson, October 3, 1966, WHCF, Whitney Young Name File, box 41. John D'Emilio, *Lost Prophet: The Life and Times of Bayard Rustin* (New York: Free Press, 2003).

44. John Dittmer, "The Politics of the Mississippi Movement, 1954–1964," in *The Civil Rights Movement in America*, ed. Charles Eagles (Jackson: University of Mississippi Press, 1986), pp. 65–93; Wilkins, *Standing Fast*, pp. 305–6.

45. Clayborne Carson, *In Struggle: SNCC and the Black Awakening of the 1960s* (Cambridge: Harvard University Press, 1981), p. 188.

46. Humphrey to Califano, January 22, 1966, WHCF EX HU 2, box 4; Carson, *In Struggle*, p. 189

47. On the White House Conference and its relationship to black leadership, see Steven F. Lawson, "Civil Rights" in *Exploring the Johnson Years*, ed. Robert A. Divine (Austin, University of Texas Press, 1981), pp. 110–11, and Lawson, *In Pursuit of Power: Southern Blacks and Electoral Politics, 1965–1982* (New York: Columbia University Press, 1985), pp. 43–49. The Johnson Library holds the records of this conference, and materials found in files designated WHCF EX HU 2/mc are also helpful. Oral histories with McPherson, Ben Heineman (April 16, 1970, by Joe B. Frantz), Clifford Alexander (February 17, 1972, by Joe B. Frantz), and Ramsey Clark (March 21, 1969, by Harri Baker) are also useful.

48. McPherson Oral History, pt. 4, tape 2, p. 7; John Lewis to A. Philip Randolph, December 14, 1965, White House Conference on Civil Rights, "To Fulfill These Rights" Files, box 66.

49. Dr. King joined his old civil rights comrades in criticizing SNCC. Martin Luther King, Jr., A. Philip Randolph, Roy Wilkins, and Whitney Young to Stokely Carmichael, August 3, 1966, and SNCC Central Committee to Roy Wilkins, August 4, 1966, Marvin Watson Files, box 18. I would like to thank Lewis Gould for directing me to this material.

50. Harry McPherson, *A Political Education: A Journal of Life with Senators, Generals, Cabinet Members and Presidents* (Boston: Little, Brown and Company, 1972), p. 357. He also included CORE, which was moving in the same antiwar, black nationalist direction as SNCC.

51. Kenneth O'Reilly, *"Racial Matters": The FBI's Secret File on Black America,*

1960–1972 (New York: Free Press, 1989). This book and Garrow's on the FBI and Dr. King show that the Johnson administration had a clandestine relationship with black leaders that the papers of the Johnson Library do not generally reveal. Also of interest on a more visible level, the record of a White House meeting on March 12, 1965, notes the presence of Hubert "Rap" Brown, who would become SNCC's head and a White House nemesis ("President's Schedule, March 12, 1965, Washington Civil Rights Delegation," Diary Backup Files, box 15). At the time, Brown was representing the Non Violent Action Group, a SNCC affiliate at Howard University.

52. Carson, *In Struggle*, pp. 276–77.

53. McPherson Oral History, pt. 5, tape 2, p. 9; McPherson, *Political Education*, p. 363.

54. Cabinet Dossier no. 1, Report, August 2, 1967, Cabinet Meeting Files, box 9. Carmichael was out of the country at the time.

55. When the Logan Act, barring private citizens from attempting to influence relations between a foreign government and the United States, was suggested as a possible basis for prosecution, Clark sarcastically responded that he "could make a better case against George Romney [the Republican governor and presidential aspirant who had visited Vietnam] than they could against Stokely." Larry Temple to president, January 19, 1968, Stokely Carmichael Confidential Name File, box 144; Clark Oral History, pt. 4, p. 28; see also Ralph A. Spritzer memo for Ramsey Clark, August 14, 1967, "Sedition and Inciting Rebellion: Re: Stokely Carmichael," box 75, Ramsey Clark papers. The government did prosecute H. Rap Brown for crossing state lines with a gun when he was under a felony indictment in Cambridge, Maryland. Clark thought the five-year prison sentence was too "harsh" under this "peculiar and technical statute."

56. This remark came after the August 21, 1967, cabinet meeting cited in note 54. See also Roger Wilkins, *A Man's Life* (New York: Touchstone, 1982), p. 229. The administration's frustration with and animosity toward Carmichael reached silly proportions. Presidential counselor John Roche reported that he had "planted a rumor that Stokely is really *white*" (Roche to Marvin Watson, "Eyes Only," December 22, 1967, WHCF, Stokely Carmichael Confidential Name File, box 144).

57. Allen J. Matusow, *The Unraveling of America: A History of Liberalism in the 1960s* (New York: Harper and Row, 1984), p. 253; Polly Greenberg, *The Devil Has Slippery Shoes: A Biased Biography of the Child Development Group of Mississippi* (London: Macmillan, 1969). See also the Johnson Library's Administrative History of the Office of Economic Opportunity.

58. McPherson, *Political Education*, pp. 353–55. He speculated that the Democrats would have trouble carrying the state in the 1968 presidential election, which it had already failed to do in 1964.

59. Matusow, *Unraveling of America*, p. 254; Christopher Jencks, "Accommodating Whites: A New Look at Mississippi," *New Republic*, April 16, 1966, p. 22; Nicholas Lemann, *The Promised Land: The Great Black Migration and How It Changed America* (New York: Vintage, 1991), pp. 324–27. Critics charged that McPherson engineered the deal to create the moderate Mississippi Action for Progress, (MAP), a group of loyal Johnson whites and blacks. The organization included as co-chair Aaron Henry, the NAACP leader from Clarksdale who had led the MFDP contingent at the 1964 Democratic National Convention but had moved away from the black radicals in the state (Greenberg, *Devil Has Slippery Shoes*, p. 640). On efforts to back Henry and moderate whites in capturing the Democratic party, see Lawson, *In Pur-*

suit of Power, 114–15, 196–200, and Aaron Henry Oral History Interview, September 12, 1970, by Thomas H. Baker.

60. Dittmer, "Politics of the Mississippi Movement." Since publication of this essay, Dittmer published *Local People* (Urbana: University of Illinois Press, 1994), which contains a chapter on CDGM. For Johnson Library holdings on the CDGM, see War on Poverty Files, October 14, 1966, to November, 1, 1966, and April 1, 1967, to April 20, 1967, WHCF GEN WE 9, boxes 41 and 42. Another related event that deserves further study concerns the takeover of the Greenville, Mississippi, Air Base by displaced black farm workers. See Nicholas Katzenbach to president, February 14, 1966, WHCF EX HU 2/St 24, box 27, and James C. Cobb, "'Somebody Done Nailed Us on the Cross': Federal Farm and Welfare Policy and The Civil Rights Movement in the Mississippi Delta," *Journal of American History* 77 (December 1990); 928–33.

61. Hobart Taylor, Jr., to president, November 27, 1964, Adam Clayton Powell Name File, box 280.

62. Louis Martin to Harry McPherson, December 12, 1966, box 55; Louis Martin to Jim Jones, October 3, 1966, box 47; Harry McPherson to Marvin Watson, December 12, 1966, box 55, all in Diary Backup Files; Clifford Alexander to president, November 11, 1966, WHCR EX PL 2, box 86; Clifford Alexander to president, January 19, 1966, WHCF, Louis Martin Name File, box 127.

63. McPherson Oral History, pt. 5, tape 1, p. 17.

64. Alexander Oral History, tape 2, pp. 10–11; June 4, 1973, tape 3, p. 29. The quote is drawn from a composite of statements.

65. In 1968 there were five black members of the House of Representatives, all Democrats, and one Republican in the Senate. A sixth congressman, Adam Clayton Powell, had been barred from taking his seat.

66. John P. Roche to Marvin Watson, October 4, 1967, WHCF, Carl Stokes Name File, box 588.

67. Charles V. Hamilton, *Adam Clayton Powell*; see also Wil Haygood, *King of the Cats: The Life and Times of Adam Clayton Powell, Jr.* (Boston: Houghton Mifflin, 1993).

68. Califano, *Triumph & Tragedy*, p. 207; see also Barbara Jordan and Shelby Hearon, *Barbara Jordan: A Self Portrait* (Garden City, N.Y.: Doubleday, 1979); Barbara Jordan Oral History Interview, March 28, 1984, by Roland C. Hayes; and Memorandum for the Record, February 15, 1967, Diary Backup Files, box 55.

69. See Steven F. Lawson, "Freedom Then, Freedom Now: The Historiography of the Civil Rights Movement," *American Historical Review* 96 (April 1991): 467–69.

70. Bruce Miroff, "Presidential Leverage over Social Movements: The Johnson White House and Civil Rights," *Journal of Politics* 41 (February 1981): 17.

71. Richard Goodwin to president, May 4, 1964, WHCF EX HU 2, box 2; Douglass Cater to president, May 19, 1964, WHCF, EX HU 2, box 2; Hobart Taylor, Jr., to president, July 17, 1964, WHCF, EX HU 2, box 3; Hobart Taylor to president, October 13, 1964, WHCR, EX HU 2, box 3.

72. James. C. Gaither to president, May 9, 1967, WHCF, EX WE 9; notes of president's meeting with Kenneth Crawford, *Newsweek*, July 19, 1967, Diary Backup Files, box 71; Farmer Oral History, tape 2, p. 18; Clark Oral History, March 21, 1969, tape 3, p. 16; Califano, *Triumph & Tragedy*, p. 211; claims that Wilkins blamed the riots on Communist instigation.

73. McPherson Oral History, pt. 5, tape 1, p. 12; Katzenbach Oral History, tape

1, p. 30; Burke Marshall Oral History Interview, October 28, 1968, by Thomas H. Baker, p. 27; McPherson, *Political Education*, pp. 356–58.

74. Harry McPherson to president, July 26, 1967, WHCF, EX HU 2, box 5.

75. Harry McPherson to president, September 7, 1966, McPherson Files, box 22; McPherson to George Christian, August 1, 1967, WHCF, EX HU 2, box 6. Though White House Press Aide Andrew Hatcher, who was black, recommended a presidential meeting with black militants other than Carmichael and Brown, he also suggested that the government should establish an "almost CIA type operation to keep watch over the ghettos." George Christian to president, July 31, 1967, WHCF, EX HU 2, box 6. McPherson still wanted to collaborate with traditional African American leaders. Admitting that they "have not much more contact with, or power of persuasion over the terrorists than NAM [National Association of Manufacturers] does," he saw them representing "whatever Negro leadership there is in the country." Prominent in civil rights, business, labor, religious, educational, and political affairs, they might speak out in support of using "lawful means for gaining their legitimate ends." McPherson argued for this approach in terms the chief executive best understood: Just "as in a period of labor strife the White House talks with representatives of labor and industry," he counseled, "in a racial revolt we should talk to responsible representation of the Negro community." LBJ liked the idea, but the proposed meeting apparently never took place. McPherson to president, July 26, 1967, and Louis Martin memo for McPherson, July 25, 1967, both in WHCF, EX HU 2, box 5. See attached list containing the names of fifty-three people whom McPherson, Louis Martin, and probably the president viewed as legitimate black leaders. The plan called for these leaders to invite the president to meet with them.

76. McPherson, *Political Education*, p. 375. One inquiry for future research should concern the extent to which the White House used the Justice Department's Community Relations Service to establish communication with ghetto activists to head off potential explosions. Its director, Roger Wilkins, argued that the president refused to rely on this agency to build bridges to grassroots leaders who articulated real grievances. The question remains why. See Wilkins, *A Man's Life*, pp. 185, 242.

77. Sherwin Markman to president, August 14, 1967, WHCF, EX WE 9, box 28.

78. Harry McPherson to president, August 14, 1967, WHCF, EX HU 2, box 6.

79. Sherwin Markman to president, May 9, 1967, WHCF, EX WE 9, box 28 or 29. For another report that commented on the lack of interest in Vietnam within the ghetto, see Thomas E. Cronin to president, May 31, 1967, WHCF, EX WE 9, box 29.

80. James Gaither to president, May 9, 1967, WHCF, EX WE 9, box 29; Bill Graham to president, June 16, 1967, James C. Gaither Files, box 252.

81. James Gaither to president, May 9, 1967, WHCF, EX WE 9, box 29; Sherwin Markman to president, August 15, 1967, Gaither Files, box 352; Markman to president, March 14, 1967, WHCF, EX WE 9, box 28; McPherson Oral History, pt. 4, tape 2, p. 18.

82. McPherson, *Political Education*, p. 376; Alexander Oral History, tape 2, p. 14.

83. Farmer Oral History, tape 2, p. 27.

84. Sherwin Markman to president, February 1, 1967, WHCF,EX WE 9, box 28.

85. Alexander Oral History, tape 2, p. 22. In an otherwise revealing article, Kenneth O'Reilly writes that following the 1967 riots the FBI argued that moderates had paved the way for the radicals, and Johnson became "fully committed to smearing the civil rights movement." However, I have not found this to be the case with respect to Johnson's attitude toward Wilkins, Young, and their allies. See Kenneth

O'Reilly, "The FBI and the Politics of Riots," *Journal of American History* 75 (June 1988): 104.

86. Whitney Young Oral History, p. 13; Wilkins, *Standing Fast*, p. 313. Alexander, in Oral History, tape 2, pp. 13, 15, 22, observed the same phenomenon but attributed some of the blame to Roy Wilkins for not doing more to keep Johnson from taking the riots as a personal affront. See also Roger Wilkins, *A Man's Life*, p. 231. **309**

87. Minutes cabinet meeting, August 2, 1967, Cabinet Papers, box 9.

88. Harry McPherson to president, August 14, 1967, WHCF, EX HU 2, box 6. Califano, in *Triumph & Tragedy*, p. 219, maintains that the president created the commission to head off an independent congressional investigation that might produce a negative political fallout for the administration. In addition to Kerner, Wilkins, and Brooke, the members of the commission were I. W. Abel, James C. Corman, Fred R. Harris, Herbert Jenkins, John V. Lindsay, William M. McCulloch, Katherine Graham Peden, and Charles B. Thornton.

89. Califano, *Triumph & Tragedy*, pp. 261–262.

90. Harry McPherson to Califano, March 1, 1968, McPherson Files, box 32; McPherson to president, March 18, 1968, McPherson Files, box 53; Wilkins Oral History, p. 21. The papers of the Kerner Commission are housed at the Johnson Library. It is questionable whether the chief executive would have responded to the commission more favorably even if the tone of the report had not offended him. He was in no mood to advocate sweeping increases in expenditures for domestic programs while the Vietnam War continued. In 1966 his White House Conference on Civil Rights recommended big public spending programs that the president chose to ignore; instead he concentrated on passing legislation that would not require great expenditures: protection of civil rights workers and fair housing.

91. McPherson Oral History, pt. 5, tape 1, p. 13; Califano, *Triumph & Tragedy*, p. 277; Lyndon B. Johnson, *The Vantage Point: Perspectives of the Presidency, 1963–1969* (New York: Holt, Rinehart and Winston, 1971), p. 175; Harry McPherson to Joseph Califano, April 5, 1968, 3:30 A.M., James Gaither to president, April 5, 1968, 8:30 A. M., Diary Backup Files, box 95. Also attending the meeting were Judge Leon Higginbotham (see his Oral History Interview, October 7, 1976, by Joe B. Frantz), Clarence Mitchell III, and Bishop George Baber; from the administration: Warren Christopher, Thurgood Marshall, whom Johnson had appointed to the U.S. Supreme Court, Robert Weaver, and Steve Pollak; from Congress: Senators Mike Mansfield and Thomas Kuchel, Speaker John McCormack and Congressmen Carl Albert and William McCulloch. Mayor Carl Stokes of Cleveland, Charles Evers, and A. Philip Randolph could not attend. Tom Johnson to president, April 7, 1968, Tom Johnson's Notes of Meetings, box 2.

92. James Gaither to president, April 5, 1967, 4:50 A. M., Joseph Califano to president, April 5, 1967, 11:22 A. M., Diary Backup Files, box 95; "Handwritten Notes" (Joseph A. Califano's) folder, n.d., Diary Backup Files, box 96; McPherson, *Political Education*, p. 365; Martin Oral History 34–37. The two men who accompanied McKissick were Roy Innis and Wilfred Ussery.

93. Tom Johnson to president, "Notes of the President's Meeting with Negro Leaders," with attachments, April 7, 1968, Tom Johnson's notes of meetings, box 2. For security reasons, Johnson did not attend King's funeral and sent Vice-President Humphrey in his place to head a delegation of administration officials; he also arranged for Roy Wilkins and Whitney Young to accompany them. Joseph Califano to president, April 8, 1968, Diary Backup Files, box 95. Roger Wilkins does not recall the

White House cooperating in facilitating participation of federal officials at the funeral (Wilkins, *A Man's Life*, p. 214). For the president's public remarks on the assassination, see *Public Papers of the Presidents: Lyndon B. Johnson*, vol 1 (Washington, D.C.: Government Printing Office, 1970), p. 493. After proclaiming a national day of mourning, Johnson canceled a planned address to Congress scheduled for April 8.

94. Harvard Sitkoff, *The Struggle for Black Equality, 1954–1980* (New York: Hill and Wang, 1982), p. 221.

95. Lawson, *In Pursuit of Power*, chapter 3.

96. Ralph David Abernathy, *And the Walls Came Tumbling Down* (New York: Harper and Row, 1989), p. 502; Fairclough, *To Redeem the Soul*, pp. 363–65.

97. Cabinet minutes, May 1, 1968, Cabinet Papers, box 13; Califano, *Triumph & Tragedy*, p. 287; McPherson Oral History, pt. 5, tape 2, p. 2.

98. Cabinet minutes, May 1, 1968, Cabinet Papers, box 13. See also minutes of April 3, 1968, in box 13; Matthew Nimetz to Califano, April 25, 1968, and Nimetz to Warren Christopher, April 18, 1968, James Gaither Presidential Task Force Files, box 36. For a harsh view of King and the SCLC, see Larry Temple to president, February 14, 1968, WHCF, EX HU 2, box 7.

99. Matthew Nimetz to Joseph Califano, May 16, 1968, Gaither Presidential Task Force Files, box 36, with enclosed pages 256–65 from Arthur Schlesinger's *Crisis of the Old Order* depicting the 1932 march.

100. Joseph Califano to president, May 21, 1968, Gaither Presidential Task Forces Files, box 36. Knowing the chief executive, Califano made it clear that the changes were based not on pressure but on their merits and had "been in the works for some time."

101. In early June, Bayard Rustin had taken over as organizer of the June 19 rally, which pleased the administration as the best way to achieve a peaceful demonstration. Frustrated with SCLC officials, Rustin subsequently stepped down. Ramsey Clark to Larry Levenson, June 3, 1968, box 34, Clark Papers.

102. Califano, *Triumph & Tragedy*, p. 287; James Gaither to Harry McPherson, June 21, 1968, Gaither Presidential Task Force Files, box 36; McPherson to president, June 20, 1968, McPherson Files, box 53. Also in attendance at the peaceful rally were moderates such as Whitney Young and Roy Wilkins as well as several administration representatives.

103. Clark Oral History, tape 5, p. 17.

104. Clarence Mitchell, the NAACP's premier lobbyist, epitomized Johnson's model of leadership. Dubbed the "101st Senator," Mitchell thought protests could be helpful in publicizing grievances, but the real work of resolving them took place on Capitol Hill. As Johnson came under assault for not acting swiftly enough to combat long-standing racial and economic ills, Mitchell stood "militantly" with him and became "increasingly disillusioned with . . . [those] who urge new programs but are unwilling to concentrate on passage of proposed programs." Barefoot Sanders to president, April 29, 1968, Clarence Mitchell Name File; Watson, *Lion in the Lobby*, p. 592; McPherson, *Political Education*, p. 300; Johnson, *Vantage Point*, p. 177. See also Jack Valenti to president, January 26, 1965, WHCF, Clarence Mitchell Name File, box 480; Jim Jones to president, October 18, 1967, Diary Backup Files, box 76; Clarence Mitchell Oral History Interview, April 30, 1969, by Thomas H. Baker, p. 18.

105. Harry McPherson to president, July 26, 1967, EX HU 2, box 5.

106. Cabinet minutes, August 2, 1967, Cabinet Papers, box 9. For the influence

of FDR on Johnson and other post–New Deal presidents, see William E. Leuchtenburg, *In the Shadow of FDR: From Harry Truman to Ronald Reagan* (Ithaca, N.Y.: Cornell University Press, 1983).
107. Farmer Oral History, p. 27. Despite his break with Johnson, Farmer was an insightful critic.
108. Quoted in Greenberg, *Devil Has Slippery Shoes*, p. 513.
109. Wilkins, *A Man's Life*, p. 229.

311

FROM BOYCOTTS TO BALLOTS

1. Steven F. Lawson, *Black Ballots: Voting Rights in the South, 1944–1969* (New York: Columbia Univ. Press, 1976), 102; L. D. Reddick, *Crusader without Violence: A Biography of Martin Luther King, Jr.* (New York: Harper, 1959), 196; Manning Marable, *Black American Politics: From the Washington Marches to Jesse Jackson* (London: Verso, 1985), 121.
2. Studies by sociologists include Doug McAdam, *Political Process and the Development of Black Insurgency, 1930–1970* (Chicago: Univ. of Chicago Press, 1982), and Aldon D. Morris, *The Origins of the Civil Rights Movement: Black Communities Organizing for Change* (New York: Free Press, 1984). By political scientists, see Daniel M. Berman, *A Bill Becomes a Law: Congress Enacts Civil Rights Legislation* (New York: MacMillan, 1966), and Earl Black and Merle Black, *Politics and Society in the South* (Cambridge: Harvard Univ. Press, 1987; Harry Holloway, *The Politics of the Southern Negro: From Exclusion to Big City Organization* (New York: Random House, 1969), Everett C. Ladd, *Negro Political Leadership in the South* (Ithaca, N.Y.: Cornell Univ. Press, 1966); Donald R. Matthews and James W. Prothro, *Negroes and the New Southern Politics* (New York: Harcourt, Brace and World, 1966); Frederick Wirt, *Politics of Southern Equality*, (Chicago: Aldine, 1970). By historians, see Human V. Bartley and Hugh D. Graham, *Southern Politics and the Second Reconstruction* (Baltimore: Johns Hopkins Univ. Press, 1975); Adam Fairclough, *"To Redeem the Soul of America": The Southern Christian Leadership Conference and Martin Luther King, Jr.* (Athens: Univ. of Georgia Press, 1987). By journalists, see Jack Bass and Walter DeVries, *Transformation of Southern Politics: Social Change and Political Consequence since 1945* (New York: Basic Books, 1976; Richard Kluger, *Simple Justice: The History of* Brown v. Board of Education *and Black America's Struggle for Equality* (New York: Knopf, 1976); Pat Watters and Reese Cleghorn, *Climbing Jacob's Ladder: The Arrival of Negroes in Southern Politics* (New York: Harcourt, Brace and World, 1967). David Garrow, a political scientist, has written extensively on Martin Luther King in the vein of an historian; for example, see *Bearing the Cross: Martin Luther King, Jr., and the Southern Christian Leadership Conference* (New York: Morrow, 1986). Also the historian August Meier and the sociologist Elliott Rudwick have collaborated on many works related to the movement. For example, see *CORE: A Study of the Civil Rights Movement, 1942–1968* (New York: Oxford Univ. Press, 1973).
3. See Lawrence J. Hanks, *The Struggle for Black Political Empowerment in Three Georgia Counties* (Knoxville: Univ. of Tennessee Press, 1987), for the diversity in the Peach State. See also the documentary film by Alan Bell and Paul Stekler, *Hands That Picked the Cotton: The Story of Black Politics in Today's Rural South* (1984).
4. Eric Foner, "Comment," in Darlene Clark Hine, ed., *The State of Afro-Ameri-*

can History: Past, Present, and Future (Baton Rouge: Louisiana State Univ. Press, 1986), 77; W.E.B. Du Bois, *The Souls of Black Folk* (New York: New American Library, 1969), 91. "Negroes must insist continually, in season and out of season, that voting is necessary to modern manhood," Du Bois wrote.

5. William Hastie, "Appraisal of *Smith v. Allwright*," *Lawyers' Guild Review* 5 (Mar. -Apr. 1945): 66; Darlene Clark Hine, *Black Victory: The Rise and Fall of the White Primary in Texas* (New York: KTO Press, 1979).

6. Morris, *Origins of the Civil Rights Movement*, chap. 5; Patricia Sullivan, "The Voting Rights Movement in South Carolina during the 1940s" (Paper delivered at the Annual Meeting of the Southern Historical Association, Houston, 15 Nov. 1985).

7. Charles V. Hamilton, "Foreward," in Michael B. Preston, Lenneal J. Henderson, Jr., and Paul Puryear, eds., *New Black Politics: The Search for Political Power* (New York: Longman, 1982), xviii.

8. On SNCC, see Clayborne Carson, *In Struggle: SNCC and the Black Reawakening of the 1960s* (Cambridge: Harvard Univ. Press, 1981); Howard Zinn, *SNCC: The New Abolitionists* (Boston: Beacon Press, 1964); Cleveland Sellers with Robert Terrell, *The River of No Return: The Autobiography of a Black Militant and the Life and Death of SNCC* (New York: Morrow, 1973); Mary King, *Freedom Song: A Personal Story of the 1960s Civil Rights Movement* (New York: Morrow, 1987).

9. Bob Moses, "Speech to Organizers Training Center," San Francisco, 5 June 1987, 10–11, courtesy of Joseph Sinsheimer; Joseph Sinsheimer, "Never Turn Back: An Interview with Sam Block," *Southern Exposure* 15 (Summer 1987): 43; Fannie Lou Hamer to Dear Friends, 11 May 1976, addition 78, folder 31, Eugene Cox Manuscripts, Mississippi State University. See also Carson, *In Struggle*, 171.

10. Watters and Cleghorn, *Climbing Jacob's Ladder*, 54; Minion K. C. Morrison, *Black Political Mobilization: Leadership, Power, and Mass Behavior* (Albany: State Univ. of New York Press, 1987), 51.

11. August Meier, "The Dilemmas of Negro Protest Strategy," *New South* 21 (Spring 1966): 14; J. Mills Thornton, "Challenge and Response in the Montgomery Bus Boycott of 1955–1956," *Alabama Review* 33 (1980): 163–235; Fairclough, *To Redeem*; Robert J. Norrell, *Reaping the Whirlwind: The Civil Rights Movement in Tuskegee* (New York: Knopf, 1985); William H. Chafe, *Civilities and Civil Rights: Greensboro, North Carolina, and the Black Struggle for Freedom* (New York: Oxford Univ. Press, 1980).

12. Fairclough, *To Redeem*, 52.

13. David J. Garrow, *Protest at Selma: Martin Luther King, Jr., and the Voting Rights Act of 1965* (New Haven: Yale Univ. Press, 1978), 18; Lawson, *Black Ballots*, 283.

14. For a fuller discussion of this issue, see Steven F. Lawson, *In Pursuit of Power: Southern Blacks and Electoral Politics, 1965–1982* (New York: Columbia Univ. Press, 1985), chap. 2.

15. Lester M. Salamon, "Leadership and Modernization: The Emerging Black Political Elite in the American South," *Journal of Politics* 35 (1973): 615–46; Richard D. Shingles, "Black Consciousness and Political Participation: The Missing Link," *American Political Science Review* 75 (1981): 79–91.

16. Lawson, *Pursuit*, 297; Thomas E. Cavanagh, *Inside Black America: The Meaning of the Black Vote in the 1984 Elections* (Washington, D.C.: Joint Center for Political Studies, 1985), 22; U.S. Department of Commerce, Bureau of the Census, *Statistical Abstract of the United States*, 1987 (Washington D.C.: GPO, 1986), 245.

17. Thomas E. Cavanagh, *Impact of the Black Vote* (Washington, D.C.: Joint Center for Political Studies, 1984), 2–3; Chandler Davidson, *Biracial Politics: Conflict and Coalition in the Metropolitan South* (Baton Rouge: Louisiana State Univ. Press, 1972), 92; Richard Murray and Arnold Vedlitz, "Race, Socioeconomic Status, and Voting Participation in Large Southern Cities," *Journal of Politics* 39 (1977): 1070; Minion K. C. Morrison, *Black Political Mobilization*, 1975; Sidney Verba, Norman Nie, and Jae-on Kim, *Participation and Political Equality* (Cambridge: Cambridge Univ. Press, 1978), 13; Paul Jeffrey Stekler, "Black Politics in the New South: An Investigation of Change at Various Levels" (Ph.D. diss., Harvard Univ., 1982), 31; Hanes Walton, *Invisible Politics: Black Political Behavior* (Albany: State Univ. of New York Press, 1985).

18. Janet C. Shortt, "Mississippi Tour," 22, 24, 28–30 June 1972, Voter Education Project Office Files, Atlanta Univ. Library: Hanks, *The Struggle for Black Political Empowerment*, 38. Hanks concludes: "Organization, with an emphasis on group consciousness and a sense of group efficacy, is a bypassing agent around low black [socioeconomic status]."

19. More voters were enrolled in counties that received federal examiners but did not have a local registration drive than in counties that only had a suffrage campaign without federal registrars. The best results occurred when the two operated in tandem. See Watters and Cleghorn, *Climbing Jacob's Ladder*, 255, and Harold W. Stanley, *Voter Mobilization and the Politics of Race: The South and Universal Suffrage, 1952–1984* (New York: Praeger, 1987), 96.

20. Howard Ball, Dale Krane, and Thomas P. Lauth, *Compromised Compliance: Implementation of the 1965 Voting Rights Act* (Westport, Conn.: Greenwood Press, 1982); Lawson, *Pursuit*; Abigail M. Themstrom, *Whose Votes Count? Affirmative Action and Minority Voting Rights* (Cambridge: Harvard Univ. Press, 1987).

21. Michal R. Belknap, *Federal Law and Southern Order: Racial Violence and Constitutional Conflicts in the Post-Brown South* (Athens: Univ. of Georgia Press, 1987); Lawson, *Pursuit*, chap. 2.

22. Leonard A. Cole, *Blacks in Power: A Comparative Study of Black and White Elected Officials* (Princeton: Princeton Univ. Press, 1976), 101; Robert C. Smith, "Black Power and the Transformation from Protest to Politics," *Political Science Quarterly* 96 (1981): 431–43.

23. Alton Hornsby, Jr., "The Negro in Atlanta Politics, 1961–1973," *Atlanta Historical Bulletin* 21 (Spring 1977); William R. Keech, *The Impact of Negro Voting* (Chicago: Rand McNally, 1968); Ladd, *Negro Leadership*; Norrell, *Reaping the Whirlwind*.

24. Tom McCain, quoted in Themstrom, *Whose Votes*, 239.

25. Mrs. Geneva Collins, quoted in Julian Bond, *Black Candidates: Southern Campaign Experiences* (Atlanta: Southern Regional Council, 1968), 8.

26. *New Pittsburgh Courier*, 21 Feb. 1970, p. 6: John Conyers, Jr., "A Black Political Strategy for 1972," in Nathan Wright, Jr. *What Black Politicians Are Saying* (New York: Hawthorn Books, 1972), 164. For an analysis of "clientage politics," see Martin Kilson, "Political Change in the Negro Ghetto, 1900–1940's," in Nathan I. Huggins, Martin Kilson, Daniel M. Fox, eds., *Key Issues in the Afro-American Experience* 2 (New York: Harcourt, Brace, Jovanovich, 1971): 171, and Kilson, "The New Black Political Class," in Joseph Washington, Jr., ed., *Dilemmas of the Black Middle Class* (n. p., 1980), 81.

27. Quoted in Walton, *Invisible*, 155. For a critical assessment of the performance of black elected officials, see Marable, *Black American Politics*, 244.

28. Paul Jeffrey Stekler, "Electing Blacks to Office in the South—Black Candidates, Bloc Voting and Racial Unity Twenty Years after the Voting Rights Act," *Urban Lawyer* 17 (1985): 485; Holloway, *The Politics of the Southern Negro*, 177.

29. Bass and DeVries, *The Transformation of Southern Politics*, 54. This pragmatism surfaced in the support George C. Wallace received during the 1970s and 1980s from black officials, such as Mayor Johnny Ford of Tuskegee. According to Ford, "it's business with me—no emotion. What you must do is penetrate the system and, once within the system, learn how it works. And then work it well" (quoted in Neil R. Peirce, *The Deep South States of America: People, Politics, and Power in the Seven Deep South States* (New York: Norton, 1974), 281–82.

30. Margaret Edds, *Free at Last: What Really Happened When Civil Rights Came to Southern Politics* (Bethesda, Md.: Adler and Adler, 1987), 97.

31. Ibid., 109; Peter K. Eisinger, *The Politics of Displacement: Racial and Ethnic Transition in Three American Cities* (New York: Academic Press, 1980), 74; Marable, *Black American Politics*, 244. On Arrington, see Jimmie Lewis Franklin, *Back to Birmingham: Richard Arrington and His Times* (Tuscaloosa: Univ. of Alabama Press, 1989).

32. Joint Center for Political Studies, *Black Elected Officials: A National Roster, 1987* (Washington, D.C., 1987), 11, 16–17; U.S. Commission on Civil Rights, *The Voting Rights Act: Unfulfilled Goals* (Washington, D.C.: CPO, 1981), 17.

33. Chandler Davidson and George Korbel, "At-Large Elections and Minority Group Representation: A Reexamination of Historical and Contemporary Evidence," *Journal of Politics* 43 (1981): 982–1005.

34. Earl Black, *Southern Governors and Civil Rights: Racial Segregation as a Campaign Issue in the Second Reconstruction* (Cambridge: Harvard Univ. Press, 1976).

35. Thernstrom, *Whose Votes*, 77–78. On the tension between individual and group rights, see William H. Chafe, "The End of One Struggle, the Beginning of Another," and J. Mills Thornton, "Commentary," in Charles W. Eagles, ed., *The Civil Rights Movement in America* (Jackson: Univ. Press of Mississippi, 1986), 127–48, 148–55.

36. Thernstrom, *Whose Votes*, 242; Katharine I. Butler, "Denial or Abridgement of the Right to Vote: What Does It Mean?" in Lorn S. Foster, ed., *The Voting Rights Act: Consequences and Implications* (New York: Praeger, 1985), 56.

37. Lawson, *Pursuit*, 194; William J. Crotty, *Decision for the Democrats: Reforming the Party Structure* (Baltimore: Johns Hopkins Univ. Press, 1979); Byron E. Shafer, *Quiet Revolution: The Struggle for the Democratic Party and the Shaping of Post-Reform Politics* (New York: Russell Sage Foundation, 1983).

38. Lawson, *Pursuit*, 196.

39. Voter Education and Registration Action, Inc., *Harassment of Black Elected Officials: Ten Years Later* (Washington, D.C., 1987).

40. Eisinger, *Displacement*, 150. In 1982 a Senate staff member described voting rights for blacks as "the purest brand of motherhood" (Thernstrom, *Whose Votes*, 113). On the issue of citizenship and legitimacy, see Milton D. Morris, *The Politics of Black America* (New York: Harper and Row, 1975), 86–89. Many whites could still not bring themselves to vote for black candidates, but they could indirectly support them by staying away from the polls and not voting for their white opponents. This happened in the 1986 congressional contest in Mississippi, in which Mike Espy became the first black since Reconstruction to win a seat in the U.S. House of Representatives ("Political Trendletter," *Focus* 14 [Nov.-Dec. 1986]: 1).

41. Eddie N. Williams, "Black Political Progress in the 1970s: The Electoral

Arena," in Preston, Henderson, and Puryear, *New Black Politics*, 75; Manning Marable, *Race Reform and Rebellion: The Second Reconstruction in Black America* (Jackson: Univ. Press of Mississippi, 1984), 169. See also Adolph L. Reed, Jr., *The Jesse Jackson Phenomenon: The Crisis in Afro-American Politics* (New Haven: Yale Univ. Press, 1986), 123–27.   **315**

42. Moses, "Speech," 10; Stekler, "Black Politics," 194ff., 262; John Dittmer, "The Politics of the Mississippi Movement, 1954–1964," in Eagles, *Civil Rights Movement*, 91–91; Lawson, *Pursuit*, 114–15, 196–99, 202–3.

43. Edds, *Free*, 112; Margaret K. Latimer and Robert S. Montjoy, "Overcoming the Politics of Polarization in Birmingham," in Thomas E. Cavanagh, ed., *Strategies for Mobilizing Black Voters* (Washington, D.C.: Joint Center for Political Studies, 1987), 91; Morris, *Politics of Black America*, 296ff.

44. Thernstrom, *Whose Votes*, 241. For a different view from a black politician who actively sought white votes, see Edds, *Free*, 188–89. In the Atlanta congressional race of 1986, John Lewis defeated his former SNCC ally Julian Bond in the Democratic Party primary, capturing 82 percent of the white vote and 40 percent of the black electorate. In his general election victory against a white Republican, Lewis received only 47 percent of the white vote ("Political Trendletter," *Focus* 14 [Sept. 1986]: 2; ibid. [Oct.-Nov. 1986]: 4).

45. In 1989 Douglas Wilder won the position of governor of Virginia. In 1987 four black judges were elected to the highest court in the states of Alabama, Florida, Mississippi, and North Carolina. In the North blacks had been elected to various statewide positions, including lieutenant governor of California (Mervyn Dymally), U.S. senator from Massachusetts (Edward Brooke), secretary of state of Michigan (Richard Austin), and comptroller of Illinois (Roland Burris).

46. Black and Black, *Politics*, 204–6; Robert Emil Botsch, *We Shall Not Overcome: Populism and Southern-Blue Collar Workers* (Chapel Hill: Univ of North Carolina Press, 1980), 204–5; Bartley and Graham, *Southern Politics and the Second Reconstruction*, 195. In contrast, see Davidson, *Biracial*, 215; Richard Murray and Arnold Vedlitz, "Racial Voting Patterns in the South: An Analysis of Major Elections from 1960 to 1977 in Five Cities," *Annals of the American Academy of Political and Social Sciences* 439 (Sept. 1978): 34. See also Alexander P. Lamis, *The Two Party South* (New York: Oxford Univ. Press, 1984), 39, 62; Marable, *Black American Politics*, 61.

47. Lamis, *Two Party*, 54.

48. Lawson, *Pursuit*, 252; *Raleigh News and Observer*, 4 Oct. 1987, p. 5A. In 1987 there were twenty-three black congressman, with four from the South.

49. Raleigh News and Observer, 10 Jan. 1988, p. 2D; Black and Black, *Politics*, 143, 296.

50. Shirley Chisholm campaigned for the Democratic nomination in 1972 with far less support and success.

51. Sheila D. Collins, *The Rainbow Challenge: The Jackson Campaign and the Future of U.S. Politics* (New York: Monthly Review Press, 1986); Bob Faw and Nancy Skelton, *Thunder in America: The Improbable Presidential Campaign of Jesse Jackson* (Austin: Texas Monthly Press, 1986); Thomas Landess and Richard Quinn, *Jesse Jackson and the Politics of Race* (Ottawa, Ill.: Jameson Books, 1985); Reed, *Jesse Jackson Phenomenon*; Barbara A. Reynolds, *Jesse Jackson: America's David* (Washington, D.C.: JES Associates, 1985); Lucius J. Barker, *Our Time Has Come: A Delegate's Diary of Jesse Jackson's 1984 Presidential Campaign* (Urbana: Univ. of Illinois Press, 1988).

52. Edds, *Free*, 83, 97. See also Norrell, *Reaping the Whirlwind*, chap. 13.

53. Kilson, "New Black Political Class," 87; Albert Karnig and Susan Welch, *Black Representation and Urban Policy* (Chicago: Univ. of Chicago Press, 1980), 90; L. Bart Landry, "The Social and Economic Adequacy of the Black Middle Class,"in Washington, *Dilemmas*, 10–11.

54. Collins, *Rainbow Challenge*, 175–76; Marguerite Ross Barnett, "The Strategic Debate over a Black Presidential Candidate," *PS* 16 (1983): 490. In 1984 many black political leaders chose to endorse Walter Mondale for his strong record on civil rights issues. In contrast, four years later, blacks did not identify any white candidate with the cause of civil rights.

55. Dittmer, "Politics of the Mississippi Movement," in Eagles, *Civil Rights Movement*; Joseph Sinsheimer, "COFO and the 1963 Freedom Vote: New Strategies for Change in Mississippi," *Journal of Southern History* 55 (1989): 217–44; Edds, *Free*, 179ff., concerning generational splits in Greene County, Alabama.

56. Cavanagh, *Inside*, 6; Black and Black, *Politics*, 70–72, 139–40; Stanley, *Voter Mobilization*, 145. The upsurge in white participation stemmed from more than a racial backlash in the wake of the 1965 Voting Rights Act. Long-term trends, such as revived two-party competition, urbanization, and improved socioeconomic conditions, played the most important roles. These factors became especially significant with the increased passage of time since the civil rights movement.

57. This is usually most evident in at-large elections. Ironically, the Republican Party, as the minority party in the South, has benefited from black challenges to at-large and multimember district elections. See Thernstrom, *Whose Votes*, 224. Sometimes southern blacks did get elected with white votes in citywide elections in which blacks were the minority. For example in 1983, Harvey Gantt, the first black to desegregate Clemson University, was elected mayor of Charlotte, North Carolina. After winning reelection in 1985, he was defeated two years later. For a study that minimizes the phenomenon of racial polarization at the polls, see Charles S. Bullock III, "Aftermath of the Voting Rights Act: Racial Voting Patterns in Atlanta-Area Election," in Foster, *Voting Rights Act*, 203.

58. Norrell, *Reaping the Whirlwind*. Two other important case studies are Chafe, *Civilities and Civil Rights*, and David T. Colburn, *Racial Change and Community Crisis: St. Augustine, Florida, 1877–1980* (New York: Columbia Univ. Press, 1985).

59. Jo Ann Robinson, *The Montgomery Bus Boycott and the Women Who Started It: The Memories of Jo Ann Gibson Robinson* (Knoxville: Univ. of Tennessee Press, 1987). On Unita Blackwell, see Morrison, *Black Political Mobilization*, chap 4.

60. Cavanagh, *Inside*, 18. Unfortunately, for purposes of comparison, the figures for white woman officeholders are not similarly available. According to the National Women's Political Caucus, 15.6 percent of state legislative seats in the nation and 11.1 percent of the mayor's posts in cities over 30,000 people were occupied by women (National Women's Political Caucus, *1987 National Directory of Women Elected Officials* [Washington, D.C., 1987], 10).

61. A starting point for drawing any such comparison should be William Chafe, *Women and Equality: Changing Patterns in American Culture* (New York: Oxford Univ. Press, 1977), chaps. 3 and 4.

62. For a valuable attempt to weave together the economic and political strands of the black freedom struggle, see Jack M. Bloom, *Class, Race, and the Civil Rights Movement* (Bloomington: Indiana Univ. Press, 1987).

63. Moses, "Speech," 5. In a similar vein, Vincent G. Harding has written: "We

are entrenched in many parts of the public sector of the political, economic, and cultural life. Nowhere can we be invisible again" (Harding, *The Other American Revolution* [Los Angeles: Center for Afro-American Studies, 1981], 204).

317

PRESERVING THE SECOND RECONSTRUCTION

1. *Allen et. al. v. State Board of Elections et. al.*, 393 U.S. 595 (1969).

2. Chuck Stone, *Black Political Power in America* (New York 1970, rev. ed.), 252.

3. A. Philip Randolph, "An Open Letter to Black Voters," n.d., Box 68, Chicago Office Files, Everett Dirksen MSS, Dirksen Library, Pekin, Illinois. See also, Vernon E. Jordan, Jr., "End of the Second Reconstruction?" *Vital Speeches* 38 (1 July 1972), 553.

4. William Gillette, *Retreat From Reconstruction 1869–1879* (Baton Rouge and London, 1979), chapters 1 and 2; Robert H. Wiebe, "White Attitudes and Black Rights from *Brown* to *Bakke*," in Michael V. Namorato, ed., *Have We Overcome? Race Relations Since* Brown (Jackson, Miss., 1979), 157–58.

5. Numan V. Bartley and Hugh D. Graham, *Southern Politics and the Second Reconstruction* (Baltimore, 1976), 109–10; Earl Black, *Southern Governors and Civil Rights: Racial Segregation as a Campaign Issue in the Second Reconstruction* (Cambridge, Massachusetts, 1976), 326, 329; Vinton M. Prince, Jr., "Black Voting Strength in Mississippi: The Case of the Unreal Advantage," paper delivered to the Symposium on Southern Politics, The Citadel, Charleston, South Carolina, 1978. For population figures in the Civil War and Reconstruction era see W.E.B. Du Bois, *Black Reconstruction in America 1860–1880* (New York, 1935), *passim*. In 1960, approximately seventy-five counties had a majority black voting age population.

6. Wiebe, "White Attitudes" p. 147; George M. Frederickson, *White Supremacy: A Comparative Study in American and South African History* (New York, 1981), 182–83, 198.

7. On the passage of the Voting Rights Act see David J. Garrow, *Protest at Selma: Martin Luther King, Jr., and the Voting Rights Act of 1965* (New Haven, 1978) and Steven F. Lawson, *Black Ballots: Voting Rights in the South, 1944–1969* (New York, 1976), Chapter 10. The formula was based on voter registration and turnout at the polls in the 1964 presidential election with the statistical threshold set at 50 percent. The electoral submissions subject to preclearance could be found defective if they had a racially discriminatory purpose or effect. The act covered Alabama, Georgia, Louisiana, Mississippi, South Carolina, Virginia, and thirty-four North Carolina counties.

8. Ramsey Clark Oral History Interview, Lyndon Baines Johnson Library (LBJL).

9. 27 May 1967. On the connection between the administration's racial policies and Vietnam see Louis Martin to Marvin Watson, 16 August 1965, ND 19/LO 312; Bill Moyers to the President, 30 August 1965, ExHu 2, Box 3, Clifford Alexander to the President, 6 January 1966, ExHu 2, Box 3; Harry McPherson to the President, 4 April 1967, Box 14, McPherson Files; George Christian to the President, 8 April 1967, ExHu 2, Box 4, LBJL.

10. Howard W. Smith to Joe C. Culp, 20 May 1966, Box 100, Howard W. Smith Mss., University of Virginia.

11. Matthew Nimitz Oral History Interview, LBJL. See the exchange of correspondence between Nicholas Katzenbach and Harry McPherson, 12, 17, 20 September 1966, Box 21, Harry McPherson Files, LBJL.

12. Bruce Miroff, "Presidential Leverage over Social Movements: the Johnson White House and Civil Rights," *The Journal of Politics* 43 (February 1981), 2–23.

13. "Address by Nicholas deB. Katzenbach to the Southern Regional Council, Atlanta, Georgia, February 28, 1966," press release, (Civil Rights), Will Sparks Files, LBJL.

14. *Public Papers of the President, Lyndon B. Johnson*, 1968 (Washington, 1969), 1354.

15. Bayard Rustin, "From Protest to Politics: The Future of the Civil Rights Movement," *Commentary* 39 (February 1965), 25.

16. Martin Luther King, Jr., "Martin Luther King Defines 'Black Power'" *New York Times Magazine* (June 11, 1967), 101; King, *Where Do We Go From Here: Chaos or Community?* (New York, 1967), 15.

17. Stokely Carmichael and Charles V. Hamilton, *Black Power: The Politics of Liberation in America* (New York, 1967), 104. The Student Nonviolent Coordinating Committee, the organization Carmichael chaired, was active in the early voter registration drives and in creating black dominated political parties in Mississippi and Alabama. After Carmichael became head of SNCC in 1966, the organization shifted its black political power orientation from the rural South to urban ghettoes. On this transformation see Clayborne Carson, *In Struggle: SNCC and the Black Awakening of the 1960s* (Cambridge, Mass., 1981).

18. Ruby Magee Interview, Mississippi Oral History Program, University of Southern Mississippi. See also Joyce Ladner, "What Black Power Means to Negroes in Mississippi," in August Meier, ed., *The Transformation of Activism* (New York, 1970), 145.

19. Gary Orfield, *The Reconstruction of Southern Education: The Schools and the 1964 Civil Rights Act* (New York, 1969), 308–09.

20. In *Climbing Jacob's Ladder* (New York, 1967), 262, Pat Watters and Reese Cleghorn claim that in determining where to send examiners the Justice Department sought not to antagonize powerful senators like Richard Russell of Georgia and James Eastland of Mississippi. The evidence on this point remains inconclusive, but for some testimony of the southern political clout on the enforcement program see Richard Russell to Carey Williams, 17 February 1966, IF IA, Dictation, Richard B. Russell MSS, Russell Library, University of Georgia, and *Delta Democrat-Times*, 22 April 1966, cited in U.S. Congress, House of Representatives, Committee on the Judiciary, *Hearings* (Civil Rights), 89th Congress, Second Session, p. 1488.

21. John Doar, Memo for the Attorney General, 19 August 1965, Civil Rights Division office files, Washington, D.C. On Kennedy's civil rights policies consult Carl M. Brauer, *John F. Kennedy and the Second Reconstruction* (New York, 1977).

22. For a cogent treatise on the enforcement role adopted by the Justice Department in race relations, see Burke Marshall, *Federalism and Civil Rights*, (New York, 1964).

23. Testimony of John Doar, 5 October 1965, Special Equal Rights Committee, Box 91, Democratic National Committee Records, LBJL.

24. Allan Wolk, *The Presidency and Black Civil Rights: Eisenhower to Nixon* (Rutherford, New Jersey, 1971), 75.

25. Nicholas Katzenbach to William Taylor, 4 December 1965, Box 3, Lee White Files, LBJL; William Taylor, Memo, to the United States Commission on Civil Rights, 15 December 1965, Box 67, Theodore M. Hesburgh MSS., Notre Dame University

Law Library. The attorney general could dispatch examiners if he received twenty meritorious complaints of discrimination; this option was not utilized.

26. John Doar to Bradford J. Dye, 26 January 1966, Civil Rights Division office files.

319

27. Nicholas Katzenbach to state and local registration officials, 8 January 1966, 23 April 1966, Department of Justice Administrative History, volume VII, LBJL; John Doar to L. O. Aulds, 28 April 1967, CRD office files. On the impact of the judiciary in devising a "freezing" concept to overcome the effects of past disfranchisement tactics, see Frank T. Read and Lucy S. McGough, *Let Them Be Judged: The Judicial Integration of the Deep South* (Metuchen, New Jersey, 1978), chapter 7.

28. John Doar to St. John Barrett, 21 May 1967, CRD office files.

29. Wolf, *The Presidency and Black Civil Rights*, p. 77; John Doar, "Civil Rights and Self Government," in Dona Baron, ed., *The National Purpose Reconsidered* (New York, 1978), 112.

30. Wolk, Ibid., p. 76. This attempt to function impartially also applied to decisions involving the assignment of federal observers provided under the 1965 act. In April 1966 Attorney General Katzenbach explained the department's rationale in exercising restraint in sending federal personnel to monitor Alabama elections: "We cannot afford widespread charges of fraud or intimidation of voters. Nor do I wish to 'interfere' in local elections. By and large I am attempting to do the least that I can safely do without upsetting civil rights groups. But the fact that observers are not going into any but the most difficult counties will, I think, show we are both knowledgeable and even-handed." Nicholas Katzenbach, Memo for the President, 26 April 1966, Ex P1/St1, LBJL. For criticism of the deficiencies in the observer program, see United States Commission on Civil Rights, *Political Participation* (Washington, D.C., 1968), 183–84.

31. *Crisis* 73 (January 1966), 41–2; Thurgood Marshall to the President, 14 January 1966, ExHu 2, Box 3, LBJL. For a favorable comment on the success of the act, see the testimony of Joseph Rauh, U.S. Congress, House of Representatives, Committee on the Judiciary, *Hearings* (Voting Rights Act Extension), Ninety-First Congress, First Session, p. 179.

32. U.S. Congress, House of Representatives, Committee on the Judiciary, Ibid., p. 193.

33. Testimony of Lawrence Speiser, Director, Washington Office, American Civil Liberties Union, U.S. Congress, Senate Judiciary Committee, *Hearings* (Amendment to the Voting Rights Act of 1965), Ninety-First Congress, First and Second Session, p. 158. According to Bayard Rustin, "in civil rights there is a situation in which if the party you prefer is in and if the President is one you happen to think is doing a good job, it is under those circumstances you have to be even harsher on him than at any point. So when you have a guy in who is literally no good, you just dismiss him as a small fungus and proceed." Bayard Rustin Oral History Interview, LBJL.

34. Penn Kimball, *The Disconnected* (New York, 1972), 3, 272; Garrow, *Protest at Selma*, p. 191.

35. U.S. Congress, Senate Judiciary Committee, Ibid., p. 444; Leon E. Panetta and Peter Gall, *Bring Us Together: The Nixon Team and the Civil Rights Retreat* (Philadelphia, 1971), 106. For a different version of the southern strategy, see Harry Dent, *The Prodigal South Returns to Power* (New York, 1978), 75, 96, 177.

36. Richard Russell to Olin L. Spence, 31 January 1969, Box 5, Russell MSS.

37. Panetta, *Bring Us Together*, p. 92; Richard Harris, Justice: *The Crisis of Law, Order, and Freedom in America* (New York, 1970), 151–52; Kevin Philips, *The Emerging Republican Majority* (New Rochelle, N.Y., 1969). More than twenty of Strom Thurmond's friends took key positions in the Nixon administration according to Neal R. Pierce, *The Deep South States of America: People, Politics, and Power in the Seven Deep South States* (New York, 1974), 39.

38. U.S. Congress, House of Representatives, Committee on the Judiciary, *Hearings*, Ninety-First Congress, First session, pp. 219–269. The Mitchell proposal virtually freed the seven southern states from coverage under the 1965 law. Unless the original terms of the statute were extended for an additional number of years, the covered jurisdiction could easily bail out by demonstrating that it had not employed a literacy test or device during the previous five years. Without renewal, the tough provisions of the Voting Rights Act would have expired on 6 August 1970. However, even if the states extricated themselves, the federal district court in Washington, D.C., would retain jurisdiction for five years. Before President Johnson left office, he had recommended a simple five year extension of the act.

39. *Public Papers of the President, Richard Nixon, 1970* (Washington, D.C., 1971), 512. In contrast to the celebration five years earlier, Nixon signed the bill without fanfare and with only one of his aides present. *New York Times* 23 June 1970, p. 31. For a concise account of the passage and the forces shaping it, see Gary Orfield, *Congressional Power: Congress and Social Change* (New York, 1975), 97–101. In the Senate 33 Republicans joined 31 Democrats in supporting the final version of the bill, and in the House, 59 Republicans and 165 Democrats formed the majority.

40. *New Pittsburgh Courier*, 11 July 1970, p. 10.

41. Orfield, *Congressional Power*, p. 102. On the final 64–12 vote in the Senate four southerners, two from Tennessee and one each from Arkansas and Virginia voted for the bill. Hollings kept his private reservations to himself and voted no. The bill passed the House 224–183 and included twenty-seven southerners in the majority. Senator John Stennis, T.V. Transcript, 1 March 1970, John Stennis MSS., Mitchell Memorial Library, Mississippi State University. For assessment of the sometimes confusing posture of the White House, see Roy Reed, *New York Times*, 11 June 1969; Warren Weaver, Jr., *New York Times*, 28 June 1969, p. 12; E. W. Kenworthy, *New York Times*, 14 December 1969, IV, p. 2; Panetta, *Bring Us Together*, p. 221; Jonathan Schell, *The Time of Illusion* (New York, 1976), pp. 40–44.

42. Washington Research Project [David Hunter], *The Shameful Blight: The Survival of Racial Discrimination in Voting in the South* (Washington, D.C., 1972), *passim*. The attorney general had failed to disallow the Mississippi Open Primary law, which stipulated that all candidates for office compete in a single election with a run-off required if no candidate received a majority of the ballots. The law would reduce the chances for winning of independent party candidates like Charles Evers, who might triumph by solidly gaining the minority black vote while white opponents divided the white electorate. The Justice Department refused to object, because it could not reach a decision within the sixty days mandated by section five. Jerris Leonard to Julius L. Lotterhos, Jr., 16 October 1970, Notebook, Voting Rights Act Hearings, CRD office files; Howard Glickstein to John Mitchell, 30 November 1970, Box 74, Jerris Leonard to Howard Glickstein, 12 November 1970, Box 74, Howard Glickstein to Jerris Leonard, 12 February 1971, Box 75, Theodore Hesburgh MSS.

43. *Allen v. State Board of Elections*, 393 U.S. 565 (1969). On the evolution of section five enforcement see John J. Roman, "Section 5 of the Voting Rights Act: The Formation of an Extraordinary Federal Remedy," *The American University Law Review* 22 (Fall 1972), 111–33; Armand Derfner, "Racial Discrimination and the Right to Vote," *Vanderbilt Law Review* 26 (April 1973), 523–84; Richard L. Engstrom, "Racial Vote Dilution: Supreme Court Interpretations of Section 5 of the Voting Rights Act," *Southern University Law Review* 4 (Spring 1978), 139–64; Gayle Binion, "The Implementation of Section 5 of the 1965 Voting Rights Act: A Retrospective on the Role of the Courts," *The Western Political Quarterly* 32 (June 1979), 154–73.

321

44. On the influence of the CRD attorneys and the circumstances surrounding their interest in pressing for section five enforcement, see Howard Ball, Dale A. Krane, Thomas P. Lauth, Jr., "Judicial Impact on the Enforcement of Voting Rights Policy By Attorneys in the Department of Justice," paper delivered at the Southern Political Science Association meeting , 1977, and see also their Comprised Compliance: *Implementation of the 1965 Voting Rights Act* (Westport, Conn., 1982), 44–58; Abigail M. Thernstrom, "The Odd Evolution of the Voting Rights Act," *The Public Interest* 55 (Spring 1979), 58.

45. BW [Burt Wides] to PAH (Philip A. Hart), n. d. (1971), Box 185, CR 3f, Philip A. Hart MSS, Michigan Historical Collection, University of Michigan; Burt Wides to Bill Hildebrand, 7 April 1971, S3 54, Hugh Scott MSS, University of Virginia Library. The bipartisan coalition was led by Senators Philip Hart (D. Michigan), Hugh Scott (R. Pennsylvania), the minority leader, and Jacob Javits (R. New York). They were joined by the congressional Black Caucus, the staff director of the United States Commission on Civil Rights, Howard Glickstein, and representatives of civil rights groups, especially Armand Derfner of the Lawyers' Committee for Civil Rights Under Law. The ruling which reversed the Justice Department's position in handling the clearance of the Mississippi Open Primary law was *Evers v. State Board of Election Commissioners*, 327 F. Supp. 640 (S. D. Miss. 1971). Congressman Don Edwards, a California Democrat, did conduct public hearings on the enforcement of the act even after the Justice Department decided to heed the objections of the liberals. U.S. Congress, House of Representatives, Committee on the Judiciary, The Civil Rights Oversight Subcommittee, *Hearings on the Enforcement and Administration of the Voting Rights Act of 1965, As Amended*. Ninety-Second Congress, First Session. Washington Research Project, Shameful Blight, p. 144.

46. William E. Leuchtenburg, "The White House and Black America: From Eisenhower to Carter," in Namorato, ed., *Have We Overcome?*, p. 142. The figures on section five were computed from data in Comptroller General of the United States, *Voting Rights Act— Enforcement Needs Strengthening* (Washington, D.C., 1978), 57, and U.S. Congress, Senate Judiciary Committee, *Hearings* (Extension of the Voting Rights Act of 1965), Ninety-Fourth Congress, First Session, p. 597. The proportion of voting-age blacks registered to vote in the seven covered states held virtually steady at 57 percent when Nixon resigned. This is impressive because the percentage is drawn from the larger pool of eligible but unregistered voters created by the enfranchisement of eighteen- to twenty-year-olds. Before the end of the Johnson years, CRD attorneys considered their task in voter registration "substantially complete both by means of federal registration efforts and by the impetus that federal registration had given to local registrars to go ahead and register people." Ball, et. al., *Compromised Compliance*, p. 58.

47. U.S. Congress, House of Representatives, Committee on the Judiciary, *Hearings* (Extension of the Voting Rights Act), Ninety-Fourth Congress, First Session, p. 338.

48. U.S. Congress, House of Representatives, The Civil Rights Oversight Subcommittee, *Hearings*, pp. 63, 19, 44. From 1965 to 1975 of the five assistant attorneys general in charge of the CRD, three had been recruited from within the division and one, J. Stanley Pottinger, Norman's successor, came directly from HEW where he had been responsible for civil rights enforcement. Only Leonard lacked civil rights credentials and came from outside the Washington bureaucracy. Gerald Jones, the chief of the Voting Rights Section throughout this period, was also a career lawyer with the CRD.

49. Janet Wells, "Voting Rights in 1975," *Civil Rights Digest* 7 (Summer 1975), 19.

50. Ball, et al., "Judicial Impact on the Enforcement of Voting Rights Policy," p. 23. Section five had a deterrent effect warning southern officials against adopting changes that the CRD would most likely reject. U.S. Congress, House of Representatives, Committee on the Judiciary, *Hearings*, Ninety-Fourth Congress, First Session, pp. 280ff; Derfner, "Racial Discrimination and the Right to Vote," 580. For criticism of the Justice Department's ability to monitor section five submissions, see Comptroller General of the United States, *Voting Rights Act*, chapter 3 and the reply from David Hunter, "The Administrators' Dilemmas In The Enforcement of Section 5 of the Voting Rights Act of 1965," paper delivered to the National Conference of the American Society for Public Administration, 1978.

51. A. Stanley Halpin, Jr. and Richard L. Engsgrom, "Racial Gerrymandering and Southern State Legislative Redistricting: Attorney General Determinations Under the Voting Rights Act," *Journal of Public Law* 22 (1973), 65–66.

52. The Democrats actively instituted affirmative action guidelines for selecting delegates to their national conventions. The GOP did not do nearly as much, but they did not completely disregard the issue. William J. Crotty, *Decision for the Democrats: Reforming the Party Structure* (Baltimore, 1979); Jack Bass and Walter DeVries, *The Transformation of Southern Politics: Social Change and Political Consequence Since 1945* (New York, 1976), 214; Mary Costello, "Minority Voting Rights," *Editorial Research Reports* 1 (28 February 1975), 156.

53. Birmingham *News*, 22 February 1973, clipping in Voter Education Project office files, Atlanta, Georgia. Of the combined vote approving the extension in 1975, seventy-three southerners favored and fifty-three opposed it. Bass and DeVries, Ibid., pp. 377–78.

54. Lester M. Salamon, "Leadership and Modernization: The Emerging Black Political Elite in the American South," *Journal of Politics* 35 (August 1973), 615–46; Charles S. Bullock, III, "The Election of Blacks in the South: Reconditions and Consequences," *American Journal of Political Science* 19 (November 1975), 727–39; James David Campbell, "Electoral Participation and the Quest for Equality: Black Politics in Alabama Since the Voting Rights Act of 1965," Ph.D. diss., University of Texas, 1976. David Campbell and Joe R. Feagin, "Black Politics in the South: A Descriptive Analysis," *The Journal of Politics* 37 (February 1975), 129–62.

55. Phil A. Garland, "A Taste of Triumph for Black Mississippi," *Ebony* 23 (February 1968), 27; James David Campbell, "Electoral Participation," p. 244ff. James Button and Richard Scher, "Impact of the Civil Rights Movement: Elite Perceptions of Black Municipal Service Charges," paper, University of Florida, 1978; Earl Black, *Southern Governors and Civil Rights, passim.*

56. United States Commission on Civil Rights, *The Voting Rights Act: Unfulfilled Goals* (Washington, D.C. (1981)) 251. See also United States Commission on Civil Rights, *The Voting Rights Act: Ten Years After* (Washington, D.C. 1975).

57. Edgar Taplin, Intern Report, 1969, Voter Education Project, Office Files, Atlanta, Georgia.   **323**

58. Charles Evers, *Evers* (New York, 1971), 189.

59. Thernstrom, "The Odd Evolution of the Voting Rights Act;" Gerald P. Goulder, "The Reconstructed Right to Vote: Neutral Principles and Minority Representation,:" *Capital University Law Review* 9 (1979), 31–96; R. Perry Sentell, Jr., "Federalizing Through the Franchise: The Supreme Court and Local Government," *Georgia Law Review* 6 (Fall 1971), 34–73; Davis D. Carr, "Vote Dilution Challenges After *Washington v. Davis,*" *Alabama Law Review* 30 (Winter 1979), 396–418; Christopher Peters, "At-Large Elections of Parish Officials," *Alabama Law Review* 26 (Fall 1973), 163–76; Morton J. Horwitz, "The Jurisprudence of *Brown* and the Dilemmas of Liberalism," in Namorato, ed., *Have We Overcome?*, pp. 173–87; James E. Conyers and Walter L. Wallace, *Black Elected Officials* (New York, 1976); *City of Mobile v. Bolden,* 44 U.S. 55 (1980).

THE UNMAKING OF THE SECOND RECONSTRUCTION

1. Harvard Sitkoff, *The Struggle for Black Equality* 1954–1980 (New York, 1981), 94.

2. Southern Christian Leadership Conference, "The Ultimate Aim Is The Beloved Community," in August Meier, Elliot Rudwick, and Francis L. Broderick, eds., *Black Protest Thought in the Twentieth Century* (Indianapolis, 1971), 302–6; John J. Ansbro, *Martin Luther King, Jr.: The Making of a Mind* (Maryknoll, New York, 1982).

3. Haig Bosmajian, "The Letter from Birmingham Jail," in C. Eric Lincoln, ed., *Martin Luther King, Jr.: A Profile* (New York, 1970), 136.

4. August Meier, "On the Role of Martin Luther King, Jr.," *New Politics* 4 (Winter 1965):52–59.

5. W.E.B. DuBois, *The Souls of Black Folk* (New York, 1969), 45–46.

6. William H. Chafe, *Civilities and Civil Rights: Greensboro, North Carolina and the Black Struggle for Freedom* (Oxford, 1981), 83.

7. See Elizabeth Jacoway and David R. Colburn, eds., *Southern Businessmen and Desegregation* (Baton Route, 1982) for a variety of responses by southern communities to racial protest during the 1960s.

8. Anne Moody, *Coming of Age in Mississippi* (New York, 1968), 265–67.

9. Chafe, *Civilities,* 100; Steven F. Lawson, "From Sit-in to Race Riot: Businessmen, Blacks, and the Pursuit of Moderation in Tampa, 1960–1967," in Jacoway and Colburn, eds., *Southern Businessmen,* 264, 280.

10. Carl M. Brauer, *John F. Kennedy and the Second Reconstruction* (New York, 1977), 33.

11. Ibid, 47–50; Harris Wofford, *Of Kennedys and Kings: Making Sense of the Sixties* (New York, 1980), chapter one.

12. Steven F. Lawson, *Black Ballots: Voting Rights in the South, 1944–1969* (New York, 1976), 289.

13. Sitkoff, *Struggle for Black Equality,* 106.

14. Lawson, *Black Ballots,* 175.

15. Catherine A. Barnes, *Journey From Jim Crow: The Desegregation of Southern Transit* (New York, 1983), 188.

16. Brauer, *John F. Kennedy*, 260.

17. Ibid, 267.

18. Sitkoff, *Struggle for Black Equality*, 164.

19. For critical accounts of Kennedy's civil rights program that share this judgment, see Bruce Miroff, *Pragmatic Illusions: The Presidential Politics of John F. Kennedy* (New York, 1976), 269–70; David Burner, "Kennedy: A Cold Warrior," in Robert D. Marcus and David Burner, eds., *America Since 1945*, 2ded. (New York, 1977), 190–93, 195–96; Roy Wilkins with Tom Mathews, *Standing Fast: The Autobiography of Roy Wilkins*, (New York, 1982), 277, 294. It should be noted that when Richard Nixon ran for the presidency in 1960 he had compiled a strong civil rights record as vice-president. Yet his campaign exhibited the features of his "southern strategy" that would achieve success in 1968.

20. Nathan Glazer, *Affirmative Discrimination: Ethnic Inequality and Public Policy* (New York, 1975), 45. According to Title VII of the law, employers were not required to grant preferential treatment to any individual or group on the basis of race, color, religion, sex, or national origin "on account of an imbalance which may exist with respect to the total or percentage of persons of any race, color, religion, sex or national origin employed by an employer."

21. Allen J. Matusow, "From Civil Rights to Black Power: The Case of SNCC, 1960–1966," in Barton J. Bernstein and Allen J. Matusow, eds., *Twentieth Century America: Recent Interpretations* (New York), 1972), 507, 509; Cleveland Sellers with Robert Terrell, *The River of No Return: The Autobiography of a Black Militant and the Life and Death of SNCC* (New York, 1973). On the issue of women in the civil rights movement, see Sara Evans, *Personal Politics: The Roots of Women's Liberation in the Civil Rights Movement and the New Left* (New York, 1980), chapter four. Black activists may have become cynical about whites, but they had invited their participation for tactical reasons in the first place. The organizers of the summer project expected casualties and believed that violence against northern white volunteers would push the federal government to take stronger action against racism in Mississippi. Neil R. McMillen, "Black Enfranchisement in Mississippi: Federal Enforcement and Black Protest in the 1960s," *Journal of Southern History* 43 (August 1977): 367.

22. James Forman, The Making of Black Revolutionaries (New York, 1972), 265.

23. On this point see Joseph Rauh Oral History, Lyndon B. Johnson, Presidential Library.

24. Lawson, *Black Ballots*, 300; David J. Garrow, *Protest At Selma: Martin Luther King, Jr., and the Voting Rights Act of 1965* (New Haven, 1978), chapters two and three.

25. *Public Papers of the Presidents, Lyndon B. Johnson, 1965* (Washington, D.C., 1966), 1: 284.

26. Initially, the state of Alaska, three counties in Arizona, one county in Hawaii, and one county in Idaho were covered under the formula of the act because of the presence, not of blacks, but of Indian, Eskimo, or Asian minorities. By 1968 these jurisdictions had removed themselves through litigation. United States Commission on Civil Rights, *Political Participation* (Washington, D.C., 1968), 11.

27. Frank T. Read and Lucy S. McGough, *Let Them Be Judged: The Judicial Integration of the Deep South* (Metuchen, New Jersey, 1978), 300ff.

28. Increased black political participation produced a white counterreaction. While the number of black registrants was growing by 1.5 million during the late 1960s, the number of white registrants rose by 4.4 million. Garrow, *Protest At Selma*, 302, n. 33. Also on this point, see Numan V. Bartley and Hugh Davis Graham, *Southern Politics and the Second Reconstruction* (Baltimore, 1975), 109.

29. *Public Papers of the President, Lyndon B. Johnson, 1965*, 1: 636; Harry McPherson Oral History, Lyndon B. Johnson Presidential Library.

30. Lee Rainwater and William L. Yancey, *The Moynihan Report and the Politics of Controversy* (Cambridge, Mass., 1967) for a highly critical account of the conference.

31. *New York Times*, 7 January 1966, 2. For the transformation of SNCC and CORE into black power groups, see Clayborne Carson. *In Struggle: SNCC and The Black Awakening of The 1960s* (Cambridge, Mass., 1981) and August Meier and Elliott Rudwick, *CORE: A Study in the Civil Rights Movement, 1942–1968* (New York, 1973).

32. Sellers with Terrell, *The River of No Return*, 162, 166–67.

33. Matusow, "From Civil Rights to Black Power," 514–17. Stokely Carmichael and Charles V. Hamilton, *Black Power: The Politics of Liberation In America* (New York, 1967), 30–31.

34. Martin Luther King, Jr., *Where Do We Go From Here: Chaos or Community?* (New York, 1967), 30–31.

35. Carson, *In Struggle*, 221.

36. In 1963, 64 percent of the nation's whites thought blacks were pushing too quickly for equality. Robert H. Wiebe, "White Attitudes and Black Rights from *Brown* to *Bakke*," in Michael V. Namorato, Ed., *Have We Overcome? Race Relations Since Brown* (Jackson, Mississippi, 1979), 156.

37. William L. O'Neill, *Coming Apart: An Informal History of America in the 1960s* (New York, 1975), 389.

38. Harry McPherson to Nicholas Katzenbach, 20 September 1966, Box 21 (2), Harry McPherson Files, Lyndon B. Johnson Presidential Library. On the complexities of the riots and their varying effects on governmental policy, see James Button, *Black Violence* (Princeton, 1978).

39. McCulloch is quoted in the *Congressional Record*, 89th Cong. 2nd Sess., 17112. Horace Kornegay to James W. Morrison, 21 July 1966, Box 39, Horace Kornegay Papers, Southern Historical Collection, University of North Carolina Library.

40. For an extended treatment of the passage of the 1968 law, see Steven F. Lawson, *In Pursuit of Power: Southern Blacks and Electoral Politics, 1965–1982* (New York, 1985), chapter 3. For less favorable assessments of Johnson's role after 1965, see James C. Harvey, *Black Civil Rights During the Johnson Administration* (Jackson, Mississippi, 1973), and Allen J. Matusow, *The Unraveling of America: A History of Liberalism in the 1960s* (New York, 1984), 206–8. Matusow has emphasized the weaknesses in the enforcement provisions concerning equal housing. The act failed to give the Department of Housing and Urban Development power to issue cease and desist orders. Undoubtedly, this omission limited the effect of the law, and housing segregation remains a substantial problem today. Nevertheless, it is difficult to see how the Johnson administration could have obtained passage of a stronger housing section, given the legislative climate of opinion. The results of the law notwithstanding, Johnson's legislative achievement, in the face of serious obstacles, was extraordinary.

41. Glazer, *Affirmative Discrimination*, 46–47; Harvey, *Black Civil Rights*, 117–18. Despite these guidelines the federal government failed to live up to its promises.

Allen Matusow has concluded that in the late 1960s and 1970s "the direct effects of federal enforcement on the vast and complex American job market were small." Matusow, *Unraveling of America*, 211. Also see Harvey, *Black Civil Rights*, 123–48. Besides the Department of Labor, the Equal Employment Opportunity Commission, created by the 1964 Civil Rights Act, played a major role in challenging job bias. Since 1972, when Congress expanded the EEOC's enforcement powers, it has become more effective in implementing affirmative action programs. For a history of affirmative action, see Citizens' Commission on Civil Rights, *Affirmative Action to Open the Doors of Job Opportunity* (Washington, D.C., 1984), chap. 1.

326

42. Glazer, *Affirmative Discrimination*, 220.

43. Richard Polenberg, *One Nation Divisible: Class, Race, and Ethnicity in the United States Since 1938* (New York, 1980), 246.

44. *Green v. County School Board of New Kent County*, 391 U.S. 430, 437–38 (1968).

45. J. Harvie Wilkinson, III, *From* Brown *to* Bakke: *The Supreme Court and School Integration 1954–1978* (Oxford, 1981), 117.

46. *Alexander v. Holmes County Board of Education*, 396 U.S. 19, 20 (1969). For an insider's account of the bureaucratic struggle, see Leon E. Panetta and Peter Gall, *Bring Us Together: The Nixon Team and the Civil Rights Retreat* (Philadelphia, 1971).

47. *Swann v. Charlotte-Mecklenburg Board of Education*, 402 U.S. 1, 25 (1971).

48. Gary Orfield, *Must We Bus? Segregated Schools and National Policy* (Washington, D.C., 1978), 115–16; Polenberg, *One Nation Divisible*, 239.

49. On the complexities of white flight, see Orfield, *Must We Bus?* 100, 413, and Diane Ravitch, "The 'White Flight' Controversy," in Nicolaus Mills, ed., *Busing U.S.A.* (New York, 1979), 238–55.

50. *Public Papers of the Presidents, Richard M. Nixon, 1971* (Washington, D.C., 1972), 597.

51. Orfield, *Must We Bus?*, chapters eight to ten, 267. In the final days of the Nixon administration, Congress passed legislation restraining the courts from ordering the busing of students beyond the closest or next closest schools. After Nixon resigned, President Gerald Ford signed the bill into law. The practical effect of the measure was minimal, however, because Congress could not restrict courts from enforcing the constitutional rights of minority students through busing. The law did limit federal agencies from implementing busing by simple legislation.

52. *Congressional Quarterly Almanac*, 28 (1972), 680.

53. *Milliken v. Bradley*, 418 U.S. 717 (1974).

54. Charles S. Bullock, III, "Equal Education Opportunity," in Charles S. Bullock, III and Charles M. Lamb, eds., *Implementation of Civil Rights Policy* (Monterey, California, 1984), 72.

55. Orfield, *Must We Bus?*, 417. Two recent histories of educational desegregation disagree over the value of busing. George R. Metcalf, *From Little Rock to Boston: The History of School Desegregation* (Westport, Connecticut, 1983), finds busing an effective remedy and criticizes the federal government for not implementing it more fully. In contrast Raymond Wolters, *The Burden of* Brown: *Thirty Years of School Desegregation* (Knoxville, 1984), considers busing a misguided solution and condemns the judiciary for promoting its use. For the case of Atlanta, where blacks preferred increasing their control over the school district rather than supporting massive busing, see Orfield, 369–70.

56. *Allen v. State Board of Elections*, 393 U.S. 544, 565 (1969).

57. U.S. House of Representatives, Committee on the Judiciary, Civil Rights Oversight Subcommittee, *Hearings on the Enforcement and Administration of the Voting Rights Act of 1965, As Amended*, 92nd Cong., 1st Sess., 1971, 91.

58. *Allen v. State Board of Elections*, 393 U.S. 585 (1969).

59. Abigail M. Thernstrom, "The Odd Evolution of the Voting Rights Act," *Public Interest* 55 (Spring 1979): 59–60. For two divergent views of the issue, see Abigail M. Thernstrom, *Whose Ballots Count? Affirmative Action and Minority Voting Rights* (Cambridge, Ma.: Harvard University Press, 1987) and J. Morgan Kousser, *Colorblind Injustice: Minority Voting Rights and the Undoing of the Second Reconstruction* (Chapel Hill: University of North Carolina Press, 1999).

60. *City of Mobile v. Bolden*, 446 U.S. 55 (1980), for the court opinion that made it difficult for civil rights plaintiffs to prove suffrage discrimination in at-large elections.

61. Burt Wides to Philip A. Hart, n. d. (1971), Box 185, CR 3f, Philip A. Hart MSS., Michigan Historical Collection, University of Michigan. In the area of political party organization, however, the Democrats compiled a much better record than did the Republicans. Following the MFDP challenge, the Democratic Party adopted affirmative action guidelines to ensure blacks and other minority groups fair representation in the selection of delegates to the national convention. Although Democratic chieftains did not make quotas mandatory, they wrote guidelines that suggested proportional representation as a goal for achieving equality in selection procedures. This reform reached its peak in 1972 with the nomination of George S. McGovern. Since the disastrous defeat in the general election of that year, the Democrats have retreated somewhat from applying their earlier standards, but black participation within party affairs is at a much higher level than in the GOP. See William J. Crotty, *Decision for the Democrats: Reforming the Party Structure* (Baltimore: 1979).

62. *Lau v. Nichols*, 414 U.S. 563 (1974), involved Chinese-speaking children in San Francisco. For purposes of busing to achieve school desegregation, the Supreme Court equated Mexican-American children with black students and ordered them integrated with Anglos. *Keyes v. School District No. 1., Denver, Colorado*, 413 U.S. 189 (1973). For a discussion of bilingualism and biculturalism in the education of Hispanic-Americans, see Orfield, *Must We Bus?*, chapter 7. According to the 1975 extension of the Voting Rights Act, a jurisdiction was eligible for federal examiners and observers and subject to preclearance review if it used English-only registration and election materials on 1 November 1972 and less than 50 percent of the voting-age citizens were registered on 1 November 1972 or voted in the presidential election of 1972, and more than 5 percent of the citizens of voting age belonged to a sizable language minority group. In addition, if more than 5 percent of citizens were part of a sizable language minority and the illiteracy rate of such group was higher than the national average, then registration and election materials had to be furnished in the language of the applicable minority group as well as in the English language. To those areas already covered, the act added Texas and parts of California, Colorado, Connecticut, Florida, Hawaii, Idaho, Kansas, Maine, Michigan, Minnesota, Montana, Nebraska, Nevada, New Mexico, North Dakota, Oklahoma, South Dakota, Utah, Washington, Wisconsin, and Wyoming. The protected groups included, Spanish, American Indian, Chinese, and Filipino.

63. Joel Dreyfuss and Charles Lawrence, III, *The Bakke Case: The Politics of Inequality* (New York, 1979). For a different view, see Norman Podhoretz, *Breaking Ranks: A Political Memoir* (New York, 1980), 293–94.

64. Seymour Martin Lipset and William Schneider, "An Emerging National Consensus," *New Republic*, 15 October 1977, 8: "Disadvantaged Groups, Individual Rights," *New Republic*, 15 October 1977, 8.

65. *Griggs v. Duke Power Co.*, 401 U.S. 424 (1971); Alan P. Sindler, *Bakke, DeFunis, and Minority Admissions: The Quest for Equal Opportunity* (New York, 1978), 239; Polenberg, One Nation Divisible, 241.

66. *Washington v. Davis*, 426 U.S. 229 (1976); Sindler, *Bakke*, 184–86.

67. Although Bakke scored higher on the entrance qualifications than did most of the minority students admitted through the special program, he still might not have been accepted because other whites had been rejected with even higher ratings than he had.

68. *Regents of the University of California v. Bakke*, 438 U.S. 265, 298 (1978).

69. Ibid., 400–401, 407.

70. *United Steelworkers of America v. Weber*, 443 U.S. 193 (1979); *New York Times*, 13 June 1984, B12 for Hooks's statement and the opinion of the Court in *Firefighters v. Stotts*. The Court has approved congressional legislation establishing a quota for granting contracts in public works projects to minority-owned firms in order to rectify past discrimination. *Fullilove v Klutznick*, 448 U.S. 448 (1980).

71. For the Carter administration's uneven performance in civil rights and the Bakke case, see Joseph A. Califano, Jr., *Governing America: An Insider's Report from the White House and Cabinet* (New York, 1981), 243; Dreyfuss and Lawrence, *Bakke*, 166ff. ; and Sindler, *Bakke*, 246–51. In 1980 Carter did act forcefully in threatening to veto a bill passed by both houses of Congress that prohibited the Justice Department from seeking busing remedies in the courts. Congress backed down and the measure was withdrawn. Under the Reagan administration it was revived and passed by the Republican-controlled Senate but was defeated in the House.

72. "Quotas Under Attack," *Newsweek*, 25 April 1983, 95–96; Tampa *Tribune*, 30 April 1983, 9A.

73. Dreyfuss and Lawrence, *Bakke*, 144; Lipset and Schneider, "An Emerging National Consensus," 8–9.

74. Dreyfuss and Lawrence, *Bakke*, 198. For a prominent exception of a black who opposed most affirmative action programs, see Thomas Sowell, "A Black Conservative Dissents," *New York Times Magazine*, 8 August 1976, 15, 43.

75. Sitkoff, *Struggle for Black Equality*, 232–33. Of all the areas of civil rights, the situation had perhaps improved the least in housing. For a balanced assessment, see Charles M. Lamb, "Equal Housing Opportunity," in Bullock and Lamb, eds., *Implementation of Civil Rights Policy*, 148–83.

76. Sitkoff, *Struggle for Black Equality*, 234–36; Polenberg, One Nation Divisible, 275; Harrell R. Rodgers, Jr., "Fair Employment Laws for Minorities: An Evaluation of Federal Implementation," in Bullock and Lamb, eds., *Implementation*, 93–117; Dorothy K. Newman, et al, *Protest, Politics, and Prosperity: Black Americans and White Institutions, 1940–1975* (New York, 1978), passim.

77. William J. Wilson, *The Declining Significance of Race: Blacks and Changing American Institutions* (Chicago, 1978), 154–64; Thomas Sowell, *Race and Economics* (New York, 1975), 156. Sowell blames affirmative action for contributing to the economic decline of disadvantaged blacks, but Wilson discounts this as a causal factor and stresses the changing structure of the economy. See Wilson's review of Sowell's *Civil Rights: Rhetoric or Reality?* (New York, 1984), in "Hurting the Disadvantaged," *New York Times Book Review* 89 (24 June 1984): 28.

78. Raymond Wolters, *Right Turn: William Bradford Reynolds, the Reagan Administration, and Black Civil Rights* (New Brunswick, N.J.: Transaction, 1996); Hugh Davis Graham, *The Civil Rights Era: Origins and Development of National Policy* (New York: Oxford University Press, 1990).

79. *Wards Cove Packing Company v. Atonio* 490 U.S. 642 (1989). For a different view, see Wolters, *Right Turn*, pp. 280-85.

80. *City of Richmond v. J. A. Croson* 488 U.S. 469 (1989).

81. *Adarand Constructors v. Pena* 515 U.S. 200 (1995); *Adarand Cosntructors v. Mineta* 534 U.S. 103 (2001).

82. *Hopwood v. State of Texas* 236 F. 3d 256 (2000). William G. Bowen and Derek Bok, *The Shape of the River: Long-term Consequences of Considering Race in College and University Admissions* (Princeton: Princeton University Press, 1998), p. 14.

83. *Katuria Smith v. University of Washington Law School* 233 F. 3d 1188 (2000); *Grutter v. Bollinger* 288 F. 3d 732 (2002).

84. *Johnson v. Regents of the University of Georgia* 263 F. 3d 1234 (2001).

85. Noah Grand and Timothy Kudy, "Action Reaction: Affirmative Action has Controversial History," *The Daily Bruin*, 12 March 2001; Bob Laird, "Bending Admissions to Political Ends," *The Chronicle of Higher Education*, 17 May 2002, p. 11; Pamela Burdman, "Diversity Drama at the University of California," *Salon. com*, 24 June 2002.

86. Bob Edwards, National Public Radio transcript, 23 July 2002. Found in http://web. lexis-nexis. com. See also, Rick Bragg, "Florida Governor Offers Plan for Diversity," *New York Times* 10 November 1999, p. A18; Rick Bragg, "Florida Plan Would End Race Based Admissions," *New York Times* 11 November 1999, p. A2; Rick Bragg, "Affirmative Action Ban Meets a Wall in Florida," 7 June 1999, p. A16

87. Greg Winter, "Schools Resegregate, Study Finds," *The New York* Times, January 21, 2003, p. A14; Carey Goldberg, "Busing's Day Ends: Boston Drops Race in Pupil Placement," *New York Times* 14 July 1999, p. A1. John Newsom, "Dismantling Desegregation," *News and Record* (Greensboro, NC) 19 August 2001, p. A1.

88. The North Carolina cases are *Shaw v. Reno* 509 U.S. 630 (1993) and *Easley v. Cromartie* 532 U.S. 1076 (2001). The Georgia case was *Miller v. Johnson* 515 U.S. 952 (1995); the Texas case was *Bush v. Vera* 517 U.S. 952 (1996).

89. Kousser, *Colorblind Injustice*, passim.

90. David A. Bositis, "Black Elected Officials: A Statistical Summary 2000," (Washington, D.C.: Joint Center for Political and Economic Studies, 2002), pp. 12, 20.

91. Robert Pear, "Number of People Living in Poverty Increases in U.S.," *New York Times* 25 September 2002, p. A1, A19; U.S. Census Bureau report "The Black Population in the United States," March 1999, p. 1.

92. U.S. Census Bureau report "The Black Population in the United States," March 1999, p. 3.

93. Incarceration statistics taken from the Joint Center for Economic and Political Studies web site http://www.jointcenter.org. The report is titled, "African Americans and the Correctional System."

FLORIDA'S LITTLE SCOTTSBORO

I would like to acknowledge David R. Colburn and Darryl Paulson as coauthors of this chapter.

329

1. The white primary case was *Smith v. Allwright*, 321 U.S. 649 (1944); Steven F. Lawson, *Black Ballots: Voting Rights in the South, 1944–1969* (New York, 1976), 100.

2. Reported in "Major Racial Issues at Stake in Trial of three Florida Negroes," *Christian Science Monitor*, clipping, n.d., Franklin H. Williams scrapbooks, in possession of Franklin Williams, hereinafter cited as FHW scrapbooks. See Also Edward L. Ayers, *Vengeance and Justice; Crime and Punishment in the Nineteen Century American South* (New York, 1984).

3. Gloster Current, "Martyr for a Cause," *Crisis* 59 (February 1952), 72–81; Lawson, *Black Ballots*, 134.

4. L. Allen, "Lake County, Florida," Federal Writer's Project, *American Guide*, Orlando, December 12, 1939, 12.

5. Interview with Franklin Williams by David Colburn and Steven Lawson, February 11, 1985, CRG 2 AB, University of Florida Oral History Archives, Florida State Museum, Gainesville. Colburn-Lawson interview with Williams hereinafter cited as Franklin Williams interview. "Report on Groveland," 1, Box 192, Workers Defense League Files, Archives of Labor, History, and Urban Affairs, Wayne State University, hereinafter cited as WDL files; James W. Ivy, "Florida's Little Scottsboro: Groveland," *Crisis* 56 (October 1949), 266; Interview with Mabel Norris Reese [Chesley] by Franklin Williams, n.d., copy in possession of authors.

6. Mabel Norris Reese [Chesley], "Lake County Personalities," *Mount Dora Topic*, July 28, 1949, I; Dudley Clendenin, "The Legend of Iceman McCall Chills the Air in Lake County," *Floridian, St. Petersburg Times*, November 5, 1972, 22; Rowland Watts to Mr. Baskin, "September 15, 1949, Box 192 1, WDL Files.

7. Ivy, "Florida's Little Scottsboro," 266; "Mobile Violence: Motorized Mobs in a Florida County," *New South* 4 (August 1949), 1–2.

8. *Orlando Sentinel-Star*, September 4, 1949, 2.

9. *Orlando Sentinel*, July 17, 1949, 1 and July 27, 1949, 1; *Mount Dora Topic*, July 17, 1949, 1; *New York Times*, July 27, 1949, 48; "Mobile Violence," 5.

10. *Miami Herald*, July 18, 1949, 1, July 19, 1949, 1, July 20, 1949, 1; "Mobile Violence," 2–3; *Pittsburgh Courier*, August 23, 1949, 1.

11. *Orlando Sentinel*, July 18, 1949, 1, July 19, 1949, 1; "Mobile Violence," 3–5; *New York Times*, July 19, 1949, 1, July 20, 1949, 14, July 25, 1949, 30; *Lakeland Ledger*, July 20, 1949, 1; Franklin Williams interview.

12. "Mobile Violence," 6.

13. Edna B. Kerin, "Another Chance for the Groveland Victims," *Crisis* 58 (May 1951), 319; *New York Times*, July 20, 1949, clipping, FHW scrapbooks; Ted Poston, "'A Good Nigger'—But They Ruined Him Too," *New York Post*, September 3, 1949, clipping, FHW scrapbooks.

14. Jacqueline Dowd Hall, "'The Mind That Burns In Each Body': Women, Rape, and Racial Violence," in Ann Snitow, Christine Stansell, and Sharon Thompson, eds., *Powers of Desire: The Politics of Sexuality* (New York, 1983), 334. The myth of the black rapist was at least as significant as the actual incidence of interracial rape in justifying lynching. The figures show that from 1882–1968, twenty-five per cent of lynchings involved rape or attempted rape. The largest percentage of lynchings, nearly forty-one per cent, stemmed from homicides. Jacqueline Dowd Hall, *Revolt Against Chivalry: Jesse Daniel Ames and the Women's Campaign Against Lynching* (New York, 1979), 149; Robert L. Zangrando, *The NAACP Crusade Against Lynching, 1909–1950* (Philadelphia, 1980), 8. See Ayers, *Vengeance and Justice*.

15. "Report of Investigation Made in Florida on the Groveland Case by Pro-

fessor Hornell Hart, Duke University, School of Religion, and Reverend Paul Moore, Jr., Grace Episcopal Church, Jersey City, New Jersey," n.d., Box 192–1, WDL Files.

16. Hall, *Revolt Against Chivalry*, 235–36; Zangrando, *The NAACP Crusade Against Lynching*, 213–215; James R. McGovern, *Anatomy of a Lynching: The Killing of Claude Neal* (Baton Rouge, 1982), 138–39. Between 1920 and 1939, there were 1,067 reported lynchings in contrast to forty-six between 1940 and 1968. Calculated from figures in Zangrando, 6–7.

17. *Orlando Sentinel*, July 17, 1949, 1.

18. Dan T. Carter, *Scottsboro: A Tragedy of the American South* (New York, 1971).

19. Franklin Williams interview; *Chicago Defender*, September 17, 1949, clipping, FHW scrapbooks; Ivy, "Florida's Little Scottsboro," 267, 285: M. C. Thomas to Watts, May 11, 1951, Box 192–6, WDL Files; article by Stetson Kennedy for *Droit et Liberte*, n.d., typewritten copy, Stetson Kennedy files, Southern Labor Archives, Georgia State University.

20. M. C. Thomas to Watts, May 11, 1951, Box 192–6, WDL Files; Interview with Mabel Norris Reese [Chesley], by Franklin Williams. There was additional speculation that Singleton paid protection money to McCall, that the sheriff wanted to punish Ernest Thomas for pocketing money, and that he led the posse out of his jurisdiction to silence Thomas. No evidence of these charges has surfaced.

21. Franklin Williams interview; *Orlando Sentinel*, July 17, 1949, 1; Ivy, "Florida's Little Scottsboro," 267–68.

22. "Mobile Violence," 3; *St. Petersburg Times*, April 8, 1950, 17; Franklin Williams interview.

23. *St. Petersburg Times*, April 8, 1950, 17.

24. *Orlando Sentinel*, July 19, 1949, 1, July 21, 1949, 1, 3; *Mount Dora Topic*, July 21, 1949, 1. Thomas had brought Greenlee to Lake County from Alachua and left him at the gasoline station. When local police arrested Greenlee several hours later at the station they found the gun on him.

25. Franklin Williams interview; transcript of testimony, *State of Florida v. Charles Greenlee, Walter Irvin, and Samuel Shepherd*, Florida Supreme Court, Tallahassee, Florida, 2.

26. Franklin Williams interview; interview with Alex Akerman, by David Colburn, May 31, 1984, CRG 1 A, University of Florida Oral History Archives, Florida State Museum, Gainesville.

27. Franklin Williams interview; Ivy, "Florida's Little Scottsboro," 268.

28. *Orlando Sentinel*, September 1, 1949, 1; *Mount Dora Topic*, July 29, 1949, 1.

29. *Orlando Sentinel*, September 3, 1949, 1, 2, September 4, 1949, 1, 2; *St. Petersburg Times*, April 7, 1950, 13, April 8, 1950, 17.

30. Transcript of testimony, Florida Supreme Court, 467–76; *Orlando Sentinel*, September 3, 1949, 1, 2, September 4, 1949, 1.

31. Transcript of testimony, Florida Supreme Court, 538–41; Bill Harris to LeRoy Collins, n.d., 7–9, 13–14, LeRoy Collins Papers, University of South Florida, *Orlando Sentinel*, September 3, 1949, 2; *Mount Dora Topic*, September 8, 1949, 5.

32. Harris to Collins, 9, Collins Papers.

33. Interview with Alex Akerman by Franklin Williams, 17, FHW scrapbooks. A Lake County grand jury reviewing the case in 1955 concluded that it would have been impossible for a doctor to furnish clinical proof of rape because Norma Padgett had gone home and "cleaned herself up before the doctor ever saw her." "Present-

ment of the Grand Jury to Honorable T. G. Futch," 11, Governor T. LeRoy Collins Administrative Correspondence, Box 25, Laf-Leg. 1955–56, Rg 102, Series 7776a, State Archives, Tallahassee.

34. *Mount Dora Topic*, September 8, 1949, 1–2; *Orlando Sentinel*, September 3, 1949, 2, September 4, 1949, 2.

35. *Mount Dora Topic*, September 8, 1949, 1–2, 8; *Orlando Sentinel*, September 4, 1949, 2; Franklin Williams interview.

36. Ivy, "Florida's Little Scottsboro," 268; *Mount Dora Topic*, n.d., clipping, FHW scrapbooks; *Orlando Sentinel*, September 4, 1949, 1.

37. *New York Post*, September 19, 1950, April 6, 1950, April 7, 1950, clippings. FHW scrapbooks; Ivy, "Florida's Little Scottsboro," 267; *Orlando Sentinel*, April 19, 1950, 1–2. Poston described a high-speed chase from Tavares to Orlando in which a car he was riding in with another black reporter and the two black attorneys was pursued by a carload of whites.

38. "Florida Shooting," *Crisis* 58 (December 1951), 638.

39. "Resolutions Adopted by Forty-Third Annual Convention of the NAACP at Oklahoma City, Oklahoma, June 28, 1952," *Crisis* 59 (August-September 1952), 448. The criticism of the FBI leveled by the NAACP resulted from numerous instances of postwar violence against blacks.

40. *St. Petersburg Times*, April 7, 1950, 13, April 8, 1950, 17.

41. *Shepherd v. State*, 46 So. 2d. 1950, 880, 883, 884; *Orlando Sentinel*, April 17, 1950, 1.

42. *Shepherd v. Florida*, 341 U.S. 50 (1950), 55. The jury included farmers and businessmen from the county. No women were included in the jury.

43. *Orlando Sentinel*, April 10, 1951, 1, 7: *Tampa Tribune*, April 10, 1951; *New York Times*, April 10, 1951, 1, 25; Mabel Norris Reese, "Lake County Personalities," *Mount Dora Topic*, September 8, 1949, 1.

44. Sworn statements of Willis McCall and James L. Yates, 59–68, 51–58, Box 53, Lab-Lar, Rg 102, S 235, Governor Fuller Warren Administrative File, Governor Fuller Warren Papers, Florida State Archives, Tallahassee: *Orlando Sentinel*, November 7, 1951, 1, November 8, 1951, 1, 9; *Mount Dora Topic*, November 8, 1951, 1.

45. Affidavit of Walter Lee Irvin, 1–5, Box 53, Governor Fuller Warren Administrative Correspondence; *Orlando Sentinel*, November 9, 1951, 1, 11; *Mount Dora Topic*, November 15, 1951, 1.

46. Interview with Mabel Norris Reese [Chesley], by Franklin H. Williams, 14, FHW scrapbooks.

47. J. J. Elliott to Fuller Warren, November 21, 1951, Box 53, Lab-Lar, Rg 102, S 235, Governor Warren Administrative File, Warren Papers. Stetson Kennedy, a journalist, charged that Elliott had been a member of the Ku Klux Klan in Georgia. Stetson Kennedy, *I Rode With the Klan*, (London, 1954), 245–247.

48. *Mount Dora Topic*, November 29, 1951, clipping, FHW scrapbooks; interview with Mabel Norris Reese [Chesley], by Franklin Williams, 13–15, FHW scrapbooks.

49. Interview with Alex Akerman, by David Colburn.

50. Both statements are quoted in "Answer to Vishinsky," *Crisis* 58 (December 1951), 666–67.

51. *Mount Dora Topic*, December 6, 1951, 1, 4; *New York Times*, December 7, 1951, 30.

52. Harry T. Moore to Warren, November 15, 1951, Box 53, Rg 102, 1949–51, Governor Warren Administrative Correspondence, Warren Papers.

53. "Terror in Florida," *Crisis* 59 (January 1952), 35.

54. The FBI initially conjectured that Moore may have been killed by either the NAACP or the Communist party "for propaganda purposes." However, its investigation led the Bureau in a more sensible direction to five members of the Ku Klux Klan; but in 1953, when a federal judge threw out indictments against them on related charges of perjury, the Justice Department decided not to pursue the case. On September 16, 1955, the case was officially closed. This account was reconstructed from files obtained under the Freedom of Information Act by WTSP Channel 10, St. Petersburg-Tampa. The material was inspected at the office of the station. For an update, see Ben Green, *Before His Time: The Untold Story of Harry T. Moore, America's First Civil Rights Martyr* (New York: Free Press, 1999).

333

55. *Mount Dora Topic*, February 14, 1952, 1, 8; *Orlando Sentinel*, February 12, 1952, 1, 11, February 13, 1951, 1, 13, February 14, 1952, 1, 7, February 15, 1952, 1, 3; *New York Times*, February 17, 1952, 22.

56. *Orlando Sentinel*, February 13, 1952, 1, 13, February 14, 1952, 1, 7; *New York Times*, February 14, 1952, 28.

57. *Leesburg Commercial*, December 10, 1962, 1, December 21, 1962, 1.

58. *Orlando Sentinel*, February 15, 1952, 1, 2; *New York Times*, February 15, 1952, 42; *Irvin v. State*, 66, So 2d 288 (1953); *Irvin v. Florida*, 346 U.S. 927 (1954).

59. *St. Petersburg Times*, February 21, 1954, 4.

60. Interview with Reverend Ben F. Wyland, by Darryl Paulson, December 8, 1981, St. Petersburg. Interview in possession of authors.

61. *Crisis* 61 (December 1954), 18: Harris to LeRoy Collins, 7–10, Collins Papers; Lula L. Mullikan to L. F. Chapman, File—Irvin, Walter, Death Warrant, Governor LeRoy Collins Papers, Florida State Archives.

62. Thomas Wagy, *Governor LeRoy Collins of Florida: Spokesman of the New South* (University, AL, 1985), 66–68; *Orlando Sentinel*, March 15, 1956, 1; *Tampa Tribune*, May 5, 1956, 1; "Presentment of the Grand Jury to Honorable T. G. Futch," 15, Box 29, Laf-Leg, 1955–56, Rg 102, Series ba, Governor LeRoy Collins Administrative Correspondence, Collins Papers, Florida State Archives.

63. McCall to Herbert S. Phillips, July 8, 1955, Box 5, Herbert S. Phillips Family Papers, University of South Florida.

64. *Tampa Tribune*, January 1, 1956, 5; Phillips to Collins, March 23, 1955, Box 5, Phillips Family Papers.

65. Franklin Williams interview; Clendenin, "The Legacy of Iceman McCall," 23.

66. Hall, *Revolt Against Chivalry*, 153.

67. "Florida Governor Errs on NAACP, Lawyer Says," Press Release, December 15, 1955, GOF II, A 229, NAACP Papers, Library of Congress, Washington, D.C.

68. Stetson Kennedy, "Ocala: Old Trials in New Bottles," typed manuscript, Stetson Kennedy Papers, Southern Labor Archives, Georgia State University.

INVESTIGATIONS AND MASSIVE RESISTANCE

1. Statement by Gov. LeRoy Collins, November 19, 1956, PUT-RAC, box 33, RG 102, ser. 776A, T. LeRoy Collins Papers, Florida State Archives, Tallahassee.

2. Numan V. Bartley, *The Rise of Massive Resistance: Race and Politics in the South during the 1950s* (Baton Rouge, 1969), 241.

3. Theodore R. Gibson to the editor of *Look*, May 21, 1958, Branch III, Florida, NAACP Papers, Library of Congress, Washington, D.C.

334

4. Bartley, *The Rise of Massive Resistance*, 119, 170–71, 245.

5. Wilson Record, *Race and Radicalism: The NAACP and the Communist Party in Conflict* (Ithaca, N.Y., 1964), 164, 212; Walter F. Murphy, "The South Counterattacks: The Anti-NAACP Laws," *Western Political Quarterly* 12 (1959): 389.

6. American Jewish Congress, Commission on Law and Social Action, *Assault upon Freedom of Association: A Study of the Southern Attack on the National Association for the Advancement of Colored People* (New York, 1957), 19, 21; Harry Kalven, Jr., *The Negro and the First Amendment* (Columbus, Ohio, 1965), 70–71.

7. Collins to Edward O. Davis, July 2, 1956, PUT-RAC, box 33, Collins Papers. See also William C. Havard and Loren P. Beth, *The Politics of Mis-Representation: Rural-Urban Conflict in the Florida Legislature* (Baton Route, 1962), 6, 43, 80.

8. Thomas R. Wagy, *Governor LeRoy Collins of Florida: Spokesman of the New South* (University, Ala., 1985), 77,80, 88 (quotation from 77). See Ben C. Willis to Collins, February 9, 1956, PUT-RAC, box 33, Collins Papers, for views similar to the governor's.

9. *Laws of Florida*, chap. 31498 (1956), 396–97.

10. Bonnie Stark, "McCarthyism in Florida: Charley Johns and the Florida Legislative Investigation Committee, July, 1956 to July, 1965" (master's thesis, University of South Florida, 1985), 13–16. The bill passed thirty-four to one in the Senate and seventy-two to fifteen in the House. *Tampa Tribune*, August 22, 1956, 1; *Florida Times Union*, February 3, 1957, 22.

11. A. J. Musselman, Jr., to LeRoy Collins, July14, 1956, PUT-RAC, box 33, Collins Papers.

12. Stark, "McCarthyism in Florida," 16; *Tampa Tribune*, August 23, 1956, 24. He did so on the ground that the establishment of the committee was a legislative matter.

13. Robert Saunders to Roy Wilkins, February 27, 1957, and Francisco A. Rodriguez to Jack Greenberg, August 22, 1956, *Gibson v. Florida Legislative Investigation Committee*, Legal Files, NAACP Papers. See also Robert L. Carter to William A. Fordham, June 4, 1956, and Fordham to R. A. Gray, July 19, 1956 (registered), ibid. ; Saunders to Wilkins, August 23, 1956, "Reprisals in Florida," Administration II, NAACP Papers; and typewritten report, n.d., n.p., Robert Saunders Papers, University of South Florida, Tampa.

14. *Miami Herald*, September 12, 1956, 20A; *Tampa Tribune*, February 5, 1957, 14B; Ibid., February 25, 1957, 12; Havard and Beth, *The Politics of Mis-Representation*, 158; Stark, "McCarthyism in Florida," 18.

15. Press release, February 7, [1957], Ruth Perry Files, in possession of the author; Stark, "McCarthyism in Florida," 22. The Perry Files are deposited at the University of South Florida Library.

16. Florida Legislative Investigation Committee (FLIC), *Transcript of Testimony*, 1957, NAACP Investigation Files, 1957–60, Florida Bar Association Papers, Department of Archives, Tallahassee, Fla., 949.

17. Wilkins to Henry Land, reprinted in Ibid., 1612. William Fordham had told the committee in Tallahassee on February 4 that the branch files had been rounded up for safekeeping. Ibid., 71, 121–22. For Perry's and Graves's testimony, see Ibid., 1143–77, 1180–86, 1360; and Grattan E. Graves, Jr., to Thurgood Marshall, February 25, 1957, Branch III, Florida, NAACP Papers. One last unsuccessful attempt was made before the close of the hearings to secure the pertinent records from the

NAACP's Florida field secretary, Robert W. Saunders. See FLIC, *Transcript*, 1957, 1944–2075.

18. *Tampa Tribune*, February 9, 1957, 6.

19. Ibid., quoting Sen. Dewey Johnson, April 17, 1957, 11. See also Stark, "McCarthyism in Florida," 27–28.

20. A Louisiana legislative committee had reportedly supplied the FLIC with evidence of Communist activities in Florida. *Tampa Tribune*, April 16, 1957, 11. During the Tallahassee and Miami hearings, Charley Johns routinely had asked NAACP officials if they were members of the Communist party. FLIC, *Transcript*, 1957, 668, 1068, 1139, 1161.

21. The governor added that the committee "would bring serious harm if its procedure is changed radically." As he had done a year earlier, Collins allowed the bill to become law without his signature. *Miami Herald*, April 21, 1957, 2; *Tampa Tribune*, May 16, 1957, 14A; Stark, "McCarthyism in Florida," 28.

22. *Laws of Florida*, chap. 57–125 (1957), 204.

23. *Tampa Tribune*, June 1, 1957, 6.

24. Mark R. Hawes to Baya M. Harrison, September 26, 1957, and George W. Atkinson to Harrison, February 13, 1958, Box 2, NAACP Investigation Files, Florida Bar Association Papers. Though the lawyers represented individual plaintiffs in these cases, the report found that they actually were paid and supervised by the NAACP, contrary to the code against associational lawyers representing clients in personal matters.

25. Paul B. Comstock to Ralph C. Dell, July 22, 1958, box 2, NAACP Investigation Files, Florida Bar Association Papers. See also Dell to O. B. McEwan, July 31, 1958; Jack A. Abbott, "Report of Unauthorized Practice of Law Committee of the Florida Bar," received May 15, 1959; "Findings and Report before the Grievance Committee from the Seventh Judicial Circuit Division 'A,'" June 24, 1960; "Alleged Unethical Conduct by Members of the Florida Bar Reported by Legislative Investigation Committee, Report of Seventh Judicial Circuit Grievance Committee 'A,'" November 4, 1960; all in ibid. The bar association did believe that the NAACP as an organization was guilty of the unauthorized practice of law, but the record does not show that formal charges were ever brought.

26. *Miami News*, February 7, 1958, 1C.

27. *Miami Herald*, February 11, 1958, 1A, 2C. For a skeptical assessment of Matthews, see *Tampa Tribune*, February 13, 1958, 14A.

28. *Miami News*, June 18, 1958, clipping, Perry Files.

29. *Miami Herald*, February 27, 1958, 1A; Ibid., February 28, 1958, 1A; *Tampa Tribune*, February 27, 1958, 1; Ibid., February 28, 1958, 15A. The lawyer was Howard Dixon, who worked with the American Civil Liberties Union (ACLU).

30. Robert W. Saunders to Robert L. Carter, February 13, 1958, *Gibson*, Legal Files, NAACP Papers. See also Saunders to Roy Wilkins, November 19, 1957, "Reprisals in Florida," Administration II; ibid.

31. "Preliminary Statement by Mrs. Ruth Perry to the Florida Legislative Investigation Committee at Miami, Florida, February 26, 1958," Perry Files.

32. Petition for Writ of Certiorari to the Supreme Court of Florida, Brief of Petitioners, *Theodore R. Gibson, Ruth Perry. Vernell Albury and Grattan E. Graves, Jr., v. Florida Legislative Investigation Committee*, U.S. Supreme Court, October Term, 1958, no. 873, pp. 11–3.

33. Ruth W. Perry, "Along Freedom's Road," *Miami Times*, March 8, 1958, clipping, Perry Files. See also *Miami Herald*, March 1, 1958, 2A; and Ruth W. Perry, interview with author, May 24, 1986, Miami. Perry feared that her defiance of the committee might cost her her job as a Miami Beach librarian. Robert Carter to Perry, March 7, 1958, Perry Files; Perry to Carter, March 2 and April 7, 1958, *Gibson*, Legal Files, NAACP Papers.

34. *Miami Times*, March 1, 1958, 1, clipping, Perry Files.

35. In the Supreme Court of Florida, *Edward T. Graham v. Florida Legislative Investigation Committee*, Brief of Appellant, May 16, 1958, no. 29,493, p. A-10. See also In Re Petition of Graham, 104 So. 2d 16 (1958); and *Tampa Tribune*, February 22, 1958, 16 (for the position of the ACLU, whose attorneys, Tobias Simon and Howard Dixon, represented Graham).

36. The *Miami Herald*, February 27, 1958, 1A, speculated that the names of suspected Communists came from a Dade County grand jury probe in 1954. See also Stark, "McCarthyism in Florida," 42–43.

37. *Tampa Tribune*, August 2, 1958, 16. The use of the Fifth Amendment during the 1950s was a tactic employed not only by alleged Communists but also by suspected mob figures brought before congressional committees. In 1956 the Florida Bar Association had adopted a resolution condemning lawyers who invoked the Fifth Amendment in refusing to answer questions about Communist activities. "The Proposal Re 'Fifth Amendment Lawyers,'" *Florida Bar Journal* 30 (1956): 318. Though the *Tampa Tribune* distinguished the NAACP from "Fifth Amendment Communists," it condemned the group's "unwarranted display of arrogance against the authority of the State of Florida" and argued that its "hostile tactics generate suspicion," March 1, 1958, 6. One notable dissent came from Jack Bell, a popular *Miami Herald* columnist, who recognized the right of the FLIC to investigate NAACP activities but lambasted it for "drag[ging] out the old 'were you ever a Communist' bromide." "The Town Crier," *Miami Herald*, March 9, 1958, clipping, Perry Files.

38. *St. Petersburg Times*, February 19, 1958, 9A. Perhaps in recognition that the committee was singling out the NAACP for attack, its members voted to launch a probe of the Ku Klux Klan. In doing so, they placed the NAACP in the same camp with "all racial troublemakers," according to the *Florida Times-Union*, March 1, 1958, 20.

39. *Watkins v. United States*, 354 U.S. 178 (1957); *Sweezy v. New Hampshire*, 354 U.S. 234 (1957); *Pennsylvania v. Nelson*, 350 U.S. 497 (1956).

40. *NAACP v. Alabama*, 357 U.S. 449, 466 (1958). In this instance the court could not find that disclosure of the names of NAACP members was necessary to implement the foreign registration act.

41. In the Supreme Court of Florida, Brief of Appellants, *Theodore R. Gibson, Ruth Perry, Vernell Albury and Grattan E. Graves, Jr., v. Florida Legislative Investigation Committee*, September Term, 1958, no. 29, 491, pp. 20, 24 (quotation from 20). See also *Tampa Tribune*, July 3, 1958, 3.

42. Supreme Court of Florida, Brief of Appellants, Gibson et al., 1958, 24, 27, 29. Graves also claimed the attorney-client privilege as a basis for not divulging communications between himself and association members.

43. Supreme Court of Florida, Brief of Appellant, Graham, 1958, 4–5.

44. In the Supreme Court of Florida, Brief of Appellee, *Theodore R. Gibson, Ruth Perry, Vernell Albury and Grattan E. Graves, Jr. v. Florida Legislative Investigation Committee*, no. 29, 491, August 25, 1958, 27.

45. Ibid., 34. In June 1958 the committee had conducted hearings of the Ku

Klux Klan, but in contrast to its efforts against the NAACP, the panel did not recommend any new measures to restrict the white-supremacist group. Stark, "McCarthyism in Florida," pp. 47–48; "Report of Florida Legislative Investigation Committee to 1959 Session of the Legislature," 19–21, photocopy courtesy of Bonnie Stark. At these hearings Sheriff Hugh Lewis of Suwanee County, an admitted member of the Ku Klux Klan, took the Fifth Amendment and refused to testify about his possible involvement in a flogging of a black in 1955. For Collins's cautious reaction to this case, see Collins to Charley Johns, September 15, 1958; *Tampa Tribune*, September 22, 1958, clipping; and Bill Durden to Bill Killian, February 11, 1959, "Race Relations, 1959–1960"; all in LeRoy Collins Papers, University of South Florida Library, Tampa.

46. *Gibson v. Florida Legislative Investigation Committee*, 108 So. 2d 737, 741 (1958).

47. Ibid., 739–40, 743.

48. Ibid, 744, 745. The suspected Communists, Anna Rosenberg and Bertha Teplow, were represented by Robert Ramer. The courts also ruled that the attorney-client privilege invoked by Grattan Graves, Jr., did not enable him to avoid answering questions required of his clients. However, the justices asserted that vaguely drawn questions could not satisfy the pertinency requirement. It was not permissible to ask: "Do you know Bertha Teplow?" Rather, the committee had to state the connection between the person and the subject of the inquiry, in this instance that Teplow was a suspected member of the Communist party. See *Tampa Tribune*, December 23, 1958, 12, for praise of Thornal's decision safeguarding both "the order and security of the state . . . [and] the rank and file of the NAACP membership from a random and potentially capricious committee search."

49. SNS to J. M. Harlan, Bench Memo, "*Gibson v. Florida Legislative Investigation Committee*," no. 873, May 29, 1959, John Marshall Harlan Papers, Princeton University Library, Princeton, N.J. Robert Carter, the NAACP's attorney, correctly guessed the Court's reasoning. Carter to Vernell Albury, Theodore Gibson, Grattan E. Graves, Jr., and Ruth Perry, June 25, 1959, *Gibson*, Legal Files, NAACP Papers. Three justices, Earl Warren, Hugo Black, and William O. Douglas, one short of those required to grant review, voted to hear the case.

50. Perry to Robert L. Carter, June 23, 1959, *Gibson*, Legal Files, NAACP Papers.

51. FLIC, *Transcript of Testimony*, November 4, 1959, 17–19, photocopy courtesy of Bonnie Stark; "Report of Florida Legislative Investigation Committee to 1959 Session," 12, 16–17.

52. FLIC, *Transcript*, 1959, 40, 46, 50, 117–40.

53. Ibid., 63, 86. See also Ibid., 89ff. ·

54. This distinction drew mixed reviews. The *Pittsburgh Courier*, a black newspaper, suggested that the issue was not really Communism but the destruction of the NAACP, and "once in possession of the membership lists, the Cracker dictatorship would immediately proceed to launch a 'cold war' against every NAACP member." November 14, 1959, 13. In contrast, the *Tampa Tribune* pointed out that had the civil rights leaders cooperated, they could have permitted examination of their records "without revealing the entire membership." November 7, 1959, 10.

55. *Florida Legislative Investigation Committee v. Gibson*, no. 16821, Circuit Court, 2d Circuit, Leon County, July 19, 1960, 1. See also Circuit Court, *Transcript of Hearing*, May 1960, 41, 70, 77–78, 81, 90–91, 158; and Mark Hawes, Memo, June 11, 1960, and Howard W. Dixon and Tobias Simon, Memo of Respondent, June 23,

1960, *Florida Legislative Investigation Committee v. Graham*, no. 16820, Circuit Court, Leon County.

56. FLIC, *Transcript of Hearing*, July 27, 1960, in *Florida Legislative Investigation Committee v. Gibson*, no 16821, Circuit Court, 2d Circuit, Leon County; *Tampa Tribune*, August 31, 1960, 16.

57. In the Supreme Court of Florida, Brief for Appellant, *Theodore R. Gibson v. Florida Legislative Investigation Committee*, September Term, 1960, no. 30,661, p. 29.

58. In the Supreme Court of Florida, Reply Brief of Appellant, *Edward T. Graham v. Florida Legislative Investigation Committee*, September Term, 1960, no. 30,660, p. 1. See also Supreme Court of Florida, Brief of Appellant, Gibson, 1960, 32; *Bates v. Little Rock*, 61 U.S. 461 (1960); and Kalven, *The Negro and the First Amendment*, 97.

59. In the Supreme Court of Florida, Brief of Appellee, *Theodore R. Gibson v. Florida Legislative Investigation Committee; Edward T. Graham v. Florida Legislative Investigation Committee*, September Term, 1960, nos. 30,660, 30,661, pp. 3, 8 (quotation from 3).

60. *Gibson v. Florida Legislative Investigation Committee*, 26 So. 2d 129, 132, 136 (1960).

61. Wilkins to Harry Belafonte, March 2, 1961, "Reprisals in Florida," Administration II, NAACP Papers.

62. *Shelton v. Tucker*, 364 U.S. 497 (1960); *NAACP v. Louisiana*, 366 U.S. 293 (1961); Kalven, *The Negro and the First Amendment*, 74–75, 97–100.

63. *Barenblatt v. United States*, 360 U.S. 109 (1959); *Wilkinson v. United States*, 356 U.S. 399 (1961); *Braden v. United States*, 365 U.S. 431 (1961); *Uphaus v. Wyman*, 360 U.S. 72 (1959); Robert E. Cushman and Robert F. Cushman, *Cases in Constitutional Law*, 3d ed. (New York, 1968), 121; Paul L. Murphy, *The Constitution in Crisis Times* (New York, 1972), 331–34, 345–46; Anthony Lewis, *New York Times*, December 6, 1961, 28.

64. Petition for Writ of Certiorari to the Supreme Court of Florida, *Theodore R. Gibson v. Florida Legislative Investigation Committee*, Supreme Court of the United States, October Term, 1960, 21.

65. Brief for Petitioner, *Theodore R. Gibson v. Florida Legislative Investigation Committee*, Supreme Court of the United States, October Term, 1961, no. 70 (6), p. 20. See also Brief for Petitioner, Gibson, Certiorari, U.S. Supreme Court, 1960, 18–19.

66. Brief for Petitioner, Gibson, U.S. Supreme Court, 1961, 25; Brief for Petitioner, Gibson, Certiorari, U.S. Supreme Court, 1960, 17.

67. Brief of Respondent, *Theodore R. Gibson v. Florida*, Supreme Court of the United States, October Term, 1961, no. 70 (6), pp. 4 (quoting Hawes), 18, 20.

68. MHB, Bench Memo, "*Gibson v. Florida Legislative Investigation Committee*," n.d., 10–11, box 232, Earl Warren Papers, Library of Congress. See also TBD, Bench Memo, "*Gibson v. Florida Legislative Investigation Committee*," n.d., ibid. ; and CF, Bench Memo, "*Gibson v. Florida Legislative Investigation Committee*," March 5, 1961, Harlan Papers.

69. Draft opinion, *Gibson v. Florida Legislative Investigation Committee*, March 13, 1962, 11, Harlan Papers, Potter Stewart to John Marshall Harlan, March 15, 1962, and notations of Tom Clark, March 14, 1962, and Felix Frankfurter, n.d., can be found in the margins of ibid. Shortly before Frankfurter resigned, the conservatives also had lost Charles Whittaker to retirement. His place was taken, however, by Byron White, who supported their position.

70. Earl Warren, memorandum to Justices Black, Douglas, Clark, Harlan, Brennan, Stewart, and White, April 25, 1962, box 351, Hugo Black Papers, Library of Congress; Anthony Lewis, *New York Times*, March 26, 1963, 1.

71. *Gibson v. Florida Legislative Investigation Committee*, 372 U.S. 539 (1963) at 548, 555, 557.

339

72. Ibid., 572. See also William O. Douglas, "The Right of Association," *Columbia Law Review* 63 (1963): 1378-79.

73. *Gibson v. Florida Legislative Investigation Committee*, 372 U.S. at 579, 580. White also dissented because the "net effect of the Court's decision is . . . to insulate from effective legislative inquiry and preventive legislation the time-proven skills of the Communist Party in subverting and eventually controlling legitimate organization." Ibid., 585. See also Kalven, *The Negro and the First Amendment*, 113.

74. Kalven, *The Negro and the First Amendment*, 116; "The Supreme Court 1962 Term," *Harvard Law Review* 77 (1963): 120; Gerald F. Richman, "Constitutional Law: Associational Privacy Afforded to Legitimate Organizations notwithstanding Subversive Infiltration," *University of Florida Law Review* 16 (1963): 496-97; Cushman and Cushman, *Cases*, 122.

75. "The Supreme Court 1962," 122. See also Kalven, The *Negro and the First Amendment*, 119; and Anthony Lewis, *New York Times*, March 26, 1963, 1, and June 23, 1963, 64.

76. FLIC, *Report*, 1961, photocopy courtesy of Bonnie Stark; Stark, "McCarthyism in Florida," 77-78. The focus of the hearings was on Carl Braden, a leader of the Southern Conference, who had been cited for contempt of HUAC and whose conviction was upheld by the U.S. Supreme Court. Despite the FLIC's assumption, the NAACP had tried to steer clear of Braden and his group. Robert W. Saunders to Ruby Hurley, November 30, 1959, Saunders Papers.

77. *Miami Herald*, March 27, 1963, 6A; *Miami News*, March 27, 1963, 16A. See the *Tampa Tribune*, March 27, 1963, 6B, for a slightly different view. Several years earlier, the FLIC had shifted its attention toward hunting for subversives and homosexuals on the campuses of the University of Florida and the University of South Florida. These probes generated a good deal of political animosity and negative publicity. See Stark, "McCarthyism in Florida," chaps. 3 and 4.

78. Ruth W. Perry to Roy Wilkins, October 31,1958; Branch III, Florida; Perry to Robert Carter, June 23, 1959, *Gibson*, Legal Files; Lucille Black to Theodore R. Gibson, June 7, 1960, Branch III, Florida; all in NAACP Papers.

79. Ruth Perry, "Along Freedom's Road," *Miami Times*, April 11, 1959, clipping, Perry Files. See also Perry interview; and Robert W. Saunders, interview with author, September 9, 1986, Tampa, Fl. The figures on membership in Florida were not published separately but were included along with the totals for Georgia, Mississippi, North Carolina, South Carolina, Tennessee, and, until 1957, Alabama. The aggregate figures for this region were 52,365 in 1955; 44,447 in 1956; 26,775 in 1957; 30,245 in 1958; 37,273 in 1959; 44,842 in 1960; 45,007 in 1961; 49,597 in 1962; and 57,450 in 1963. See NAACP, *Annual Report*, 1955-63. The impressionistic evidence suggests that Florida enrollments did not improve until the early 1960s. Robert W. Saunders to Robert Carter, December 7, 1959, Saunders Papers. For promotion of the *Gibson* suit, see Roy Wilkins to Harry Belafonte, March 2, 1961, "Reprisals in Florida," Administration II; Robert L. Carter to Wilkins and Henry Lee Moon, August 31, 1960, "Reprisals in Florida," Administration II; Jesse DeVore to editors, columnists, and writers, January 4, 1961, "Reprisals in Florida," Administration II;

Otis D. James and George A. Simpson to Gloster B. Current, March 9, 1961, Branch III, Florida; and Current to Theodore R. Gibson, June 15, 1961, Branch III, Florida; all in NAACP Papers.

80. On the ranking of Florida in qualities of southernness, see Hugh D. Price, *The Negro and Southern Politics: A Chapter in Florida History* (New York, 1957), 8–9.

81. Saunders interview. By targeting the NAACP for harassment, southern white segregationists inadvertently may have strengthened its image among many blacks as the leading organization fighting for racial equality. See Adam Fairclough, *"To Redeem the Soul of America": The Southern Christian Leadership Conference and Martin Luther King, Jr.* (Athens, Ga., 1987), 22–23. On the negative side, some NAACP leaders undermined their more radical civil rights competitors by cooperating with the FBI to provide a source of inside information that could be used against them. David Colburn, *Racial Change and Community Crisis: St. Augustine, Florida, 1877–1980* (New York, 1985), 85.

82. *Gibson v. Florida Legislative Investigation Committee*, 372 U.S. at 544, quoting *Bates v. Little Rock*.

FROM SIT-IN TO RACE RIOT

1. Morton Inger, *Politics and Reality in an American City: The New Orleans School Crisis of 1960* (New York: Center for Urban Education, 1969), 82–85; Robert L. Crain, *The Politics of School Desegregation: Comparative Case Studies of Community Structure and Policy-Making* (Chicago: Aldine, 1968), 3, 302–305; Numan V. Bartley, *The Rise of Massive Resistance: Race and Politics in the South During the 1950's* (Baton Rouge: Louisiana State University Press, 1969), 313.

2. C. Vann Woodward, "New South Fraud is Papered by Old South Myth," Washington *Post*, July 9, 1961, p. E3; Richard Cramer, "School Desegregation and New Industry: The Southern Community Leaders' Viewpoint," *Social Forces*, XLI (May, 1963), 387.

3. Jack L. Walker, "The Functions of Disunity: Negro Leadership in a Southern City," *Journal of Negro Education*, XXXII (Summer, 1963), 227–36.

4. Tampa *Tribune*, November 13, 1960, p. 1A, June 22, 1960, p. 4A, July 3, 1961, p. 6A.

5. This composite profile is based on the careers of Blythe Andrews, Sr., and Blythe Andrews, Jr., publishers of the *Florida Sentinel-Bulletin*, a black biweekly newspaper, and prominent figures in the inappropriately named Lily White Benevolent Association, a fraternal group that provided health and burial services—Perry Harvey, Sr., who was president of International Longshoremen's Association Local 1402; A. Leon Lowry, Robert Saunders, Francisco Rodriguez, Charles Stanford, and Robert Gilder, who spearheaded the NAACP; and James Hammond and Charles Jones, who guided the Young Adults for Progressive Action. *Florida Sentinel-Bulletin*, September 3, 1960, p. 4.

6. *Florida Sentinel-Bulletin*, September 3, 1960, p. 4, September 29, 1962, p. 5. See Tampa *Tribune*, July 20, 1960, p. 14, for expectations of increased tourism. A. Leon Lowry, interviewed by the author on September 5, 1977, stated that black leaders used the economic arguments in discussions with white civic leaders.

7. Interview with Julian Lane by the author, January 16, 1978; Tampa *Times*, October 14, 1959, p. 6; *Florida Sentinel-Bulletin*, October 10, 1959, p. 4, November 3,

1959, p. 4; "Uncle Fed's Notebook," January, 1960, in Cody Fowler Files, University of South Florida Library, Tampa (USFL); Cody Fowler to members of Biracial Committee, December 24, 1959, in Robert Thomas Files, USFL. Among the white businessmen selected to the committee were Robert Thomas, a port developer, and Sandy A. Moffitt, a supplier of building materials. Along with Fowler they provided the most sustained interest and leadership. Besides Lowry, the most important blacks were Blythe Andrews, Sr., and Perry Harvey, Sr.

341

8. Interview with Cody Fowler by the author, December 5, 1977; interview with Robert Thomas by the author, December 7, 1977; untitled manuscript on Progress Village, in Thomas Files; Tampa *Times*, October 14, 1959, p. 6. During the late fifties, Andrews and Harvey had cooperated with Fowler and Thomas in establishing a segregated but upgraded housing development in Progress Village in order "to prevent racial friction . . . caused by invasion of white districts by Negroes." See Andrews, "So They Tell Me," *Florida Sentinel-Bulletin*, January 10, 1961, p. 1.

9. Cody Fowler, Address to the Empire Club, Toronto, Canada, December 10, 1964, in Fowler Files. Robert Thomas bluntly recalled that he was not an integrationist. Thomas interview.

10. *Florida Sentinel-Bulletin*, August 30, 1960, p. 4, June 28, 1960, p. 4.

11. Tampa *Times*, March 1, 1960, p. 4; Tampa *Tribune*, March 1, 1960, p. 1; *Florida Sentinel-Bulletin*, March 1, 1960, p. 16; interview with Clarence Fort by the author, January 29, 1978; interview with Robert Saunders by the author, September 17, 1977.

12. Tampa *Tribune*, March 2, 1960, p. 1, March 3, 1960, p. 1A; *Florida Sentinel-Bulletin*, March 5, 1960, p. 13.

13. Tampa *Tribune*, March 2, 1960, p. 12; *Florida Sentinel-Bulletin*, March 5, 1960, p. 4.

14. Tampa *Tribune*, March 1, 1960, p. 1., March 2, 1960, p. 1, March 12, 1960, p. 9; Tampa *Times*, March 1, 1960, p. 1. However, there was a disparity in the outcome of the two arrest cases. Both youths were convicted for disturbing the peace, but the Negro was sentenced to eighty days in jail and given a six-hundred-dollar fine. The white man received a one-hundred-dollar fine and fifty days in prison.

15. Tampa *Tribune*, March 22, 1960, p. 14.

16. A. Leon Lowry to Merchants Association, March 14, 1960, in Thomas Files. See also Cody Fowler to Members of Biracial Committee, March 7, 1960, in Thomas Files; Lowry interview; Tampa *Tribune*, March 10, 1960, p. 8A.

17. Tampa *Tribune*, March 22, 1960, p. 7; Commission of Community Relations, "Historical Background of the Biracial Committee and the Commission of Community Relations," 3, n.d., in Thomas Files; Robert Saunders, "Monthly Report of Activities," March, 1960, in Robert Saunders Files, USFL; Tampa *Tribune*, April 28, 1960, p. 11A. See also Robert Thomas to Cody Fowler, March 29, 1960, in Thomas Files.

18. "Statement by Cody Fowler, Chairman, Commission on Race Relations," press release, May 27, 1960, in Fowler Files; Tampa *Tribune*, March 21, 1960, p. 1, May 29, 1960, p. 1A.

19. Tampa *Tribune*, May 18, 1960, p. 31; interview with Melvin Stein by the author, January 13, 1978; "Proposed Method of Desegregation of Down Town Lunch Counters, Also Ybor City and Sears," August, 1960, in Thomas Files; *Florida Sentinel-Bulletin*, September 10, 1960, p. 4.

20. Tampa *Tribune*, September 15, 1960, p. 1A; *Florida Sentinel-Bulletin*, Sep-

tember 17, 1960, p. 1; Fort interview; Lowry interview. There was some minor opposition. Criminal Court Judge L. A. Grayson suggested a white boycott of the participating stores, and he turned in his credit cards. Tampa *Times*, September 15, 1960, p. 1; Stein interview.

21. Tampa *Tribune*, September 3, 1960, p. 10, September 15, 1960, p. 1A, September 16, 1960, p. 22A.

22. Robert Saunders to Blythe Andrews, Jr., June 26, 1962, in Saunders Files; *Florida Sentinel-Bulletin*, May 4, 1963, p. 4, June 8, 1963, p. 1., August 20, 1963, p. 1, November 16, 1963, p. 1, January 11, 1964, p. 3, February 11, 1964, p. 3, May 4, 1963, p. 4, May 22, 1965, p. 2; NAACP, "Report of Assignment," August 15–September 15, 1963, and Charles Stanford to Gene Diego, March 9, 1964, both in Saunders Files; Tampa *Times*, July 3, 1964, p. 1; Robert Thomas to Cody Fowler, January 13, 1964, and Commission of Community Relations, "Minutes," May 22, 1966, both in Thomas Files; Tampa *Tribune*, March 5, 1965, p. 2B, November 24, 1967, p. 1B.

23. On the committee during most of the 1960s was Leon Lowry of the NAACP and Jim Hammond of the Young Adults for Progressive Action. The business community was represented by Colby Armstrong, Robert Thomas, Leonard Hutchinson, regional manager of Sears, and Sandy Moffitt.

24. James A. Hammond to Colby Armstrong, October 30, 1962, in Merchants Association Files, USFL; Tampa *Tribune*, September 13, 1961, p. 12B, September 14, 1961, p. 10A, September 18, 1961, p. 10A, September 20, 1961, p. 12A; interview with James Hammond by the author, September 12, 1977.

25. James Hammond to Colby Armstrong, November 24, 1962, and "Minutes," Equal Job Opportunities Committee, February 21, April 17, June 6, 1963, all in Merchants Association Files.

26. Colby Armstrong to Joseph D. Kelly, August 6, 1963, in Merchants Association Files. Evidence about whether black graduates succeeded in obtaining employment is inconclusive. *Women's Wear Daily*, October 2, 1963, reported: "Some are known to have taken some of the positions in the stores." However, results of a survey conducted by the merchants immediately after the course indicated that participants enjoyed the training but most had not secured jobs.

27. *Florida Sentinel-Bulletin*, June 22, 1963, p. 24; Tampa *Tribune*, June 21, 1963, p. 1A; Tampa *Times*, June 22, 1963, p. 9.

28. Tampa *Times*, June 21, 1963, pp. 1, 7; Tampa *Tribune*, June 22, 1963, p. 2A; Fowler interview; interview with Francisco Rodriguez by the author, January 11, 1978. Rodriguez was an NAACP attorney who represented the Youth Council.

29. Colby Armstrong to James Hammond, June 27, 1963, in Merchants Association Files; Robert Saunders, "Report of Assignment, August 15–September 15, 1963," in Saunders Files.

30. Fischer Black to Colby Armstrong, August 14, 1963, in Merchants Association Files; Tampa *Tribune*, August 24, 1963, p. 1B.

31. Mayor's Biracial Committee to Nick Nuccio and Ellsworth Simmons, September 21, 1964, in Thomas Files; *Florida Sentinel-Bulletin*, November 27, 1965, p. 4; Tampa *Tribune*, January 29, 1964, p. 1B.

32. Robert L. Gilder to Paul S. Walker, June 24, 1965, in Saunders Files; *Florida Sentinel-Bulletin*, July 19, 1966, p. 4.

33. *Florida Sentinel-Bulletin*, June 26, 1965, p. 3; Robert Gilder to Paul S. Walker, June 24, 1965, in Saunders Files.

34. NAACP, "Report of Labor and Industry Committee," July 29, 1962, in Saunders Files; Florida Advisory Committee to the United States Commission on Civil Rights, *Report* (Washington, D.C.: Government Printing Office, 1973), 29–30; James Hammond to CCR, July 28, 1966, and "Continuing Employment Feeder Workshop," n. d. [*ca.* 1967], both in Thomas Files.

35. *Florida Sentinel-Bulletin*, February 22, 1966, p. 4. See also issue of June 4, 1966, p. 4.

36. Tampa *Tribune*, May 19, 1960, p. 1A.

37. Tampa *Times*, August 23, 1962, p. 12A; Tampa *Tribune*, November 14, 1967, p. 11A. On school desegregation see United States Commission on Civil Rights, "Hillsborough County School Desegregation," March, 1976, Washington, D.C., staff report in possession of the author.

38. *Florida Sentinel-Bulletin*, October 15, 1966, p. 4; Tampa *Times*, September 23, 1966, p. 2.

39. Minutes, Commission of Community Relations, August 31, 1966, in Thomas Files; Administrator's Report, Commission of Community Relations, September 26, 1966, in Commission of Community Relations Files, CCR Office.

40. Quoted in Tampa *Tribune*, November 24, 1966, p. 2B; Administrator's Report, October 19, 1966, December 21, 1966, in CCR Files; Tampa *Tribune*, November 4, 1966, p. 2B, January 13, 1967, p. 16A; *Florida Sentinel-Bulletin*, February 11, 1967, p. 4; James Hammond to Commission of Community Relations, September 28, 1966, and James Hammond to Commissioners, Community Relations, April 21, 1967, including "Budget for 1967–68 as Proposed," both in Thomas Files.

41. National Advisory Commission on Civil Disorders, *Report* (New York: Bantam, 1968), 42–44; *Florida Sentinel-Bulletin*, October 11, 1966, p. 4, May 5, 1967, p. 4; *Bureau of the Census, Census Tracts Tampa-St. Petersburg, 1960* (Washington, D.C.: Government Printing Office, 1961), 72–97. On police brutality see *Florida Sentinel-Bulletin*, October 11, 1966, p. 4, May 13, 1967, p. 4.

42. *Florida Sentinel-Bulletin*, January 21, 1967, p. 4.

43. Ibid., September 24, 1966, p. 3, July 4, 1967, p. 4. Statistical evidence confirmed this assessment. Since 1960, little had improved for the residents of the Central Park Village neighborhood where the riot first broke out. In 1969, 48 percent of the families lived below the poverty level; median family income was around $3,000; and the median years of school completed was a little over 8. 0. Bureau of the Census, *Census Tracts Tampa-St. Petersburg, 1970* (Washington, D.C.: Government Printing Office, 1971), 78. For a full discussion of riot causation and political ideology see Joe R. Feagin and Harlan Hahn, *Ghetto Revolts* (New York: Macmillan, 1973).

44. Gayle Everett Davis, "Riot in Tampa" (M. A. thesis, University of South Florida, 1976), 88; Commission of Community Relations, "Historical Background of the City Youth Patrol (White Hat Concept) 'Tampa Technique,'" June 27, 1967, in Thomas Files; Tampa *Tribune*, June 14, 1967, p. 8B; Tampa *Times*, June 16, 1967, p. 16; Hammond interview.

45. Tampa *Tribune*, June 13, 1967, p. 4B, June 16, 1967, p. 11C, June 18, 1967, p. 17A; Tampa *Times*, June 13, 1967, p. 14; National Advisory Commission on Civil Disorders, *Report*, 163; Permanent Subcommittee on Investigations of the Senate Committee on Government Operations, *Riots, Civil and Criminal Disorders*, 90th Cong., 1st Sess. (1967), Part 1, Insert, 14. The *Tribune* assessed the property losses at $1. 5 million. Whatever the actual figure, Tampa escaped with fewer monetary damages,

deaths, and injuries than did most of the eight cities—Buffalo, Cincinnati, Detroit, Milwaukee, Minneapolis, Newark, Plainfield, Tampa—which the Kerner Commission identified as having experienced major convulsions in 1967.

46. "Continuing Employment Feeder Workshop," in Thomas Files.

47. Tampa *Tribune*, June 14, 1967, p. 8B.

48. Davis, "Riot in Tampa," 99–101. Just in case these measures failed to snuff out the fires of insurrection, the city spent forty-five thousand dollars to augment its antiriot arsenal with the latest equipment. Davis, "Riot in Tampa," 104; Tampa *Tribune*, December 9, 1967, p. 2B, December 12, 1967, p. 4B.

49. "Continuing Employment Feeder Workshop," in Thomas Files; Frank Johnson to Cody Fowler, April 5, 1968, Cody Fowler to James Hammond, April 16, 1968, both in Fowler Files; interview with Charles Jones by the author, January 9, 1978.

50. Tampa *Tribune*, December 1, 1967, p. 1B, December 2, 1967, p. 10A.

51. Ibid., September 18, 1963, p. 4B; interview with Scott Christopher by the author, January 9, 1978; interview with Fred Learey by the author, January 20, 1978; *Florida Sentinel-Bulletin*, April 16, 1963, p. 4.

52. $1000 Lane Bryant Awards Group Winner," press release, November, 1967, in Fowler Files.

ROCK 'N' ROLL, THE PAYOLA SCANDAL, AND THE POLITICAL CULTURE OF CIVIL RIGHTS

1. On congressional anti-communism, Robert Griffith, *Politics of Fear: Joseph McCarthy and the Senate* (Amherst, Mass., 1987); William Howard Moore, *The Kefauver Committee and the Politics of Crime, 1950–1952*, (Columbia, Missouri, 1974); and James Gilbert, *A Cycle of Outrage: America's Reaction to the Juvenile Delinquent in the 1950s*, (New York, 1986); Kent Anderson, *Television Fraud: The History and Implications of the Quiz Show Scandals*, (Westport, Conn., 1978).

2. Quoted in Kerry Seagrave, *Payola in the Music Industry: A History, 1880–1991*, (Jefferson, North Carolina, 1994), p. 12. Seagrave dates the first appearance of the word payola in 1938, p. 1. John A. Jackson, *Big Beat Heat: Alan Freed and the Early Years of Rock & Roll*, (New York, 1991), p. 245, dates it to 1916, but gives no specific reference. Whenever the term formally appeared, it is clear that the concept was well known around the turn of the century. See also, R. H. Coarse, "Payola in Radio and Television Broadcasting," *Journal of Law and Economics*, 22 (October, 1979): 32; Marc Eliot, *Rockonomics: The Money Behind the Music*, (New York, 1993) p. 10; *Billboard*, November 23, 1959, p. 4.

3. Seagrave, *Payola*, p. 29; Coarse, "Payola," 286; Steve Chapple and Reebee Garofalo, *Rock 'n' Roll is Here to Pay: The History and Politics of the Music Industry*, (Chicago, 1977), p. 55.

4. *Variety*, November 11, 1959, p. 55. Chapple, *Rock 'n ' Roll*, p. 60. Eliot, Rockonomics, p. 42.

5. Jackson, *Big Beat*, p. 252; Dorothy Wade and Justin Picardie, *Music Man: Ahmet Ertegun, Atlantic Records, and the Triumph of Rock 'n' Roll*, (New York, 1990), p. 89; Fredric Dannen, *Hit Men: Power Brokers and Fast Money Inside the Music Business*, (New York, 1990), p. 43ff. For example, in 1909, New York made it illegal

for anyone either to offer or accept a gratuity "with intent to influence" an employee's behavior without the employer's knowledge. However, this statute was aimed at department stores and not music industry practices.

6. Quoted in Coarse, "Payola," 276. See also Coarse, 278, 279, 280, 283, 285; Seagrave, *Payola*, p. 16; Hazel Meyer, *The Gold in Tin Pan Alley*, (Philadelphia, 1958), p. 155. Over the years the MPPA proved ineffective in curbing payola; without enforcement power it could not stop publishers from trying to gain an advantage at the expense of their competitors by reviving payoffs. An abortive effort to curb the practice came with an anti-payola provision inserted in the music business code under the New Deal's National Recovery Administration. Before the code could go into effect, the Supreme Court declared the NRA unconstitutional in 1935.

7. *Variety*, July 21, 1954, p. 35, July 28, 1954, p. 107, August 11, 1954, pp. 43, 49

8. *Variety*, February 23, 1955, p. 2.

9. Quoted in Gilbert, *Cycle*, p. 201; Grace Palladino, *Teenagers: An American History*, (New York, 1996), pp. 53, 156–57; Thomas Doherty, *Teenagers and Teenpics*, (Boston, 1988) pp. 6, 54. David Szatmary, *Rockin' in Time: A Social History of Rock-And-Roll*, (Englewood Cliffs, New Jersey, 1991), p. 24; Jonathan Kamin, "Parallels in the Social Reactions to Jazz and Rock," *Journal of Jazz Studies* 2 (1974): 121; Eliot, *Rockonomics*, p. 65.

10. Gilbert, *Cycle*, p. 176.

11. Ibid., pp. 10, 13–14; Elaine Tyler May, *Homeward Bound: American Families in the Cold War Era*, (New York, 1988), chapters 4 and 5.

12. Greenfield, *No Peace, No Place*, (Garden City, New York, 1973), pp. 29, 56. On high schools as an institution to keep working class and ethnic influences away from middle class whites and at the same time promote values of tolerance, see William Graebner, *Coming of Age in Buffalo: Youth and Authority in the Postwar Era*, (Philadelphia, 1990); Gertrude Samuels, "Why They Rock 'n' Roll—And Should They?," *New York Times Magazine*, January 12, 1958, 19. Doherty, *Teenpics*, p. 81; Palladino, *Teenagers*, p. 124; Carl Belz, *The Story of Rock*, (New York, 1972), p. 20.

13. King in *Ebony*, April, 1958, p. 104; Joe Bostic in *Amsterdam News*, March 5, 1955, p. 26. On the belief that "'bad' working-class teenagers were leading the rest astray," see Simon Frith, *Sound Effects: Youth, Leisure, and the Politics of Rock 'n' Roll*, (New York, 1981), p. 186. George Lipsitz, *Time Passages: Collective Memory and American Popular Culture*, (Minneapolis, 1990), p. 123 and "Ain't Nobody Here but us Chickens: The Origins of Rock and Roll," in George Lipsitz, ed., *Rainbow at Midnight: Labor and Culture in the 1960s*, (Champaign-Urbana, Illinois, 1994), p. 330; Jackson Lears, "A Matter of Taste: Corporate Hegemony in Mass Consumption Society," in Lary May, ed., *Recasting America: Culture and Politics in the Age of Cold War*, (Chicago, 1989), p. 53; Palladino, Teenagers, p. 152; Michael Bane, *White Boys Singin' the Blues*, (New York, 1982), pp. 125–26; Wini Breines, *Young, White, and Miserable: Growing Up Female in the Fifties*, (Boston, 1992), p. 20.

14. May, *Homeward Bound*, chapter 5.

15. Greenfield, *No Peace*, p. 53.

16. John A. Jackson, *American Bandstand: Dick Clark and the Making of a Rock 'n' Roll Empire*, (New York, 1997), p. 217, quoting Philadelphia disk jockey Hy Lit.

17. Charlotte Grieg, *Will You Still Love Me Tomorrow? Girl Groups from the Fifties On*, (London, 1989), p. 26.

18. For many teenagers rock 'n' roll became, as Wini Breines asserts, "a symbol

of youth rebellion against authority, with sex and race the not-so-hidden-narrative." Breines, *Young*, p. 155; Susan J. Douglas, *Where the Girls Are: Growing Up Female with the Mass Media*, (New York, 1994), p. 84.

19. "Warning to the Music Business," *Variety*, February 23, 1955, p. 2. As it developed in the 1950s, rock 'n' roll evolved into a hybrid of rhythm and blues and the country flavored sounds of rockabilly as exemplified in the music of Elvis Presley, Jerry Lee Lewis, Carl Perkins, and Buddy Holly.

20. Russell Sanjek, *American Popular Music and its Business in the 20th Century*, (New York, 1988), p. 326; Shane Maddock, "Whole Lotta Shakin' Goin' On: Racism and Early Opposition to Rock Music," *Mid-America*, 78 (Summer 1996): 182; Peter Guralnick, *Last Train to Memphis: The Rise of Elvis Presley*, (Boston, 1994), pp. 39–40.

21. Breines, *Young*, pp. 153–54; Jerry Wexler and David Ritz, *Rhythm and the Blues: A Life in American Music*, (New York, 1993), p. 286; Richard A. Peterson, "Why 1955? Explaining the Advent of Rock Music," *Popular Music* 9 (1990): 99, 101; Szatmary, *Rockin'*, p. 23; Palladino, *Teenagers*, p. 152; Chappell, *Rock 'n' Roll*, p. 41; *Variety*, July 6, 1955, p. 43.

22. Frye Gaillard, *Race, Rock, and Religion: Profiles from a Southern Journalist*, (Charlottesville, Virginia, 1982), p. 74; Charlie Gillett, *The Sound of the City: The Rise of American Rock and Roll*, (New York, 1983), p. 38

23. Nelson George, *The Death of Rhythm & Blues*, (New York, 1988), p. 63.

24. Wexler, *Rhythm*, p. 90; Graebner, *Buffalo*, 29; George Lipsitz, "Land of a Thousand Dances: Youth, Minorities and the Rise of Rock and Roll," in May, *Recasting America*, p. 273; Jackson, *Big Beat*, p. 335; David Nasaw, *Going Out: The Rise and Fall of Public Amusements*, (New York, 1993) p. 244; Trent Hill, "The Enemy Within: Censorship in Rock Music in the 1950s," in Anthony DeCurtis, ed., *Present Tense: Rock & Roll and Culture*, (Durham, North Carolina, 1992), p. 53. Otis, a musician as well as deejay, was an interesting case. Of Greek origin, he identified himself as culturally black, and his show in Los Angeles appealed to Latinos as well as blacks and whites.

25. Brian Ward, *Just My Soul Responding: Rhythm and Blues, Black Consciousness, and Race Relations*, (Berkeley, California, 1998), p. 128.

26. Robert Palmer, "The '50s," *Rolling Stone*, April 19,1989: 48; Richard Welch, "Rock 'n' Roll and Social Change," *History Today*, 40 (February 1990): 32; Breines, *Young*, p. 152; Hill, "Enemy," 50.

27. Ward, *Just My Soul*, pp. 129–30; Martha Bayles, *Hole in Our Soul: The Loss of Beauty and Meaning in American Popular Music*, (Chicago, 1994), p. 115.

28. *Shreveport Journal*, November 12, 1959, clipping, Box 1149, Oren Harris Papers, University of Arkansas, Fayetteville.

29. Ward, *Just My Soul*, p. 103; *Newsweek*, April 23, 1956, p. 32.

30. Gerald Early has written: "These were the years . . . in which America recognized and cringed before, the social reality . . . of a miscegenated culture in which, beneath the mask of inhuman racial etiquette where everyone supposedly was as separated as the twin beds in the bedroom of nearly every 1950s T.V. sitcom, there lurked an unquenchable thirst for mixing." Quoted in Breines, *Young*, p. 152; Lipsitz, "Land of," pp. 273, 280–81; Robert Palmer, *Rock & Roll: An Unruly History*, (New York, 1995), p. 139; Frith, *Sound*, p. 24; Szatmary, *Rockin'*, p. 25.

31. Linda Martin and Kerry Seagrave, *Anti-Rock: The Opposition to Rock 'n' Roll*, (Hamden, Conn., 1988), p. 41. 103. See *Christian Century*, April 11, 1956, p. 444 and

Chicago Defender, April 14, 1956, p. 13 for critical responses to Carter's charges. Carter's group, extremist even by Alabama standards, went beyond mere words and resorted to violence to protect white virtue. On April 10, 1956, several of its members attacked Nat King Cole while he was performing to a white's-only audience in the Birmingham Municipal Auditorium. Cole was hardly a rock 'n' roll crooner, but he shared the stage with a white woman singer, which according to Carter posed the same threat as authentic rock 'n' roll performers who also took their shows to Birmingham. After all, Carter reasoned, it marked only "a short step . . . from the sly, nightclub technique vulgarity of Cole, to the openly animalistic obscenity of the horde of Negro rock and rollers." Ward, *Just My Soul,* p. 100.

32. *Congressional Record,* 85th Cong., 1st Sess., August 15, 1957, Appendix, 6288. John Charles Hajduk, "Music Wars: Conflict and Accommodation in America's Culture Industry, 1940–1960," unpublished doctoral dissertation, State University of New York at Buffalo, 1995, p. 432; Martin, *Anti-Rock,* pp. 37, 53; Maddock, "Whole Lotta Shakin": 189–90; *Variety,* June 13, 1956, p. 51, September 5, 1956, p. 33; Life, "Rock and Roll," p. 168; *Time,* June 18, 1956, p. 54.

33. New York *Amsterdam News,* July 14, 1956, p. 12; *Pittsburgh Courier,* October 6, 1956, p. 9; *Ebony,* December 1956, p. 80.

34. Hajduk, "Music Wars," chapter two.

35. The information on ASCAP and BMI in these two paragraphs comes from, Hill, "Enemy," 58–59; Sanjek, *American Popular Music,* pp. 308, 328; Hajduk, "Music Wars," p. 481; Chapple, *Rock 'n'Roll,* p. 65; Eliot. *Rockonomics,* p. 57; Ward, *Just My Soul,* p. 119; Coarse, "Payola," 315.

36. Seagrave, *Payola,* pp. 104–05.

37. Chapple, *Rock 'n'Roll,* p. 46; Hajduk, "Music Wars," p. 479; *Billboard,* April 7, 1958, p. 10.

38. House of Representatives, Antitrust Subcommittee of the Committee of the Judiciary, Hearings, "Monopoly Problems in Regulated Industries," 84th Cong., Second Sess., (Washington, D.C., 1957), pp. 4141, 4425, 4426, 4427, 4428.

39. In 1957, the Celler Committee issued a report concluding that as "disk jockeys are responsible for selecting much of the music played on the air . . . BMI has made the effort to influence them to favor its music." House of Representatives, Committee on the Judiciary, Hearings, "Television Broadcasting Industry, Report of the Antitrust Subcommittee," 85th Cong., 1st Sess., (Washington, D.C., 1957), p. 122.

40. The Smathers bill was S. 2834 and it sought to amend the Communications Act of 1934. At around the same time, Congressman James Roosevelt conducted hearings before the Select Committee on Small Business in the House into charges by dissident ASCAP members that the society favored a small group of large music publishing firms. Though proving inconclusive, the investigation heard ASCAP officials brag that ASCAP had few composers of rock 'n' roll. House of Representatives, Subcommittee No. 5 of the Select Committee on Small Business, Hearings, "Policies of American Society of Composers, Authors, and Publishers," 85th Cong., 2nd Sess., (Washington, D.C. 1958), pp. 1, 16–17. Defensive about its internal management practices, ASCAP had another incentive for continuing its war with BMI and welcoming investigations into payola. Sanjek, *American Popular Music,* p. 421.

41. United States Senate, Committee on Interstate and Foreign Commerce, Subcommittee on Communication, Hearings, "Amendment to the Communications Act of 1934," [Pastore Hearings], 85th Congress, 2nd Sess., (Washington, D.C., 1958), p. 107; Daniel Horowitz, *Vance Packard and American Social Criticism,* (Chapel Hill,

North Carolina, 1994), p. 199; Vance Packard, *The Hidden Persuaders,* (New York, 1957).

42. Pastore Hearings, p. 136.

43. Pastore Hearings, p. 995.

44. Pastore Hearings, p. 541.

45. Pastore Hearings, pp. 150, 607, 1181, 1184, 1218; Hajduk, Music Wars," p. 494. Six months after the hearings ended, a federal court dismissed ASCAP's complaint that BMI had engaged in a conspiracy against it, but upheld the plaintiffs right to sue BMI for discriminating against its members compositions. In any event, the networks began to divest their ownership of BMI and left control in the hands of the independent stations. Sanjek argues that network executives did not want to become embroiled in the widening payola scandal and its association with "unsavory rock 'n' roll." Sanjek, *American Popular Music,* pp. 431, 432.

46. Anderson, *Television Fraud, passim;* Richard S. Tedlow, "Intellect on Television: The Quiz Show Scandals of the 1950s," *American Quarterly* (28) Fall 1976): 483–95.

47. Richard N. Goodwin, *Remembering America: A Voice From the Sixties,* (New York, 1989), p. 63. Goodwin soon joined Kennedy's staff as a speech writer.

48. Stephen Whitfield, *The Culture of the Cold War,* (Baltimore, 1991), pp. 176–77; Greenfield, *No Peace,.* p. 142.

49. Walter Karp, "The Quiz Show Scandal," in Leonard Dinnerstein and Kenneth T. Jackson, eds. *American Vistas 1877 to the Present,* 6th edition (New York, 1991), p. 330; Hajduk, *Music Wars,* p. 502, n. 66; Karal Ann Marling, *As Seen on T.V.: The Visual Culture of Everyday Life in the 1950s,* (Cambridge, Mass., 1994), p. 183.

50. Whitfield, *Culture,* p. 177. Steinbeck's concern about moral declension also emerged in his novel, *The Winter of Our Discontent* (New York, 1961).

51. Coarse, "Payola," 291; House of Representatives, Subcommittee on Legislative Oversight, *Interim Report,* [No. 1258] "Investigation of Regulatory Commissions and Agencies," 86th Cong., 2nd Sess., (Washington, D.C., 1960), p. 37; Sanjek, *American Popular Music,* p. 439; Seagrave, *Payola,* pp. 100–101; *Variety,* November 11, 1959, 1.

52. Subcommittee on Legislative Oversight, *Interim Report,* p. 37.

53. Oren Harris to A. Reed, January 21, 1950, Box 1109; William Colmer to Oren Harris, February 24, 1950, and Harris to Colmer, February 27, 1950, Box 1109; Harris to B. W. Mitchell, June 14, 1949, Box 1109, Harris Papers, Special Collections Division, University of Arkansas Library, Fayetteville.

54. Harris Speech, February 22, 1950, Box 1109, Harris Papers.

55. Roy Reed, *Faubus: The Life and Times of An American Prodigal,* (Fayetteville, Ark., 1997), pp. 249, 263; Oren Harris to O. D. Johnson, September 30, 1957, Harris to A. G. Davis, September 16, 1957, Harris to George F. Edwards, October 21, 1957, Box 1136, Harris Papers. For other examples of Harris's racial views see, Ward, *Just My Soul,* p. 169; *Arkansas Gazette,* August 14, 1960, A4; Oren Harris to Alvy Edwards, July 8, 1959, Box 1143, Harris Papers.

56. *American Nationalist* attached to Oren Harris to J. J. Babb, January 5, 1960, Box 1149, Harris Papers. Babb lived in Arkansas, but the *American Nationalist* originated from California.

57. Oren Harris to J. J. Babb, January 5, Box 1960, 1149, Harris Papers. On the bottom of the copy of the *American Nationalist,* Babb, from El Dorado, Arkansas, had penned: "Dear Oren: Is this angle too hot to handle?"

58. On the "fallow years" of King and civil rights protest, see Adam Fairclough, To *Redeem the Soul of America: The Southern Christian Leadership Conference and Martin Luther King, Jr,* (Athens, Ga, 1987), chapter two. On the unsteady progress toward the ballot during the 1950s, see Steven F. Lawson, *Black Ballots: Voting Rights in the South, 1944–1969* (New York, 1976).

349

59. Bernard Schwartz, *The Professor and the Commissions,* (New York, 1959), pp. 9, 96. "Statement of Dr. Bernard Schwartz," February 10, 1958, Box 1298, Harris Papers. Harris declared that he fired Bernard Schwartz for insubordination. "Statement of Honorable Oren Harris Upon Assuming Chairmanship of Special Subcommittee on Legislative oversight, Wednesday, February 12, 1958," Box 1298, Harris Papers.

60. Besides Harris, Democrats included Peter Mack of Illinois, Walter Rogers of Texas, John J. Flynt of Georgia, and John Moss of California. On the Republican side were John B. Bennett of Michigan, William Springer of Illinois, Steven B. Derounian of New York, and Samuel L. Devine of Ohio.

61. John E. Moss interview by Donald B. Seney, State Government Oral History Program, copy in Bancroft Library, University of California at Berkeley, pp. 6, 12–13, 183. "Memo from Moss," April 14, 1960, June 16, 1960, Scrapbook clippings, John E. Moss Papers, University Archives, California State University at Sacramento.

62. U.S. House of Representatives, Subcommittee on Legislative Oversight, Committee on Interstate and Foreign Commerce, "Responsibilities of Broadcasting Licensees and Station Personnel," [Payola Hearings], 86th Cong., 2nd Sess., (Washington, D.C., 1960), pp. 192, 870.

63. *Public Papers of the President, Dwight David Eisenhower, 1959* (Washington, D.C., 1960, p. 277. At the same time, Eisenhower tried to quell the public outcry over the decline of public morality by commenting at a news conference on November 4, 1959, that he did not think "that America has forgotten her own moral standards." He compared the quiz show scandal to the Chicago Black Sox scandal of the 1919 World Series.

64. "Report to the President by the Attorney General on Deceptive Practices in Broadcasting Media, December 30, 1959," in Subcommittee on Legislative Oversight, *Interim Report,* Appendix E, pp. 63, 65, 70. *New York Times,* January 1, 1960, p. 1; *Billboard,* January 11, 1960, p. 1; William Boddy, *Fifties Television: The Industry and its Critics* (Urbana, Illinois, 1990), p. 224.

65. Payola Hearings, pp. 183, 620 for representative testimony of Cleveland's Wes Hopkins and Bob Clayton from Boston.

66. See testimony of Samuel Clark, Payola Hearings, p. 485, for the view of what the record company hoped to get from payola.

67. Payola Hearings, pp. 1, 331–32.

68. Payola Hearings, pp. 92, 247; *Billboard,* February 15, 1960, p. 2; Sanjek, *American Popular Music,* 448.

69. Payola Hearings, pp. 247, 252; *Broadcasting,* February 15, 1960, p. 54. Lee Gorman to Oren Harris, March 14, 1960 and Harris to Gorman, March 19, 1960, Box 1297, Harris Papers about employment for Richards in the wake of the investigation. For two opposing views on the ritual of confession and anticommunism see Victor S. Navasky, *Naming Names,* (New York, 1980) and William L. O'Neill, *A Better World: The Great Schism: Stalinism and the American Intellectuals,* (New York, 1982).

70. Both federal agencies conducted their own investigations of payola, with the FTC uncovering payoffs to 255 disk jockeys in twenty-six states and issuing

complaints against more than one hundred record companies and distributors to cease engaging in the unfair practice. Nevertheless, ASCAP had no more success against its BMI adversary in the administrative realm than it had in the judicial. Although the Justice Department eventually filed an antitrust suit against BMI in 1964, the government accepted an agreement that allowed broadcasters to retain ownership of BMI. Jackson, *Big Beat*, p. 322. *Variety*, March 9, 1960, p. 61, March 23, 1960, p. 24; December 9, 1959, p. 53; *Billboard*, May 23, 1960, p. 2;*Broadcasting*, February 22, 1960, pp. 36, 40; *New York Times*, August 8, 1960, p. 13; *New York Post*, December 3, 1959, pp. 5, 64; Hajduk, "Music Wars," p. 513; Seagrave, *Payola*, pp. 135, 138; Sanjek, *American Popular Music*, p. 449; Payola Hearings, p. 641.

71. During the hearings in mid March, Eisenhower accepted the resignation of his appointed chairman of the FCC, John C. Doerfer, who had testified before the Harris Committee of taking a Florida vacation aboard the yacht of George Storer, a wealthy owner of radio and television stations licensed by the FCC. Republicans on the committee, led by John Bennett of Michigan sought to move up the timetable for bringing the disk jockey Dick Clark to the nation's capital to testify in order to deflect attention away from this scandal tainting the GOP administration. Harris and the Democrats, however, did not act for another month and a half. Payola Hearings, March 4, 1960, pp. 652, 725; *New York Post*, March 13, 1960, p. 5; *New York Times*, March 21, 1960, pp. 1, 28; "Statement of John B. Bennett," March 21, 1960; "Statement by Congressman Peter F. Mack and Congressman John E. Moss," March 21, 1960; Robert Lishman to Oren Harris, March 16, 1960, miscellaneous, Moss Papers.

72. Berry had been convicted on a morals charge allegedly for transporting a fourteen-year-old girl across state lines in violation of the Mann Act. Little Richard turned to the ministry. Szatmary, *Rockin'*, pp. 56–59.

73. Steven F. Lawson, "The Florida Legislative Investigation Committee and the Constitutional Readjustment of Race Relations, 1956–1963," in Kermit L. Hall and James W. Ely, Jr., ed, *An Uncertain Tradition: Constitutionalism and the History of the South*, (Athens, Ga., 1989): 296–325; John Dittmer, *Local People: The Struggle for Civil Rights in Mississippi* (Urbana, Ill., 1994), pp. 80–83.

74. Jackson, *American Bandstand*, p. 60; Davidson, "Dick Clark," 111.

75. Dick Clark, *Your Happiest Years*, (New York, 1959) p. 17; Dick Clark and Richard Robinson, *Rock, Roll, and Remember*, (New York, 1976), p. 146.

76. Clark, *Rock, Roll*, p. 67; *New York Times*, March 5, 1960, p. 40; Belz, *Story of Rock*, p. 104; Jackson, *American Bandstand*, p. 69; Henry Schipper, "Dick Clark Interview," *Rolling Stone*, April 19, 1990, p. 68.

77. Jackson, *American Bandstand*, p. 66. Even with his squeaky clean visage, Clark could not entirely remove himself from the negative images identified with rock and roll. He was called "The Czar of the Switchblade Set," "The Kingpin of the Teen-age Mafia," and "the Pied Piper of Bedlam." Pete Martin, "I Call on Dick Clark," *Saturday Evening Post*, October 10, 1959, p. 27; Bill Davidson, "The Strange World of Dick Clark," *Redbook*, March 1960, p. 111.

78. Clark, *Rock, Roll*, p. 82; Martin, *Anti Rock*, p. 107; Schipper, "Dick Clark," 126; Donald Clarke, *The Rise and Fall of Popular Music*, (New York, 1995), pp. 422–23.

79. Letter from Dorothy Simmons, *Pittsburgh Courier*, September 5, 1959, p. 22, quoted in G. E. Pitts column. See also Jackson, *American Bandstand*, p. 141.

80. Clark recalled: "You can't live and eat and sleep next to people in a bus . . . and not begin to feel these are my people, we are together." Clark, *Rock Roll*, pp. 58,

135–36; Jackson, *Bandstand*, pp. 204–5; Schipper, "Dick Clark," 70; New York *Amsterdam News*, May 21, 1960, p. 17. However, in 1960, Clark suspended operation of the tours into the Southeast after encountering opposition from whites. Clark, *Rock, Roll*, p. 245.

81. Ward, *Just My Soul*, p. 168.

82. Eliot, *Rockonomics* quoting Joe Smith, p. 86.

83. *New York Times*, May 20, 1960, p. 62; Greenfield, *No Peace*, p. 47; Martin, *Anti Rock*, p. 95.

84. Jackson, *Big Beat*, pp. 34, 42, 73; Ward and Picardie, *Music Man*, pp. 76, 85; Martin, *Anti-Rock*, p. 95; Rick Sklar, *Rocking America: An Insider's Story*, (New York, 1984), p. 21. Reinforcing this image, the *Pittsburgh Courier* gave Freed a special Brotherhood Award for promoting black talent.

85. The charges were later dropped but not before Freed incurred huge legal fees. Jackson, *Big Beat*, pp. 200 212, 247; "Rock 'n' Riot," *Time* May 19, 1958, p. 50; Palmer, *Rock and Roll*, p. 136.

86. Jackson, *Big Beat*, p. 168; Martin, *Anti-Rock*, p. 97.

87. Jackson, *Big Beat*, pp. 105–6; Ward and Picardie, *Music Man*, p. 82; Palmer, *Rock & Roll*, p. 138; Wexler, *Rhythm*, pp. 129–31; Chuck Berry, *The Autobiography*, (New York: Simon & Schuster), 1987, p. 107; *Amsterdam News*, November 20, 1954, pp. 8, 27, July 7, 1956, p. 20, November 24, 1956, p. 14; George, *Death*, p. 91. When he first came to New York City he drew fire from Gotham's black press for slicing into the radio and concert market of black deejays, including emceeing programs at the famed Apollo Theater in Harlem.

88. *Pittsburgh Courier*, December 19, 1959, pp. 1, 23; New York *Amsterdam News*, February 6, 1960, p. 15.

89. "Now Don't Cry," *Time*, December 7, 1959, p. 47; *Variety*, November 25, 1959, p. 1; Chapple, *Rock 'n'Roll*, p. 63.

90. Jackson, *Big Beat*, pp. 279–80; *New York Post*, November 23, 1959, p. 41. Freed attributed the different treatment to the fact that Clark appeared on some three hundred stations and earned $12 million dollars for the television network, while he broadcast on one radio station and brought in only $250,000 in revenue.

91. Jackson, *Big Beat*, p. 285; *New York Post*, April 25, 1960, p. 5. Jackson was given access to Freed's testimony which the committee never released as part of its published hearings. Such testimony is closed to researchers for fifty years unless the House clerk grants permission. After many attempts to obtain permission, my request was denied.

92. On the Clark-Van Doren comparison, *New York Post*, May 2, 1960, p. 4; Clark, *Rock, Rolls*, p. 219; Payola Hearings, p. 1341.

93. Payola Hearings, testimony of Joseph Tryon, pp. 1013, 1015, 1017; Doherty, *Teenpics*, p. 224; R. Serge Denisoff, *Tarnished Gold: The Record Industry Revisited*, (New Brunswick, New Jersey, 1986), p. 238.

94. *Billboard*, May 9, 1960, p. 1.

95. *Washington Post*, April 30, 1960, pp. Al, A3. The Republican Steven B. Derounian judged Clark guilty of "royola." Payola Hearings, p. 1159.

96. *New York Post*, March 31, 1960, p. 12.

97. Payola Hearings, pp. 1168, 1169, 1170, 1176, 1182, 1211.

98. Payola Hearings, p. 1351; Dick Clark to Oren Harris, May 4, 1960, Harris to Clark, May 6, 1960, Box 1149, Harris Papers.

99. Schipper, "Dick Clark," p. 70; "Teen Agers' Elder Statesman," *TV Guide*,

August 29–September 4, 1959, p. 21; *Variety,* May 4, 1960, pp. 1, 50; Mary McGrory, "No Business Like," *New York Post,* May 3, 1960, p. 2 (magazine). Despite his escape, Clark came away bitter. He said the experience taught him "to protect your ass at all times." Clark, *Rock Roll,* p. 225; Leonard H. Goldenson with Marvin J. Wolf, *Beating the Odds,* (New York, 1991), pp. 164–65.

100. Of the seven others indicted with Freed, three were local black deejays. Two of the black disk jockeys also admitted wrongdoing, while the remaining African American and three whites had the charges dropped. In contrast, Clark avoided prosecution in an investigation into payola undertaken by the Philadelphia district attorney, which produced admissions of guilt from over twenty disk jockeys and several of Clark's business associates. Moreover, in cooperation with law enforcement officials, Clark agreed to head a local organization of disk jockeys that pledged to draw up a code of ethics to stamp out payola. Jackson, *Big Beat,* pp. 298–315; Jackson, *American Bandstand,* p. 191; *Billboard,* August 29, 1960, p. 1; New York *Amsterdam News,* May 28, 1960, p. 1.

101. Seagrave, *Payola,* p. 157; Coarse, "Payola," p. 298; Eliot, *Rockonomics,* p. 83; *Billboard,* June 13, 1960, p. 1; Minutes, Committee on Interstate and Foreign Commerce, 86th Cong, 2nd Sess., June 9, 1960, RG 233, Box 207, National Archives; House of Representatives, Committee on Interstate and Foreign Commerce, "Report to accompany S. 1898, Communication Act Amendments, 1960," 86th Cong., 2nd Sess., (Washington, D.C., 1960), p. 47; *Broadcasting,* July 4, 1960, p. 60, August 29, 1960, p. 3; *New York Times,* August 26, 1960, p. 1, August 31, 1960, p. 19.

102. *Billboard,* December 19, 1960, pp. 1, 3, 4; *Variety,* October 26, 1960, p. 57.

103. The target of payola shifted from deejays to program directors who compiled the play lists. Coarse, "Payola," p. 206; Hill, "Enemy," p. 67.

104. The phrase comes from a quote by an anonymous record company executive, *Billboard,* January 18, 1960, p. 2.

105. The introduction of Rap and Hip Hop music in the late 1980s and 1990s, with the civil rights movement in secular decline, revived attacks against black musical forms considered offensive to [white] middle-class standards of decency. Tricia Rose, *Black Noise: Rap Music and Black Culture in Contemporary America* (Hanover, New Hampshire, 1994).

WOMEN, CIVIL RIGHTS, AND BLACK LIBERATION

1. Charles Payne, "Men Led, But Women Organized: Movement Participation of Women in the Mississippi Delta," in Vicki Crawford, Jacqueline Anne Rouse, and Barbara Woods, eds., *Women in the Civil Rights Movement: Trailblazers and Torchbearers, 1941–1965* (Brooklyn, New York: Carlson Publishing, 1990), p1.

2. Kathryn L. Nasstrom, "Down to Now: Memory, Narrative, and Women's Leadership in the Civil Rights Movement in Atlanta, Georgia," *Gender and History* 11 (1999): 132.

3. Paula Giddings, *Where and When I Enter: The Impact of Black Women in Race and Sex in America* (New York, 1984), p. 262.

4. Sara Evans, *Personal Politics: The Roots of Women's Liberation in the Civil Rights Movement and New Left* (New York, 1980), p. 29.

5. Ibid., p. 34.

6. Deborah L. Schultz, *Going South: Jewish Women in the Civil Rights Movement* (New York, 2001), p. 4.

7. Barbara A. Woods, "Modjeska Simkins and the South Carolina Conference of the NAACP, 1939–1957," in Crawford, et. al. eds., *Women and the Civil Rights Movement*, p. 114.

8. Evans, *Personal Politics*, pp. 233–4.

9. Ibid., p. 87.

10. Ibid., p. 239.

11. Chana Kai Lee, *For Freedom's Sake: The Life of Fannie Lou Hamer* (Urbana, Illinois, 1999), p. 76.

12. Evans, *Personal Politics*, p. 81.

13. Belinda Robnett, *How Long? How Long? African-American Women and the Struggle for Freedom and Justice* (New York, 1997), p. 205.

SELECT BIBLIOGRAPHY

GENERAL

Carson, Clayborne. *In Struggle: SNCC and the Black Awakening of the 1960s*. Cambridge, Mass.: Harvard University Press, 1981.

Eagles, Charles. "Toward New Histories of the Civil Rights Era," in *Journal of Southern History*, LXVI (November 2000): 815–48.

Fairclough, Adam. *Better Day Coming: Blacks and Equality, 1890–2000*. New York: Viking Press, 2001.

Greenberg, Cheryl. *A Circle of Trust: Remembering SNCC*. New Brunswick, N.J.: Rutgers University Press, 1998.

King, Richard. *Civil Rights and The Idea of Freedom*. New York: Oxford University Press, 1992.

Lawson, Steven F. *Running for Freedom: Civil Rights and Black Politics in America, Since 1941*. Second Edition, New York: McGraw-Hill, 1997.

Lawson, Steven F. and Payne, Charles. *Debating the Civil Rights Movement 1945–1968*. Lanham, Maryland: Rowman & Littlefield, 1998.

Meier, August, and Rudwick, Elliott. *CORE: A Study of the Civil Rights Movement, 1942–1968*. New York: Oxford University Press, 1973.

Moses, Robert P., and Cobb, Charles E. Jr. *Radical Equations: Math Literacy and Civil Rights*. Boston: Beacon Press, 2001.

Powledge, Fred. *Free At Last?* New York: Little, Brown, 1991.

Riches, William T. Martin. *The Civil Rights Movement: Struggle and Resistance*. New York: St. Martin's Press, 1997.

Robinson, Armstead L. and Sullivan, Patricia, eds. *New Directions in Civil Rights Studies*. Charlottesville: University Press of Virginia, 1991.

Salmond, John A. *My Mind Set On Freedom: A History of the Civil Rights Movement, 1954–1968*. Chicago: Ivan R. Dee, 1997.

Sitkoff, Harvard. *The Struggle for Black Equality, 1954–1992*. New York: Hill & Wang,1993.

Townsend, Davis. *Weary Feet, Rested Souls: A Guided History of the Civil Rights Movement*. New York: W. W. Norton, 1998.

Verney, Kevern. *Black Civil Rights in America*. New York: Routledge, 2000.

Ward, Brian and Badger, Tony, eds. *The Making of Martin Luther King and the Civil Rights Movement*. New York: New York University Press, 1996.

Weisbrot, Robert. *Freedom Bound*. New York: E.P. Dutton, 1990.

Wofford, Harris. *Of Kennedys and Kings: Making Sense of the Sixties*. New York: Farrar, Straus and Giroux, 1980.

AUTOBIOGRAPHY 355

Barnard, Hollinger F., ed. *Outside the Magic Circle: The Autobiography of Virginia Foster Durr*. Alabama: University of Alabama Press, 1985.

Bates, Daisy. *The Long Shadow of Little Rock: A Memoir*. Reprint Edition. Fayetteville: University of Arkansas Press, 1987.

Beals, Melba Patillo. *Warriors Don't Cry: A Searing Memoir of the Battle to Integrate Little Rock's Central High*. New York: Pocket Books, 1994.

Braden, Anne. *The Wall Between*, 2nd ed. Knoxville: University of Tennessee Press, 1999.

Carson, Clayborne, ed. *Autobiography of Martin Luther King Jr., 1929–1968*. New York: Warner Books, 1998.

Clark, Septima. *Echo in My Soul*. New York: E.P. Dutton, 1962.

Dent, Tom. *Southern Journey: A Return to the Civil Rights Movement*. New York: W. Morrow, 1996.

Evers, Charles. *Have No Fear: The Charles Evers Story*. New York: John Wiley and Sons, 1997.

Farmer, James. *Lay Bare the Heart: An Autobiography of the Civil Rights Movement*. New York: Arbor House, 1985.

Forman, James. *The Making of Black Revolutionaries*. New York: McMillan, 1972.

Garrow, David, ed. *The Montgomery Bus Boycott and the Women Who Started It: The Memoir of Jo Ann Gibson Robinson*. Knoxville: University of Tennessee Press, 1987.

Graetz, Robert S. *Montgomery: A White Preacher's Memoir*. Minneapolis: Fortress Press, 1991.

Hemphill, Paul. *Leaving Birmingham: Notes of a Native Son*. New York: Viking Press, 1993.

Henry, Aaron, with Curry, Constance. *The Fire Ever Burning*. Jackson: University Press of Mississippi, 2000.

Hudson, Winson, and Curry, Constance. *Mississippi Harmony: Memoirs of a Freedom Fighter*. New York: Palgrave Macmillan, 2002.

Hunter-Gault, Charlayne. *In My Place*. New York: Farrar, Straus, and Giroux, 1992.

King, Mary. *Freedom Song: A Personal Story of the 1960s Civil Rights Movement*. New York: William Morrow & Company, 1987.

Lewis, John, and D'Orso, Michael. *Walking With the Wind: a Memoir of the Movement*. New York: Simon & Schuster, 1998.

Mason, Gilbert R. *Beaches, Blood, and Ballots: A Black Doctor's Civil Rights Struggle*. Jackson: University Press of Mississippi, 2000.

Moody, Anne. *Coming of Age in Mississippi*. New York: Dell Publishing, 1968.

Motley, Constance Baker. *Equal Justice Under Law: an Autobiography*. New York: Farrar, Straus and Giroux, 1998.

Murray, Pauli. *Pauli Murray: The Autobiography of a Black Activist, Feminist, Lawyer, Priest, and Poet*. Knoxville: University of Tennessee Press, 1989.

Parks, Rosa, with Jim Haskins. *My Story*. New York: Dial Books, 1992.

Segrest, Mab. *Memoir of a Race Traitor*. Boston: South End Press, 1994.

Sellers, Cleveland, with Terrell, Robert. *The River of No Return: The Autobiography of a Black Militant and the Life and Death of SNCC*. New York: William Morrow, 1973.

Shakoor, Jordana Y. *Civil Rights Childhood*. Jackson: University Press of Mississippi, 1999.

Saunders, Robert W. *Bridging the Gap: Continuing the Florida NAACP Legacy of Harry T. Moore, 1952–1966*. Tampa: University of Tampa Press, 2000.

Wilkins, Roy, with Tom Matthews. *Standing Fast*. New York: Viking, 1982.

Young, Andrew. *An Easy Burden: The Civil Rights Movement and the Transformation of America*. New York: HarperCollins, 1996.

BIOGRAPHY

Anderson, Jervis. *Bayard Rustin: Troubles I've Seen: A Biography*. New York: HarperCollins, 1997.

Branch, Taylor. *Parting the Waters: America in the King Years 1954–63*. New York: Simon & Schuster, 1988.

Branch, Taylor. *Pillar of Fire: America in the King Years, 1963–1965*. New York: Simon & Schuster, 1998.

Bass, Jack. *Taming the Storm: The Life and Times of Judge Frank M. Johnson, Jr. and the South's Fight over Civil Rights*. New York: Doubleday, 1993.

Burner, Eric. *And Gently He Shall Lead Them: Robert Parris Moses and Civil Rights In Mississippi*. New York: New York University Press, 1994.

Carter, Dan T. *The Politics of Rage: George Wallace, the Origins of the New Conservatism, and the Transformation of American Politics*. Baton Rouge: Louisiana State University Press, 2000.

Chafe, William H. *Never Stop Running: Allard Lowenstein and the Struggle to Save American Liberalism*. New York: Free Press, 1993.

Cone, James. *Martin & Malcolm & America: A Dream or a Nightmare*. New York: Orbis, Maryknoll, 1991.

Curry, Constance. *Silver Rights*. Chapel Hill: Algonquin Books, 1995.

D'Emilio, John. *Lost Prophet: The Life and Times of Bayard Rustin*. New York: Free Press, 2003.

Dickerson, Dennis. *Militant Mediator: Whitney M. Young, Jr.* Lexington: The University Press of Kentucky, 1998.

Dyson, Michael Eric. *I May Not Get There With You: The True Martin Luther King Jr.* New York: Free Press, 2000.

Eagles, Charles W. *Outside Agitator: Jon Daniels and the Civil Rights Movement in Alabama*. Chapel Hill: University of North Carolina Press, 1993.

Fairclough, Adam. *To Redeem the Soul of America: The Southern Christian Leadership Conference and Martin Luther King, Jr.* Athens: University of Georgia Press, 1987.

Fleming, Cynthia Griggs. *Soon We Will Not Cry: The Liberation of Ruby Doris Smith Robinson*. Lanham, Md.: Rowman & Littlefield, 1998.

Fost, Catherine. *Subversive Southerner: Anne Braden and the Struggle for Racial Justice in the Cold War South*. New York: Palgrave Macmillan, 2002.

Frady, Marshall. *Martin Luther King Jr.* New York: Penguin Group, 2002.

Garrow, David J. *Bearing the Cross: Martin Luther King, Jr., and the Southern Christian Leadership Conference*. New York: William Morrow & Co., 1986.

Garrow, David J. *The FBI and Martin Luther King, Jr.* Norton: New York, 1981.

Grant, Joanne. *Ella Baker: Freedom Bound.* New York: Wiley, 1998.

Green, Ben. *Before His Time: The Untold Story of Harry T. Moore, America's First Civil Rights Martyr.* New York: Free Press, 1999.

Hamilton, Charles V. *Adam Clayton Powell, Jr.: The Political Biography of an American Dilemma.* New York: Maxwell, Macmillan, 1991.

Lewis, David Levering. *W.E.B. DuBois: The Fight for Equality and the American Century, 1919–1963.* New York: Henry Holt, 2000.

Lee, Chana Kai. *For Freedom's Sake: The Life of Fannie Lou Hamer.* Urbana: University of Illinois Press, 1999.

Lesher, Stephan. *George Wallace: American Populist.* Reading, Mass.: Addison-Wesley, 1994.

Levine, Daniel. *Bayard Rustin and the Civil Rights Movement.* New Brunswick, N.J.: Rutgers University Press, 2000.

Ling, Peter J. *Martin Luther King, Jr.,* London: Routledge, 2002.

Manis, Andrew M. *A Fire You Can't Put Out.* Tuscaloosa: University of Alabama Press: 1999.

Mills, Kay. *This Little Light of Mine: The Life of Fannie Lou Hamer.* New York: Dutton, 1993.

Ransby, Barbara. *Running Against the Storm: Ella J. Baker and the Black Radical Tradition.* Chapel Hill: University of North Carolina Press, 2003.

Reed, Roy. *Faubus: The Life and Times of an American Prodigal.* Fayetteville: University of Arkansas Press, 1997.

Rowan, Carl Thomas. *Dream Makers, Dream Breakers: The World of Justice Thurgood Marshall.* New York: Little, Brown, 1993.

Spritzer, Lorraine Nelson, and Bergmark, Jean B. *Grace Towns Hamilton and the Politics of Southern Change.* Athens: University of Georgia Press, 1997.

Stanton, Mary. *From Selma to Sorrow: The Life and Death of Viola Liuzzo.* Athens: University of Georgia Press, 2001.

Tyson, Timothy B. *Radio Free Dixie: Robert F. Williams and the Roots of Black Power.* Chapel Hill: University of North Carolina Press, 2000.

Tushnet, Mark V. *Making Civil Rights Law: Thurgood Marshall and the Supreme Court, 1936–1961.* New York: Oxford University Press, 1994.

Watson, Denton. *Lion in the Lobby: Clarence Mitchell Jr.'s Struggle for the Passage of Civil Rights Laws.* New York: Morrow, 1990.

White, Marjorie L., and Manis, Andrew M. *Birmingham Revolutionaries: Fred Shuttlesworth and the Alabama Christian Movement for Human Rights.* Macon, Ga.: Mercer University Press, 2000.

COMMUNITY STUDIES

Bayor, Ronald H. *Race & the Shaping of Twentieth-Century Atlanta.* Chapel Hill: University of North Carolina Press, 1996.

Burns, Stewart. *Daybreak of Freedom.* Chapel Hill: University of North Carolina Press, 1997.

Chafe, William H. *Civilities and Civil Rights: Greensboro, North Carolina, and the Black Freedom Struggle.* New York: Oxford University Press, 1981.

Colburn, David R. *Racial Change and Community Crisis: St. Augustine, Florida, 1877–1980.* New York: Columbia University Press, 1985.

Davis, Jack E. *Race Against Time: Culture and Separation in Natchez Since 1930.* Baton Rouge: Louisiana State University Press, 2001.

357

De Jong, Greta. *A Different Day: African American Struggles for Justice in Rural Louisiana 1900–1970.* Chapel Hill: University of North Carolina Press, 2002.

Dittmer, John. *Local People: The Struggle for Civil Rights in Mississippi.* Urbana: University of Illinois Press, 1994.

Eick, Gretchen Cassel. *Dissent in Wichita: The Civil Rights Movement in the Midwest.* Urbana: University of Illinois Press, 2001.

Eskew, Glenn T. *But For Birmingham: The Local and National Movements in the Civil Rights Struggle.* Chapel Hill: University of North Carolina Press, 1997.

Fairclough, Adam. *Race and Democracy: The Civil Rights Struggle in Louisiana, 1915–1972.* Athens: University of Georgia Press, 1995.

Godwin, John L. *Black Wilmington and the North Carolina Way: Portrait of a Community in the Era of Civil Rights Protest.* Lanham, Md.: University Press of America, 2000.

Halberstam, David. *The Children.* New York: Random House, 1998.

Harmon, David A. *Beneath the Image of the Civil Rights Movement and Race Relations: Atlanta, Georgia, 1946–1981.* New York: Garland Press, 1996.

Katagiri, Yasuhiro. *The Mississippi State Sovereignty Commission: Civil Rights and States' Rights.* Jackson: University Press of Mississippi, 2001.

McWhorter, Diane. *Carry Me Home: Birmingham, Alabama: The Climactic Battle of the Civil Rights Revolution.* New York: Simon & Schuster, 2001.

Mills, Nicolaus. *Like A Holy Crusade: Mississippi 1964—The Turning of the Civil Rights Movement in America.* Chicago: Ivan R. Dee, 1992.

Morris, Aldon D. *The Origins of the Civil Rights Movement: Black Communities Organizing for Change.* New York: Free Press, 1984.

Norrell, Robert J. *Reaping the Whirlwind: The Civil Rights Movement in Tuskegee.* New York: Knopf, 1985.

O'Brien, Gayle Williams. *The Color of Law: Race, Violence, and Justice in the Post-World War II South.* Chapel Hill: University of North Carolina Press, 1999.

Payne, Charles. *I've Got the Light of Freedom: The Organizing Tradition and the Mississippi Freedom Struggle.* Berkeley: University of California Press, 1995.

Rabby, Glenda Alice. *The Pain and the Promise: The Struggle for Civil Rights in Tallahassee, Florida.* Athens: University of Georgia Press, 1999.

Rogers, Kim Lacy. *Righteous Lives: Narratives of the New Orleans Civil Rights Movement.* New York: New York University Press, 1993.

Thornton, J. Mills III. *Dividing Lines: Municipal Politics and the Struggle for Civil Rights in Montgomery, Birmingham, and Selma.* Tuscaloosa: University of Alabama Press, 2002.

Tuck, Stephen, G.N. *Beyond Atlanta: The Struggle for Racial Equality in Georgia, 1940–1980.* Athens: University of Georgia Press, 2001.

Whitfield, Stephen J. *A Death in the Delta: The Story of Emmett Till.* Baltimore: Johns Hopkins University Press, 1991.

Wilson, Bobby M. *Race and Place in Birmingham: The Civil Rights and Neighborhood Movements.* Lanham, Md.: Rowman & Littlefield Publishers, 2000.

FEDERAL GOVERNMENT

Ball, Howard, Krane, Dale, and Lauth, Thomas P. *Compromised Compliance: Implementation of the 1965 Voting Rights Act.* Westport, Conn.: Greenwood Press, 1982.

Belknap, Michal R. *Federal Law and Southern Order: Racial Violence and Constitutional Conflict in the Post-Brown South*. Athens, Ga.: University of Georgia Press, 1987.

Berman, William C. *The Politics of Civil Rights in the Truman Administration*. Columbus: Ohio State University Press, 1970.

359

Brauer, Carl. *John F. Kennedy and the Second Reconstruction*. New York: Columbia University Press, 1977.

Burk, Robert F. *The Eisenhower Administration and Black Civil Rights*. Knoxville, Tenn.: University of Tennessee Press, 1984.

Davidson, Chandler, and Grofman, Bernard, eds. *Quiet Revolution in the South: The Impact of the Voting Rights Act, 1965–1990*. Princeton: Princeton University Press, 1994.

Gardner, Michael. *Harry Truman and Civil Rights*. Carbondale, Il.: Southern Illinois University Press, 2002.

Graham, Hugh Davis, *The Civil Rights Era: Origins and Development of National Policy*. New York: Oxford University Press, 1990.

Kotlowski, Dean J. *Nixon's Civil Rights: Politics, Principle, and Policy*. Cambridge, Mass.: Harvard University Press, 2001.

Kousser, J. Morgan. *Colorblind Injustice: Minority Voting Rights and the Undoing of the Second Reconstruction*. Chapel Hill: University of North Carolina Press, 1999.

Landsbert, Brian K. *Enforcing Civil Rights: Race Discrimination and the Department of Justice*. Lawrence: University Press of Kansas, 1997.

Lawson, Steven F. *Black Ballots: Voting Rights in the South, 1944–1969*. Lanham, Md.: Lexington Books, 1999.

Lawson, Steven F. *In Pursuit of Power: Southern Blacks and Electoral Politics, 1965–1982*. New York: Columbia University Press, 1985.

McCoy, Donald R., and Reutten, Richard T. *Quest and Response: Minority Rights and the Truman Administration*. Lawrence: University of Kansas Press, 1973.

Meyer, Stephen Grant. *As Long As They Don't Move Next Door: Segregation and Racial Conflict in American Neighborhoods*. Lanham, Md.: Rowman & Littlefield, 2001.

O'Reilly, Kenneth. *"Racial Matters": The FBI's Secret File on Black America, 1960–1972*. New York: Free Press, 1989.

Parker, Frank R. *Black Votes Count: Political Empowerment in Mississippi after 1965*. Chapel Hill: University of North Carolina Press, 1990.

Pauley, Garth E. *The Modern Presidency and Civil Rights*. College Station: Texas A&M University Press, 2001.

Reed, Merl E. *Seedtime for the Modern Civil Rights Movement: The President's Committee on Fair Employment Practice, 1941–1968*. Baton Rouge: Louisiana State University Press, 1991.

Sitkoff, Harvard. *A New Deal for Blacks: The Emergence of Civil Rights as a National Issue*. New York: Oxford University Press, 1978.

Stern, Mark, *Calculating Visions: Kennedy, Johnson, and Civil Rights*. New Brunswick, N.J.: Rutgers University Press, 1992.

Thernstrom, Abigail M. *Whose Votes Count? Affirmative Action and Minority Voting Rights*. Cambridge, MA.: 1987.

Whelan, Charles and Whelan, Barbara. *The Longest Debate: A Legislative History of the 1964 Civil Rights Act*. New York: New American Library, 1986.

Wolters, Raymond. *Right Turn: William Bradford Reynolds, the Reagan Administration, and Black Civil Rights*. New Brunswick, N.J.: Transaction, 1996.

GENDER, WOMEN, AND SEXUALITY

Braukman, Stacy. "Nothing Else Matters but Sex: Cold War Narratives of Deviance and the Search for Lesbian Teachers in Florida, 1959–1963," *Feminist Studies* 27 (Fall 2001): 553–75.

Chateauvert, Melinda. *Marching Together: Women of the Brotherhood of Sleeping Car Porters.* Urbana: University of Illinois Press, 1998.

Collier-Thomas, Bettye, and Franklin, V. P., eds. *Sisters in the Struggle: African American Women in the Civil Rights–Black Power Movement.* New York: New York University Press, 2001.

Crawford, Vicki, Rouse, Jacqueline Anne, and Woods, Barbara, eds. *Women in the Civil Rights Movement: Trailblazers and Torchbearers, 1941–1965.* New York: Garland Publishing, 1990.

Curry, Constance, ed. *Deep In Our Hearts: Nine White Women in the Freedom Movement.* Athens: University of Georgia Press, 2000.

Davis, Angela Y. *Women, Race and Class.* New York: Random House, 1981.

Evans, Sara. *Personal Politics: The Roots of Women's Liberation in the Civil Rights Movement and the New Left.* New York: Vintage Books, 1980.

Giddings, Paula. *When and Where I Enter: The Impact of Black Women on Race and Sex in America.* New York: William Morrow, 1984.

Howard, John. *Men Like That: A Southern Queer History.* Chicago: University of Chicago Press, 1999.

Ling, Peter, and Monteith, Sharon, eds. *Gender in the Civil Rights Movement.* New York: Garland Publishing, 1999.

Lynn, Susan. *Progressive Women in Conservative Times: Racial Justice, Peace, and Feminism, 1945 to the 1960s.* New Brunswick, N.J.: Rutgers University Press, 1992.

Nasstrom, Kathryn L. "Down to Now: Memory, Narrative, and Women's Leadership in the Civil Rights Movement in Atlanta, Georgia," *Gender and History* 11 (1999): 113–44.

Norman, Martha Prescod. "Shining in the Dark: Black Women and the Struggle for the Vote, 1955–1965," in Ann Gordon with Bettye Collier-Thomas et al. (eds.), *African American Women and the Vote, 1837–1965.* Amherst: University of Massachusetts Press, 1997, 172–99.

Olson, Lynne. *Freedom's Daughters: The Unsung Heroines of The Civil Rights Movement From 1830–1970.* New York, Scribner, 2001.

Robnett, Belinda. *How Long? How Long? African-American Women in the Struggle for Civil Rights.* New York: Oxford University Press, 1997.

Schultz, Debra L. *Going South: Jewish Women in the Civil Rights Movement.* New York: New York University Press, 2001.

White, Deborah Gray. *Too Heavy a Load: Black Women in Defense of Themselves, 1894–1994.* New York: Norton, 1999.

INTERNATIONAL POLITICS

Borstelmann, Thomas. *The Cold War and the Color Line.* Cambridge: Harvard University Press, 2001.

Dudziak, Mary L. *Cold War Civil Rights.* Princeton: Princeton University Press, 2000.

Krenn, Michael L. *Black Diplomacy: African Americans and the State Department, 1945–1969.* Armonk, N.Y.: M. E. Sharp, 1999.

Krenn, Michael L., ed. *The African American Voice in U.S. Foreign Policy since World War II*. New York: Garland Publishers, 1998.

Layton, Azza Salama. *International Politics and Civil Rights Policies in the United States, 1941–1960*. New York: Cambridge University Press, 2000.

Lawrence, Scott P. *Double V: Civil Rights Struggle of Tuskegee Airmen*. East Lansing: Michigan State University Press, 1994.

Plummer, Brenda Gayle. *Rising Wind: Black Americans and US Foreign Affairs, 1935–1960*. Chapel Hill: University of North Carolina Press, 1996.

Savage, Barbara. *Broadcasting Freedom: Radio, War, and The Politics of Race, 1938–1948*. Chapel Hill: University of North Carolina Press, 1999.

Von Eschen, Penny M. *Race Against Empire: Black Americans and Anticolonialism, 1937–1957*. Ithaca: Cornell University Press, 1997.

LABOR

Arnesen, Eric. *Brotherhoods of Color: Black Railroad Workers and the Struggle for Equality*. Cambridge, Mass.: Harvard University Press, 2001.

Bates, Beth Tompkins. *Pullman Porters and the Rise of Protest Politics in Black America, 1925–1945*. Chapel Hill: University of North Carolina Press, 2001.

Draper, Alan. *Conflict of Interests: Organized Labor and the Civil Rights Movement in the South, 1954–1968*. Ithaca, N.Y.: ILR Press, 1994.

Honey, Michael. *Southern Labor and Black Civil Rights*. Urbana: University of Illinois Press, 1993.

Kelley, Robin G. *Hammer and Hoe*. Chapel Hill: University of North Carolina Press, 1990.

Korstad, Robert. *Civil Rights Unionism: Tobacco Workers and the Struggle for Democracy in the mid-Twentieth-Century South*. Chapel Hill: University of North Carolina Press, 2003.

Minchin, Timothy. *The Color of Work: The Struggle for Civil Rights in the Southern Paper Industry: 1945–1980*. Chapel Hill: University of North Carolina Press, 2001.

———. *Hiring the Black Worker: The Racial Integration of the Southern Textile Industry, 1960–1980*. Chapel Hill: University of North Carolina Press, 1999.

Nelson, Bruce. *Divided We Stand*. Princeton: Princeton University Press, 2001.

Stein, Judith. *Running Steel, Running America*. Chapel Hill: University of North Carolina Press, 1998.

POPULAR CULTURE

Smith, Suzanne. *Dancing in the Streets: Motown and the Cultural Politics of Detroit*. Cambridge, Mass.: Harvard University Press, 1999.

Van Deburg, William L. *New Day in Babylon: The Black Power Movement and American Culture, 1965–1975*. Chicago: University of Chicago Press, 1992.

Ward, Brian. *Just My Soul Responding: Rhythm and Blues, Black Consciousness and Race Relations*. London: UCL Press, 1998.

Ward, Brian, ed. *Media, Culture, and the Modern African American Freedom Struggle*. Gainesville: University Press of Florida, 2001.

RELIGION

Alvis, Joel L. Jr. *Religion and Race: Southern Presbyterians, 1946–1983.* Tuscaloosa: University of Alabama Press, 1994.

Bass, Jonathan S. *Blessed are the Peacemakers: Martin Luther King Jr., Eight White Religious Leaders and the "Letter From a Birmingham Jail."* Baton Rouge: Louisiana State University Press, 2001.

Bauman, Mark K., and Kalin, Berkley, eds. *The Quiet Voices: Southern Rabbis and Black Civil Rights.* Tuscaloosa: University of Alabama Press, 1997.

Collins, Donald E. *When the Church Bell Rang Racist: The Methodist Church and the Civil Rights Movement in Alabama.* Macon, Ga.: Mercer University Press, 1998.

Findlay, James F. Jr. *Church People in the Struggle: The National Council of Churches and the Black Freedom Movement.* New York: Oxford University Press, 1993.

Friedland, Michael B. *Lift Up Your Voice Like a Trumpet: White Clergy and the Civil Rights and Antiwar Movements, 1954–1973.* Chapel Hill: University of North Carolina Press, 1998.

Lischer, Richard. *The Preacher King: Martin Luther King Jr. and the Word that Moved America.* New York: Oxford University Press, 1995.

Marsh, Charles. *God's Long Summer: Stories of Faith and Civil Rights.* Princeton: Princeton University Press, 1997.

Miller, Keith D. *Voice of Deliverance: The Language of Martin Luther King Jr. and Its Sources.* New York: Free Press, 1992.

Schneier, Rabbi Marc. *Shared Dreams: Martin Luther King Jr. and the Jewish Community.* Woodstock, Vt.: Jewish Lights Publishing, 1999.

Shattuck, Gardiner, H. Jr. *Episcopalians and Race: Civil War to Civil Rights.* Lexington: The University Press of Kentucky, 2000.

Webb, Clive. *Fight Against Fear: Southern Jews and Black Civil Rights.* Athens: University of Georgia Press, 2001.

SCHOOL DESEGREGATION

Cecelski, David. *Along Freedom Road: Hyde County, North Carolina and the Fate of Black Schools in the South.* Chapel Hill: University of North Carolina Press, 1994.

Clark, E. Culpepper. *The Schoolhouse Door: Segregation's Last Stand at the University of Alabama.* New York: Oxford University Press, 1995.

Douglas, Davidson M. *Reading, Writing, and Race: The Desegregation of the Charlotte Schools.* Chapel Hill: University of North Carolina Press, 1995.

Doyle, William. *An American Insurrection: The Battle of Oxford Mississippi, 1962.* New York: Doubleday, 2001.

Greenberg, Jack. *Crusaders in the Courts:* New York: Basic Books, 1994.

Keller, William Henry. *Make Haste Slowly: Moderates, Conservatives, and School Desegregation in Houston.* College Station: Texas A&M University Press, 1999.

Kirk, John A. *Redefining the Color Line: Black Activism in Little Rock, Arkansas, 1940–1970.* Gainesville: University Press of Florida, 2002.

Klarman, Michael J. "How *Brown* Changed Race Relations: The Backlash Thesis," *Journal of American History,* LXXXI (June 1994): 81–118.

Kluger, Richard. *Simple Justice: The History of* Brown v. Board of Education *and Black America's Struggle for Equality.* New York: Vintage, 1975.

Ladino, Robyn Duff. *Desegregating Texas Schools: Eisenhower, Shivers, and the Crisis at Mansfield High.* Austin: University of Texas Press, 1996.

Leidholdt, Alexander. *Standing Before the Shouting Mob: Lenoir Chambers and Virginia's Massive Resistance to Public School Integration.* Tuscaloosa: University of Alabama Press 1997.

Patterson, James T. Brown v. Board of Education: *A Civil Rights Milestone and Its Troubled Legacy.* New York: Oxford University Press, 2001.

Pratt, Robert. *We Shall Not Be Moved: Desegregation of the University of Georgia.* Athens: University of Georgia Press, 2002.

Pratt, Robert A. *The Color of Their Skin: Education and Race in Richmond, Virginia.* Charlottesville: University of Virginia Press, 1992.

Roche, Jeff. *Restructured Resistance: The Silbey Commission and the Politics of Desegregation in Georgia.* Athens: University of Georgia Press, 1998.

WHITES AND THE CIVIL RIGHTS MOVEMENT

Bartley, Numan V. *The Rise of Massive Resistance.* Baton Rouge: Louisiana State University Press, 1970.

Chappell, David L. *Inside Agitators: White Southerners in the Civil Rights Movement.* Baltimore: John Hopkins University Press, 1994.

Egerton, John. *Speak Now Against the Day: The Generation Before the Civil Rights Movement in the South.* Chapel Hill: University of North Carolina Press, 1994.

Frederickson, Kari. *The Dixiecrat Revolt and the End of the Solid South, 1932–1968.* Chapel Hill: University of North Carolina Press, 2001.

Jacoway, Elizabeth, and Colburn, David R., eds. *Southern Businessmen and Desegregation.* Baton Rouge: Louisiana State University Press, 1982.

Marsh, Charles. *The Last Days: A Son's Story of Sin and Segregation at the Dawn of the New South.* New York: Basic Books, 2001.

McAdam, Doug. *Freedom Summer.* New York: Oxford University Press, 1988.

McMillen, Neil R. *The Citizens' Council: Organized Resistance to the Second Reconstruction, 1954–1964.* Urbana: University of Illinois Press, 1971.

Polsgrove, Carol. *Divided Minds: Intellectuals and the Civil Rights Movement.* New York: Norton, 2001.

Sullivan, Patricia. *Days of Hope: Race and Democracy in the New Deal Era.* Chapel Hill: University of North Carolina Press, 1996.

PERMISSIONS

INDEX